The Babylon Complex

The Babylon Complex

Theopolitical Fantasies of War, Sex, and Sovereignty

Erin Runions

FORDHAM UNIVERSITY PRESS

NEW YORK 2014

Library of Congress Cataloging-in-Publication Data is available
from the publisher.

Printed in the United States of America

16 15 14   5 4 3 2 1

First edition

CONTENTS

ACKNOWLEDGMENTS

I am always indebted to encouraging, supportive, and critical readers of my work; they see things that I don't see and push me to make it better. Friends and colleagues who have suggested sources, read, questioned, or otherwise engaged with this work include Fiona Black, Michael Casey, Elizabeth Castelli, Oona Eisenstadt, Adrienne Gibb, Jennifer Glancy, Jione Havea, Maude Gleason, Chris Guzaitis, Andrew Jacobs, Janet Jakobsen, Zayn Kassam, Karen King, Scott Kline, Jennifer Knust, Aaron Kunin, John Kutsko, Carleen Mandolfo, Ian Moyer, Todd Penner, Tina Pippin, Kathleen Skerrett, Yvonne Sherwood, Darryl Smith, Althea Spencer Miller, Lesleigh Cushing Stahlberg, Chloë Taylor, Kyla Tompkins, Andrew Wilson, Vincent Wimbush, and Caroline Vander Stichele. I greatly appreciate the gifts of time, energy, and intellect that these colleagues have given me. The members of my writing group at Pomona College have been instrumental in motivation and feedback, as well as being inspiring in their own work and writing: Anne Dwyer, Pardis Mahdavi, Dara Regaignon, and Tomás Summers Sandoval. Their friendship, scholarship, and political savvy make life so much better. My colleagues in the department of Religious Studies at Pomona College—Oona Eisenstadt, Jerry Irish, Zayn Kassam, Zhiru Ng, and Darryl Smith—have been incredibly supportive of me in every way and have engaged thoughtfully and insightfully on many levels. Our administrative assistant, Vicki Hirales, is a friend and a huge support in administrative tasks and creating a wonderful work environment.

A number of other friends and colleagues in Southern California have provided important intellectual community: Pam Bromley, Eileen Cheng, Vin de Silva, Karen Derris, Vince Faraone, Bob Gaines, Stephan Garcia,

Erin Gratz, Chris Guzaitis, Ko Honda, Gizem Karaali, Peter Kung, April Mayes, Carol Ockman, Anne Pandey, Amit Pandey, Masha Prokopenko, Greg Regaignon, Val Thomas, Peggy Waller, the Lincoln Park book club, and United Voices of Pomona.

Several editors of earlier versions of the chapters were instrumental in getting me writing, and they offered incredibly helpful ideas and feedback: J. J. Collins, Noreen Giffney, Myra Hird, Charles Mathewes, Stephen Moore, and Mayra Rivera. Earlier versions of the ideas developed here appear as: "Empire's Allure: Babylon and the Exception to Law in Two Conservative Discourses," *Journal of the American Academy of Religion* 77 (3) 2009: 680–711; "Tolerating Babel: The Bible, Film, and the Family in U.S. Biopolitics," *Religious Studies and Theology* 29 (2) 2010: 143–69; "Disco-Reggae at Abu Ghraib: Music, the Bible, and Torture," *Religion Dispatches*, June 22, 2009; "Torture by the Book: On the Bible and 'Enhanced Interrogation Techniques,'" *The Ecumenist* 46 (4) 2009: 16–18; "Queering the Beast: The Antichrists' Gay Wedding," in *Queering the Non-Human*, ed. Noreen Giffney and Myra Hird, 97–110, Aldershot: Ashgate, 2008; "Detranscendentalizing Decisionism: Political Theology after Gayatri Spivak," *Journal of Feminist Studies in Religion* 25 (2) 2009: 67–85; "Effects of Grace: Detranscendentalizing," in *Planetary Loves: Spivak, Postcoloniality, and Theology*, ed. Stephen D. Moore and Mayra Rivera, 225–37, New York: Fordham University Press, 2011. I am grateful to Joe Marchal and Jay Twomey for their helpful and affirming reviews of the full manuscript. I am thankful to my editors and the staff at Fordham University Press, Helen Tartar, Tom Lay, Eric Newman, and Katie Sweeney, whose work I value and appreciate very much. I thank Teresa Jesionowski and Katrina Van Heest for their outstanding copyediting.

I also thank Hannah Crumme, Steven Mears, James Page, Leah Rediger Schulte, and Katrina Van Heest for their valuable research assistance at various points in the process. I especially thank Rina Sadun, who was a phenomenal research assistant for almost two years and whose efficiency and ability at tasks large and small were appreciated beyond measure. Students whose insights I have included and noted are Zev Gurman and Emily Marantz. Former graduate students, and now scholars in their own rights, Tom Crawford, Jacqueline Hidalgo, Richard Lindsay, and Katrina Van Heest have also been important in pushing my thinking on scripturalization, many of them in their work with the Institute for Signifying Scriptures at Claremont Graduate University.

The first proposal for the book was done on a summer research stipend from the Wabash Center for Teaching and Learning in Theology and Religion. My "ten-year" Wabash cohort and facilitators have been a bastion of wisdom and a source of pedagogical inspiration and learning. I also thank Pomona College for generous research funding on several occasions.

Finally, this book would not have seen the light of day without the persistent encouragement and mentoring of Elizabeth Castelli, who is a model of academic brilliance, erudition, and generosity. She has tirelessly read, commented on, and advocated for this project in its many forms. Likewise, my partner, Michael Casey, has been encouraging at every stage; he has given feedback on multiple drafts, discussed ideas, kept me up to speed on life and the world, encouraged me to take breaks with RR&P (the critter crew) or in the gym, and, in short, has helped make this book more complex and also more readable.

Introduction: Babylon and the Crisis of Sovereignty

The "war on terror" and a renewed fear of sexuality have marked the years following the attacks on the World Trade Center in New York City. War and sex feed into a general sense of moral panic that creates assent for new kinds of political, economic, and military policies and actions.[1] Torture becomes a necessity. Economic interests take precedence over human well-being. Sexual expression and domestic arrangements become constitutional matters. Military action, economic policy, and sexual regulation are frequently given authority in the United States by means of the Bible and, more particularly, by popularized and sometimes secularized modes of Protestant biblical interpretation. This book argues that invocations of biblical authority smooth the way for the continual attempts to reassert U.S. power in a world where national sovereignty must bow before the transnational circuits

---

1. The term "moral panic" is Stanley Cohen's ([1972] 2011).

of capital and power. Yet in the contradictory way that power is networked throughout the population—heterogeneous yet homogenizing, conscious and unconscious, strategized and unplanned—biblical interpretation discordantly authorizes U.S. sovereignty and at the same time undermines it by participating in the larger transnational networks of power and capital that organize populations, markets, and political relations on a global scale. The moral panic associated with terror and sexuality may be symptomatic of a loss of national power and the concurrent national insistence on the very market forces that produce this loss.

These political currents, although sometimes muddied by the speed at which they seem to travel in opposite directions, become visible in the freeze-frame of one composite biblical figure—Babylon. It is a figure that has surprising ubiquity as an icon and metaphor in U.S. culture and politics. What better book to name and ease moral panic than the Bible? Biblical interpretation is a powerful means by which to express and manage tensions between national sovereignty and economic spread. The theopolitical discourse that emerges under the multitextured sign of Babylon authorizes a renewed nationalism and simultaneously produces subjects shaped for neoliberal global markets, all the while obscuring how the latter also affect national sovereignty. The power and the contradictory uses of the symbol are produced, in part, through a tradition of interpretation that has conflated the various and conflicting biblical depictions of Babylon. These include the Tower of Babel, that enviable collective human achievement disrupted by God to produce cultural and linguistic diversity; the conquering yet seductive empire of Nebuchadnezzar II—with its architecturally stunning city of Babylon—that takes Israel into exile and destroys the temple; the alluring, genderqueer, bloodfiend Whore of Babylon as an allegory for Rome; and the mostly nonbiblical, charismatic yet frightening non/human antichrist who is said to reside in Babylon. When its component parts are kaleidoscopically recombined, as they tend to be, Babylon comes to serve a remarkable number of rhetorical needs.

The United States has a Babylon complex: Babylon becomes a site of identification and an object of intense counteridentification.[2] Great city,

---

2. A physical Babylon Complex exists in The Hague. It includes a shopping center, an office building, a meeting center, a gym, dining facilities, and the Eden Babylon Hotel. See

successful empire, queenly Whore, ambitious building project, united char-ismatic power, and failed achievement, Babylon is both vilified and glamor-ized. It is condemned (as immoral, undemocratic, inhuman) and imitated (as sensational, titillating, tolerant, diverse, and unifying). Babylon appears in shifting configuration in debates over the individual and the collective, law and exception to law, liberty and equality, moral control and economic expedience, tolerance and assimilation. In the war on Iraq, Babylon is the site of literal destruction. In Hollywood, it becomes a symbol for the film industry and cinema's potential, as well as of the excesses and perversities of success. Although Babylon's appearances are highly labile and seem to indicate contradictory affective responses (fascination, admiration, self-righteousness, revenge), there are consistencies: Babylon and the Bible are used to authorize military action and policy in war, shape the population via sexual regulation, and negotiate the meaning of social collectivity and de-mocracy in ways that are consistent with globally expanding free markets. Invariably allusions to Babylon touch on the dangers of sex, the necessity of war, or the problems of governance. The heterosexual family, the military, and limited democracy are promoted as necessary forces for life, morality, truth, and economics; these institutions are used to stimulate the economy *and* govern its unruly aspects. A motivator for such political necessities, Babylon represents what might be considered central fears within U.S. lib-eral democracy: that sexual, moral, ethnic, or political diversity will disrupt national unity or, conversely, that some totalitarian system will curtail freedom and force homogeneous unity. These conflicting fears, over too much diversity and too much unity, appear in debates about the nature of governance and democracy, about sexual morality, about truth, and about the role of the U.S. military in the world. It is precisely within this complex of contradictions that allusions to Babylon can represent and assuage the crisis of dwindling national sovereignty in the process of a highly promoted economic globalization.

---

http://www.newbabylon.nl/. Unlike this physical complex, the U.S. Babylon complex de-scribed in this book operates on the level of conscious and unconscious, as well as religious and secular, political and cultural discourse, policy, and aspiration. It has a range of compo-nents, mechanisms, and symptoms that include but are not limited to the global market forces that make the physical place in The Hague possible and attractive.

Sovereignty and Spread

Multiple cultural forces, among them religious discourse, prime the U.S. population to expect national cohesion and superiority in the face of globalization's economic diffusion of power. As many political theorists and social scientists have argued, however, national sovereignty is increasingly a fiction in a globalized world; political hegemony now goes beyond borders, operating through a transnational system of capital (see, e.g., Brown 2010; Hardt and Negri 2000, 2004; Ong 2006; Povinelli 2006; Sassen 1998). These scholars have traced the slow shift in the loci of sovereignty that ironically commenced with colonialism, the very force that secured nationalisms.[3] As Elizabeth Povinelli puts it, recapitulating W. E. B. Du Bois's earlier insight, "the location of the United States and Europe and their economic and discursive wealth, capital, and political power was not self-evident and was certainly not anchored in their own borders" (2006, 17).[4] From the outset, nations have relied on obtaining resources external to them. As globalization has developed, a new form of empire has emerged in the network of transnational capital, as Michael Hardt and Antonio Negri have famously argued (2000); with the extraction of resources and underpaid labor from around the world, the global flow of capital is far more imperial than any nation-state. Even as the United States tries to consolidate its status as superpower in the world, centralized national power is becoming a fiction. Yet as Saskia Sassen writes, nation-states are willing participants in their undoing in that they have responded by "guarantee[ing] the domestic and global rights of capital" (1998, xxvii). Nations are less concerned with their citizens' rights, their cultural production, and their technological achievements, than with offering docile bodies, compliant political subjectivities, mobile populations, and unregulated resources as capital and for capitalism. These "biopolitical" power relations—to use Michel Foucault's

3. In this book I do not engage the whole history of sovereignty, from monarchy to biopolitics, which others have done so well. For such a history, see Hardt and Negri 2000, 67–204.

4. For instance, Du Bois says, "Why, then, is Europe great? Because of the foundations which the mighty past have furnished her to build upon: the iron trade of ancient, black Africa, the religion and empire-building of yellow Asia, the art and science of the 'dago' Mediterranean shore, east, south, and west, as well as north" (1920a, 40). For more on Du Bois's analysis of colonialism, see Kaplan 2002, 171–212.

conceptual nomenclature—are focused on producing *life* and *populations* in accord with the needs of the market. People, power, and capital move and circulate beyond the confines of nation-states, in the diffuse realm of the transnational. This new power dynamic operates on two registers: those who collect profit and those who produce it at cost to themselves. Aihwa Ong describes this differential as "graduated sovereignty" with "graduated citizenship" so that geographic regions and populations are "developed" or protected differently, within and between nations. As she puts it, political states have moved "from being administrators of a watertight national entity to regulators of diverse spaces and populations that link with global markets" (2006, 78). Citizenship and sovereignty are dispersed, no longer clearly aligned with nations.[5]

The U.S. national imaginary, however, tends to acknowledge its transnationally constructed and dependent power only through the prism of its own sovereignty and superiority. As Wendy Brown points out, the United States theatrically maintains a sense of bordered cohesion, through militarized walls and homeland security. Although the nation demands the immigration and cheap labor provided by globalization, it polices movement and tries at least to look as if it is fortified against the deterritorializations and political breakdowns in national sovereignty (2010, 90–102). Brown perceptively suggests that walls project a theopolitical image, wherein sovereignty, like God, is "the source, condition, and protector of civic life" (58). In Brown's words, "Walls optically gratify the wish for intact sovereign power and protection" (132).

Similarly, the United States makes continued militarized attempts to maintain its position of world dominance. This ambition was perhaps most clearly verbalized in the seminal report of the neoconservative Project for the New American Century, *Rebuilding America's Defenses: Strategy, Forces and Resources for a New Century* (Kagan, Schmitt, and Donnelly 2000). The report, which provided the ideology by which the post-2001 wars were fought, is chiefly concerned with preserving the United States as an economic and ideological superpower. Much is made of the need to preserve the nation's geopolitical

5. Similar kinds of observations about the decreased power of the state and its varying effects on regions within states have been made by those working on theorizing and problematizing the concept of "global citizenship." See, e.g., Axtmann 2002, 107–9.

and military "preeminence." The premise of the report is that the military capacity required to preserve American dominance is declining and that without it "the happy conditions [peace and prosperity] that follow from it will be inevitably undermined" (2000, i). A fear of loss motivates the need for superiority. As will be shown, Babylon is sometimes invoked to justify military efforts to this end. This theopolitical response to the loss of national superiority might be one of what Georges Dreyfus calls countermovements to the demise of the nation-state, which include "religious nationalisms" (2011, 135). The Bible is used to buttress national superiority.

Still, opening up markets has been a chief aim of the military project since 2001. In 2002, the G. W. Bush administration's security strategy revealed its economic messianism in proclaiming that its military tactics were designed "to *bring the hope of democracy, development, free markets, and free trade* to every corner of the world" (White House 2002, ii, emphasis mine). Likewise, in 2010, the Obama administration's security strategy speaks of U.S. military policy as "leadership," in "a world in which our prosperity is inextricably linked to global prosperity" (White House 2010, 2). Part of the 2010 security strategy is to "pursue bilateral and multilateral trade agreements that advance our shared prosperity, while accelerating investments in development that can narrow inequality, expand markets, and support individual opportunity and state capacity abroad" (4). The goals of *expanded markets*, *individual opportunity*, and *state capacity* indicate the tension between centering and decentering that Babylon comes to mediate. Yet even while the market is increasingly important for U.S. security, loss of sovereignty is central. As the same 2010 security strategy puts it, "Shocks to the global economy can precipitate disaster—including the loss of jobs, a decline in standards of living in parts of our country, and instability and a loss of U.S. influence abroad" (White House 2010, 28). It is this loss of superior sovereignty within a global economy that produces moral panic, fueling a messianic pursuit of war, certainty, religion, and sexual regulation.

Biopolitical fragmentation of sovereignty includes increased mobility of populations, a particular shaping of political subjectivity toward economic interest, and securitization. Where others have given excellent detailed accounts of these consequences of globalization, my aim is to illuminate a particular and pervasive *theopolitics* that accompanies and facilitates these movements. Further complicating the argument that Brown makes—in her suggestion that the desire for walls and securitization is a holdover from a theological orientation to political sovereignty—this book looks at how a theological, scriptural orientation both upholds and undermines sovereignty. If actual walls try to manage the tension between sovereignty and spread by recalling divine omnipotence, the elusive walls of Babylon are more symbolically pliable, erected and torn down as theologically, politically, and economically necessary. Observation of the Babylon complex reveals a theopolitics that reinforces a diminishing U.S. sovereignty through war and sexual regulation, yet simultaneously promotes many of the biopolitical conditions of economic globalization that undercut that very sovereignty. This theopolitics facilitates biopolitical, market-oriented dynamics and seeks to maintain hierarchy and control in response to the proliferation of difference and the perceived potential for increased ungovernability in the new economic era. References to Babylon enable, manage, and occlude these contradictions; they cut across secular, religious, and political lines, revealing interdependencies of political positions, as well as the religious shaping of the entire political field.

Methodological Positioning

The Babylon Complex sits at the intersection of biblical studies, religious studies, and cultural studies. In these subfields, the relation between *biopolitics* and *biblical interpretation* has not yet been extensively explored. Certainly, scholars of religious studies, philosophy, and political theory have paid increased attention to the "theopolitical"—that is, the ways that religion intersects with the secular political sphere and structures of power.[6] Journalistic works have helpfully illustrated this point with reference to the U.S. situation and to the relationship between the Christian Right and Republican administrations.[7] Outside of biblical studies, however, the *Bible*'s

6. Asad 2003; Castelli 2005, 2006, 2007a, 2007b, 2007c; Connolly 2000; Crockett 2011; Crockett and Robbins 2012; Davis, Milbank, and Žižek 2005; de Vries and Sullivan 2006; Fessenden 2007; Jakobsen 2005; Jakobsen and Pellegrini 2000, 2003; Lincoln 2006; Pecora 2006; Robbins 2011; Santner 2011; Scott and Hirschkind 2006; Vatter 2011; Warner, Van-Antwerpen, and Calhoun 2010.
7. E.g., M. Goldberg 2006; Phillips 2006; Sharlet 2008, 2010.

influence is often either overlooked, or thought to be straightforward, per-haps precisely because the Bible is so familiar. The nuances of its effect are rarely explored.

Within biblical studies, the Bible's role in the theopolitical has begun to be elucidated and productively contested.[8] *The Babylon Complex* builds on the insights of these works but is unique in demonstrating how bibli-cal interpretation is implicated in biopolitical securitizing and regular-izing discourses (on war and sex), as they are yoked with national self-understandings and aspirations (of collectivity, democracy, economic hegemony). In this work, I am deeply influenced by recent interrogations by Elizabeth Castelli, Vincent Wimbush, and others of the power rela-tions at issue in the discursive operations that define and interpret "scriptures."[9] In many senses, this book seeks to show how politics and

8. Alice Bach makes connections between biblical texts, popular culture, and politics in *Re-ligion, Politics, Media in the Broadband Era* (2004). Roland Boer's *Political Myth: On the Use and Abuse of Biblical Themes* (2009) shows how the Bible is foundational in Australia and the United States for political myths of capitalism *and* socialism. In *Homeland Mythology: Biblical Narratives in American Culture* (2007), Christopher Collins extends the kinds of arguments made by Boyer (1992), Ingebretsen (1996), Keller (2005), and Runions (2004), in outlining the apocalyptically structured national mythology; importantly, he shows how it bolsters the notion of an American homeland, post 9/11. Catherine Keller works to construct a theology that pushes against the general apocalyptic themes that sustain U.S. imperialism in her book *God and Power: Counter Apocalyptic Journeys* (2005). In *The Power of the Word: Scripture and the Rhetoric of Empire* (2007), Elisabeth Schüssler Fiorenza examines the influence of the Roman Empire on the texts that became Christian scriptures; she explores forms of interpretation that can "detoxify" scriptures implicated in the logic of empire. A collection of papers titled "Bush's Bible" (Sherwood 2006) explores the Bible's effect on understandings of law and sexuality—issues that beg to be further developed. These works are part of a larger emerging cultural studies and reception history approach within biblical studies, e.g., Avalos, Melcher and Schipper 2007; Bailey, Liew and Segovia 2009; Bailey, Kirk-Duggan, Masenya, and Sadler 2010; Bal 2008; Beal 2001; Beal and Linafelt 2005; Berlinerblau 2005; Black 2006, 2012; Boer 2007, 2008, 2009; Callahan 2006, 2008, 2009; Castelli 2004, 2005, 2006, 2007a, 2007b, 2007c; Crawford 2011; Crossley 2008, 2010, 2012; Culbertson and Wainwright 2010; Exum and Moore 1998; Fewell, Phillips, and Sherwood 2008; Harding 2012; Hawkins and Stahlberg 2009; Hidalgo 2010; Hornsby and Stone 2011; Kittredge, Aitken, and Draper 2008; Liew 2008; Liew and Yee 2002; Linafelt 2000; Lindsay 2012; Moore 1996, 2002, 2010; Page 1998, 2009; Pyper 2010a, 2010b, 2012; Ruffin 2010; Runions 2003, 2004, 2005; Sawyer 2006; Schüssler Fiorenza 2007; Shepherd 2008; Sherwood 2000, 2006, 2008; Stahlberg 2008a, 2008b; Twomey 2007, 2009a, 2009b; Van Heest 2011; Wimbush 2008b, 2012.

9. E.g., Bielo 2009; Castelli 2004; Crawford 2011; Hidalgo 2010; W. C. Smith 1993; Van Heest 2011; Wimbush 2008b, 2012. See also the journal *Postscripts: The Journal of Sacred Texts and Contemporary Worlds*, edited by Elizabeth Castelli.

"scripturalization"—the human activity of treating texts in an elevated way—are intertwined.[10]

Outside of biblical and religious studies, my argument has been shaped through engagement with political philosophy, queer theory, and cultural studies.[11] I use these theoretical frameworks and insights to illuminate an archive of biblicized and scripturalizing theopolitical machinations that propel an internally combusting U.S. imperialism. The examples that animate my analysis come from a wide array of cultural locations and forms: film, television, libertarian philosophers, neoconservative ideologues, prophecy writing, conservative Christian theologies, reports of events in the war on terror, tabloids, presidential speeches and campaigns, evangelical prayer rallies, and online blogs and jokes. Most of these moments are taken from the years 2001–11 but some are connected with earlier iterations to show that there is continuity with long-term trends in religious and political discourse. I juxtapose cultural artifacts, interpretive traditions, layers of texts, philosophical overlays, and theoretical analyses to present a discursive diorama of the Babylon complex. Over the course of the book, I show the cumulative theopolitical effect of Babylonian interpretive fantasies. I hope that the exhibition of this pastiche archive will be as intriguing for those interested in cultural studies and politics as it will be for scholars of religion.

Empire's Repellent Allure

In the rest of this introductory chapter, I wish more fully to introduce the figure of Babylon. Without hoping to be exhaustive, I give a sense of the wide prevalence and malleability of this image in U.S. culture and politics,

---

10. For arguments about the process of scripturalization in general, see W. C. Smith 1993. As Wimbush (2008a) elaborates, for Smith, scripture is not text per se but the *human activity* of treating text in a particular way (W. C. Smith 1993, 18). Wimbush is interested in the power dynamics of scripturalization as they have affected minority groups; see also Wimbush 2012.

11. E.g., Agamben (1995) 1998, (2003) 2005; Brown 2005, 2006; Butler 1997, 2004a, 2004b; Connolly 2000, 2005; Derrida (1989–90) 2002, (1996) 2002, (2003) 2005; Duggan 2003; Edelman 2004; Foucault (1975) 1995, (1976) 1990, (1978) 1991, 2003, 2008; Hardt and Negri 2000, 2004; Kaplan 2002; Lefort 2006; Mbembe 2003; Ong 2006; Puar 2007; Rana 2011; Rancière 2006; Santner 2011; and Spivak 1995, 1999, 2001, 2004.

indicating the patterns of its signification. I show that conflicting reactions to Babylon (love and hate) come through an original biblical ambiguity that has made it an excellent figure for representing and managing the centering and decentering tensions of a biopolitical capitalist polity with messianic aspirations. Beginning with an overview of the ambiguous biblical texts that crystallize into the culturally recognizable figure of Babylon, I then demarcate the field of Babylon's ambiguous thematics in U.S. culture; finally, I turn to the biopolitical theoretical framework that illuminates these dynamics and that I elaborate further throughout the book.

Babylon is intriguing in the way that it is both loved and hated, often in tandem. This affective variance begins in the biblical text itself and is carried on throughout the history of its interpretation, three strands of which I outline before turning to contemporary uses. Most texts and interpretations are hostile to Babylon, but circumscribed admiration and attraction for Babylon emerge as well. This originary love and hate of Babylon goes a long way in establishing the Babylon complex.

LIVING IN BABYLON

Biblical representations of the complicated colonial relationship between Judah and Babylon are themselves conflicted. The Hebrew Bible's historical and prophetic books tell how the neo-Babylonian empire of Nebuchadnezzar II (626–539 B.C.E.) conquers Judah. The king of Babylon takes the southern Israelite (Judean) elite into exile in 597 and puts a puppet king, Zedekiah, on the throne in Jerusalem. When Judah rebels by making an alliance with Egypt, Nebuchadnezzar besieges Jerusalem and eventually destroys the city and temple in 587 B.C.E., exiling the rest of the elite.[12] Babylon is therefore the purveyor of a deep trauma for the Judean people, one with which many biblical texts wrestle. It also becomes the home for the exiled Judeans and a place of learning for them, leaving its mark on their writings.[13]

12. See 2 Kings 24–25; 2 Chronicles 36; Jeremiah 37; Ezekiel 17:11–20. The Babylonian Chronicles record Nebuchadnezzar's first conquest of Jerusalem in 597.
13. As biblical and ancient Near Eastern scholars have amply demonstrated, Old Babylonian and Neo-Babylonian myths were deeply influential for the authors of the biblical texts. Most obvious are similarities between Genesis and The Epic of Gilgamesh and the Babylonian creation myth, the Enuma Elish.

It is difficult to say whether the exiled Judeans were oppressed or comfortable in their exile; scholars disagree on this point. For instance, Daniel Smith-Christopher argues that the text and archaeological record indicate that the Babylonian conquest of Jerusalem and exile was catastrophic and traumatic, during both neo-Babylonian and Persian rule. Nebuchadnezzar's inscriptions, which boast that he used labor conscripted from his conquests for his building projects, suggest to Smith-Christopher that the Judeans may have been subject to such labor (2002, 66–67).[14] Others, like Hans Barstad suggest that even slaves in Babylon lived in relative comfort, with their families and with a degree of freedom, although it is difficult to know whether or not the Judeans were slaves or of higher social standing in their exile (1996, 75).[15] The proto-apocalyptic prophetic book of Daniel indicates the latter, in its descriptions of the young Judean men (Daniel, Hananiah, Mishael, and Azariah) at the service of a capricious and cruel Nebuchadnezzar. Although the stories in Daniel were likely written in the much later Greek period and have a fabricated folk quality to them (the young men survive the fiery furnace and the lion's den into which they are thrown at the whim of the king; Dn 3, 6), they provide the fullest biblical approximation of life in exile; they indicate at least that some Judeans may have been integrated into the Babylonian court as literati. In my view, it is possible and even likely that those who became the biblical writers and editors had varying experiences and attitudes toward the exile, which therefore might spawn inconsistency in its representation. Whatever the conditions in Babylon, a community of Judeans preferred to remain there even after Cyrus of Persia conquered the city of Babylon (539 B.C.E.) and allowed Judeans to return to Jerusalem to rebuild the temple. Almost a thousand years later, the community that stayed behind completed the Babylonian Talmud.

During and after the exile, authors and editors of the Hebrew scriptures certainly borrowed from Babylonian traditions, even while they criticized

---

14. Likewise, Pinker suggests that exiles from Judea may have labored on Nebuchadnezzar's reconstruction of the ziggurat Etemenanki, and were both awed by it and depressed by their hard labor (2000, 9). For Nebuchadnezzar's inscriptions, see George 2011, discussed in note 21 below.

15. A collection of essays edited by Ben Zvi and Levin 2010, suggest that the Hebrew scriptures were largely shaped by a position of privilege within the exile (the *golah* community that formed in Babylon and imposed itself on return to Yehud).

them. One such text is the well-known story in Genesis 11 of the proliferation of language at Tower of Babel. In this mythic prelude to the story of
the chosen people, humans build a city and a tower. God sees the people's
building, worries about unstoppable human potential, and so multiplies language, dividing and dispersing humanity across the face of the earth. The
word *Babel* is the Hebrew word for Babylon (*bbl*); it plays on both the Hebrew
verb *bll*, "to confound or confuse," and also on the Babylonian *bab-ili*, "gate of
the gods" (Blenkinsopp 1992, 91; R. E. Friedman 2001, 46; Sarna 1989, 84;
Van Seters 1992, 183–85).[16]

The story of the Tower of Babel clearly mimics the Babylonian creation
epic, the Enuma Elish (Fox 1983, 43; Gressman 1928, 5–6). It tells of the
Babylonian gods using bricks to build the city of Babylon and a ziggurat.[17]
Marduk, the patron god of Babylon, says, "I shall make a house to be a
luxurious dwelling for myself. . . . Whenever you come down from the sky
for an assembly, your night's resting place shall be in it, receiving you all. I
hereby name it Babylon, home of the great gods" (Tablet V).[18] The gods
then take up this idea; they make bricks and build the temple Esagil—
Sumerian for "House Whose Top Is High" (Marzahn 2008, 48)—as a shrine
for Marduk (Tablet VI).[19] When completed, "The Lord invited the gods his
fathers to attend a banquet in the great sanctuary which he had created as
his dwelling. [He says,] 'Indeed, Babili is your home too! Sing for joy there,
dwell in happiness'" (Tablet VI). Although not mentioned by name in the
Enuma Elish, the ziggurat, Etemenanki—"The Foundation Stone of Heaven
and Earth" (Koldewey 1914, 183)—may be implied there. Excavations un-
covered the base of this giant ziggurat adjacent to the Esagil complex (Koldewey 1914, 183–215).[20] Biblical scholars assume that the Tower of Babel

16. Fokkelman and Sarna note that the first common plural cohortative form of the verb *bll*
(rendering *nblh* "let us confuse") plays on the word for brick, *lbnh* (Fokkelman 1975, 37; Sarna
1989, 84).
17. Kramer (1968) suggests that the biblical version also alludes to a Sumerian myth of one
language. Alternatively, Alster understands the Sumerian text as describing a future day,
rather than a past myth, in which all nations will "submit to Sumer and speak the Sumerian
language" (1973, 105).
18. Trans. Dalley 1989; see also Landsberger and Wilson 1961.
19. Trans. Dalley 1989.
20. The Esagil Tablet, dated to 229 B.C.E., but thought to be copied from an earlier source,
explicitly links Esagil with Etemenanki. The tablet is a mathematical exercise for students,
to calculate area based on the dimensions of Esagil and Etemenanki (George 2008, 128–30).

story has Etemenanki in mind, especially since Nebuchadnezzar was involved in rebuilding the great ziggurat.[21] City and tower, home of the patron god Marduk, and resting place for the pantheon, Babylon is the seat of divine and political empire.

The allusion to the Enuma Elish and Babylonian architecture in the story of the Tower of Babel clearly indicates Israelite knowledge of Babylonian traditions but is surprisingly obscure in its judgments. Richard Elliot Friedman points out that Genesis 11 "has ambiguity at its center": It does not explain what the people plan with the tower, why they do not want to be scattered, or why the Israelite God, Yahweh, wants humans to be limited (2001, 46). God's actions seem insecure. In mimicking the Babylon story, Genesis 11 may imply that the Hebrew God has power over the Babylonian gods, and over Babylon itself, so that Babylon is mere babble. Alternatively, it could be read as subtly criticizing Yahweh's (and Judea's) jealousy of human and Babylonian technical capacity. When it is interpreted through other Hebrew texts or later Christian texts, however, it becomes a straightforward cautionary tale about human and political ambition or pride.[22]

The most obviously dichotomous biblical views about Babylon can be found in the prophetic book of Jeremiah, which provides a window into differing Judean attitudes. In Jeremiah—a composite text with portions originating from varying circumstances and time periods but unified under the name of one prophet[23]—Babylon is praised, accommodated, and cursed. John Hill has shown that Babylon functions dually in Jeremiah as "a metaphor for landlessness, exile and death" and "the possibility of a future for Judah" (1999, 55). On one hand, Babylon and Nebuchadnezzar are closely

21. For Nebuchadnezzar's inscriptions about Etemenanki see George 2011. These include a stele that has come to be known as the Babel Stele because of its reference to Etemenanki and its plans for the building; the four-column foundation cylinder for Etemenanki; as well as the three-column foundation cylinder from Nebuchadnezzar's north palace in Babylon that mentions Etemenanki and the ziggurat at Borsippa.

22. Scholars have enumerated the early Jewish and Christian texts that turn the Babel story into one about prideful war against God and punishment: These include *The Book of Jubilees*, *3 Baruch*, Philo's *Questions and Answers in Genesis* and *On the Confusion of Tongues*, Josephus's *Antiquities of the Jews*, Pseudo-Philo's *Biblical Antiquities*, the *Targum Neophyti*, and early Christian theological works such as Chrysostom's *Homilies on Genesis* and Augustine's *City of God* (Graves and Patai 1964, 125–29; Kugel 1997, 123–30; Louth 2001, 166–70).

23. See Carroll 1981, 1986; Kessler 2004; Mowinckel 1913; Perdue and Kovacs 1984; Sharp 2003; Thelle 2009a.

associated with Yahweh. The prophet says that Yahweh has subjected all nations, people, and even animals to Babylon (chaps. 27–28). Several speeches of Yahweh refer to Nebuchadnezzar as "my servant" (Jer 25:9; 27:6; 43:10). Jeremiah wishes Babylon well and urges the exiles in Babylon to settle down in their exile: "Seek the prosperity of the city to which I have carried you into exile. Pray to Yahweh for it, because if it prospers, you too will prosper" (29:7). On the other hand, the hatred of Babylon for its destruction of Jerusalem are also prominent in the book, especially in portions like the oracles against Babylon (chaps. 50–51). There Babylon is accused of arrogance and of oppressing Israel (50:31–34), for which God promises to punish and destroy it. Babylon will be broken so badly that it cannot heal (51:8–9); Israel will be returned home (50:19).

The historical reason for the violent response to Babylon in Jeremiah 50–51 and the shift in attitude from a pro-Babylonian stance has been an object of scholarly speculation.[24] The city of Babylon was not actually *destroyed* by Cyrus's Persian conquest (Carroll 1986, 68; Bellis 1995, 15; Kessler 2003, 206). It did not suffer the kind of devastation the text imagines until the reign of Xerxes I of Persia (486–65 b.c.e.) who dismantled the ziggurat Etemenanki in response to a Babylonian rebellion in 484 (Kessler 2003, 196–97, 206; George 2008, 56). Most scholars' dating for the final edition of Jeremiah, however, places it fairly close to the time of the exile, long before the time of Xerxes's destruction of Babylon. At the very least, as Robert Carroll has suggested, the divergence in response to Babylon might indicate varying political and geographic interests—of the commu-

---

24. Sharp (2003) suggests that the book reveals a struggle for authority between the community that was exiled to Babylon in 597 and those that remained behind in Jerusalem. Hill (2009) suggests that Jeremiah was redacted in the Persian period and its ambiguities indicate a group of editors located outside of the Jerusalem community in Mizpah, who were opposed to the reestablishment of the Davidic monarchy and the rebuilding of the temple. Carroll suggests that the lack of realism of the oracles suggests a detachment from the actual situation, indicating a Persian date. Although aware of the problems of dating the passage, he does suggest that perhaps Babylon is used here as a symbol for "imperial powers ranged against Israel" (1986, 68). See also Thelle 2009b, 218. For essays that discuss the differing attitudes toward Babylon in Jeremiah within an understanding of the book's overall coherence, see Kessler 2004. For a summary of the scholarship on whether the anti-Babylonian sentiments in Jeremiah 50–51 are authentic or a later addition, see Keown, Scalise, and Smothers 1995, 357–61. For literary readings of Jeremiah 50–51 that suggest they are consistent with the book's overall message, see Aitken 1983; Bellis 1995; Hill 1999; Smelik 2004; Thelle 2009b; Van Hecke 2003.

nity remaining in Babylon, the community returning from Babylon, the community in Jerusalem—that are later redacted together (1986, 69–74).

Whatever the causes for a sea change toward Babylon in the book of Jeremiah, it is significant that in the hostile sections Babylon's fate is imagined as *revenge* for the destruction of Jerusalem and Judah. The prophetic voice inveighs against Babylon: "Shout against her, surrounding her. She has given up her hand; her bulwarks have fallen, her walls are torn down. This is the vengeance of Yahweh. Take vengeance on her, do to her as she has done" (50:15). This revenge fantasy has affective power in its reception and reinterpretation; as we will see, it circulates through the imagery of the Whore's destruction in Revelation and then into the contemporary moment (chapter 4).

Even within the revenge fantasy against Babylon in the book of Jeremiah, there is an implicit identification between Babylon and Judah, representing an ambiguity between them. In the middle of the oracles against Babylon, we find a short poem that seems to speak positively of Babylon as God's weapon (51:20–23), "You are my war club, my weapon for battle; with you I shatter nations, with you I destroy nations" (51:20).[25] Conversely, a negative identification between Judah and Babylon occurs, as Hill notices, when the oracles against Babylon mimic the language of the earlier oracles against Judah (Jer 2–6, 10): "Both are portrayed as sinful and guilty" (1999, 173).

The prophetic texts of Isaiah and Ezekiel likewise represent a conflicted stance toward Babylon. As in Jeremiah, Babylon is both the servant of Yahweh and destined for destruction, in Ezekiel. Babylon is the shining sword of Yahweh (21:15), which, when it has done its duty conquering Jerusalem, will be sheathed, judged, and punished (21:14–32). Other passages in Ezekiel condemn the time when Babylon's puppet king of Judah broke covenant with Babylon and appealed to Egypt for help. Surprisingly acquiescent to Babylon's rule, the prophet says that Yahweh will strengthen Babylon who will conquer Egypt (chaps. 29–32).[26] Isaiah is far less pro-Babylon. A text in

25. For a discussion of the ambiguity of the addressee of Jer 51:20–23, see Lundbom 1999, 451–52. Reimer (1993, 226) reads the poem as addressing Babylon, as do Bellis (1995, 146–48) and Keown, Scalise, and Smothers (1995, 370). Carroll calls it an unidentified power (1986, 842). Holladay reads the addressee as a postexilic Israel (1989, 406–7).

26. See Allen 1990, 101–39; Joyce 2007, 181–89; Odell 2005, 275–79, 375–76, 386–90. Mein suggests that Ezekiel reflects the views of Judah's political and religious elite who were

Isaiah associated with Cyrus's conquest of Babylon, describes the city as a humiliated woman (Is 47).[27] The prophet lambastes Babylon, who has boasted about her security in the past. In an another passage in Isaiah—written earlier, possibly around the time that Assyria occupied Babylon and was attacking Israel and Judah (740–722, 701 B.C.E.)[28]—a still angry but more divided assessment emerges. A famous verse, known primarily through Christian interpretations of Lucifer, describes the precipitous decline of the king of Babylon: "How you are fallen from heaven, O morning star, son of the dawn. You have been cut down to earth, one who defeated nations" (Is 14:12). The writer accuses him of arrogance: "You said in your heart, 'I will ascend to heaven, I will raise my throne above the stars of God'" (v. 13). As part of an oracle against Babylon, this verse certainly indicates enmity, but it also implies a kind of one-time admiration. Babylon's king was apparently considered a shining light, *son of the dawn*. It is perhaps not surprising that this verse is eventually interpreted to be about the *attractive, yet fallen*, Lucifer, thrown from heaven (a much later mythic development).[29]

SEDUCTIVE TYRANTS IN BABYLON

That Babylon is both enticing and repugnant makes it highly serviceable for mythic representations of social anxiety and moral panic. A second apocalyptic strand of biblical representation cosmically inflates Babylon to produce the dangerous magnetism of the Whore of Babylon and the deceptive

---

concerned not so much with loyalty to Babylon as with upholding Yahweh's honor and "the oath of vassalage . . . sworn in YHWH's name" (2001, 88). Mein points out that Ezekiel 17 indicates the view that "in breaking his covenant with Nebuchadnezzar, Zedekiah has in effect broken his covenant with YHWH himself. 'As I live, surely *my oath* which he despised, and *my* covenant which he broke' (17:19)" (87).

27. The sexualization of Babylon develops as early as the Greek Septuagint translation of Isaiah 47:8. In the Hebrew, the term used to describe her is obscure; elsewhere this term appears as the masculine proper name Adin (Ez 2:15, 8:6, Neh 7:20, 10:17). In the Septuagint Greek translation, she is negatively described as the voluptuous or luxuriant one (*ē truphera*). This translation is further amplified in later English translations, so that Babylon becomes "one given to pleasures" (KJV), "the sensual one" (NAS), and "wanton creature" (NIV).

28. See Erlandsson 1970; Peters 1919; Sweeney 1996, 232–33.

29. For a discussion of this development through subsequent readings of this passage as about Satan in the Christian New Testament, early Christian theology, and beyond, see Kelly 2006, 191–214.

charisma of the antichrist. In the Christian apocalyptic text of Revelation, the Roman empire of the first century c.e. is figured as Babylon and as Whore (chaps. 17–18). There she is castigated for every imaginable evil: drinking the blood of the saints, committing adulteries with the kings of the earth, reveling in excessive luxuries that line the pockets of the merchants of the earth, and providing shelter for every imaginable evil. The seer calls God's people to resist her and prophesies that they will be avenged in her violent destruction. The call for revenge on the Whore is one that repeats and amplifies the revenge imagined by the Hebrew prophets, making revenge a biblically approved thematic in both Jewish and Christian testaments. At the same time, as Chris Frilingos (2004) and Stephen Moore (2006) have shown, the book of Revelation indicates a certain attraction to and involvement with the Roman empire (see chapter 6).

In the contemporary era, the Whore of Babylon is drawn into a larger religious narrative in which she is conflated with the figures of Babel and the empires of Babylon and Rome. The apocalyptic (premillennialist, dispensationalist) mode of biblical interpretation that gained prominence in Protestantism in the early twentieth century synthesizes and elaborates bits and pieces of text found throughout the Bible into a much larger narrative about the end time.[30] The key elements of this thought—built from Revelation but supplemented by other biblical texts—are that the world will finally come to an end when Christ returns, judges all people, banishes Satan, and establishes his new and glorious kingdom. Although apocalyptic interpreters differ in the details, many agree that in the not-too-distant future a spiritualized center of danger, Babylon/Babel, will be restored as a center of the antichrist's world control. Babylon must be rebuilt before the return of Christ, when it will be destroyed again. The question is, where will it be rebuilt? Some prophecy writers—the self-described niche of those interpreting biblical prophecy in terms of imminent events—argue that Babylon is Rome, or the Roman Catholic Church; some say New York, or the United States, and others argue that it will be reestablished in ancient Babylon in Iraq. Oddly, there is hopeful *anticipation* for the reemergence of wicked

---

30. For lengthy discussions of the effect of apocalyptic thinking on U.S. American culture, see Boyer 1992; Ingebretsen 1996; Long 2005.

Babylon, in this interpretation, because it would be a sign of the imminent return of Christ.[31]

A rebuilt Babylon becomes the home of the attractive, deceptive, and ultimately tyrannical world leader: the antichrist. In Revelation 17, the Whore famously rides "the beast," who is interpreted as the antichrist. Babylon and its prince the antichrist are then used to describe licentious and tyrannical, if attractive, governments or political ideas (foreign or domestic) that will mark the end times. Those fooled by such deceptions will be entrapped into an oppressive totalitarian regime. The antichrist becomes an embodiment of Satan, who is the spiritual enemy behind a new Tower of Babel, a one-world, neutralized, homogenized order in its various guises as liberalism, Communism, technology, or, more recently, in the United States, Islam, or terror.[32] The perverse sexuality of the Whore has even extended to the antichrist, so that many apocalyptic interpreters now imagine him as "homosexual" (see chapter 5).

In the U.S. national myth, ancient Israel (Judah) becomes the United States, while Babylon becomes a symbol of tyranny and evil that must be fought by any means necessary. Babylon becomes more than the ancient empire; it becomes the cosmic symbol of political and sexual evil, against which U.S. messianism pitches its battle and shines its light for the world. Catherine Keller argues that there is a subliminal "apocalyptic unconscious" working behind the United States' "messianic imperialism" (2005, 37).[33] This messianism, she suggests, is "a space akin to terror that can only be maintained by extreme violence." The violent imagery of God punishing the wicked and their environs helps this messianic imperialism to function: "This violence at the edges of our collective consciousness is where any cruelty can be justified by the threat of 'Barbarians,' 'terrorists,' 'infidels,' or 'unbelievers'" (38). Any party at odds with the United States or its frequently espoused values (capitalism, democracy, heterosexuality) can be apocalyptically coded as Babylonian, while the actions of the United States

31. For examples of prophecy writing on these themes, see Baxley 2005; Hitchcock 2003; James 1997; LaHaye 1999.
32. For the way the antichrist has figured in U.S. political thought, see Boyer 1992, 282–84, 328–30; Fuller 1995; Keller 2005, 71–73, 136–60. For descriptions of the antichrist's one-world politics, see James 1997.
33. See also Runions 2004, 2005.

are fully vindicated by their association with God. When these apocalyptic figures are integrated into *secular* political debate, as will be shown in chapters 4 and 5, they create an affective theological force field: The stakes go up on decision-making processes, and the implicit spiritual threats generate support for strong action. Babylon offers a reason for the United States to reassert its global superiority. It can be read as a figure of the fear of loss of U.S. sovereignty, eclipsed by another power.

ORIENTALIST STUDY OF BABYLON

Onto these alluring colonial and sexualized assessments of Babylon is grafted a third strand of representation: knowledge about ancient Babylon produced by archaeological and textual sources. Study of these sources, pioneered in the orientalism of the early twentieth century, has produced qualified appreciation for the ancient empire. The city of Babylon was an important center in Mesopotamia from its founding in 1894 B.C.E. up until the time of Alexander the Great, who conquered the city and briefly made it his capital. The brief but influential Old Babylonian Empire (c. 1764–1750 B.C.E.) produced Hammurabi's famous law code (much of which biblical law resembles).[34] Under the Neo-Assyrian Empire in the seventh century B.C.E., the city was destroyed in 689 B.C.E. by Sennacherib (704–681 B.C.E.) and then rebuilt by his grandson Ashurbanipal (668–627 B.C.E.), who was a devotee of Babylon's god, Marduk. The Neo-Babylonian Empire that succeeded the Assyrian Empire has been much admired, especially the achievements of Nebuchadnezzar II (605–562 B.C.E.), who is legendary for his astonishing building projects in the city. These include the famed Hanging Gardens described by Herodotus; the rebuilding of the ziggurat Etemenanki; and the stunningly beautiful and colossal Ishtar Gate—the ornamental gate to the city—with its blue and gold glazed bricks, patterned

---

34. Wright (2009) argues for dependence of the Covenant Code (Exodus 20:23–23:19) on the Laws of Hammurabi. He suggests that the Israelite authors would have come into contact with these laws beginning in the neo-Assyrian period. Van Seters likewise argues that the Yahwistic writer of the Covenant Code would have had access to ancient Babylonian law codes, although unlike Wright, he suggests that it was written in exile (2003, 45). For bibliography on those scholars who do not wish to see any dependence on the Babylonian law codes, see Wright 2009, chap. 1, nn. 32–35).

with lions, bulls, and dragons (Finkel and Seymour 2008; see also Oates 2008).

The archaeological and textual study of Babylon is, as Edward Said has shown of orientalism in general, bound up with the projects of colonialism and nationalism. The excavation and study of Babylon is fully integrated into this project. Interest in the excavation of the ancient city of Babylon started as a sideline to British colonial interest,[35] but by the beginning of the twentieth century it had become a major archaeological coup for Germany in the production of German nationalism. Frederick Bohrer's immensely informative study of orientalism and visual culture in nineteenth-century Europe explains how Germany laid claim to ancient Babylon, just as England had done with Assyria (2003, 272–313).[36] The Ishtar Gate and the ancient Processional Way—on which processions in honor of Babylon's patron god Marduk took place—were excavated from 1899 to 1912 by the German archaeologist Robert Koldewey (Lyon 1918, 309, 311; Koldewey 1914, vi–ix, 25). Bohrer shows how the groundbreaking biblical scholar and philologist Friedrich Delitzsch secured support from Kaiser Wilhelm II for the Babylon excavation and publicized the work of the excavation (279–82).[37] Delitzsch was central to the use of Babylon as a "tool for Germany's parvenu entry into the imperial contest" (272).[38] Now, a century later, the spectacular Ishtar Gate is housed in the Museum of the Ancient Near East in the Pergamon Museum in Berlin, where it has been "re-created to approximately the original dimensions by meticulously re-assembling the

35. The first nineteenth-century drawings of the ancient site of the city of Babylon were undertaken by the British Baghdad resident Claudius James Rich, with help from a Captain Lockett. As Julian Reade points out, Rich was in Baghdad to protect British interests in India (2008, 35). While he was there, he pursued his interest in Babylon.

36. Sir Austen Henry Layard excavated Nimrud and Nineveh in the late 1840s and published his findings throughout the 1840s and '50s, bringing ancient Assyria into the English intellectual domain.

37. Delitzsch also provided translations of inscriptions Koldewey found there (Koldewey 1914, ix), substantially forming the interpretation of them.

38. As Bohrer argues, German archaeology of Babylon was closely linked to the influential field of German biblical study and philology, yet academic study of the Bible came under fire from more conservative communities of faith, which also affected cultural reception of the figure of Babylon. In his "Babel-Bibel" lectures, Delitzsch drew on the still-current argument that Babylon was formative for the Bible; he took the argument to untenable conclusions, suggesting that the Mesopotamians were Aryan and not Semitic (Bohrer 2003, 291). German Christians responded to his questioning of divine revelation via pamphlets and articles that satirized Babylon and made it an object of loathing (289–97).

many broken pieces of excavated glazed bricks."[39] Only the base remains in Iraq.

U.S. Americans were also interested in Mesopotamia in the late nineteenth and early twentieth centuries. As Bruce Kuklick (1996) details, scholars under the auspices of the U.S. Babylon Exploration Fund excavated at Nippur (southeast of the city of Babylon) in the 1890s. They found it to be a center of Sumerian culture; they excavated many clay tablets, including the earliest Sumerian version of the Epic of Gilgamesh (not actually translated until the 1940s). The excavated tablets were eventually curated and controlled by Hermann Hilprecht, of the University of Pennsylvania, a German who had trained under Delitzsch and who consulted with Koldewey in the course of the excavations. These excavations did not do the same work for U.S. scholarship and nationalism as it had for Germany, but for a short time they raised the position of U.S. academia with respect to the growing field of Near Eastern studies.[40]

These sorts of orientalist approaches to Babylon are central to the modern period, as Nicholas Mirzoeff argues: "The legend of the fallen city of grandeur haunts and inspires modernity" (2005, 9).[41] Making a similar argument, the Pergamon Museum, home of the Ishtar Gate, ran an exhibition in 2008 called "Babylon: Myth and Truth" in conjunction with the Louvre, the French Réunion des musées nationaux, and the British Museum (see Finkel and Seymour 2008). The exhibition aimed to show the truth of ancient Babylon and the myth of the fallen hubristic city in European art and culture. Exhibiting a certain degree of self-awareness, the curators wrote that "the story is not one of a historical truth about Babylon, but of a truth about a civilisation that needs the myth of Babel in order to understand itself."[42] (Perhaps not surprisingly, Europe became aware of its own problematic relation to orientalism at the time that it responded

---

39. Preußischer Kulturbesitz 2012.

40. Kuklick gives a detailed account of the intellectual shifts and academic power struggles to which this work gave rise. Although this work raised the profile of U.S. biblical scholarship for a while, it still remained in the shadow of German scholarship. Thomas Joseph Crawford traces the rise of U.S. biblical scholarship to the (postwar) study of the Nag Hammadi texts by James M. Robinson and others (2011, 92–100).

41. Mirzoeff points to the appearance of Babylon in historical arguments by early twentieth-century scholars and cultural critics such as Walter Benjamin, via Max Nordau, and Théophile Gautier (2005, 92–94).

42. Preußischer Kulturbesitz 2008.

increasingly negatively to the U.S. war on Iraq.) Orientalism creates a Babylon onto which national desires and fears can be projected.

Babylon in U.S. Culture

When these threads are woven together into a tale about the current moment, Babylon has multiple and competing significations. The shifting response to Babylon in the biblical text is amplified by past and present orientalism, making it exceedingly pliable in its application. Let me now indicate the manifold ways that Babylon and Babel appear in a wide variety of U.S. cultural sites. The Tower of Babel is used to negotiate varying attitudes toward difference within the political sphere. As an apocalyptic symbol, Babylon provides a cosmology in which transcendent good and evil can be made to correspond to any political position under critique. It frequently symbolizes political opponents deemed too powerful, making extreme military or legal measures palatable and even necessary if the United States is to fulfill its self-proclaimed role of world savior. Sexualized as the Whore, Babylon can also be invoked to censor disapproved forms of excess and sexuality. Yet the lure of Babylon's power is strong as an ancient empire advanced in military strategy, knowledge, law, architecture, and engineering. Babylon becomes a kind of mirror for the United States, even while it provides a foil for its messianism. As in the tradition of Jeremiah, the United States can shift between *being* Babylon (the servant of Yahweh, the great site of culture) and standing firm *against* it (the place of evil, oppression and excess). Babylon is tyrannical, colonizing, beguiling, technologically and culturally sophisticated, and spiritually threatening.

E PLURIBUS UNUM?

The Tower of Babel appears in political and religious discourse when people want to think about what holds the United States together in the face of its racial and cultural diversity. Because the Babelian creation of diverse languages is typically read as both *God's will* and at the same time *a punishment*, the story lends itself well to representing a range of attitudes about difference. A confusing ambivalence about unity and about too much diversity emerges. Via the Babel story, Babylon is sometimes used to promote tolerance toward sexual and ethnic difference, insofar as U.S. Americans see themselves as benevolent toward difference. At other times it is used to stigmatize and attack difference as embodying a problematic unity without moral distinctions. It is also used by minority groups to indicate anger at their lack of inclusion and at color-blind descriptions of national progress. These vacillations can be read as symptoms of anxieties that emerge in the tension between globalization and nationalism. Globalization produces and requires difference, while the nation-state tries to contain it; those branded as different negotiate their standing as valued diversity, while those afraid of difference counterintuitively call it an oppressive *unity*. For those bothered by the increasing diversity that appears within the nation as a result of globalization, Babel is a negative term. For instance, the conservative Pat Buchanan consistently applies the image to complain about difference: that the United States is converting from a Christian nation into the Tower of Babel (1997) or that love of diversity is producing the tower of Babel and destroying the idea of America (2009). In his official website, Buchanan writes, "Without the assent of her people, America is being converted from a Christian country, nine in 10 of whose people traced their roots to Europe as late as the time of JFK, into a multiracial, multiethnic, multilingual, multicultural Tower of Babel not seen since the late Roman Empire" (2009).[43] Buchanan is nostalgic for a unity that represents national power and white European roots.

Ostensibly more liberal voices worry about diversity in similar ways. For instance, the historian and political pundit Arthur M. Schlesinger Jr. refers to Babel while reflecting on multiculturalism. He asks, "Will the center hold? Or will the melting pot yield to the tower of Babel" (1998, 22). He wonders, "When does obsession with difference begin to threaten the idea of an overarching American nationality" (81). Although committed to "interplay of diverse traditions" (144), he nonetheless concludes that the United States needs a more narrowly conceived unity. He thus worries about whether schools should teach "racial and ethnic pride" (81). In his view, the

---

43. In October of 2011, Color of Change and CREDO Action launched a successful campaign for MSNBC to fire Buchanan for his racist views, as promoted in his book *Suicide of a Superpower* (2012), which contains a chapter titled "The End of White America."

United States ought fully to accept and "master" its European origins before it can successfully integrate difference; the core of the melting pot
must be understood to be European (145). Schlesinger models "tolerance,"
with its characteristic prioritization of the self against the tolerated other
(see chapter 3).

African American speculative fiction writers voice strong disagreement
with the assumptions of Schlesinger and others that U.S. culture and achievement is primarily Anglo-European, to which all other ethnicities must
adapt or be expulsed. Rather they mark the founding contributions of African Americans to the nation and trouble a myth of color-blind progress.
The cultural critic Darryl Smith has drawn attention to the way African
American fiction writers have long used the Babel story to parody the myth
of national unity and belonging, as part of their critique of science fiction's
myth of progress. Smith beautifully elucidates how writers such as W. E. B.
Du Bois, Amiri Baraka, and Derrick Bell are critical of the science fiction
dream of a speculative "spike," or "singularity," that will take humans into
posthuman cybernetics. A history of conscription to forced labor for the
making of "progress" makes these authors clear-eyed about the hazards of
scientific, national, and fictional utopic projects. The idea of a universal
"spike" does not take into account existing inequalities. These authors' works
are not begging for inclusion into an already established national unity, but
rather critically appraising the aspiration of reaching for unity and offering
another option. Smith puns, "If the motto of Anglo-European sf [science fic-
tion] has been 'Excelsior!' ('Ever onward and upward!'), then the rebel yell of
Afro-Diasporic sf has been 'Excavate!' ('Dig it!')" (2007, 202). They wish to
place value on the diversity of Babel.

To take an example with strong Babelian allusions, Du Bois's 1920
story "The Comet" indicates how difference is excluded from national
belonging unless it serves a dominant interest. The story tells of an African American bank messenger, Jim, who has been sent into the lower
vaults of the bank—where no one else wants to go and where no one of
value is sent. Of this scene Smith writes, "Like being trapped in the grav-
ity well of a singularity . . . Jim's descent is complete before he begins it"
(2007, 208). While Jim is in the vault, a comet's tail hits New York. Only
he and a wealthy white woman, Julia, survive. Searching the city for life
and family, Jim and Julia eventually ascend the Metropolitan Tower to set

off flare rockets. There she realizes a shift in her consciousness toward the black man beside her: "He was no longer a thing apart, a creature below, a strange outcast of another clime and blood, but her Brother Humanity Incarnate, Son of God, and great All-Father of the race to be" (Du Bois 1920b, 15). That is, until they hear the "babel of voices" (16) signifying the presence of her father, her fiancé, their search party, and the inevitable crash of a spike, or singularity, beyond race. Julia drops Jim, barely muttering words to counteract her family's racist suspicions of him. They pay him, and, "for Jim, the Inverted Spike is restored" (D. Smith 2007, 210); he is back where he started, isolated in the lower vaults of the tower of "progress." Difference is always already excluded from unity, the story implies; neither tower nor resulting "babel" can adequately accommodate otherness.

In contrast, political commentators who refuse to recognize the assertions made by African Americans and other minority groups about their rightful place within the nation sometimes represent diversity as an oppressive controlling *unity* that is compared to the Tower of Babel. In conservative discourse, economic, sexual, and political diversity is frequently represented as a neutralizing—and therefore mindlessly tyrannical—unity (chapters 1 and 2). Those who interpret the tower in this way argue for the sharp distinctions of truth, the testing of which will propel strong military, economic, or moral action. Many times these actions require exception to law (see chapter 2). Without fail, such allusions to Babel seek to consolidate national, familial, and/or God's sovereignty, as well as open up areas for free trade, democracy, freedom, and individual rights of accumulation and consumption. A similar fear of groupthink unity finds its way into a fictional narrative that ruminates on religious, linguistic, and sexual difference. Neal Stephenson's cyberpunk *Snow Crash* features a computer virus that causes the world to linguistically revert to a time before Babel. The novel depicts Babylonian unity as irrational control of human thought. As the story goes, an electronically transmitted virus—the Snow Crash virus—taps into humans' linguistic infrastructure, essentially the brain stem, and controls them. As it turns out, Snow Crash is a new high-tech version of an ancient "Asherah virus," which "coil[s] around the brainstem like a serpent around a tree" (1992, 399). Stephenson evokes the story of the snake in the garden of Eden, as he tropes on the strong biblical prohibitions against the Canaanite goddess Asherah.[44] In the fictional world, the Asherah virus brings an original mother tongue closer to the surface and makes people subject to control by other viruses and viral ideas, including irrational religion. It also "makes them sexually promiscuous." The antidote to this controlling unity is linguistic diversity—the fall of the tower—and, paradoxically, "rational" *monotheistic* religions and their systems of written text and law. *Snow Crash* values diversity, but only if it is familiar, sexually regulated, and monotheistic. In this respect, Stephenson also follows an orientalist trend of relating sexual diversity to lack of self-control in allusions to Babylon and a theopolitical trend of containing diversity by means of religion.

WAR ON BABYLON

President Barack Obama also uses Babel to think about national unity in ways that tend toward military defense of national superiority. His exhortations to set aside ideological disagreements for unity end up allying with unprecedented military action and an anti-Babylonian theopolitics. In his 2010 address to the National Prayer Breakfast, Obama expresses hope that the nation can avoid the results of Babel (see chapter 1). He worries that "in this Tower of Babel [of ideological disputes] we lose the sound of God's voice." He asks citizens and politicians to move beyond their divisions and to look for what forms the common good of the nation. Although Obama's philosophy of national unity seems to take a benign middle road, a more violent underside emerges in his 2012 State of the Union address, which reiterates the theme of unity in difference. Obama opens his 2012 address by recalling the assassination of the U.S. archenemy Osama bin Laden. He applauds the team work of the U.S. special forces and holds it up as edification for the nation: "They're not consumed with personal ambition. They don't obsess over their differences. They focus on the mission at hand. They work together" (2012). National unity is imagined through nonegotistical

---

44. Archaeological, but not biblical, sources show Asherah to have been the consort of Yahweh, the God of the Israelites (Dever 2005). Biblical scholarship has hypothesized that Asherah was related to a cult of fertility (i.e., orgiastic sex), but such a cult is not attested in the archaeological data (see Hillers 1985; Noll 2001, 259–61). Stephenson associates Canaan with Babylon, a move that conflates the Canaanites, whom the Israelites boast of colonizing and whose customs they abhor, with Babylon, which colonizes Judah.

teamwork that sets aside difference, which is said to be the result of *ambition* and not, for instance, cultural location or systemic imbalance. Notably, unity is achieved in the *extrajudicial* mission to execute bin Laden (the relationship between Babylon and exception to law is one I develop in chapter 2). In religious commentary on bin Laden's death that is indicative of the prevalence of Babylon in the theopolitics I am discussing, bin Laden was given Babylonian coding (see chapter 4). National unity is forged, then, by excluding Babel from the United States and by killing Babylon overseas.[45]

Literally speaking, Babylon was already substantially destroyed by the time Obama took office in the war on Iraq. In April of 2003, the ancient site of Babylon, modernized and rebuilt to some degree by Saddam Hussein, was occupied by Coalition Forces. In September of 2003, it became Camp Alpha, where Polish troops were stationed until December of 2004 (Torchia and Al-Musawi 2008). According to a 2009 UNESCO report assessing damages, the ancient site was badly harmed. The military had dug trenches, cut into unexcavated mounds, leveled such mounds, covered them with sand and gravel, and treated them with chemicals. Parking lots and helipads were constructed (2009, 13–17). Heavy vehicles compacted the earth and broke ancient paving stones. The remains of the Ishtar Gate and the ancient Processional Way were both damaged.[46] In addition, the museums that Saddam Hussein had built on the site were looted and ransacked; all papers, including archaeological records, were burned (6).[47]

Arguably, the blatant disregard for ancient Babylon in the war has to do with apocalyptic subtexts, wherein the United States understands itself on the side of God, fighting the forces of evil associated with ancient and future (rebuilt) Babylon. The relation between Iraq and the site of the apocalyptic Babylon has been popularized by Timothy LaHaye, author of the enormously popular Christian *Left Behind* series set in apocalyptic end times. LaHaye suggests in novels and nonfiction writing that the ancient city of

45. I am indebted to Pardis Mahdavi and Elizabeth Castelli for reminding me of these themes in the 2012 State of the Union address.

46. Bricks were smashed on nine of the animal reliefs on the Ishtar Gate, when someone tried to remove them (UNESCO 2009, 18; McCarthy and Kennedy 2005). The Processional Way had three rows of two-ton concrete blocks placed onto it (UNESCO 2009, 18).

47. For discussion of how U.S. military forces failed to secure the antiquities in the National Museum of Iraq, see Rothfield 2009.

Babylon will be rebuilt and the antichrist will rule there before the return of Christ. Saddam Hussein's activities in rebuilding the ancient city were taken, by LaHaye, as a sign of the end times. In *Revelation Unveiled* (1999), he writes, "Saddam Hussein, the megalomaniac dictator of the country, has spent over one billion dollars on the rebuilding of that ancient city, which I believe will be taken over one day by the Antichrist, titled New Babylon, and made the governmental, commercial, and religious center of the world" (283).[48] Given that LaHaye's *Left Behind Series* sold over 63 million copies,[49] it seems hardly incidental that, in the war on Iraq, ancient Babylon has been badly damaged. As I show in chapters 4 and 5, many of the political statements and military actions in the second U.S. war on Iraq suggest that this apocalyptic vision is very much present as a motivating rhetoric.[50]

U.S. orientalism toward Babylon also feeds into the war on Iraq, along with market interests, as Mirzoeff has shown in *Watching Babylon: The War in Iraq and Global Visual Culture* (2005). Mirzoeff looks at the media coverage of the war as it interacts with other cultural images of Babylon, and as it affects military action in Iraq, globalization, and suburban U.S. life (focusing on Babylon, New York). He notes the ambivalence toward Babylon, the love and hate toward it produced by orientalism, and its function within modern circuits of power. If I am suggesting that an apocalyptic theopolitics consolidates a sense of U.S. nationalism within global monetary circuits, Mirzoeff shows how the war in Iraq worked in tandem. He suggests that the Iraq war was fought so that Iraq would "become a denationalized zone for the operation of global capital" (2005, 156) and that its televisual presentation in the United States "embodies a stabilized and centralized viewpoint on globalization as the drama of the Western subject and its sufferings" (75). As we will see throughout *The Babylon Complex*, Babylon is very much used to shore up U.S. subjectivity and nationalism in its wars, in

---

48. Another prophecy writer, Mark Hitchcock, makes the same argument in *The Second Coming of Babylon* (2003), arguing that his view is not based on the unfolding war in Iraq. He claims consistency with tradition, citing theologians and preachers from the nineteenth and early twentieth centuries who also believed Babylon would be rebuilt on its ancient site.

49. This statistic is given on the series' website (http://www.leftbehind.com).

50. Even as far back as 1997, the view of Iraq as an apocalyptic threat emerged in the secular press. *The Economist* ran an editorial piece on Iraq's supposed biological-weapons capacities; the article had no religious content but was titled with a reference to the book of Revelation, "The Whore of Babylon and the Horseman of the Plague" (1997).

its religious and orientalist framing; moreover, it manages to do so in a way that both encourages and obfuscates the decentering of U.S political subjectivity and the crisis of national sovereignty.

BABYLON / AMERICA

Not all interpreters believe that spiritual Babylon is so closely aligned with Iraq. For those who discern moral or political corruption in the United States, Babylon is an apt descriptor, especially the Whore of Babylon. Babylon and the United States are closely aligned in jeremiads of the religious right and the secular left. Again, the figure is used to contend with unmet (and divergent) desires for unity or diversity. When the religious right refers to the ills of Babylon, it is to condemn the fracturing of a single Christian morality in the United States; when the secular left refers to Babylon it is to decry the abuses of an antidemocratic, capitalist system.

The religious critique of immorality follows a trend—popularized in the nineteenth century, in sensationalized tabloid and fiction writing—of scrutinizing behaviors and religious beliefs as evidence that a particular city (often New York) is the Whore of Babylon.[51] Pastor Mike Bickle of the International House of Prayer provides a twenty-first-century exhibit of this tendency. He calls the moral stances of most U.S. citizens—which he thinks are too tolerant and lacking in rigor—"Harlot Babylon religion." When, in August of 2011, Bickle gave his support to the prayer rally of the Republican presidential hopeful Rick Perry, this teaching came to light under public scrutiny. (Political commentators and watchdog groups such as Rightwing Watch circulated a clip of one of his sermons in which he called Oprah Winfrey a representative of this harlot religion.) In Bickle's teaching, Harlot Babylon is a one-world religion, first practiced at the Tower of Babel but now practiced at large in the United States. It is the religion of tolerance, the religion in which everyone is accepted and everyone is happy; it is a humanistic and humanitarian religion. According to Bickle, "This counterfeit justice movement will feed the poor and be involved in humanitarian projects, and will appear to be filled with compassion" (2011). But this movement is a

51. See University of Virginia Library 1999–2000.

trap; after people join, they "will be forced to worship Satan in the Anti-christ religion." Those who blindly follow the Harlot's tolerance will find themselves part of a much larger, totalitarian one-world system. In this Bickle picks up on a prominent fear of one-world systems for the religious and political Right, and on a neoconservative hatred of liberalism (chapters 1, 2, 5). Here again, Babylon is used to represent a bellicose fear of unity, a fear of mindless control; as in the conservative discourse discussed above, it is those practices that differ from the supposed moral norm that get called mindless unity.

Left-wing and secular groups also make use of Babylon, picking up on the way African American slaves used the term in the antebellum period. Slaves sometimes described themselves in religious terms as exiled to Babylon, awaiting return. For instance, Keith Miller notes the "popular slave sermon, 'Dry Bones in the Valley' . . . that portrays the Hebrews captive in Babylon as skeletal remains in a desolate valley whom God miraculously revives" (2007, 407–8).[52] Likewise, Allen Dwight Callahan points out that in 1833 Maria Stewart—the first woman to write politically in the United States—compared the United States to the Whore of Babylon in "An Address Delivered at the African Masonic Hall" (Callahan 2009, 53). Stewart said:

> It appears to me that America has become like the great city of Babylon. . . .
> She is, indeed a seller of slaves and the souls of men; she has made the Africans drunk with the wine of her fornication; she has put them completely beneath her feet, and she means to keep them there. (1987, 63)[53]

In a reversal of the usual national myth, the United States is Babylon, who enslaves the children of God.

Building on these kinds of interpretations, Babylon becomes a name for colonial oppression in Africana resistance movements. The Rastafarian tradition uses the term *Babylon* to describe "a systemic reality that alienates the descendants of Africa from their real selves and homeland [which they called Zion]" (Davidson 2006). Rastafarians famously wish to "chant down

---

52. The sermon takes Ezekiel 37:1–14 as a starting point and combines it with the Babylon trope.
53. For a contemporary womanist reading of the Whore of Babylon that also focuses on the U.S. history of slavery and its similarity to the exploitations of the Whore, see C. Martin 2005.

Babylon" in order to bring in a second, messianic exodus from oppression (Middleton 2000, 186; Murrell 2000, 30). The Black Panther movement similarly used the term to denote the U.S. state and its systemic attempts to disenfranchise African Americans. The Panthers believed that the people of Babylon could overturn Babylon (Self 2003, 14).

Drawing on Africana traditions, secular, antistatist, and anticolonial discourses refer to Babylon to represent the United States as a place of captivity and its government as an oppressive force. Babylon becomes a trope in antitransnational, anticapitalist, and environmental organizing as well. The antiglobalization movement sometimes refers to capitalism and its global workings as Babylon (Wall 2005), evoking both the apocalyptic and imperial histories of the city. The environmental, countercultural, peace, and free-love Rainbow movement uses the term *Babylon* to refer to the strictures and violence of mainstream society.[54] Likewise, the notion of Babylon as an oppressive government system has found its way into mainstream secular liberal commentary, as in Alexander Cockburn and Ken Silverstein's *Washington Babylon* (1996), which argues that "both major political parties have been bought up by big money from corporations and wealthy Americans" (1996, ix).[55] Babylon comes to represent corruption from outside the state system—from corporations.

In varying degrees, these identifications of Babylon with the United States criticize the United States as complicit with harm. They also indicate that Babylon goes beyond the borders of the United States; it becomes a symbol for malevolent global forces (sometimes real, sometimes imagined) that wish to constrain the freedoms of U.S. citizens or harm the planet. These negative identifications of Babylon with the United States all at least point to the fact that U.S. power is implicated in a global network. While my own political sympathies lie with the antistatist and anticolonial organizers, in

54. In contrast to other uses, the Rainbow gathering is unique in making Babylon a metaphor for sexual constraint. I am grateful to my student Emily Marantz for pointing me to the Rainbow Gatherings.

55. Silverstein kept the designation *Washington Babylon* alive as the name of a blog column until he resigned as *Harper's* Washington editor in 2012. Other political commentators have taken up the phrase *Washington Babylon* too. For instance, Judy Bachrach so titled her column on the indictment of California Republican Congressperson Duke Cunningham for accepting $2.4 million in bribes (2006).

my view, the secular use of biblical language is unfortunate because it can so easily and perhaps unconsciously be allied with the theopolitics I am uncovering.

BABYLON IN HOLLYWOOD

The last si(gh)ting of Babylon in U.S. culture that I want to mention, before returning to the theoretical framing for the book, is perhaps the one that gives it the most traction: popular visual culture. Given the negative tendency of allusions to Babylon, it is unexpected, perhaps, to find it a place of great fascination for popular culture. Nonetheless, Babylon is an object of desire, *in* film, *as* Hollywood (in its many layers as a physical, conceptual, and discursive space), and in television. In the orientalist tradition of reluctant awe for all things Babylonian, Hollywood popularizes the great city as a representation of the lure and dangers of economic success, sexuality, and political ambition. It represents the place of capitalism's *possibilities*, signaling the economic and cultural interests that can be pursued and desired by U.S. citizens. It provides a cautionary tale about the very pursuit of those interests, allowing viewers concomitant identification and counteridentification with Babylon. Hollywood Babylon generates capital and entices viewers to particular freedoms—primarily in the realms of sexual and economic fantasy—all the while displaying the dangers of too much freedom. Hollywood thus keeps alive the moral panic that Babylon comes to represent: the desired excess and tempting seduction that bring destruction and the political tyranny against which a U.S. messianism can be imagined. Although this book deals with film only in chapter 3, it is important to note here the ways in which Hollywood makes Babylon a public figure. Hollywood (narrowly) educates the public about the biblical, archaeological, artistic, and filmic iconography of Babylon, and emphasizes the ideological overlay I have been discussing.

Babylon was most famously celebrated in conjunction with cinema in the 1916 film *Intolerance*, directed by the chief progenitor of Hollywood film style, D. W. Griffith (best known for his deeply racist film *Birth of a Nation*). In this box-office failure, which was nonetheless hugely influential, Babylon is depicted as a place of luxury, sensuality, and joy, and as a metaphor for the universal language of film (M. Hansen 1991). The set itself was a feat, and it remained standing for years as a landmark of film history and neglect at the corner of Hollywood and Sunset boulevards in Los Angeles. Two double arches in ancient Near Eastern style formed the backdrop, before which a great hall stretched, over a mile long with (faux) Babylonian iconography (and some additional elephants).[56] In her autobiography, film star Lillian Gish recalls, "The walls enclosing the court of Belshazzar were over 200 feet high. The court . . . was flanked by two colonnades supporting columns fifty feet high, each column in turn supporting a great statue of the elephant got erect on its hind legs" (1969, 169). Yet despite the fact that Griffith admires Babylon, he makes much of the fact that Babylon is ultimately unsuccessful and destroyed. American film can do what Babylon could not; it can create a universal language; it can also offer sexual pleasures while modeling the correct morality of the nuclear family (for a detailed discussion of this film, see chapter 3).

The association of Hollywood with Babylon was intensified by Kenneth Anger in his infamous book of scandal, *Hollywood Babylon* (1975).[57] In this book of gossip, published first in France in 1959, Anger revealed the inner workings of Hollywood as a place of decadence, intrigue, and despair. Since Anger was himself a renowned underground queer filmmaker who made use of occult themes and was fond of the high life, the book does not appear to be making typical moral judgments so much as making money (see Bhattacharya 2004). Anger reinvigorates a certain sensibility about Hollywood and simultaneously creates distance from it, using Babylon as a central prop. He opens with a reference to *Intolerance* that captures this ambivalence:

56. Bernard Hanson notes that Griffith's set designer told him that elephants were not authentic but that Griffith insisted. Hanson suggests that he may have taken the idea from the 1914 Italian spectacular *Cabiria* (1972, 500). For more on Griffith's influences and style, see Merritt 1979; F. Martin 1983. Griffith does not seem to be deeply concerned about realism, since the images on the set are Assyrian, not Babylonian; they are similar to those found at the ancient Assyrian palace of Ashurnasirpal II at Nimrud in northern Iraq. This substitution may be because there was more scholarship available on Assyria than on Babylon; Koldewey's excavations of Babylon were only published in 1914 and had not yet been analyzed in the way that the Assyrian artifacts had been, when Griffith was making *Intolerance*. At the same time, it does betray the orientalist mind-set that allows all ancient Near Eastern culture to be lumped together.

57. For the tradition of Hollywood gossip that this book comes out of, see Slide 2010.

Long after Belshazzar's court had sprouted weeds and its walls had begun to peel and warp in abandoned movie-set disarray . . . still it stood: Griffith's *Babylon, something of a reproach and something of a challenge* to the burgeoning movie town—something to surpass and something to live down. (1975, 6, emphasis mine)

Babylon beckons and rebukes, even in Anger's own writing. He suggests that Hollywood is best viewed from a distance because its glamour consistently produces personal, financial, and relational tragedy. Yet even while he criticizes the shallowness of Hollywood culture, Anger continually laments the censor of the Motion Picture Production Code, and, in a way, his book serves as a kind of protest against it.

Babylon also regularly makes an appearance *in* Hollywood film. Most iconically, Babylon appears in German filmmaker Fritz Lang's *Metropolis* (1927), first released in Germany with an edited version released a few months later in the United States by Paramount. Metropolis is a fictional towering city—inspired by New York—sustained underground by enslaved workers and machines. The film's heroine, Maria (Brigitte Helm), exhorts workers with the story of Babel, warning against a repeat of a fictive biblical scenario in which the workers who built Babel rose up violently against the brains of the operation. Instead, she calls for peaceful mediation between workers and bosses. Meanwhile, an evil inventor creates a robot in Maria's likeness, who seduces and incites the workers to revolt, sabotages the machines, and destroys the city. Robot Maria is eroticized as the Whore of Babylon, through a seductive burlesque dance, and through an iconic shot of her sitting upon a dragon, hands held high. This film exhibits fear about workers' demands for rights that are not controlled and contained.[58]

In less influential films than *Intolerance* and *Metropolis*, Babylon exhibits anxieties about various kinds of sexual or political excess and ambition and, ultimately, heroic escape from these dangers. This thematic constellation is exploited in *Two Weeks in Another Town* (Vincente Minnelli, 1962), which draws parallels between Hollywood's corruption and Babylon, and in *The Devil's Advocate* (Taylor Hackford, 1997), where New York/Babylon is the seductive home of Satan's law firm. Other films imagine fighting foreign

58. See Bachmann 2000.

imperial control; in them Babylon appears as a quasi-historical city in which soft, feminized tyrants rule slaves, and harems are liberated by hard, masculine, freedom-loving heroes (primarily Alexander the Great): *Alexander* (Oliver Stone, 2004); *Alexander the Great* (Robert Rossen, 1956); *Slaves of Babylon* (William Castle, 1953). These films ideologically inflate the historic Greek conquest of Persian Babylon and associate the United States with Greece. They display the characteristic orientalism in which "the West" (Greece, the United States) is considered superior to "the East" (Persia and Babylon), and which can give voice to U.S. messianism. More nuanced, Alejandro González Iñárritu's 2006 film *Babel* recognizes the problems of *U.S.* imperialism and tries to think about how film can solve the problems of difference and misunderstanding across borders (chapter 3 explores the limits of this effort).

Indebted as it is to film, television has also capitalized on Babylon's enticements and dangers, again with varying degrees of love and hate. Several TV shows pick up on the associations of sexual and material excess associated with Hollywood and/or Babylon. *Californication*'s Whore of Babylon episode pokes fun at a novelist's attempts to whore himself out to Hollywood, emphasizing the exploitative nature of Hollywood (season 1, episode 3). In *Carnivàle*'s Babylon episode, the town of Babylon's zombie inhabitants brutally attack and kill one of the showgirls after the cooch show, making Babylon an indicator of such otherworldly deviance that it destroys even ol' timey sexual exhibitionism, which the viewer is left to desire (season 1, episode 5). More positively, "Club Babylon" is the center of much of the action on *Queer as Folk*, picking up on Griffith's and Anger's respective depictions of Babylon as a place of uncensored or not necessarily heteronormative sexual expression. Referencing more bellicose Babylonian fantasies, the 1990s cult sci-fi TV series *Babylon V* imagines a space station where mutual respect and diversity between alien species and humans was attempted. By season three of the five-season series, however, the optimism voiced in the opening tagline—"the last, best hope for peace"—is shown to be faulty and replaced with war: The space station becomes "the last, best hope for *victory*."[59]

59. A British TV comedy, *Hotel Babylon*, follows the intrigues and escapades of the hotel staff in their interactions with their clients' excesses. The less popular U.S. show *Supernatural*

Babylon and Biopolitics

I have tried to indicate thus far how Babylon and the Bible are used to characterize various constituencies within the nation, to imagine political and spiritual enemies, to authorize military action and policy in war, to comment on sexual morality, and to negotiate the meaning of individual freedoms and state governance in ways that are consistent with the tension between sovereignty and spread in globalization. The complexity and slipperiness of interpretation within these large trends—with alternating value placed on unity and diversity—give Babylon its multivalence. It is an image flexible enough to mediate and contain these political tensions. It becomes an antagonist against which to claim transcendent sovereignty and authority, and also a model for immanent subjectivities that facilitate capitalism—shaped for consumption, family, and war.

In theoretical terms, these shifting dynamics are symptomatic of what Foucault has called biopolitics, that is, the nurture of populations for market relations. Beginning in the seventeenth century, Foucault famously argues, power shifts from mastery via the threat of death to mastery via the control of life ([1976] 1990, 135–45). Biopolitics enables the smooth functioning of capital throughout and between populations. In *History of Sexuality* and in his posthumously published lectures given at the Collège de France in the late 1970s, Foucault describes the aims, configurations, networks, and tactics of biopolitical power, as well as accompanying modes of subjectivity. He argues that, within secular liberalism, power is mobilized so that *populations* are produced, regularized, and classified as different kinds of human capital (Foucault 2003, 2008). As Foucault puts it, biopolitics is concerned with "the investment of the body, its valorization, and the distributive management of its forces" ([1976] 1990, 141). Eventually, as economies expand in the twentieth century, biopolitics functions globally, allowing populations to be "regularized" through the control of birthrates, mortality rates, and longevity (2003, 2008). In biopolitics, populations are cultivated as capital via racialization, mobility, sexual regulation, and secu-

---

also has a Hollywood Babylon episode (season 2, episode 18): Its main characters investigate the haunting of a Hollywood set by the ghost of a woman who had been mistreated by a corrupt studio executive.

ritization. Populations are characterized and hierarchized through racialization and economic advantage, encouraged to travel from their homes as laborers, managers, or owners, and controlled through sexual regulation and securitization.

In the context of globalization, some populations are positioned as disposable, some as commodity-labor forces, and some as investors. Michael Dillon and Julian Reid have glossed this point with reference to securitization and war, which they see as central to liberal governance and its ostensible drive to protect "species life." They write, "Liberal governance requires constant auditing and sorting of life to determine which life forms are productive and which not" (2009, 43); if something is judged to "systematically endanger life," it must be eradicated, often through war. Less-than-good life is said not to value human life.[60] As Dillon and Reid point out, this project cannot avoid racializing (49–50). The disposability of certain populations, as Achille Mbembe (2003) has pointed out, creates zones of death, or, *necropolitics*. We will see throughout the book how the figure of Babylon appears to characterize the lives of those to be killed or tortured as less than good, somehow spiritually suspect, racializing and demonizing in the process. Conversely, those forms of life that are considered good are nurtured in (U.S.) *families*. Time and time again, the evil associated with Babylon is thought to be remedied by the nuclear family, usually backlit by the racialization and sexualization of nonnormative families, ethnic groups, or nations under attack.

Foucault further complicates this picture by describing a change in political subjectivity that accompanies biopolitics, which helps explain the slipperiness between unity and diversity, equality, and hierarchy that I have been discussing. Foucault suggests that as biopolitics develops, people shift from understanding themselves as *subjects of right* to *subjects of interest*. The subject of right submits to a social contract or law (a type of socially agreed-upon unity) in exchange for access to rights. In order to facilitate the social contract and become the possessor of universal rights, the subject agrees to

---

60. To give one example, Hillary Clinton, then U.S. Secretary of State, said this about the Algerian hostage crisis in January 2013: "But when you deal with these relentless terrorists, *life is not in any way precious to them*" (Sterling and Botelho 2013, emphasis mine). The fact that life was lost in freeing the hostages seems immaterial in this view.

relinquish some individual rights (Foucault 2008, 276). The renunciation of personal desires that this exchange requires is partially shaped through the bodily and affective disciplines of modernity, as instilled, for instance, in schools, factories, and armies.[61] The subject of interest, in contrast, is governed by economic and personal interest rather than by social contract. The subject of interest, or "*homo oeconomicus*," is no longer beholden to the unity of social contract; s/he makes atomistic choices according to (mainly) economic interest (Foucault 2008, 272–76). This creates the potential for populations not beholden to laws or social contracts or political power in general, and, as we will see, produces a generalized fear of loss of control. Ironically, though, because interests can be manipulated from the outside, in Foucault's view, the subject of interest is very governable (270).

Biblical interpretation works in tandem with biopolitics, particularly in acculturating the population to the newer arrangements of power and forms of subjectivity. Biopolitics requires openness and closure, diversity and unity, inclusion and exclusion. These are tensions that, as I have been showing, the image of Babylon represents and manages in various formations.

Religion, the Bible, and Babylon help shore up what Foucault calls *liberal governmentality*, which facilitates biopolitics outside of traditional norms of social contract and national sovereignty.[62] As Wendy Brown glosses it, governmentality is that "mode of governance encompassing but not limited to the state . . . that produces subjects, forms of citizenship and behavior" (2005, 37). The governmentality of biopolitics "has as its target population, as its principal form of knowledge political economy, and as its essential technical means apparatuses of security" (Foucault [1978] 1991, 102). Governmentality generates structures of control and regulation within the transnational context of globalization. It works variously through security, the economy, disciplines, surveillance, structures of government, the family, the law, and, it should be added, *religion*. In Foucault's view, the biopolitical focus on bodies and populations means that everyday dangers such as disease, hygiene, and degeneration replace the traditional "apocalyptic threats of plague,

---

61. As outlined in Foucault's *Discipline and Punish* ([1975] 1995).
62. In fact, Foucault speaks of the processes of governmentality much more than he does biopolitics, which is the larger term for "the attempt . . . to rationalize the problems posed to governmental practice . . . [in] forming a population" (2008, 317).

death, and war." In his words, "the horsemen of the Apocalypse disappear" (2008, 66). But do apocalyptic threats really disappear?[63] References to Babylon suggest otherwise. The apocalyptic worldview—which frequently features Babylon—is regularly used to gloss dangers to collective interests, both from within the United States and also from without. In the United States, Christianity continues to be particularly close to the surface. Babylon evokes an apocalyptic cosmos that imagines transcendence outside the political sphere that can usefully be called upon to express dangers to the smooth functioning of biopolitics.

While apocalyptic threats remain an active part of religious and secular discourse, they are integrated into a military and economic structure that negotiates between interests and control. In Foucault's words, "strategies of security . . . ensure that the mechanism of interests does not give rise to individual or collective dangers" (2008, 65). Order must be kept, even while individual interests are lauded. Biopolitics operates through "procedures of control, constraint and coercion which are something like the counterpart and counterweights of different freedoms" (67). Securitization (e.g., war, militarization, incarceration, and border policing) and disciplinary surveillance (e.g., sexual regulation, racial profiling, and workplace-management policies) replace traditional forms of sovereign protection, and eventually also the social contract. For Foucault, securitization works together with the disciplines to negotiate conflicts between individual and collective interests. A sense of danger, at times blurred between religious and secular danger, continues to animate these tactics. The strategies of securitization and disciplinary sexual regulation are two trends that popular modes of biblical interpretation also tend to follow, frequently with racializing effects. Many of the chapters in this book show how notions of national security, unity, and mission are bound up with the religious production of the nuclear family in opposition to the nonnormative sexual and nonnational other—the spiritual and military enemy.

This tension between the centering and decentering of power (control and interests) is one that Babylon is particularly apt to represent and manage,

---

63. As Michael Lackey points out, Foucault is one of the progenitors of the idea that Christianity continued to inform the secular, even as people no longer believed in it (2009, 130–32).

with both its unitary towering achievement and its eventual dispersal envied and eschewed. As Colin Gordon points out, for Foucault, liberalism embodies a tension between "the essential incompatibility between the nontotalizable multiplicity of economic subjects of interest and the totalizing unity of the juridical sovereign" (Foucault 2008, 282; Gordon 1991, 22). Put another way, the challenge of liberalism is to make economically driven subjects of interest (multiplicity) accountable to law (a form of social unity) without getting in the way of the market. How to construct social unity and control while pursuing a market driven laissez-faire atomism? As Gordon glosses this point, "Liberalism undertakes . . . the construction of a complex domain of governmentality, within which economic and juridical subjectivity can alike be situated as relative moments, partial aspects of a more englobing element" (22). For market processes of globalization to take hold, sometimes national juridical sovereignty is needed, and sometimes it is a hindrance. We will see how this ideological dance takes place via the alternating value on unity and diversity imagined through reference to Babel.

As will become apparent, biblical interpretation of Babylon resists the idea that power might no longer be localized in the nation-state (and in the United States); but it can also conveniently bolster the very tactics on which biopolitics relies. Longing for the certainties of national sovereignty (and theological truth) is articulated with an insistence on the openness of the market. Babylon is often used as the antithesis of U.S. sovereignty, with the effect of negatively characterizing spaces and people outside of the auspices of U.S. sovereignty as morally suspect or downright evil. Meanwhile, spectacular Babylon and the diversity of Babel are both used to celebrate the subject of interest and multiplicity.

In some ways, the fact that Babylon is loved as well as hated corresponds to what Eric Santner has written about the shift in sovereignty from the king to the people, in his theoretically energizing book: *The Royal Remains: The People's Two Bodies and the Endgames of Sovereignty*. Santner provides an excellent account of how, in the shift from monarchical to democratic sovereignty, the "fleshy" bodies of "the people" are invested with the embodied power that once belonged to the king (2011). Describing this shift as something like the psychoanalytic theory of castration, Santner writes,

When the sovereign thing, whether phallus, father, or king, [or state], can no longer discharge the duties of its office, it discharges the remains of the flesh it has heretofore pretended or appeared to embody. . . . The secret of the master/ sovereign . . . becomes a kind of chronic, spectral secretion of the social body at large, one registered as a surplus of immanence that oscillates between the sublime and the abject and calls forth the apparatuses of biopolitical administration. (2011, 81)

For Santner, biopolitics manages the "vicissitudes of flesh" (98) that are discharged in the transition from monarchy to republic. Babylon assists in this management. Bodies, particularly sexualized bodies, are both invested and vilified, via Babylon, according to how they correspond to the aims of the nation-state (the people). Although Santner focuses on the investiture of people's bodies in modernity, he does not go as far as to explore what happens to this investiture of the flesh once sovereignty moves outside of the people to the corporation, driven by global market forces.

What we see with references to Babylon is that the cosmological and spiritual are used to try to contain, localize, and hierarchize flesh for capital in a globally graduated sovereignty that is always attempting to place the United States at the top of the hierarchy. If sovereignty has now moved beyond the people, beyond the nation-state, then the beyond of the apocalyptic cosmological order figures this shift, but the secular uses of Babylon still navigate the push and pull between economic globalization and state.

Roadmap

Much of this book shows that Babylon and the interpretive tradition in which it has been elaborated come to manage the position of the United States within a biopolitical, globalized world. These conditions include political ideals (exception to law, class and patriarchal hierarchies, theistic sovereignty), military tactics (occupation and torture), sexual regulation (homophobia, sexualized racialization, the continual valorization of the heterosexual nuclear family), and economics (tactics that direct global movements of capital and labor). The book ends with a queer exploration of the most wicked elements in the Babylon narrative (the antichrist and the

Whore), in order to push back against the family-oriented cultivation of biopolitical health through sexualization and the transcendental guarantors of U.S. national power.

The first three chapters deal primarily with elaborations of the Babel story. Chapter 1 looks at how the Tower of Babel becomes a facilitator of biopolitics. The Jewish historian and Roman apologist Josephus, writing in the first century of the Common Era, is the first to turn the story into one about proper modes of governance. The political ideals that Josephus conveys in his version—drawn from Greek and Roman ideals of governance and self-control and his worry over Jewish revolt—were largely transmitted via Christianity and have indelibly marked transmission of this story. Christian-inflected Josephan allusions to the Babel story can be heard in U.S. partisan politics, from the Republican tea party to Barack Obama's Democratic big tent. The Babel story is used to debate the role of government, the role of family, and the relationship between liberty and equality in democracy; it is used as a cautionary tale about self-indulgence and big government taking the place of faith in God. Both sides of the partisan divide use the story to promote what I call theodemocracy: They require faith in the Christian God, democracy that distinguishes between civil and economic equality, and heteropatriarchal sexual regulation. Faith, democracy, and sexual regulation work together to promote the biopolitical subject of interest and to secure the free flow of capital. These dynamics are illuminated by the work of the French philosopher Jacques Rancière (2006) on a certain conservative hatred of radical equality in democracy.

Chapter 2 traces ambivalences around unity and diversity in allusions to Babel in discourses about law and military aggression. This chapter tracks references to Babylon and Babel in the secular discourse of the neoconservative movement and in the religious, conservative discourse of theonomy. Despite significant philosophical and religious differences, a similar affinity for making exception to the law surfaces in both sets of writings, through the tensions, slippages, and alternating values placed on unified social action and diversity. Suspicious of political and philosophical unities, such as non-U.S. empires or secular humanism, both favor decentralization and individualism that can go beyond the law. These discourses nonetheless insist on unified truth, presented in strongly imperialist terms. When these dynamics are read alongside Carl Schmitt's genealogy of the exception in *Political Theology* ([1922] 2005) a clear picture emerges not only of their violent aspirations but also of the scripturalized structure of exception to law in U.S. liberal democracy.

Hollywood Babylon—or the national U.S. art form: film—is the subject of chapter 3. It shows how biopolitics, biblical interpretation, and the discourse of tolerance are imbricated in two important films: D. W. Griffith's 1916 film *Intolerance: Love's Struggle through the Ages*, and Alejandro González Iñárritu's 2006 film *Babel*. Both films articulate a wish to rebuild Babel: They propose cinema as a tolerant universal language. While advocating tolerance, they sexualize and negatively appraise the otherness of Babylon in ways that uphold the normative sexual relations of the white heteronormative family. The ambivalence of these films toward their central metaphor is also consistent with the overlap between disciplines and regularization in biopolitics. Together, they reveal how Bible, film, family, and tolerance discourse all work together to normalize biopolitical divisions of populations and to model subjects of interest that are free but not too free. The place of tolerance in biopolitics is theorized via Wendy Brown (2006) and Janet Jakobsen and Ann Pellegrini (2003).

The last half of the book pays attention to the impact of the apocalyptic framing of Babylon in its theopolitical machinations. These chapters show how the apocalyptic personages associated with Babylon—the Whore and the antichrist—are part of the eschatological landscape in which references to Babylon find their efficacy. Chapter 4 moves from sexual regulation (biopolitical regularization) to war (securitization). This chapter analyzes the use of the Bible in torture. Boney M's song "Rivers of Babylon"—which sets the biblical Psalm 137 to music—was played at ear-splitting volume in the attempts to break prisoners at Abu Ghraib. Examination of this generally overlooked detail reveals much about why torture has been considered both permissible and necessary in the war on terror. The use of this particular psalm as a form of torture—ending with revenge as it does—calls for an interrogation of the relationship of revenge to torture. The chapter traces the interpretive tradition that promotes violence and revenge toward Babylon. It explores the apocalyptically inflected, literalist-allegorical form of biblical interpretation that allows this text to be used as torture. "Rivers of Babylon" at Abu Ghraib reveals how allegory, scripture, torture, and revenge are used to establish the truth of U.S. sovereignty and to diminish any threat to it in the future.

The fifth chapter explores places where the war on terror and sexual regulation explicitly overlap. It looks at popular images of political enemies as homosexualized antichrists in apocalyptic thought and also at images of homosexualized Muslims in secular political humor (liberal and conservative). Building on work by Jasbir Puar (2007) and Junaid Rana (2011) on the racialization and sexualization of "terrorists," I use these images as an entry point into thinking about the way in which exception to law is bound up with notions of sexuality and the human. The apocalyptic reasoning that produces the homosexualized enemy as antichrist is the same future-oriented logic that is central to the delimitation of the in/human that enables the imperial project its dehumanizing techniques. I draw on Lee Edelman on "futurity" (2004) and its relation to normative sexuality and Giorgio Agamben on "bare life" (life considered to be borderline human) and the state of exception ([1995] 1998; [2003] 2005). The chapter argues that legal attempts to ban gay marriage from U.S. polity are integrally related to U.S. disregard for international law (the state of exception) that allows for torture overseas; both draw boundaries around the human in ways that accord with apocalyptically oriented desire.

The final chapter considers how biblical texts can be approached differently. Taking its cue from the Babel story, it outlines a reading practice that values liminality and impossibility, and that might provoke the politically productive feeling of the sublime instead of the bellicose feeling of terror. This chapter combines a deconstructive literary approach to religious narratives proposed by Gayatri Chakravorty Spivak to reread the Whore of Babylon and the antichrist, with the African American artist Charles Gaines's writing on the sublime as social connectivity and with queer theorists Lee Edelman and Tim Dean on the impossible rupture and connectivity of antisocial queer desire. The chapter draws to the fore Near Eastern mythological filiations between Christ, antichrist, and Whore. It rereads the antichrist and the Whore of Babylon as detranscendentalized queer figures that ironically disrupt the transcendent grounding for political decisions, making room for the sublime singular encounter with the political other.

Whether allusions to Babylon are born out of religious conviction (some are, some are not), they all illuminate how a deep-seated biblical stratum in

U.S. culture influences, limits, and enables political policy, expression, and action. At the largest level, this plays out in terms of attempts to reassert national sovereignty in the face of globalized markets and power structures. On a microlevel, biblical interpretation facilitates biopolitical subjectivity even as it seems to resist it. The complex set of positive and negative identifications made between the United States and Babylon mimic the story of Babel, constantly seeking to establish centralized power yet simultaneously undoing it. Contradictory in its signification, Babylon continually obscures and undoes the political work that it performs.

From Babel to Biopolitics: Josephus, Theodemocracy, and the Regulation of Pleasure

How does the Tower of Babel become a story about human power relations? How does it become the carrier of biopolitics? What interpretive legacies mold it into a figure that characterizes the political? Genesis 11 tells simply of God's fear of unlimited human *capacity* in building the Tower of Babel. Despite a habitual rendering of the story as one of poor governance, tyranny, and pride, the biblical text has nothing to say about those issues and is remarkably unforthcoming about the reasons for human or divine actions. Humans want to make a name for themselves to avoid being scattered (11:4). Yahweh confounds language and technology because, together, "all that the people plan to do will not be impossible for them" (11:6). Details are not given about why the people build the tower and under what compulsion or about why God wants to confound them. As several interpreters have suggested, one could interpret the text as displaying God's jealousy or oversensitivity to human capacity (Derrida [1980] 2002, 108; Humphreys 2001, 74–75; Kraeling 1920, 280; Paine 1892, 394).

The Jewish-Roman historian Josephus, writing in the first century C.E. in opposition to the Jewish revolt against Rome, is the first to turn the story into one about proper modes of governance. Josephus's retelling of Babel, in *Antiquities of the Jews* (*Ant.* 1:109–21), was preserved in the christian tradition and has lasting effects. He disambiguates the ancient Hebrew text and exonerates God, while delivering a polemic against rebellion and tyranny. In his version, the people misjudge the source of their comfort (God) and so are willing to follow a proud tyrant, Nimrod, in his building project. Josephus effectively contributes to an extrabiblical, yet still scripturalized, story about sin and punishment: humans' desire for comfort, their affront to God's leadership, their trust in their own governance, and God's punishment. In the long interpretive tradition that takes up these themes, Josephus is sometimes explicitly cited; most often, elements of his version are simply folded into Christianized scripture.[1]

As Josephus tells it, after the great flood, "God also commanded the people to send colonies abroad for the thorough peopling of the earth—that they might not raise seditions [*stasiazo*, to rebel or revolt]."[2] God wants them to disperse, in order to "cultivate a great part of the earth, and enjoy its fruits after a plentiful manner" (*Ant.* 1:110). Instead, they are persuaded by Nimrod—son of Cush, son of Ham, son of Noah—to rebel. Wanting to protect their own well-being, they disobey God's command to scatter and build a tower in case of another flood. They refuse what Josephus indicates as the good of diaspora. In his view, by staying together they risk self-destructive conflict.

The tyrant Nimrod is said to excite the people to *hubris* (pride, or an affront). Nimrod persuades them that God does not have their best interest at heart in telling them to disperse and that they, not God, are the reason for their current prosperity (*Ant.* 1:112–13). He plays on their interest in

---

1. Until recently, pride and punishment constituted the predominant way this story has been understood (Hiebert 2007, 29). Philo's *On the Confusion of Tongues* may be the first to turn the Babel story into a story about sin and punishment, but Josephus's version seems to have been more influential.

2. I use Whiston's 1999 translation of Josephus's complete works throughout, unless otherwise indicated. For the most part it is very readable and a good translation. In places where I feel the meaning of the Greek is better drawn out in another translation I use it and so indicate.

their own comfort. They become suspicious of being tricked by God, believing that they were "ordered to send out separate colonies, that, being divided asunder, they might the more easily be oppressed" (*Ant.* 1:112). Nimrod uses his influence to achieve the people's collective effort against God, "believing that only thus would men be free of fear of God if they would continue to use their own power" (*Ant.* 1:114; trans. Feldman 2000). Humans' collective effort for self-preservation is thus set in antagonistic relationship to God's governance.

The insertion of Noah's great-grandson into the Babel story is perhaps Josephus's most overtly influential elaboration. Nimrod is a very minor character in the biblical text, only mentioned in the genealogy of Noah's sons in Genesis 10:8–12. He is described as "a mighty hunter before the Lord . . . the beginning of his kingdom was Babel [Babylon], Erech, and Akkad" (Gn 10:9–10). The text goes on to list other cities that Nimrod built, but he is not associated with the building of a tower. The name *Nimrod* is, however, a homonym in Hebrew for "we will revolt." Josephus draws lines between textual dots (Babylon, building, revolt) so that Nimrod becomes the tower builder and instigator of rebellion. Certainly Josephus is not the first, or only, ancient writer to vilify Nimrod as a proud tyrant, defying God. [3] But Josephus is the first to elaborate his role at the Tower of Babel, and he does so in a way that turns the story into one about governance. Having introduced Nimrod into the story, Josephus is the progenitor of those who use the Tower of Babel to criticize a particular leader's hubris, or to argue that nonpious efforts at governance are destined to fail.

3. Nimrod appears as arrogant before God in the earlier text by Philo, *Questions and Answers in Genesis 2:82*, as noted by Kugel 1997, 126. Along similar lines, an unnamed tyrant appears in Philo's *On the Confusion of Tongues* 23:107. One possibly earlier connection between Nimrod and Babel is found in Pseudo-Philo's *Biblical Antiquities* 6:14 (Kugel 1997, 126n1; Spilsbury 1998, 52; van der Toorn and van der Horst 1990, 19). *Biblical Antiquities* briefly mentions Nimrod, in a version in which Abraham resists the building of the tower. Nimrod is not the chief prince or even a main character in this story—Jectan is—but Nimrod encourages Jectan to throw Abraham into a fiery furnace. The antagonism between Nimrod and Abraham is one that develops in later Jewish texts, such as *Sefer Hayashar*, see Graves and Patai 1964, 134–35. For genealogies of the development of Nimrod before and after Josephus, see Levin 2002; Pinker 1998; van der Toorn and van der Horst 1990. For ancient sources that develop the stories around Babel and Nimrod, see Feldman 2000, 40–41; Graves and Patai 1964, 125–29, 134–39; Kugel 1997, 122–30. For a discussion of the full Jewish and Christian interpretive tradition around Babel, see Bost 1985.

Careful reading of Josephus's version shows it to be infused with nuanced philosophical and political ideas, which are also inherited in later citations. A good deal of attention has been paid to the way that Josephus recodes and elaborates the biblical stories, making clear his own personal, political, and theological vision and revealing Greek and Roman influence (Feldman 1998a, 1998b; Franxman 1979; Inowlocki 2005, 2006; Mader 2000; Schwartz 1990, 23–57; Spilsbury 1998). As Sabrina Inowlocki (2006) points out in her astute article on the subject, however, not much has been written about his version of Babel. She makes the compelling argument that Josephus's retelling of Babel is really a political commentary that reflects his experiences in the Judean War, in particular the experience of factional strife and the competition of rebel leaders for power in place of the established line of priests (among whom Josephus was numbered). Building on Inowlocki's analysis, I explore further the ways in which the political values that Josephus conveys in this story of comfort, tyranny, and rebellion are drawn from Greek and Roman ideals of governance and self-control. As I will show, Josephus's version carries with it *a suspicion of democracy as an impious and tyrannical locus of moral dissolution and a threat to established hierarchies of governance.* More broadly, this chapter explores how both overt and subtle aspects of Josephus's version of the Babel story continue to affect the way it is used politically. The extent of Josephus's influence turns out to be greater than might be imagined.

Josephus's politically inflected version of the story has been surprisingly enduring, giving the Babel story enough political weight to be referenced in contemporary U.S. partisan politics, from the Republican tea party to the Democratic big tent. Allusions to the Babel story, shaped in its reception by Josephus, often mobilize opinions about self-indulgence—imagined in sexual or monetary terms—at the same time that they debate the role of government, the role of family, and the relationship between liberty and equality in democracy. Conservative voices worry over the uncontrollable power of democracy, variously called soft despotism, the tyranny of the majority, and too much state control—all of which are associated with sexual immorality. Somewhat counterintuitively, fears of self-indulgence, lack of faith, and nonstandard families can also be detected in liberal notions of the big tent and the need to find one higher value to unify the country.

Though Republican tea party proponents of small government and Democratic rhetoricians for the big tent disagree on many points, their allusions to Babel bring into relief a shared commitment to a ubiquitous and infinitely recognizable U.S. American understanding of democracy, that I rename *theodemocracy*. Theodemocracy is the theopolitical packaging for biopolitics. Some features of theodemocracy are that it criticizes conceptualizations of democracy that are not ordered by clear lines of hierarchy; it displays anxiety over the effect of uncontrolled sexuality on the healthy body politic; it ruminates over the tension between liberty and equality; and it worries about cultivating a sense of national unity. Eschewing radical equality but holding onto a republican democracy, theodemocracy requires faith in the Jewish or Christian God and sexual regulation in order to secure family lines of inheritance so that the biopolitical subject of interest can accumulate capital, protected by class stratification. Hierarchies built on the authority of transcendence must necessarily be in place for *homo oeconomicus* to be detached enough from the social contract to pursue his or her own interest (see the introduction). Families, and in particular family bloodlines, are required for the production of such hierarchies. "Biblical morality" provides the theological grounding for this regulation of the family. As in its ancient Jewish Greco-Roman context, the story of Babel is still told to salve political worries about hierarchy with assurances of filiation and transcendence.

Let me be clear that I am not trying to suggest that Josephus's retelling is always used deliberately and consciously in these discourses, although sometimes it is. Rather, because Josephus and Genesis were both transmitted by and for Christians in the Western world, it continues to influence the way the story is known. Further, Josephus drew on Greek and Roman notions that have been debated in post-Enlightenment political theory and which continue to shape political ideals. When merged with the Bible, these ideals take on extra authority. Thus familiar and authoritative in more ways than one, Josephus's version provides an easy support for Christian-centric political views that wish to reaffirm traditional structures of authority.

In what follows, I start with a detailed discussion of Josephus and the classical Greek and Roman thematics that affect his retelling of the Babel story, including suspicion of democracy and its purported connection to self-indulgence. I then move into the U.S. context of President Obama's 2009–12 term. I argue that elements of Josephus's version can be detected in conservatives' racializing critiques of Obama's big government, in tea party versions of what Jacques Rancière has called "hatred of democracy," and, finally, in the limits of President Obama's response to conservative discourse. In all of these, theodemocracy promotes the conditions that allow the subject of interest to flourish, unhindered by economic regulations, social programs, or the social contract—even while advocating abnegation in matters of pleasure.

Tyranny, Stasis, and Hubris and the Jewish Rebels

The Babel story is part of Josephus's account of Jewish history in *Antiquities of the Jews*, which begins in biblical times and moves on to give the larger picture of Jewish life in Roman-occupied Judea. In this, and in his other major work, *The Jewish War*, he tells of Jewish and Roman governance, and of the Jewish revolt against Rome that devastatingly resulted in the destruction of the Second Temple (70 C.E.).

Josephus's writings have provided scholars with an invaluable source of information about the period, but they are well recognized as fully biased in favor of Josephus's own agendas. Having himself led the Jewish resistance in Galilee before being arrested and defecting to the side of the Romans, he speaks out strongly against the Jewish resisters, whom he names zealots.[4] His critique of tyranny in the Babel story, and elsewhere, is therefore aimed not at Roman occupiers of Judea but rather at the Jewish rebels

---

4. Josephus served as the commander of the Galilean forces against the Romans, as he describes in *The Life of Flavius Josephus*, but from the beginning he urges peace with the Romans (*Life* 28–29). He has long been understood as selling out to the Romans. Even according to his own account, many in Galilee thought he planned to betray them (*Life* 132). Gleason draws attention to the ruthless tactics, violently enacted on bodies; these tactics, Josephus brags, helped him maintain control in Galilee (e.g., *Jewish War* 2:611–13; *Life* 145–48, 169–73; Gleason 2001, 53–64). Recently, however, scholars have argued that his support of the Roman empire was more circumspect and that Josephus was both aware of the rhetorical convention of irony and used it to criticize the Romans (see Mason 2005; McLaren 2005). Inowlocki suggests that the Babel story subtly criticizes both Greek *and* Roman imperial dominance (2006, 190).

who fought the Romans and tried to usurp control from the high priest-hood. He blames this unrest for Rome's eventual destruction of Jerusa-lem. Inowlocki notices that the language Josephus uses when he refers to the hubris and tyranny of Nimrod parallels his description of the zealots (e.g., *JW* 4:150) and especially John of Gischala, one of the rebel leaders with whom Josephus has a particular rivalry (e.g., *JW* 4:208, 389; Inowlocki 2006, 183).

As Inowlocki has shown, Josephus's Babelian cast commentary on his own context is subtly indicated by the use of the Greek concept-words *stasis*, *tyranny*, and *hubris*, all of which have political implications. His additions of hubris and tyranny to the story get especially amplified in the later interpretive tradition, so that they are commonly assumed to be part of the biblical story. Fear of collective effort and suspicion of people's interest in pleasure and comfort are inflated in the retelling and handed on in the interpretive tradition. For Josephus, as in the Greek world, excess pleasure, or wrongly oriented pleasure, leads to hubris, tyranny, and stasis. As it turns out, these thematics also show Josephus's disapproval of democratic aspirations by the common people and his judgment about the self-indulgent source of these political aims. Josephus's view on governance, forged in opposition to the stasis of the zealots, is highly critical of any affront to established lines of authority.

Josephus uses the term *stasis* frequently in his writings and twice in the Babel story (*Ant.* 1:110, 117), signaling it as an important concept for his message. *Stasis* in ancient Greek can extend beyond the more familiar meaning of "continuance" to the seemingly antithetical sense of civil strife, factionalism, conflict, and rebellion brought on by division or dissent. Inowlocki contends that Josephus uses the term to respond to the experiences of social unrest in the war against Rome that he describes in *Antiquities* and the *Jewish War* (Inowlocki 2006, 184). In the Babel story, Josephus uses *stasiazo* (the verb) to describe the tendency to rebellion that God tried to quell by commanding the people to spread out into colonies (*Ant.* 1:110). He later asserts that the confusion of languages throws the people into *stasis* (the noun) so that they disperse, as God had commanded (*Ant.* 1:117). Drawing on the work of Louis Feldman and Gottfried Mader, Inowlocki suggests that, when Josephus uses the word *stasis*, it is a loaded term influenced by the Greek historian Thucydides, for whom stasis and plague are the two routes to "desocialization and anomia" (Mader 2000, 57; see also Feldman 1998b, 140–43). Stasis and social disorder go together.

Josephus further associates the people's collective action with *hubris* (with its semantic range of insolence, affront, insult, and sexual assault).[5] In Josephus's view, the social ill of stasis is caused by disregard for lines of authority—namely, hubris and tyranny—which is caused in turn by prosperity or satiety (Inowlocki 2006, 178). This thematic often gets reduced in the interpretive tradition to the simplified form of "pride," but Josephus's view of *hubris* is more complicated. In general, he uses the term *hubris* to describe power grabs of which he does not approve, but *hubris* also designates some sort of immoderation. In a helpful, detailed study of the connections between hubris in classical Greek thought and Josephus's use of the term (1993), Daniel Levine notices that in ancient Greek thought hubris is not simply pride but also an affront or insult motivated by the perpetrator's desire.[6] The desire that produces hubris comes from overindulgence.[7] He argues that throughout *Antiquities* Josephus establishes the pattern "wealth leads to hubris" (1993, 62–63; e.g., *Ant.* 1:161–63). As Levine summarizes, "The notion of dangerous violence inherent in *hubris* was often seen as a result of abundant, excessive wealth or fullness . . . that engenders a blind folly . . . which in turn results in abusive behavior characteristic of *hubris*" (54). Josephus's use of the term *hubris* for the building of Babel therefore indicates a worry about the disordering effects of comfort and self-indulgence. The Greek idea that "prosperity leads to hubris" is reflected in his assertion that the people do not obey God's commands to form colonies because they misrecognize the source of their prosperity and

5. Levine (1993) and Cohen (1995) show that hubris was often used in the classical world to signify sexual violence, abuse, or harassment. Levine (67) notes that Josephus often uses the term *hubris* in relation to sexual impropriety (e.g., *Ant.* 2:56–57). Although sexual overtones are not explicit in Josephus's telling, they come through in later political ruminations on Babel and pleasure, as we will see.

6. As Aristotle writes, "[Hubris] is to do and to say things which make the victim incur shame not so that he would get something which he did not get before, but so that he would enjoy himself" (*Rhetoric* 1378b5, quoted in Levine 1993, 53). Roberts (1924) translates hubris in this passage as "insolence"; J. H. Freese (1926) translates it as "insult."

7. As Levine points out, Aristotle quotes Solon to say, "Satiety [*koros*] breeds insolence [*hubris*] when riches attend the men whose mind is not prepared" (*Athenian Constitution* 12.2, trans. Rackham 1935; Levine 1993, 55).

happiness, supposing it to be from the power of their own households (*Ant.* 1:111; Inowlocki 2006, 178).[8]

If Babel becomes a political allegory for the action of the Jewish rebels, one might wonder why excess and satiety would be an issue. The self-indulgent, excessive tyrant might be a recognizable political type, but it doesn't fit very well with the reality of the Jewish rebels at war with Rome. The constellation of terms Josephus uses in his narrative suggests that he is not simply defending Rome; more substantively, he is concerned with protecting a particular form of Jewish governance. In associating tyranny with hubris and also with an improper attitude toward comfort, as we will see, he seems to be arguing against a democratic attack on priestly authority.

Against Democracy

Certainly, maintaining priestly authority was of central concern to Josephus, himself of priestly lineage. Notably, in the *Jewish War*, Josephus likens the rebels' antiauthoritarianism to the political system of democracy. He criticizes their attempt to replace priestly birthright with something that sounds akin to ancient Athenian democracy, where public office was elected via the drawing of lots. He describes the rebels' proposed democratic method of choosing leaders as follows:

> *They undertook to dispose of the high priesthood by casting lots for it, whereas, as we have said already, it was to descend by succession in a family.* The pretense they made for this strange attempt was an ancient practice, while they said that of old it was determined by lot; but in truth, it was no better than a dissolution of an undeniable law, and a cunning contrivance to seize upon the government. (*JW* 4:153–54, emphasis mine)

Josephus condemns the zealots for conspiring to overturn the high priestly family line and imagining that leadership could be chosen on the basis of community membership rather than genealogy.

---

8. For further examples of prosperity leading to hubris in Josephus's thought, see *Ant.* 1:200, 3:223, 5:180.

Like the rebels, Josephus's Nimrod urges the people to buck God's authority and move to collective action; for these actions Nimrod is called a tyrant. Inowlocki mentions, but does not develop, the idea that Josephus's use of tyranny, stasis, and hubris also points to the classical Greek connection between democracy and tyranny (2006, 181). In this regard she references Demosthenes and Herodotus, but not Plato or Aristotle. But classical philosophy's strong association between satiety, democracy, and tyranny may also be pertinent in understanding the nuances of this passage. Certainly Josephus has knowledge of Plato, as he indicates in a number of places (Feldman 1998b, 179). Here he seems to take up Plato's famous antidemocratic insistence in book 8 of the *Republic* that democracy leads to tyranny. More particularly, for Plato, the freedom of democracy leads to excess indulgence of desire. To quote the philosopher, the one who "believes in legal equality" (8.561e)—i.e., the democratic person—"lives on, yielding day by day to the desire at hand. Sometimes he drinks heavily while listening to the flute; at other times, he drinks only water and is on a diet; sometimes he goes in for physical training; at other times, he's idle and neglects everything. . . . There's neither order nor necessity in his life, but he calls it pleasant, free, and blessedly happy, and he follows it for as long as he lives" (8.561c–d). This lack of discipline has the result of overturning the usual relations of hierarchy and wisdom, creating a state in which grave political mistakes can be made. Plato says, "The young imitate their elders and compete with them in word and deed, while the old stoop to the level of the young and are full of play and pleasantry, imitating the young for fear of appearing disagreeable and authoritarian" (8.563). Democratic "drones"—as Plato describes them in apiarian terms—do not censor themselves in political speech, and end up setting up *a tyrant* to defend them against perceived oligarchs (8.564–65). Likewise, Aristotle, in categorizing types of political constitutions in the *Politics*, associates tyranny with some forms and aspects of democracy (5.1313b; 6.1319b), although less univocally than Plato.

Josephus's Babel narrative seems to reflect this dim view of democracy. For instance, the language used to describe Nimrod's slip into tyranny hints at the interrelationships between oligarchy, democracy, and tyranny. After exciting the people to the hubris of self-governance, Nimrod moves toward tyranny. More literally, the Greek reads, "He turned away little by little toward tyranny [*kai perista de kat' oligon eis tyrannida*]" (*Ant.* 1:114). One cannot help but hear echoes of Plato's downward continuum of political good, descending from aristocracy through oligarchy, democracy, and finally tyranny. The idiom that Josephus uses to phrase Nimrod's turn is suggestive as well: The phrase "little by little toward tyranny [*de kat' oligon eis tyrannida*]" places *oligos* (the word for "little" or "few," and the root word for oligarchy) in close proximity to *tyranny*. The term *demos* or *democracy* is not used in this passage, but there is an implicit critique of the people led astray in collectivizing because of their unwillingness to sacrifice their pleasure to obedience. Thus there is a correspondence in this narrative between the general Greek view that excess leads to hubris and Plato's view that undisciplined desire and excess pleasure reside in democracy and lead to tyranny.[9]

Even as he borrows Greek ideals, Josephus distances himself from classical Greek political thought on the importance of virtue in producing happiness. His villain Nimrod sounds classically Greek when "he persuaded them not to attribute their prosperity [*eudamonein*] to God but to consider that their own virtue [*aretē*] brought this to them" (*Ant.* 1:113; trans. Feldman 2000).[10] Nimrod ventriloquizes the classical view that *aretē* (virtue) leads to *eudaimonia* (happiness, prosperity, the good life, hu-

9. Philo's interpretation of the Babel story also decries tyranny and seeks order but stands in contrast to Josephus's antidemocracy. Philo writes, "But there are two species of cities, the one better, the other worse. That is the better which enjoys a democratic government, a constitution which honors equality, the rulers of which are law and justice; such a constitution as this is a hymn to God. But that is the worse kind which adulterates this constitution, just as base and clipped money is adulterated in the coinage, being, in fact, ochlocracy [rule of the mob], which admires inequality, in which injustice and lawlessness bear sway" (*On the Confusion of Tongues* 23:108). Although it is well known that Philo admires Plato, he goes on in terms that almost seem to compare the Tower of Babel with Plato's view of the good city in *The Republic*: "'The mind, therefore, having called in these allies [the senses, and the passions] says, 'Let us build ourselves a city;' an expression equivalent to, 'Let us fortify our own things; let us fence them around to the best of our power let us divide and distribute, as into tribes and boroughs, each of the powers existing in the soul, allotting some to the rational part, and some to the irrational part; let us choose competent rulers, wealth, glory, honor, pleasure by means of which we may be able to become masters of everything'" (23:111). This Platonic city, with its designated rulers and tower are "a strong palace for the tyrant vice" (23:113).

10. The Whiston ([1828] 1999) translation obscures the philosophical undertones by translating *aretē* as "courage."

man flourishing).[11] By giving this perspective to his antagonist, Josephus appears to be criticizing the classical view that virtue is the most necessary element of successful collective life and good governance. Virtue is important for Josephus, but it should be oriented toward piety to God. As he elaborates in *Against Apion* (*AA*), Mosaic law was different from Greek philosophy in that it facilitated the virtue necessary for piety and did not see virtue as an end in itself. Moses, he writes, "did not make piety a part of virtue, but recognized and established the others [virtues] as parts of it [piety], that is, justice, moderation, endurance, and harmony among citizens in relation to one another in all matters" (*AA* 2:170; trans. Barclay 2006). Notably, what gets in the way of pious virtue at Babel is the people's attitude toward their own well-being (variously described in the text as *eudaimonia*, *euporia*, and *agathos*; *Ant.* 1:111, 113). Subtly, Josephus indicates that *eudaimonia* cannot be achieved by virtue *without piety*; the belief that *eudaimonia* is produced by virtue alone actually corrupts virtue and leads to a hubristic desire.

One can, therefore, read the political commentary of Josephus's Babel midrash on several levels. On one level, Josephus is commenting on his current situation. As in his work as a whole, the Jewish revolt against Rome is strongly criticized, and the rebels blamed for the disaster that followed. The rebel groups are said to be factional, and collective resistance to be compelled by tyranny. On a more general level, Josephus is commenting on political governance. In defending the priesthood, he vilifies democratic governance. He does not have a high view of the people, whom he describes as governed by their own perceptions and interests and easily manipulated by a tyrant.[12] Finally, he seems to be staking out the place for religion in politics and philosophy; obedience to God, he says, is more important for governance than virtue. Thus, the story of Babel becomes one that opposes revolt and collective action, associating both with gross lack of virtue and a disastrous expression of impiety.

---

11. When Aristotle considers the pursuit of *eudaimonia* in *Nicomachean Ethics*, he arrives at the conclusion that happiness (*eudaimonia*) or "human good" (*to anthropon agathon*) is ultimately attained by "activity of soul in accordance with virtue [*aretē*]" (1.1098a). Aristotle reaffirms the claim that "happiness is the realization and perfect exercise of virtue" in *Politics* (7.1332a).

12. Feldman draws out Josephus's dislike for the masses in several places (1998a, 246; 1998b, 146–47, 503).

Aristocratic Theocracy and the Repudiation of Self-Indulgence

When Josephus's Babel story is read in the context of the rest of his writing, both his particular concerns with the Jewish revolt and his general concerns with proper governance are accentuated. The allusions in his Babel story to the classical Greek political and philosophical juxtaposition of democracy and tyranny can be understood within Josephus's own desire for a system of leadership modeled on the Roman republic. In the case of Judea, he values the aristocratic, *virtuous*, and *pious* high priesthood and council of elders. For Josephus, pious leadership ought not to be separated from the (aristocratic) family line. These points, which scholars have long recognized, are worth outlining here. They clarify how Josephus's attitudes toward governance affect not only his own interpretation of the Babel story but also later citations of his version. Further, it is important to note how, for Josephus, rule by the proper authority prevents excess pleasure seeking and self-indulgence.

Josephus favors an "antimonarchical, senatorial aristocracy" (Mason 2005, 272). His ideal may be the Roman Republic, in part, but he famously invents the term *theocracy* to describe his own version in which God is understood as the director of power relations and the provider of the good life.[13] Josephus's political views are explicitly stated in reflections on biblical texts where power relations or governance are at stake. Inowlocki and Feldman both point out that in order to chastise the Jewish rebels, Josephus condemns ancient Israelite leaders, such as Korah (Nm 16) and Jeroboam (1 Kgs 11:26–12:33), who rebel against God-given structures of authority. When Josephus condemns biblical leaders gone awry, he makes much of their lack of family lineage, their confidence in their prosperity, and their attempts to lead outside of God's choosing.[14] Not surprisingly these figures and Nimrod

---

13. Feldman argues that theocracy and aristocracy are the same for Josephus, but this may be oversimplifying a little (1998b, 145).

14. Josephus's midrashim on Korah and Jeroboam, two biblical usurpers of power, make this clear. Korah, who challenges the authority of Moses and Aaron, is described as a demagogue who wants to take power away from those God appointed. Much like Nimrod, Korah is said to have "a mind to appear to take care of the public welfare; but in reality he was trying to procure to have that honor transferred by the multitude to himself" (*Ant.* 4:20). Feldman meticulously details that way in which the story of Korah is a political and philosophical statement about protecting the priesthood (1998a, 91–109); he suggests that this language

are described in similar terms (Feldman 1998a, 109, 209–11, 238; Inowlocki 2006, 180, 183, 185).

Conversely, proper modes of aristocratic governance are attributed to Moses. In recapitulating the laws for governance found in Deuteronomy, Josephus has Moses proclaim, "Aristocracy, and the way of living under it, is the best constitution" (*Ant.* 4:223). But, making concession for a king (as per Dt 17:14–20), Josephus's Moses continues, "But if you shall desire a king . . . let him be always careful of justice and other virtues; let him submit to the laws and esteem God's commands to be his highest wisdom; but let him do nothing *without the high priest and the votes of the senators*" (*Ant.* 4:223–24).[15] These lines crystallize a number of key values for Josephus: the notion of the virtuous leader whose highest value is piety and whose leadership is directed by God, the rightful leadership of the priesthood, and the notion of a senate, or council, of elite elders.[16] Best governance, for Josephus, seems to be modeled on an ideal Judean constitution rooted in the Torah, which, as Mason notes, he describes via Roman republicanism (e.g., *Ant.* 14:91; Mason 2005, 272).[17]

---

reflects "the Stoic conception of providence" (104). Korah is of the right family lineage, but he problematically bases his right to leadership on his considerable wealth (in Josephus's elaboration), not on God's choosing. Likewise, Jeroboam—who leads a coup against Solomon's son, Rehoboam—is seen as challenging the priesthood. In order to consolidate his power, Jeroboam establishes his own cultic centers, fashions golden calves to worship and appoints his own priests. Feldman suggests that Jeroboam demonstrates for Josephus the problems of democratically electing leaders from the "rabble" or crowd (237–39). He notes that Jeroboam's actions are called hubris (*Ant.* 8:316).

15. Likewise, when describing Samuel's negative prophetic response to the Israelite's request for a king in 1 Samuel 8, Josephus says, "These words greatly afflicted Samuel, on account of his innate love of justice, and his hatred of kingly government, for he was very fond of an aristocracy, as what made the men that used it of a divine and happy disposition" (*Ant.* 6:36). See Feldman 1998b, 145; Spilsbury 1998, 167.

16. Mason points out that Josephus inserts the idea of the senate's authority—frequently in combination with that of the high priest—in multiple places throughout his retelling of biblical stories (Mason 2005, 272; e.g., *Ant.* 4:186; 5:15, 55, 57, 80, 103, 115). The term used for senate is *gerousia* and indicates a council of elders, as mentioned in Jdt 4:8; 1 Macc 12:6; 2 Macc 1:10, 4:44, 11:27 and is the precursor to the Sanhedrin of the Christian Testament (Heidel [1915] 1988).

17. Josephus appreciates the structures of Roman republicanism but may not fully appreciate the Roman emperors, whom he describes elsewhere as tyrants, despite his proclaimed love for his Flavian patrons. His views on the Caesars become clear in *Antiquities* when he recounts the death of Gaius (Caligula) and the circumstances of his succession. Josephus puts his assessment into the mouth of senator Gnaeus Sentius Saturninus, who makes a passionate

Thus senatorial aristocracy must operate in the context of *theocracy*. In *Against Apion* Josephus writes:

> Some legislators have permitted their governments to be under monarchies, others put them under oligarchies, and others under a republican form; but our lawgiver [Moses] had no regard to any of these forms, but he ordained our government to be what, by a strained expression, may be termed theocracy, by ascribing the authority and power to God, and by persuading all the people to have a regard to him as the author of all the good things that were enjoyed either in common by all people, or by each one in particular. (*AA* 2:164–66)

Josephus rejects other forms of governance because they do not give God sufficient credit for human good. Of note in this passage, Moses's qualities as a leader are expressed almost in direct opposition to those ascribed to Nimrod in the Babel story. Where the tyrant Nimrod persuades (*peithō*) the people to commit hubris by not recognizing God as the source of their good (*eudaimonia, agathos, euporia*; *Ant.* 1:111, 113), Moses persuades (*peithō*) the people to give God the ultimate authority and to recognize that their good (*agathos*) comes from God (*AA* 2:166).[18]

The Israelites' frequent failure to conform to theocratic aristocracy had negative effects in Josephus's estimation and led to the corruption of virtue, which in turn led to pleasure-seeking self-indulgence and ultimately caused stasis. For instance, when Josephus criticizes the Israelites for not following God's command to kill all the Canaanites in their conquest of the land, he notes that their governance falls apart, and they are corrupted by pleasure.

> Since they got large tributes from the Canaanites and were indisposed for taking pains by their luxury, they suffered their aristocracy to be corrupted also, and did not ordain for themselves councils of elders, nor any other such magistrates as their laws had formerly required, but they were very much given to cultivating their fields, in order to get wealth; which great indolence of theirs brought a terrible sedition [*stasis*] upon them, and they proceeded so far as to fight one against another. (*Ant.* 5:134–35)

---

speech against the (eventual) succession of Claudius as emperor. He would rather return to days before the Caesars, describing "what mischiefs tyrannies have brought upon this commonwealth, discouraging all virtue, and depriving persons of the magnanimity of their liberty" (*Ant.* 19:172–73). For more on his critique of Roman rule, see McLaren 2005.

18. On further afterlives of Nimrod's persuasiveness, see Callahan 2008, 154.

The hierarchy of aristocracy is necessary to keep indulgence in check and so to preserve pious virtue and civil harmony.[19]

In this light, Nimrod shows the problem of hierarchies gone wrong, of sons led astray. Within theocracy, Josephus believed that good leaders should be wellborn (i.e., aristocratic), virtuous, and above all, chosen by God.[20] Leaders such as Nimrod, Korah, and Jeroboam fail not merely because they are on the same level as the people whom they persuade into rebellion but rather because, with hubris, they do not respect the priestly leaders whom God has chosen and do not follow God's commands, thus producing stasis. Nimrod is said to be *gennaios*, which could mean "brave and strong," or also "of noble birth" (*Ant.* 1:113).[21] But Nimrod is lacking the other virtues (courage, wisdom, temperance, justice, and especially piety) that Josephus indicates are necessary for leadership.

Although Josephus borrows heavily from Roman republicanism in imagining aristocratic senatorial governances, he differs by prioritizing piety and the priesthood. Within his own context, Josephus was torn between loyalty to the Jewish people and wanting social stability and personal security that could be granted by the Romans.[22] His conservative political leanings match his particular hybrid subjectivity as colonized and as collaborator. Before I move on to demonstrating how the Josephan Babel story gets taken up into U.S. politics, it is important to remember that he was writing at a time where full social equality was not a political option, even within democracy. It is fascinating to observe, however, what happens when his political views are imported into contemporary discussions of U.S. democracy: In the new context, fear of social equality and the need for family hierarchies are considerably amplified.

19. See Feldman 1998b, 143–44.
20. Feldman outlines the virtues that Josephus looks for in leaders, in his analysis of Josephus's descriptions of Moses, David, and Solomon (1998b, 398–425, 543–61, 579–602).
21. Inowlocki points out that Jeroboam is described in terms similar to Nimrod. Both are said to be noble (*gennaios*) and bold (*tolmēros*; *Ant.* 8:205).
22. Although he certainly can be—and has been—read as selling out to the Romans, he remained an advocate for Jews' right to worship in their diasporic locations. See Rajak (1985, 28–31) for the ways that Josephus incorporates and manipulates historical documents in *Antiquities* to argue for the Jewish right to worship in peace, as for example in *Ant.* 16:35–37; 19:283.

Nimrod's Racialized Legacy

The principles of hierarchy, filiation, and transcendent authorization to which Josephus adheres are also central to what I am calling theodemocracy, that form of democracy so conducive to biopolitics. Theodemocracy should be more than familiar for those in the U.S. context: It goes by the name and electoral structure of democracy but authorizes its policies by belief in God. What I wish to show in the remainder of this chapter is that belief in God also grounds social hierarchies that are kept in place by family lineages—all of which serve the formation of the subject of interest and the smooth biopolitical functioning of the market. The Babel story, inflected through Josephus's retelling, becomes a useful biblical support for this project. During President Obama's 2009–12 term, the renewed interest in this story further indicates the implication of theodemocracy in racial hierarchies.

The most negative feature of Josephus's legacy is the way that Nimrod, builder of Babel, has been racialized over time (Pinn and Callahan 2008). Prior to Josephus, the Jewish philosopher Philo of Alexandria identified Nimrod as Ethiopian because he was the son of Cush (a Hebrew name that designates a region in North Eastern Africa). Josephus does not pick up on this connection, likely because he uses Nimrod to criticize the infighting in his own ethnic group. Other interpreters, however, combine the racial identification initially put forward by Philo with Josephus's version, so that Babel's architect becomes a tyrant of African descent. The blackening of Nimrod is part of the tradition that reads his grandfather Ham, the cursed son of Noah, as black and inferior (Evans 2008, 18); Ham's blackness is also derived from Cush (his son). In debates over slavery in the nineteenth-century United States, the Hamitic curse was commonly used to justify slavery and a claim to white superiority (S. Johnson 2004).[23] The story of Nimrod was likewise used in this way. For instance, as Dale Andrews has shown, the proslavery northerner Josiah Priest suggested that Nimrod was the "archetype of black immoral character and human rebellion against God" (Andrews 2008, 196). Consciously or not, Priest echoes Josephus in

---

23. E.g., Priest (1843, 78–79, 325–26).

condemning Nimrod's tyranny and his tower-building rebellion, which Priest calls idolatry.[24]

Not surprisingly, this racialized legacy has found its way into some critiques of the first African American U.S. president, Barack Obama, along with critiques of "big government" intrusions by the Democrats. Obama is called Nimrod. Although some of these biblicized critiques are written for specialized conspiracy-theory and prophecy-writing websites,[25] others can be found on secular websites and in online magazines. In order to connect Babel, big government, Nimrod, and Obama, these writers must mobilize a Josephan approach to the story. As we will see, sometimes they attribute their knowledge of biblical history to Josephus, and sometimes they simply cite Josephus *as* scripture. In this discourse, the raced Nimrod provides an easy shorthand to identify and express the dangers of not conforming to theodemocracy and to raise the supposed spiritual stakes of political formation. Theodemocracy is racialized (sometimes intentionally, sometimes not) when Babel and Nimrod are used as cautionary figures in this way.

For example, the online conservative magazine *American Thinker* ran a piece called "Nimrod's Tower," in which the author, Randy Fardal (2009), outlines the similarities between Nimrod and "Barry Babble" (juxtaposing Obama's childhood nickname, "Barry," with Babel). "Mr. Obama's growing tyranny" is compared to Nimrod's motivations. Explicitly referring to Josephus's "historical" account, Fardal further glosses the story: "Initially regarded by his supporters as a great leader, Nimrod became more tyrannical as his power grew." Other (unnamed) historians are referenced to claim "that Nimrod built the tower to monitor and oppress his growing kingdom," in a way that is similar to the Obama administration's actions. The article does not specifically mention Obama's race, but the long-standing racialization of Nimrod stands in the background.

More explicitly racializing are the prodigious prophetic warnings of Craig Portwood (2010), which appeared on the professional-amateur ("pro-am")

24. For a discussion of a more positive reclamation of Nimrod by the African American historian George Washington Williams in the nineteenth century, see A. Smith 2008.
25. Participants in one discussion board spend considerable time showing the connections between Obama and Nimrod: http://www.godlikeproductions.com/forum1/message505914 /pg1.

news website Examiner.com.[26] Portwood worries about big government extending to the feared global order and rule of the antichrist. He explains, after quoting Josephus at length, that "Nimrod and his confederates were attempting to build no less than a global government and that tower would be a reminder to all of the power of man reigning over that of God. It is notable that Nimrod said he would be 'revenged on God' [*Ant.* 1:114]. This is the identical spirit one would expect to [be] seen in an Antichrist" (2010). Citing dubious reconstructions of Nimrod's ancient Near Eastern connections,[27] Portwood makes his way from Nimrod through Osiris and the giants (Nephilim) of Genesis 6, to the evil designs of the antichrist and Obama.[28] He concludes:

> Being the grandson of Ham and the Son of Cush, Nimrod was of dark complexion or as we say today, black. We do have one [?!] black world leader in place: United States President Barack Obama. If the soon anticipated Antichrist does indeed make an abrupt appearance in a world in crisis, will he be more suited to that role than is Barack Obama?

The racialization of the antichrist[29] meets the racialization of Nimrod. In this case, the Babel story is interpreted through the larger apocalyptic discourse on Babylon as the home to great evil. The stakes of distrusting Obama's leadership and government increase considerably.

Glenn Beck, Babel, and the Subject of Interest

Nimrod appears in proximity to another critique of Obama in a lengthy screed against big government and the dangerous equality that it enforces.

---

26. The website is owned by the billionaire Philip Anschutz, a generous contributor to the Republican Party. It is unclear what kind of quality checks "examiners" are required to undergo. They are paid per page view. See Lee 2010. A link to Portwood (2010) is reposted on the self-described prophecy and conspiracy website *Beacon of Truth: The Voice of the Christian Underground*, http://www.beaconoftruth.com/nimrod_obama.htm.
27. For historical data, Portwood turns to sources such as the 1853 religious pamphlet of Alexander Hislop, *The Two Babylons; or, Papal Worship Proved to Be Worship of Nimrod and His Wife*; and the alternate histories of David Hatcher Childress.
28. The connection between Nimrod and the antichrist is also made by other prophecy writers, such as Mark Hitchcock, who cites, in turn, an earlier apocalyptic writer, John Walvoord (Hitchcock 2003, 39–42); both seem to draw on the same Hislop pamphlet to which Portwood refers.
29. For more on the antichrist, see chapters 5 and 6.

On November 17, 2010, the tea-party mobilizer and television host Glenn Beck devoted an entire show to the Babel story as a metaphor for the dangers of a one-world order, equality, humanism, and big government. Assisting him in his biblical exegesis was Rabbi Daniel Lapin. Their interpretation of Babel is remarkable in the work that it does for theodemocracy: It sets up God and the market as two requirements for freedom; it contests economic and social equality; and it interpellates viewers into proper economic subjectivity—the pursuit of economic interests.

Beck and Lapin fear that the story of Babel is being repeated in Europe and warn against a U.S. occurrence. The attempt at a "one-world order"— ominously symbolized by the EU slogan, "many tongues, one family"— can only fail, says Beck, calling to mind Europe's failing economies and rising national debts. The episode opens and closes with images of the European Parliament building in Strasburg, which are compared architecturally to Pieter Bruegel's iconic painting of the Tower of Babel (1563). For Beck, the building "is the symbol of one united Europe, one language— one Europe" (EU slogan "many tongues" notwithstanding). The new world order is aiming for "an affront to God," which has dangerous consequences. Beck says, "We know what happens when big government gets control of the people. . . . It's the oldest story in the book. . . . History that will boggle your mind." Beck warns his audience that they too could face rising prices and high unemployment if they are forced into a "new world order [that] was first tried at the Tower of Babel" (2010, 8).

There is only one brief reference to Obama in the show, in a critique of his health care bill, dubbed by conservatives as "Obamacare."[30] Halfway through the show, as part of his plea to be prepared for the inflation that the global order will incur, Beck gives the example of the rising health care costs of Obamacare. He reminds his audience, "Europe is ahead of us. They're on fire because of the similar policies that they have done years ago and they have failed. . . . This may seem like a new story to you, but it is not." Babel tells us so. Obama and Obamacare are effectively linked to Europe, a global order, debt, Babel, and, by association, the tyrant Nimrod. Beck makes use of a set of connections that are certain to ignite some people's spiritual and fiscal anxieties, each reinforcing the other.

---

30. The Patient Protection and Affordable Care Act, H.R. 3590, 111th Cong. (2010).

From the beginning of the episode, Josephus's interpretation is recalibrated to fit a contemporary context and seamlessly inserted into the biblical text.[31] Beck and Lapin tell the story as follows: "A hunter, a king— Nimrod—says let's build bricks and then we'll build a tower." The problem is not in building the city and the tower, they say, because, after all, the United States is a shining city on the hill. The problem is that Nimrod builds with bricks, not stones. Stones are diverse, unique: "It takes a real artist to be able to put them all together." Proper political subjectivity and collectivity require God. Bricks, by contrast, are human made. Lapin explains, "If you want to turn people to bricks, you are able to turn them into interchangeable social economic cogs that can be plugged around society." Beck emphasizes this point: "America, I want you to think about this. . . . The king made everybody into bricks so they're all exactly the same. Everyone is equal. Everyone is equal." The United States is oddly aligned with Babel via the building of biblical city on the hill (Mt 5:14)—but a *good* Babel, one whose foundations are *not* equality.[32]

Beck tells his viewers that they are being offered a choice under impending duress, between the "yes we can" communist model (as Babelian bricks) and the "yes I can" individualist model. People must retain their individuality, agency, and belief in God. Beck declares, "I can reach out to my community . . . and I can help. And together a collection of strong eyes [*sic*] will make the strongest 'we' the world has ever seen." For Beck and Lapin, God-ordained social distinction (over and against equality) is the key to unity. In Foucauldian terms, they make a strong argument against the social contract and for the subject of interest. This dynamic is tempered, however, by the compassionate-conservative model that keeps "extra on hand, because we need to be a shelter for others."

31. It is likely that Beck's Mormon background shapes this reception of Babel, even though he does not refer to Mormonism in this episode of his show. The story of Nimrod is not developed in the Book of Mormon, but Mormon teachers, such as the influential Hugh Nibley (1988–90), do explain that the Tower of Babel was built by Nimrod; see also Miner 1996, who cites Josephus in his commentary on Ether 2 in the Book of Mormon.

32. As is well known, the city on a hill metaphor is taken from Jesus's Sermon on the Mount and has become part of U.S. national myth. It was used by the Puritan John Winthrop to describe the new community in the Americas (see Bellah 1975, 13–15; Bercovitch 1983, 221–22) and by U.S. Presidents John F. Kennedy (1961) and Ronald Reagan (1984) to describe the United States.

The fear of economic equality is palpable. Beck and Lapin tap into the conservative discourse that distinguishes individual liberty from economic equality. It is almost as if they are using the Bible to gloss the conservative opinion piece "Liberty and Equality: Are They Compatible?" that made the circuit on conservative websites (Gershowitz and Porter 2010). The authors, Hal Gershowitz and Stephen Porter, accuse Obama of big government, which they characterize as "almost tyrannical rule by a ruling class." They lament a forced economic equality in the style of now-economically-strapped European countries that wish for the EU to bail them out. Economic equality, they say, has nothing to do with equal protection and rights under the U.S. Constitution. Gershowitz and Porter write, "The left wants to create a society *based on some expanded notion of egalitarianism* which has nothing to do with equal opportunity under the law, and throw under the bus the ordered liberty which has been the bedrock principle which every generation of Americans has enjoyed" (emphasis mine). Obamacare is the latest of the "entitlement programs" that will bankrupt the country and rob hard-working individuals of their liberty and their money via taxation. Beck and Lapin also connect an expanded notion of egalitarianism to tyranny.

Moreover, for Beck and Lapin—and, as we will see, for other conservatives as well—the fear of economic equality is linked to an almost Platonic anxiety about overindulgent pleasure. Economic freedom and hierarchy are paramount, but they are coupled with caution against consumption. Beck wants to reject consumerism in favor of a higher purpose. He wants to know "what holds us together as a nation." If we are equal bricks, à la Nimrod, "then the mortar that holds it together is the stuff, the material." Consumption is not enough; it does not provide meaning: "We all know Nike. We all know the Mercedes Benz logo. We all know everything about materialism. . . . If you take that away what holds our bricks together?" Something greater, he suggests should bind us: "common experiences of spiritualist [*sic*] or even history." Lapin fills in: "Any tyranny will always begin to develop a hostility to traditional biblical faith, a hostility to the God of Abraham, Isaac and Jacob, a hostility to biblical commitment of any kind at all." Biblical faith should be what binds the nation together, their conversation implies.

Yet, despite the anxiety about excess materialism, freedom comes through the "American free-market system." Lapin opines, "One of the most beautiful expressions of freedom and independence [is] the automobile. You can buy it in whatever color you want, whatever make you want." Choice in cars is valorized over and against the Babelian equalizing of public services (transportation or public housing). The problem is not actually having material objects (although Beck vows to get rid of the $25,000 of excess stuff that he says the average household has lying around); the problem is in not believing in divinity, and, it would seem, not believing in hierarchy. Lapin says, "What any tyrant knows is that you cannot enslave a people that believe in the boss." He appears to be referring to the deity, but the formulation leaves open the possibility that other kinds of hierarchy also prevent tyranny.

In this rhetoric, Beck delivers Babel to a theodemocratic capitalism packaged through the "yes I can" subject of interest. People are encouraged to care about their own individual liberty. National unity is imagined through a shared history and a belief in God, who is the guarantor of hierarchy and nontyrannical order. Belief in God is cultivated by a worry over excess materialism, which is, oddly enough, made possible by the subject of interest that the discourse champions.

Theodemocracy and Filiation

The fear of equality leading to tyranny is a thematic frequently voiced in conservative political thought. The French philosopher Jacques Rancière (2006) calls it "hatred of democracy." Rancière shows that enforcement of political hierarchies also requires God and family lineages, both of which are held up over and against the triviality of pleasure. Rancière points to the Platonic grounding for these thematics within the conservative political imagination. His discussion helps show how conservative Platonism joins up with Josephus's Platonism, making the Babel story a perfect meeting ground.

Rancière argues that conservative critiques of democracy take two forms. Either they complain about the amount of "popular participation in discussing public affairs" or they complain about "a form of social life that turned energies toward individual satisfaction" (2006, 8).[33] These protesta-

---

33. Even Giorgio Agamben seems to accept the degenerate tendencies of democracy, when he speaks of "modern democracy's decadence and gradual convergence with totalitarian states in post-democratic spectacular societies" ([1995] 1998, 10).

tions walk a thin line, worrying of either too much collectivism or too much individualism. As Rancière summarizes, "Good democracy must be a form of government and social life capable of controlling the double excess of collective activity and individual withdrawal inherent in democratic life" (8). In the United States, the political anxieties that Rancière outlines are evident in worry over "excess democracy" (for instance, as voiced by Samuel Huntington in his coauthored report to the Trilateral Commission in 1975),[34] on the one hand, or the fear of too much consumption (also voiced in that report), on the other hand. As further elaborated in chapter 2, the Babel story has been conscripted to both of these critiques: The neoconservative progenitor Irving Kristol has spoken of the babel/babble of the unformed masses, and George W. Bush's adviser Leon Kass likened the malaise of modern life to Babel, a city filled with too much self-indulgence. Paradoxically, a suspicion of individual desires accompanies demands for individual liberty and critiques of big government.

What critics of democracy really object to, Rancière argues, is that democracy is based on chance (e.g., the Athenian drawing of lots). As he puts it, democracy is "based on nothing other than the absence of every title to govern" (2006, 41). The actual scandal of democracy is not excess indulgence but, rather, radical equality. Put another way, "Democratic excess does not have anything to do with a supposed consumptive madness. It is simply the dissolving of any standard by which nature could give its law to communitarian artifice. . . . It is the scandal of a superiority based on no other title than the very absence of superiority" (41). Or "The power of the people . . . is not the power of the population or of the majority, but the power of anyone at all, the equality of capabilities to occupy the positions of governors and the governed" (49). The lack of title to govern is, for Rancière, a kind of ungovernability that grounds politics (49). If power relations were simply natural, they would fall into place; politics would not be needed. Any power struggle, any assumption of leadership, necessarily requires some realization that people do not automatically submit to a leader's vision. They could depart from it; they could revolt or do something

34. See Crozier, Huntington, and Watanuki 1975, 113; for the larger context, see 1–10, 59–64. Notably, they refer to Tocqueville's worry that democracy will undermine itself (8).

unforeseen. Ungovernability is, in fact, the equality that is the beginning of all politics.[35]

As Rancière observes, democracy is seen by its critics as a "crime against the order of kinship" (2006, 33). Human kinship grounds hierarchy and is, he suggests, grounded in belief in a patriarchal God. Thus critics of democracy also require inherited hierarchies of kinship and God. Rancière finds a political template for this sort of antidemocratic governance based on God-ordained hierarchy in Plato's *Republic*. God, he says, has an "obstinate presence at the core of the *Republic*, where he serves as the reference point by which an opposition between good government and democratic government is established" (2006, 35). Plato requires God, if only in the form of a "noble lie," to cultivate belief in the differences between the classes that make up the ideal (aristocratic) city (34). This fable, which Plato hopes could instill the belief that governors were created partly of gold, warriors of silver, and artisans of iron and bronze, would require regulation of family lines. In Plato's words, "The first and most important command from the god to the rulers is that there is nothing that they must guard better or watch more carefully than the mixture of metals in the souls of the next generation" (*Republic* 3.415a–b). In contrast, democracy is "an organization of the human community without any relation to a God-the-father" (Rancière 2006, 32).[36] Where aristocracy adheres to social hierarchies, their inheritances, and their presumed governance structures, democracy does not need them: "It is properly the regime that overturns all the relations that structure human society" (36).

What Rancière calls the conservative hatred of democracy, therefore, shares with Josephus the reliance on God, the demand for filiation, and the Platonic suspicion of equality dressed up as overindulgent excess. Josephus turns a threat of human equality into a story about the political. He transforms a story about the ungovernability of humans and their potential equality with God into a story about unauthorized pleasure creating tyrannical

---

35. Jeffrey Robbins takes the absence of title to govern and a separation from the law of kinship as a starting point for radical democracy (2011, 57–63).
36. For work on the intersection between Rancière and queer theory that goes far beyond his stated views on kinship, see the issue of *borderlands* 8, no. 2 (Chambers and O'Rourke 2009). Rancière is used to help think through queer politics, aesthetics, relationality, and the very meaning of *queer*.

governance. Josephus does precisely what Rancière accuses both Plato and conservatives of doing: He confuses the ungovernable (human possibility) with excess pleasure. He tries to contain radical equality via hierarchies ordained by God and passed down through aristocratic family structures. Rancière does not make this point, but his critique strongly suggests a reason that sexuality is so important to the U.S. culture wars. Sexuality that is not subsumed into the hierarchy of the patriarchal family troubles lines of filiation that ground social stratification. I turn now to the pervasive fear of misdirected pleasure in conservative discourse, before looking at how it extends specifically to sexuality.

Big Government, Soft Despotism, and Tocqueville's Tower

The antidemocratic critiques of hyperindividualism, dangerous collectivity, and overindulgent pleasure correspond to concepts that conservatives draw from Tocqueville's two-volume *Democracy in America*.[37] In observing U.S. democracy of the nineteenth century, Tocqueville is impressed, but he worries about the outcomes of democracy, especially what he calls "the tyranny of the majority" and "soft despotism." The "tyranny of the majority" refers to too much collectivity, whereby minority groups might be disadvantaged by the majority opinion.[38] "Soft despotism" refers to individualist demands for equality and its pleasures, which require the state—that embodiment of the tyrant majority—to step in and adjudicate. As if channeling Josephus but amplifying the Platonic subtext, Tocqueville discusses the perils of a populace gone soft from too much comfort so that it easily accepts the elevation of a new (tower-like) despotism.

Conservatives equate "big government" with the majority tyranny and new despotism that Tocqueville describes.[39] For instance, the conservative

37. George W. Bush's infamous strategist Karl Rove (2010) lists Tocqueville's *Democracy in America* as one of the top five books that define American conservatism.
38. For an analysis of how the majority opinion becomes a new despotic democratic "religion" for Tocqueville, see Jaume 2011. For a longer discussion of Tocqueville's thinking about the place of traditional (God-centered) religion in the United States, see Robbins 2011, 155–65.
39. For a comprehensive analysis of Tocqueville's political writing, in the light of his involvement in French politics, see Wolin 2003. Wolin shows Tocqueville as a complex and

philosopher Paul Rahe, a tea-party favorite, cites Tocqueville in his book *Soft Despotism, Democracy's Drift* (2009). He argues that, following the Cold War, U.S. democracy and democracies in general have gradually undermined the principles of self-governance. Working his way through Montesquieu and Rousseau on governance, he arrives at Tocqueville's critique of democracy, which he seems to adopt as his own. Democratic citizens are likely to become too satisfied with material pleasures (178) and the search for equality, so they all become exactly alike and thus easily molded by a new form of tyranny.[40] To make this point, Rahe quotes a favorite passage from Tocqueville (its significance marked by another appearance as the epigraph to his book).

> I would like to imagine with what new traits despotism could be produced in the world. I see an innumerable crowd of *like and equal men* who turn about without repose in order to *procure for themselves petty and vulgar pleasures* with which they fill their souls. . . .
>
> *Above these is elevated an immense tutelary power*, which takes sole charge of assuring their enjoyments and of watching over their fate. It is absolute, attentive to detail, regular, provident, and gentle. It would resemble the paternal power if, like that power, it had as its object to prepare men for manhood; but it seeks, to the contrary, to keep them irrevocably fixed in childhood; it loves the fact that the citizens enjoy themselves provided that they dream solely of their own enjoyment. It works willingly for their happiness; but it wishes to be the only agent and sole arbiter of that happiness. *It provides for their security, foresees and supplies their needs, facilitates their pleasures, guides them in the principal affairs, directs their industry, regulates their testaments, divides their inheritances.* Can it not relieve them entirely of the trouble of thinking and the pain of living? (Tocqueville [1840] 2000 2.4.6.663, quoted in Rahe 2009, 187; emphasis mine)

"Soft despotism," as the elevation of the immense tutelary power that watches over people, sounds remarkably like Babel. It is impossible to know whether

---

sometimes contradictory thinker; ultimately he seeks to control the masses, and he "abhors collective action" (549, see also 445). Further, he shows that whatever enthusiasm Tocqueville shows for American democracy and civic participation in *Democracy in America* wanes as France grows closer to it in the 1848 revolution (432).

40. In Rahe's view, "as a consequence of the drift toward equality, diversity is disappearing as everyone inadvertently comes to pursue the same goal" (2009, 182).

or not Tocqueville consciously intended it as a biblical allusion, but the resonance is striking. The connection is hard to miss for those versed in the biblical story, indelibly marked by its Josephan interpretation.

Conservative pundits and philosophers link the concerns of this passage in Tocqueville and, by extension, its allusion to Babel to partisan debates. For instance, the neoconservative newsmagazine *The Weekly Standard* quotes this same passage at greater length in a piece titled "Barack Obama's America." With no comment other than the subtitle, "A Timeless Critique from Tocqueville," the article simply quotes *Democracy in America*. Beyond linking Obama with a tyrannical tower, the citation lays out themes that appear frequently in conservative discourse, in patterns that should by now be familiar. One is the fear of democracy leading to tyranny—in this case, the tyranny of big and intrusive government. A second is a fear of equality, of "like and equal men, who turn about without repose," signaling a worrisome lack of ambition, higher purpose, and social distinction. A third is wrongly directed pleasure that leads to tyranny, and the association of democracy with "vulgar pleasures." All of these echo the Platonism that reverberates through Josephus into this allusion to the Tower of Babel and Obama's big government. A fourth thematic of this critique is a fear of the suppression of individual agency, including control over estates: The state can troublesomely "divide inheritances." Here we see the importance of filiation—that is, of the family line through which money and privilege is passed.

It would seem that Tocqueville's interpreters appreciate Josephus's and Plato's aristocratic preferences. Rahe clarifies this point for an online conservative activist site[41] when he answers the question, "What is 'soft despotism,' and why should it worry us?" Contextualizing the problem, he explains that Tocqueville worried about what would fill the void after the end of aristocracy in the American and French revolutions. As Rahe tells it online, Tocqueville calls the fertile ground in which soft despotism takes root "*inquiétude*—the uneasiness and anxiety that tended to be the dominant disposition in human beings liberated from the confines of hierarchy and rank, left free to construct lives of their own choosing, and afforded all of

41. Victory NH, an online "network of activists and activist groups, dedicated to defending the principles and policies of lower taxes, smaller government, a strong national defense, and our free enterprise system," http://www.60secondupdates.com/about-us.

the opportunities and challenges that typify commercial societies" (2011). After describing the aimlessness of humans without a ranking structure and left to their own conception of the good life, Rahe goes on to say, "Tocqueville feared that, in times of crisis, men would look to the only power left standing after the disappearance of aristocracy: the all-encompassing state . . . which is, I believe, precisely what has happened." Rahe is not advocating outright for aristocracy here, but he does clearly see the lack of hierarchy as the void into which soft despotism steps. Like Josephus, Rahe and his readers seem not to want to risk the ungovernable and equality. They very strongly want to preserve social hierarchies and filiation.

Rahe explains that for Tocqueville—and, one gathers, also for himself—one of the antidotes to the unhinged desires of soft despotism is religion. Without proper religion, Rahe uses Tocqueville to say, "people give way to despair, doubting their capacity 'to resolve the greatest problems that human destiny presents'" (Tocqueville [1840] 2000, 2.1.5.418, quoted in Rahe 2009, 219). Lack of religion, and especially lack of belief in an afterlife, leads people, in Rahe's words, "to focus their attention on the immediate satisfaction of their least desires" (220). As with the loss of rank, the loss of religious authority leaves people, in Tocqueville's words, taking "fright at the prospect of an independence without limits. . . . They want at least that everything be firm and stable . . . [and so] they give themselves a master [the state]" (Tocqueville [1840] 2000, 2.1.5.418, quoted in Rahe 2009, 219). Without religion, there is no order or established rank, and so self-indulgence gives way to the tyranny of the tower.

The fear of inquietude that comes with social equality, collective action, or rebellion is not new, as Josephus shows us, nor is recourse to God the father and family in order to structure social hierarchy. In many ways, conservative discourse is nostalgic for a much older political model. What is particular to the configuration of biopolitics, however, is the focus on biology and modes of sexual expression in the critique of pleasure. It is to this dynamic that I now turn.

Filiation and the Regulation of Sexuality

As has been much commented, sexual relations that are not bound up with the hierarchies of deity and family are the object of much political energy in the United States.[42] Such sexual expression could be called ungovernable:[43] It does not guarantee lines of kinship, structures of authority, or inheritance. The fear of ungovernable sexuality produces moral panic and renewed attempts to regulate sexuality. In the political discourse I have been discussing, the connection between religion and sexual regulation is more than simple repression. Belief in the authority of God prevents human tyranny by clearly establishing earthly hierarchies. As Rancière indicates, God the father is a necessary first mover for lines of filiation. God gives people their place in the social order, which they pass on through their families. Sexuality outside this order is a danger.

It is not surprising, then, that Tocqueville's explication of soft despotism (and allusion to Babel) includes warnings about the risks of losing family and nation: "Each of them [alike and equal men] . . . exists only in himself and for himself alone, and if he still has a family, one could say at least that he no longer has a fatherland" (Tocqueville [1840] 2000 2.4.6.663; quoted in Rahe 2009, 187). Vulgar pleasure atomizes people, tempting them to abandon traditional paternal loyalties. Rahe picks up on this thematic in the closing pages to his book, when he frets that in the contemporary moment, the "moral obstacles to majority tyranny . . . have disappeared" (265). There he gives the familiar conservative complaint about the "state of American sexual mores," lamenting that "the sexual division of labor, so admired by Tocqueville, has gone by the boards," that "chastity and fidelity are no longer . . . fashionable," and that "marriage delayed generally comes too be marriage denied. . . . The overall birthrate has plummeted, especially among those who are themselves native born and the casual killing of children as yet unborn is anything but rare" (267–68). Homegrown family lines are under threat.[44]

The importance of sexual regulation to the protection of *biological* filiation is made explicit by Seana Sugrue in her essay, "Soft-Despotism and

42. See the many important analyses of the gender and sexual politics of conservative thought: Burlein 2002; Castelli 2007b; Erzen 2006; Griffith 2000; Herman 1997; Jakobsen and Pellegrini 2003; Kintz 1997.

43. As discussed in chapter 5, "raw sex" that is not incorporated into the family and the apocalyptic teleology of the nation is vilified.

44. The fear of declining "native" birthrates is linked to racialization and a fear of immigration and multiculturalism that is elsewhere made explicit in reference to Babel (e.g., Hilliker 2007; Schlesinger 1998).

Same-Sex Marriage." The essay argues that same-sex marriage will contribute to the "demise of political liberty." For Sugrue, accepting same-sex marriage would mean "subordinating ourselves to the very power that we have the most reason to fear: coercive state power" (2006, 173). Here again, the wrong kind of pleasure leads to tyranny. Same-sex marriage, she argues, "is parasitic upon the demise of conjugal society, wherein biological parents are not taking responsibility for . . . their own children" (183). Biological parents put their children up for adoption. Thus *parasitic*, same-sex couples are "crucially dependent upon the state to enforce their claim to these children as against the claims of the biological parents." Soft despotism lurks in a host of (uncited) lawsuits and adoption paperwork (in which the parents are irresponsible, litigious, or both). Sugrue turns to the same passage from Tocqueville in which the Babelian tutelage of the state paternalistically looms over those who in their self-indulgence have not learned to be independent. She writes, "Same-sex marriage requires a condition of soft-despotism to exist." This condition is based on self-gratification, not duty to children: "Self-indulgence in the realm of sexuality demands exactly the kind of gentle despotism that Tocqueville understood democracies have good reason to fear. It requires that the state increasingly step into the role of *parens patriae* to pave the way for the pursuit of self-gratification" (187). In Sugrue's account, soft despotism is *produced by* and also *facilitates* self-indulgence. Worse, what society can expect, if the demands of LGBT people for children are accommodated by the state, is "the cloning of children" (2006, 184). If soft despotism requires that everyone become alike, then taken to its logical conclusion, it requires reproduction as cloning. The fear of equality—Lapin's cogs in the machine—takes on a postapocalyptic quality.

The fight against soft despotism and for sexual regulation went public in the 2009 conservative Christian Manhattan Declaration.[45] This statement on "the sanctity of life, traditional marriage, and religious liberty" was signed

---

45. The Manhattan Declaration was drafted by Chuck Colson, founder of Prison Fellowship (after experiencing prison firsthand for his involvement in the Watergate scandal) with conservative academics Robert George (also coeditor of the volume in which Sugrue's essay appears) and Timothy George. The statement is interdenominational and was first presented by drafters for feedback and elaboration "at a meeting of Eastern Orthodox, Catholic, Anglican, and Evangelical religious leaders in Manhattan in late September, 2009." "FAQ for Sup-

by a number of religious leaders at the time, including Chuck Colson (Prison Fellowship), James Dobson (Focus on the Family), Tony Perkins (Family Research Council), Cardinal Justin Rigali (Archdiocese of Philadelphia), and Archbishop Donald Wuerl (Archdiocese of Washington, D.C.). The document—in which Tocqueville is the only footnoted source—defends and argues the need for religious values to prevent the soft despotism that will lead to tyranny. The declaration explains that the law must defend marriage, or "genuine social harms follow." Once there are restrictions on conscience, religious and individual liberties are under threat. The declaration thus buys into the discourse on religious persecution that has become so prevalent on the Christian right, as identified and analyzed by Elizabeth Castelli (2005, 2007a, 2007b, 2007c).[46] In the Manhattan Declaration, marriage must be defended, so that religious values are not curtailed. Otherwise the state can take over: "Restrictions on the freedom of conscience . . . undermine the viability of the intermediate structures of society [for instance, marriage and family], the essential buffer against the overweening authority of the state, resulting in the soft despotism Tocqueville so prophetically warned of. Disintegration of civil society is a prelude to tyranny." Defense of marriage may, therefore, require believers' resistance to unjust laws in order to prevent soft despotism.[47]

God, Family, Biopolitics

The discourse on soft despotism focuses its concerns on the pleasures enabled by equality. These pleasures are thought to draw people away from habitual structures of authority, including belief in God. Nonetheless, the larger political economy in which the discourse operates requires

---

porters of Life, Marriage, and Religious Liberty," Manhattan Declaration, http://manhattandeclaration.org/resources/faqs.

46. Castelli shows how the notion of religious persecution is linked to a championing of religious freedom, which comes to be seen as a human right above all other rights. As Castelli puts it, "Claims of religious freedom by conservative Christians have been used to underwrite the legitimacy of hierarchical gender relations, the barring of women's access to certain medical services, and discrimination against lesbians and gay men" (2007c, 675).

47. On exception to law, see chapter 2.

both pleasure and equality. To wit, the subject of interest is shaped by the liberty to pursue its interests, including its pleasures. Moreover, some notion of equality is necessary to establish the liberties of the market and the liberties of the subject of interest. For instance, as Rahe makes clear via Tocqueville, equality is important to foster independence, but too much equality creates docility that allows for despotism to creep in (2009, 192–93). Conservative sites seem to agree that an abstract legal notion of equality is necessary, alongside the liberty of consumption; but forced economic equality is an anathema (e.g., Gershowitz and Porter 2010).

Sugrue clarifies how a limited notion of equality is related to the subject of interest. Avowedly libertarian, and claiming John Locke as the progenitor not just of libertarianism but also of American values on governance, Sugrue explains that "Locke understood that the market, rooted in property rights, is premised upon the basic equality of all. Ownership in property is just, because each is capable of acquiring it through effort. . . . Each cares for the self" (2006, 178–79). Equality is, therefore, the basis on which hard work and the market can encourage the self-governance of the subject of interest. As she puts it, "Liberty, understood in the sense of taking responsibility for one's self governance, tempers the tendency toward *soft despotism*, which *arises from the desires of all to be equally comfortable and left alone*" (186, emphasis mine). Sugrue's statements indicate that while everyone has equal opportunity for acquiring property and governing the self, some differential emerges so that not all should assume the right to be "equally comfortable" or "equally . . . left alone."

The family is the key to resolving the contradictions between love of the market and restrictions on pleasure, as well as between a professed love of democracy and restrictions on equality. The family provides the right amount of liberty necessary for the self-regulation that prevents soft despotism (caused by too much liberty); it allows for acquisition but not for distracted spending; it allows for conjugal relations that produce children but not, as Lee Edelman might say, for fucking (2004, 41).[48] Subjects of interest, theoretically equal in their ability to pursue their interests but practically unequal in their ownership of property, are formed in families, whose finan-

---

48. See chapter 5.

cial legacies determine the difference in levels of comforts and appropriate accompanying desires.

The dynamics I have been describing here are consistent with the way that Foucault has described the development of the subject of interest within biopolitics. He notices that the subject of interest—which comes into view, he says, roughly with Locke (2008, 271)—wants to move away from overarching government. The subject of interest "is not satisfied with limiting the sovereign's power; to a certain extent, he strips the sovereign of power" (292). This dissatisfaction is because the subject of interest "reveals an essential, fundamental and major incapacity of the sovereign, that is to say an inability to master the totality of the economic field" (292). The economic world of biopolitics, says Foucault, is untotalizable: "Economics is a discipline without totality; economics is a discipline that begins to demonstrate not only the pointlessness, but also the impossibility of a sovereign point of view over the totality of the state that he has to govern" (282). There is no way to be sovereign over the market. Putting it another way, he says, "Economics is an atheistic discipline; economics is a discipline without God" (282). Thus, in the United States, conservative cultivation of the subject of interest—via the emphasis on individual liberties—may be symptomatic of the fact that the U.S. government cannot fully control the processes of globalization, however much it may wish to do so. People have to fend for themselves, as per Beck's "yes I can."

Recognition that the market has no sovereign may explain the hostility toward government, but what then of the marked piety that also marks these discourses? Why is God needed? Surely, in part, the notion of God hides the fact that there is no longer any center of sovereignty, that there is no longer any center of U.S. identity; it gives people some comfort in the face of a global economy. More tangibly, however, God provides a moral universe in which sexual regulation and control of family lines can be prescribed. The demands for the propertizing[49] heterosexual and biological norms of family require God to ordain them. If Foucault has famously argued that power moved away from monarchical bloodlines in the eighteenth century and began to be dispersed throughout the social body (1990,

---

49. This term is Katrina Van Heest's, from her 2011 dissertation on the property metaphors utilized by the apostle Paul.

147–50), what we see here is a frenzied attempt to return to bloodlines, but unconnected to monarchy. Self-governance within the bloodlines of family, within filiation, keeps property lines and thereby the market, going. God becomes the moral force behind the regularization and economic gradation of populations that we see in biopolitics.

These discourses that cite or allude to Babel avowedly fill the inquietude left in the wake of the Enlightenment by a return to the hierarchies of God and family. One can see how the fear of human capacity in the Babel story becomes the fear of too much democracy and the fear of unregulated sexual expression. In response, God and family enforce filiation and hierarchy. These arguments want to eviscerate, or at least radically minimize, the tower—that is, the national or political center, or big, federal government. Individual liberties are prized. The subject of interest longs to be free of state control. Instead, God and family step in to ensure that humans do not become ungovernable. Economic inequalities are passed down through families. The population is financially arranged and hierarchized by filiation that is ordained by God. People take their place in the relations of capital.

Within this arrangement, financial hierarchy tempers any notion of equality. People can be legally equal, but not economically equal. Those on the upper echelons of this kind of equality are free to pursue wealth, insofar as they temper their unruly materialism and desires by pursuing higher religious goals and as long as they are willing to practice compassionate conservatism. By contrast, big government is said to replace God with its own power, to force equality, to facilitate self-indulgence, to allow for immoral sexual expression, and to curtail liberty. In these rhetorical maneuvers, the subject of interest takes the stage, uncurtailed by national sovereignty and disavowing inherited social inequalities, and sure of the divine ordering of its position.

Babel and the Big Tent

Conservatives are not the only ones to require God and family to promote the subject of interest. President Obama has also used theodemocracy and the figure of Babel to promote the "big tent" that he is famous for invoking. Obama's interpretation of Genesis 11 does not conform exactly to Josephus's, but there are themes in common. Most notable are the struggle for power in human governance and the high value placed on piety.

In his 2010 address to the National Prayer Breakfast, President Obama referred to the Tower of Babel in appealing for national unity established through faith in God. Like Josephus, Obama seems to want to avoid civil strife, or stasis. The speech ruminates about the messiness of democracy and imagines how unity can be reached, given the pervasive divides in U.S. party politics. He particularly notes that these divides feature "arguments about the proper role of government, the relationship between liberty and equality, [and] our obligations to our fellow citizens"—themes that clearly mark the conservative discourses discussed above. In response, he advocates for hearty debate, with civility. Not surprisingly, given the occasion of the speech (the National Day of Prayer), faith and prayer are central to the project of civil debate and finding a common ground.

Like conservatives, Obama laments in his speech the lack of a higher purpose, which for him, as for other presidents before him, is sacrificial giving (by others) to people in need. Reflecting on the exemplary sacrifice of U.S. Navy corps in Haiti following the 2010 earthquake, he advocates for similar kinds of sacrifice to cross partisan divides. Sacrifice beyond self-interest (i.e., surpassing the subject of interest) is lauded.

> Sadly, though, that spirit [of sacrifice] is too often absent when tackling the long-term, but no less profound issues facing our country and the world. . . .
> We become numb to the day-to-day crises, the slow-moving tragedies of children without food and men without shelter and families without health care. We become absorbed with our abstract arguments, our ideological disputes, our contests for power. *And in this Tower of Babel, we lose the sound of God's voice.* (2010, emphasis mine)

This Tower of Babel refers to a lack of higher purpose, abstract arguments, ideological disputes, and contests for power. The metaphor implies that the United States is trapped in the tower, in its fallen state.

Obama's demand for civility might be said to resemble the kind of pluralism that goes beyond the exclusionary assumptions of tolerance.[50] He advocates "stepping out of our comfort zones in an effort to bridge

50. See chapter 3.

divisions . . . stretching out of our dogmas, our prescribed roles along the political spectrum." He insists that political lines must be softened by the recognition that "no one has a monopoly on truth." Here, in some ways, he seems to advocate something very close to what William Connolly, in advocating for deep pluralism, has called "agonistic respect." In Connolly's words, "An ethos of agonistic respect grows out of mutual appreciation for the ubiquity of faith to life and the inability . . . to demonstrate the truth of one faith over other[s]. . . . It grows out of reciprocal appreciation for the element of contestability in these domains" (2005, 123). Recognizing elements of rupture or mystery within one's own faith tradition (Connolly includes nontheists) can contribute to agonistic respect. Much as Obama asks his audience to step out of comfort zones, Connolly suggests that recognizing the contestability of belief structures can help bridge divides. Such awareness can prompt "the civic virtue of presumptive generosity" (62, 64), making it possible to "absorb the agony of having elements of your own faith called into question by others, and [to] fold agonistic contestation of others into the respect that you convey toward them" (123–24).

As much as one might want Obama to urge deep pluralism, he does not quite get there. Rather than try to find the cracks or contestability within faith, as Connolly suggests, Obama reverts to the standard theodemocratic position of using God to direct citizens' behaviors morally and to curtail individual action. Like conservatives, he eschews the inability to see a higher purpose. No more than Beck does Obama want a materialist mortar to hold together the population. What he values is "Americans of every faith, and no faith, uniting around a common purpose, a higher purpose." Prayer and faith can "remind us that [we are] . . . the children of an awesome and loving God." This awareness of positioning below God or a higher order helps people find "common ground," and it "unite[s] people to serve the common good." It also conditions them to accept demands from above. People are meant to sacrifice in the name of this good, to reach up to a higher plane in order to give up something dear to them, perhaps some source of security and pleasure. In this way, sacrifice is a value that requires God to counter the risk of ungovernable equality without hierarchy.

God is necessary not only to motivate sacrifice but also to provide a sense of common ground that extends to an understanding of the United States's role in the world. Significantly, people are not asked to sacrifice for the good of the social contract but rather for the image of the United States as conveyor of God's grace around the world. Obama indicates that, as in aid efforts in Haiti, "God's grace, and the compassion and decency of the American people is expressed . . . through the efforts of our Armed Forces, through the efforts of our entire government, through similar efforts . . . around the world." Thus, God also blesses the international efforts of the U.S. military.

Perhaps President Obama turns to God, to the military, and, as it turns out, to family, because, like conservatives, he recognizes the limitations of sovereignty within globalization and, therefore, his own conflicted role of upholding U.S. superiority in the global marketplace. Almost echoing Foucault's claim that the market undermines sovereignty, he acknowledges an "increasing recognition among progressives that government can't solve all of our problems." In the same sentence, however, as if on cue, he turns to filiation: He suggests that "values *like responsible fatherhood and healthy marriage* are integral to any anti-poverty agenda" (emphasis mine). Obama moves from the "yes we can" of national sovereignty to the "yes I can" of patriarchal family. Not unlike Sugrue and Beck, Obama suggests that it is in the privatized sphere of family and the individual that the market and compassion will work best. Obama's use of Babel reverberates with the hierarchizing filial piety of Josephus. Rather brilliantly, if inadvertently, Obama's speech typifies the way this biblical figure represents the U.S. response to the pressures of transnational capital: It links Babel with the biopolitical project of economic structuring through families and also with the need to establish U.S. authority and superiority in the world.

Containing Democratic Excess

What I have been trying to show is that the story of the Tower of Babel is used in the early twenty-first century in ways that continue to bear the marks of Josephus's retelling. These include the addition of Nimrod (racialized over time), the fear of collectivity and equality as tyrannical and self-indulgent, the reaffirmation of social hierarchy passed down through families, and the insistence on the theocratic higher power of God in ordering social relations and structures of governance. These arguments are put to work in a time when subjectivity and politics are shaped by access to global markets no longer controlled from sovereign centers within nation-states. The insistence on individual agency (along with the impossibility of economic equality) enables the market to function; the insistence on the God-ordained biological family ensures that money and power will remain with those who already have it; faith in God hides the fact that the United States is no longer a secure locus of power.

In these discourses, a Josephan-inflected Babel story operates either as a divinely authored "history," or, when translated into Tocqueville's towering state tyranny and soft despotism, as a kind of secular conservative scripture. It is a tale with a rhetorical structure that is remarkable in its ability to affirm a certain kind of diversity (the freedom of the subject of interest) while painting actual diversity as a kind of unified tyranny (i.e., the ungovernability of equality, sexual expression that is not aligned with family, and racial-ethnic difference). God and family become the insurance against democratic excess. The Babel story becomes the story of theodemocracy. Unpacking the Greco-Roman political ideologies that are encoded in a Josephan shaping of the story and its afterlives illuminates the limits of theodemocracy.

One might pause to consider why Josephus's story becomes the *Christian* story of Babel. Josephus's Jewish history is both consciously and unconsciously taken up as an authority on the story and on the present; Christian interpretations claim authenticity and historicity through Judaism. As we have seen, the Babel story is Christianized to such an extent that it is included as integral to some apocalyptic elaborations of Babylon, where Nimrod becomes the antichrist. It would appear that Josephus is cited in a fashion not unlike what Andrew Jacobs has described happening in antiquity, when "Christians staked their imperial claims on a self-conscious appropriation of Jewish space and knowledge; that is, they embedded their power and authority in the authenticated existence of a religious, political, and cultural 'other'" (2004, 14).[51] Yet, as I have shown, the Greco-Roman

---

51. Jacobs's book *Remains of the Jews* is devoted to explicating the ways in which early Christians appropriated Jewish texts, customs, and geography, as for instance in pilgrimage narratives, where any signs of living Jews are devalued or expunged, but ancient scriptural Jews are constantly referenced (2004, 103–38). I am grateful to Jennifer Knust for pointing out the connection to this contemporary moment.

(and therefore also Christian) political ideas that Josephus promotes are largely what compel conservative allusions to Josephus. The Jewish-Greco-Roman Babel story, as a story of governance, is one that bears the marks of colonization *and* empire. It is perhaps not surprising, then, that it is Christianized to become the signifier of ambiguous political struggles and attempts to grasp after sovereignty, even as it crumbles away.

Bellicose Dreams: Babylon and Exception to Law

In the previous chapter we saw how a Josephan Babel story was used along-side fear of democratic tyranny, or soft despotism, to promote an economic subjectivity (*homo oeconomicus*) that is regulated and hierarchized through the heterosexual family. In this chapter, I continue to look at conservative theopolitical discourse that refers to Babylon, in order to champion the clear access to truth—upheld by war, hierarchy, strong leaders, Christian-ity, heteronormativity, or some combination thereof—and to reject what is characterized as the mindless unity of liberalism and its laws. Babylon is frequently used to motivate the need for political or religious actors to go beyond the law or existing structures of governance, sometimes to resist empire and sometimes to facilitate it. Babylon's appearance reveals what amounts to an ambivalently imperialist theopolitics in which constantly shifting values around unity and multiplicity are bound up with a bellicose scripturalized impulse to make exceptions to the law. Unity tends to be described as totalitarianism, control, and lack of agency that must be surpassed, whereas multiplicity is alternately described as individual agency, difference, and diversity; but if difference becomes too acute, or too *equal*, it gets called unity. Here again a fluctuating value on centering and decentering corresponds to the biopolitical negotiation between social unity, juridical unity, and the freedom of the subject of interest. These oscillations are caused by an indebtedness to the very liberalism that is eschewed. As I will show, conservative references to Babylon indicate that the overlap in political values produces a *scripturalized structure that animates the need for exception to law* in U.S. liberal democracy.

Specifically under scrutiny in this chapter are secular conservative writings of neoconservatives and religious conservative writings of theonomists. Babylon appears in theonomist writing as a symbol of godless (secular) social unity against which theonomists distinguish their own drive to reestablish God's kingdom and law on earth. It appears in neoconservative texts as the symbol of post-Enlightenment humanist longing for self-sufficiency and reliance on reason. Under the pretenses of saving the social order, both groups make much of the rule of law and at the same time often seek to go beyond the law. Reporters, academics, and cultural critics became particularly concerned during the administration of George W. Bush about the imperialist, totalitarian potential of an alliance between these two conservative groups (Hedges 2004; Hendricks 2005; Yurica 2004). These commentators worried about the potential for a Christian right lobby to import conservative values and ideas into U.S. law in ways that would aid a neoconservatively shaped imperial U.S. project. This chapter examines these concerns from another angle, taking a closer look at the underlying logic of the two groups' imperializing conceptions and manipulations of law. Attention to the use of Babylon as a political symbol in these conservative writings brings into view scripture's multilayered influence on exception to law and, more importantly, the ways in which significant fault lines in U.S. liberal democracy are tied up with a scripturalized structure of law.[1]

In their predilection for bypassing the law on moral and philosophical grounds, these conservative discourses mimic the structure of scripture and

---

1. For other insights into the relation between scripture and the exception to law, see B. Johnson 2006; Sherwood 2008. For the connection of the exception to the writing of the apostle Paul, see Agamben (2000) 2005.

also what Giorgio Agamben, borrowing from Carl Schmitt, has called "the state of exception," in which the sovereign suspends law in an "emergency" situation for the purposes of consolidating power or protecting a political system under threat. As Agamben points out, for Schmitt, the sovereign's power to determine "the exception" is authorized by the law and yet contravenes it at the same time; the sovereign is both inside and outside of the law. In conservative discourse, the sovereign's right to suspend the law can also extend to individual (primarily male, patriarchal) citizens who claim some kind of moral authority to disregard the law. What seems to be disavowed in these instances is awareness of the way that individual citizens are also understood to be both inside and outside of civil law—formed and constrained by liberal conceptions of law even as they seek to bypass them.[2] This dynamic is remarkably like the relation between text and truth commonly understood to inhere in biblical texts, whereby truth is understood as coming both from inside and outside of the text. These groups' allusions to Babylon or Babel show that this scripturalized impetus of exception to law is also tied up with a sometimes dizzying attempt to negotiate ambivalence about political cohesion.

The focus on conservatism here does not absolve all things liberal. Indeed, as I will argue, these conservative discourses rely on liberal principles, and the U.S. form of liberal democracy seems to require and facilitate the scripturalized permutations of the exception. This configuration of political values is a result, in part, of competing commitments to pre- and post-Enlightenment ideas that also feed into the biopolitical tension between centering and decentering. This argument is congruent with the important work of Yvonne Sherwood (2008), who has traced the overlap between changing understandings of the Bible as mandating monarchy or liberalism. Sherwood's work has shown how space for the exception to law opens up through the competing understandings of scripture that developed as biblical interpretation adapted to changing political opin-

---

2. Certainly, theonomists and neocons are not unique in turning to a higher authority to sanction their legal transgressions; many groups on the right and the left make this move. Perhaps the question of who has authority to make and break law inheres in law itself, as is variously considered in the much larger and more extended discussion in continental and legal philosophy about the relation of law to justice. See Agamben (1995) 1998; Benjamin (1921) 1986; Derrida (1989–90) 2002; Mahlmann 2003; Maley 1999.

ions on sovereignty and law. I focus here on the way that law itself has become scripturalized in the overlap between conservative and liberal values and in the attempt to negotiate discomfort with both social agreement and difference.

In what follows, I pursue this argument by first introducing the ambiguities of the neoconservatives and theonomists more fully. I situate the main lines of their discourse with respect to sovereignty and law by comparing them to Schmitt while showing their more liberal individualist departures from his way of thinking. I then pay close attention to a number of conservative writings that refer to Babylon/Babel. I explore the ways in which an affinity for making exception to the law surfaces through the slippages, reversals, and alternating values placed on unified social action and individual agency in allusions to Babylon. In the latter sections of the chapter, the homology between scripture and law comes fully into view. The tug of war between unity and multiplicity that emerges in these references to Babylon is remarkably like the scripturalized relation between text and truth apparent in conservative legal and biblical interpretations where particular elements are raised to the status of a unifying principle that seems to come from without. In a final turn, Schmitt's own historical and theological genealogy of the exception points to the affinity between scripture and law that develops within liberalism in the overlap between pre- and post-Enlightenment thought. As he suggests, theological conceptions of transcendence continue into secular post-Enlightenment thought, so that the authority of the law, like the authority of scripture, is understood to be both interior and exterior to it, thus facilitating the exception.

A Liberal Schmittian Focus on the Family

Reporters and political analysts have recognized the hawkish views of "neocons"—such as Paul Wolfowitz, Elliot Abrams, Donald Kagan, Francis Fukuyama, Dick Cheney, Donald Rumsfeld, and the prominent Christian leader Gary Bauer—to be part of a long-term strategy for the Republican Party. Neoconservative philosophy strongly influenced the advisers, policies, and actions of the George W. Bush administration. As has been much discussed, the neocons take their philosophical bearings, if sometimes loosely, from the writing of Leo Strauss in order to focus on reinvigorating U.S. morality and leadership (see Drury 1997; Singer 2004; Crockett 2011). Although the proponents of neoconservatism for the most part claim adherence to democracy, in many ways they seem Josephan in their fear of radical equality and their adamant demand for hierarchy.

Less well known, theonomists are conservative Christians who wish to structure society based on the principles of biblical law. Theonomy is also alternately called dominion theology, after the command to humans in Genesis 1:26 to exercise dominion over the earth, or reconstructionist theology, to designate the reconstruction of a society along the Christian principles of biblical law. To quote a theonomist manifesto published by the multidenominational Coalition on Revival, this theological project wishes to "bring every society's juridical and legal systems into as close an approximation to the laws and commandments of the Bible as its citizens will allow" (Grimstead and Beisner 1986, 10). Different from other conservative Christian biblical interpretation discussed in the other chapters of this book, theonomist interpretation uses less fantastic apocalyptic language, as their beliefs are not premillennial—waiting for the rapture and tribulation before the start of the millennium—but rather postmillennial, working to complete the perfection of God's kingdom and dominion on earth (Ingersoll 2009, 183–84). Much of the rhetoric, however purportedly biblical, sounds generically right-wing: Theonomists focus on family values, the right to have and defend private property without paying tax on it, decentralized government, and constitutional originalism (thus tying an antistatist impulse to an original, now lost, form of national sovereignty). The movement began with the publication of Rousas John Rushdoony's *Institutes of Biblical Law* (1973) and since then has been popularized and softened a little through the writings of Francis Schaeffer and his many disciples (Diamond 1995, 246–48; Rogers 1994). Many highly visible Christian leaders, including Timothy LaHaye, Jack Van Impe, Pat Robertson, James Dobson, Randall Terry, Bill McCartney, and Herb Titus, have been influenced in some way by theonomy's goal of reinstating biblical law.[3]

---

3. For excellent overviews of theonomy, its theological background and influence, see McVicar 2007; Worthen 2008; Ingersoll 2009.

In many ways neocons and theonomists are quite different. But, in their critique of post-Enlightenment politics and liberalism, they both bear a startling resemblance to the thought of the German jurist and theorist of the exception Carl Schmitt (Runions 2007).[4] Like Schmitt, both groups share a critique of the *neutrality of liberalism* in favor of a world in which *strong sovereign decisions* can be made.[5] In this sense, they take up Schmitt's *decisionism*, that is, the notion that a "particular authority" (a sovereign head of state, or, in the case of the theonomists, a Christian patriarchal authority) has an obligation to make moral decisions that take legal priority over other laws ([1922] 2005, 34).[6] Like Schmitt, they advocate strong political leaders who make *exceptions to existing laws* when politically and morally necessary. Like Schmitt, their vision for politics requires *enemies, conflict, and war.* Like Schmitt, they wish to *reinvigorate weakened authorities and natural hierarchie*s. And, like Schmitt, they wish to *reclaim transcendence* as a guarantor for the decision on the exception.

Conservative allusions to Babel/Babylon, to which I turn in a moment, reflect these Schmittian dynamics, but they do so in a way that reveals their (disavowed) indebtedness to liberalism even as they criticize it.[7] In remedying what he called the endless and neutral discussions of democracy, Schmitt looked to the relationships between states rather than individuals, and to the strong decision of the sovereign of a state. Conversely, conservative critics of the neutrality of liberalism (called Babel) are, for the most part, interested in individuals' decisions to fight the battle against moral degeneration— though, to be sure, the neocons are also interested in the role of the sovereign ruler in state politics. Political sovereignty and decisionism remain

---

4. Schmitt (1888–1985) was a strong critic of the Weimar Republic; he served as a legal theorist and counsel for the Hindenburg government and, for a time, the Nazi party (see Müller 2003, 17–47). For affinities with Schmitt's thought in U.S. political discourse, see Critchley 2006; Kline 2004; McCormick 1997, 302–14; Milich 2006; Robbins 2011; Scheuerman 1999, 183–255; Wolfe 2004. Kathleen Skerrett (2008) makes an important argument, in an unpublished manuscript, about the response of the political philosopher John Rawls to the Schmittian influence on U.S. political thought.

5. For a discussion of Schmitt's critique of liberalism that takes it in the direction of a radical political theology, see Crockett 2011.

6. For a discussion of the limits of Schmitt's decisionism, see Schwab (1985) 2005; for Schmitt's own discussion of the concept, see (1922) 2005, 2–3, 31–35 52, 65–66.

7. For the argument that Schmitt was not wholly opposed to authoritarian liberalism and saw in it a possible opening for the political, see Cristi 1998.

key, but they are, for the most part, read through a stated commitment to democracy and individualism. Where Schmitt was interested in the *sovereign's suspension* of law, these discourses tend to advocate an *individualized exception* to law, which might include breaking the law—the law is bypassed in the service of a higher principle.

The conservative model for governance is a decentralized order based on the patriarchal family. The commitment to patriarchy is one of the primary ways in which the negotiation between conservatism and liberalism takes place. As shown in chapter 1, the family provides the arena in which the notion of hierarchy, important to conservative thought, is preserved but where authority is also individualized and decentralized in the subject of interest. In the conservative discourses under discussion here, a focus on the strong decision becomes important not only for a conception of the political but also for a conception of masculinity, which is, in turn, tied to the family structure.[8] In this sense, these discourses depart from what could strictly be called Schmittian. Schmitt did not focus on patriarchy, perhaps because for him the kind of *individual* decisionism envisioned in conservative conceptions of manliness is far too liberal; it is problematic in that it breeds autonomy of decision and distrust of the state, both of which, for Schmitt, would hinder the state's ability to fight the enemy ([1923] 1996, 70–71). At the same time, as will become clear, this conservative patriarchal rhetoric very much resonates with Schmitt's critique of the neutrality of liberalism, his preference for one strong political leader, his demand for the strong decision, and his bellicosity.

This individualism of conservatives is also related to the value placed on freedom, especially freedom in and of the market. Individuals are to have access to markets (recall Beck and Lapin in chapter 1), as is the United States as a nation-state. Indeed, easy (inexpensive) access to commodities for individuals is dependent on national access to markets, uninhibited by

---

8. For examples, see Mansfield 2006, or Pastor Phil Vollman's remarks in *God's Law and Society* (Alliance for Revival and Reformation 1999) about the need for strong masculine leadership. Vollman says that politicians who are not decisive suffer from "PTA, permanent testicular atrophy." For analysis of the patriarchal worldview of theonomy, see Runions 2007; Ingersoll 2009. For analyses of conservative Christian patriarchal discourse more generally, see Castelli 2007b; Kintz 1997.

excessive restrictions. The demand for free trade has been part of the motivation to consolidate national sovereignty and decisionism.[9]

In this sense, contemporary conservatives are quite different from Schmitt, who worried about the mechanism of the free market and even used the figure of the *antichrist* to denote this worry. Schmitt recognized that the market has no sovereign and worried that combined with technological development it put too much trust in the hands of the people. John McCormick (1995) has noticed the way that this mythologizing tactic helped Schmitt counter what he considered a post-Enlightenment move toward neutrality, aided by trust in technology.[10] McCormick shows how Schmitt invests a secular, materialist ("mechanistic") view of economics, politics, and technology with belief in it as something spiritually evil. This rhetoric motivates a return to hierarchical authority and the decision. For Schmitt, anything akin to economic rationalism, because of its mechanicalism and materiality, cannot make moral or political decisions—it pushes to neutralization ([1923] 1996, 15, 17; [1929] 1993, 134, 141). It provokes an eschatological fear similar to "the Protestant[s] of the sixteenth and seventeenth centuries who saw in Rome the Antichrist" ([1923] 1996, 15).[11] Schmitt calls the tendency to neutralization *technicity* (McCormick 1993, 125–27)[12] and describes it—in terms evocative of Babylon and Babel as well as the antichrist—as "perhaps an evil and demonic spirit . . . the belief in unlimited power and the domination of man over nature, even over human nature; the belief in the unlimited 'receding of natural boundaries,' in the unlimited possibilities for change and prosperity" ([1929] 1993, 141). Schmitt thus

9. As I have shown elsewhere (Runions 2005), the demand for access to markets was frequently projected onto the exchange between the cosmic figures of history and freedom in the George W. Bush era.

10. McCormick (1995) traces references or allusions to the antichrist in three texts: Schmitt (1916) 1991; (1923) 1996; (1929) 1993.

11. Neutrality and secularism are not viable politically, for Schmitt, because "there is no politics without authority and no authority without an ethos of [theological] belief" ([1923] 1996, 17).

12. Schmitt uses technicity to name a "religion of technical miracles, human achievements and the domination of nature" (Schmitt [1929] 1993, 134). As McCormick points out, Schmitt develops his critique of technicity from Weber's critique of rationalism, whereby the world becomes a mechanistic iron cage, as a result of technical and economic processes of production (1995, 56). Schmitt is able to criticize socialism, anarchism, and liberalism with his critique of mechanistic rationalism ([1923] 1996, 28–39).

takes a more negative apocalyptic view of the market and technology than do U.S. neoconservatives and theonomists, who try to balance economic freedom and political authority.

When theonomists and neoconservatives use Babel/Babylon to symbolize political systems of which they are critical, they favor a Schmittian decisionism, but one that is translated through a particular patriarchal and hierarchical strand of liberalism. This translation produces an ambiguity between controlling unity and individual agency that accompanies the impulse to go beyond the law. Both groups employ the figure of Babylon to help motivate some combination of the decision, conflict, and exception to the existing political system and its laws, which are together seen as a dangerous unity. Exception to the laws produced by secular humanism is aligned with a valued multiplicity produced in the fall of Babel. Appropriately vertiginous, the fall of Babel comes to represent some concept of valued diversity (a notion borrowed from liberal democracy) to criticize liberalism's perceived neutral unity (which is created by too much diversity). Yet in trying to negotiate the narrow straits between a problematic humanist unity and the multiplicity of moral relativity, these texts cannot help but appeal to some other kind of unity, whether of truth, God's law or *pax Americana*. Indeed, they use the Bible to struggle with the contradictory impulses of social agreement, hierarchy, and decentralization: on the one hand, they want moral unity, God's dominion, or both, which seem to aim for centralization; on the other, they tend to emphasize decentralization in political organizing.

These countermovements are produced by a certain conservatism and a mode of biblical interpretation undeniably in debt to post-Enlightenment, liberal values. As Sherwood (2006, 2008) has compellingly argued, liberalism has become a central orientation for reading the Bible and has continued to affect even more conservative readings. That the Bible is liberal (in the sense of supporting democracy) is now assumed, but as Sherwood argues through an examination of what she calls the "Absolute Monarchist's Bible" and the "Republican Bible" of seventeenth-century England (Sherwood 2006, 2008), the Bible has not always been read in democratic terms. Nonetheless, it is now read as the book of democracy. Conservative allusions to Babel/Babylon are no exception; they are drawn from the "Liberal Bible," even as they attempt to criticize the liberalism on which they rely.

The resulting blend of pre- and post-Enlightenment values allows ample room for scripture to be used to authorize exception to law, as Sherwood points out (2008, 331–35). This mixing of political values certainly carries over into conservative allusions to Babel/Babylon that endorse exception to law.

It is with attention to these shifts and slippages between unity and multiplicity, liberalism and conservatism, law and exception that I now turn to four allusions to Babel/Babylon in conservative texts. Two passing references to Babel in early neoconservative and theonomist writings show the affinities of this thought to the exception to law; both attempt to go beyond the supposed unity and neutrality of the status quo through recourse to an even higher unity. I then analyze two more substantive and more recent uses of Babel to describe the ills of the modern world; both of these illustrate the imperialist impulses of this thought, even while they argue against humanist unity and for a particular kind of patriarchal and bellicose multiplicity. All four of these allusions to Babel reveal a kind of "democratic Schmittianism" in which the mixed values of liberalism and conservatism produce the scripturalizing interplay between control and agency, law and exception. The worry over neutralizing unities is played out through what is understood as multiplicity: exception to law, individual responsibility, bellicose ambition, and a reassertion of patriarchal authority and heteronormative morality.

A Democratic Fear of a Too-Democratic Babble

In 1960, Irving Kristol published a short essay in the *Columbia Forum* titled "Democracy and Babel," which lamented the inutility of the first Kennedy-Nixon debate. Seemingly innocuous, the essay contains the seeds of the neoconservative political doctrine that came to fruition during the administration of George W. Bush, including a focus on national interest and maintaining dominance, increased power for the executive branch, and a domesticated media. This early piece of proto-neocon writing also contains prescient hints of the kind of Schmittian orientation that came to characterize the Bush II administration. Kristol argues, in the vein of Schmitt, that "the political" must be reinvigorated by the possibility of the strong sovereign's decision (Schmitt [1922] 2005, 5–15), against the neutrality of liberalism, with its constant babble.[13] Kristol does not exhibit the full Schmittian logic whereby "the exacting moral decision" based on an ability to assess evil may require exception to the law (Schmitt [1922] 2005, 5–6, 65),[14] but he does emphasize sovereign decision making on the part of the executive (which, in the neoconservative Republican years 2000–2008, becomes quite skilled at making exception to law). He wants a strong executive that can secure national interest and a pliable population, homogeneous in thought.

Kristol espouses the view that democracy requires debate between two clearly defined alternatives, and that the usual forms of political discussion, like congressional deliberation, are nothing more than Babel's babble. He refers to Babel both in the title of the essay and in the concluding paragraph, where he derisively summarizes the state of presidential debates in general: "American Democracy . . . is constantly promised a Great Debate— and is given a babel of voices—or a T.V. spectacular" (1960, 19). Kristol wants democracy, but one that doesn't *babel*. Kristol uses the Babel myth a little differently than the others I will discuss, in that he does not valorize the fall of the tower as producing a healthy multiplicity but reads it as inaugurating a fallen state of neutralization. Babel, for Kristol, seems to be a kind of unity created by the endless discussion that Schmitt describes as one of the ills of liberal democracy (Schmitt [1922] 2005, 59–63). Kristol writes: "Discussion in and of itself is as likely to confuse as to enlighten. For this discussion takes place in an area where one opinion is—or is taken to be—as good as another" (1960, 18–19). In short, if all opinions are given equal value, they are unified in their inutility.

Kristol's strategy for transforming babble into debate is to narrow the scope of legitimate political opinions and voices considerably. He wants two

---

13. In a more recent definition of neoconservatism in *The Weekly Standard*, Kristol (2003) sounds even more Schmittian, arguing for a foreign policy that works against "world government" and for political leaders to distinguish between friend and enemy.

14. Schmitt gives voice to many theological opinions about the nature of evil and the necessity for understanding its place in motivating politics through the counterrevolutionary Catholic theologians de Maistre, Bonald, and Donoso Cortés. It is clear that he does not agree with them fully, but he cites them approvingly in many cases. For a longer explanation of the place of evil in Schmitt's thought, see Runions 2007, 51–53.

clear positions and a public ready to choose one of them. In his view, too many opinions and voices confuse matters. As a case in point, the Kennedy-Nixon debate was not a real debate, he says, because "the time was too short. The audience was too large, *too heterogeneous*, to uninformed—too unintelligent" (1960, 15, emphasis mine). Kristol does not hide his disdain for a public not already molded in some way by the media. What is needed instead is a debate for which public opinion has previously been prepared in the media, in which "the alternatives must (1) be reduced to a manageable number—preferably two; and (2) be represented and articulated by political leadership capable of assuming office and implementing their policy" (1960, 19). In other words, two people potentially able to act as head of the executive should carry out the debate. Anything else is merely babble. His vision disparages both total homogeneity and total heterogeneity. He does not argue simply for one viewpoint. Rather, he wants democracy of a very particular kind: one with debate, not discussion, in which strong alternatives can be put forward for acceptance or rejection and in which public opinion is formed by the media so that it can intelligently support one of two alternatives.

Kristol is dissatisfied with the form of democratic functioning that he sees about him, and he offers another vision. He mourns the decline of Congress as a policy-making body and as a public forum (1960, 18) and suggests instead a strong executive branch. In his view, the executive can provide strong leadership determined by attention to national, rather than local, interests. He writes, "America as a world power, engaged in a struggle for survival, cannot afford to have its major policies devised by men whose prime responsibility and loyalty are to their local constituencies. . . . The national interest requires a national leadership; and this can only be provided by the Executive" (18). Note that the role of the United States as major world power is at stake here. Kristol diagnoses the need for a unified national interest over and against the diversity of local interests, but he still sees the need for democratic debate. Though he wants to strengthen the executive branch, he does not want to do so in a way that goes outside of a commitment to democracy. In wanting a strong executive, Kristol comes close to valorizing the totalitarian unity that the Babel myth usually is used to challenge. But he still favors the diversity of democracy, though only if managed through a carefully engineered political conflict.

Oddly, as we shall see, the unified neutrality of too much unqualified political debate that Kristol criticizes and allegorizes as the aftermath of the fall of Babel (i.e., the heterogeneity of endless discussion) is transformed in other conservative allusions to Babel into a kind of neutralized liberal unity of too much secular, universalizing political agreement represented by the mythic tower itself. This difference in allegorical meaning assigned to pre- and postdestruction of the tower, though seemingly contradictory, is in fact symptomatic of the continual shift and overlap between heterogeneity and homogeneity in conservative thought. The logic of exception to law, though not explicitly stated, dwells therein. A critique of unity and neutrality as a moral stance that threatens true democracy may obfuscate the commitment to a different kind of social agreement and political agency that is willing to bypass existing democratic structures.

Against Babel and the Universal Law

A passing reference to Babel in early theonomist thought uses the metaphor to envision a response to liberalism's neutrality that is similar to Kristol's, though more specifically focused on exception to law (on the part of the individual) and on the sin of building the tower. In an appendix to R. Rushdoony's formative *Institutes*, Gary North (who happens to be R. Rushdoony's son-in-law) alludes to Babel in an essay that tries to sort out what allegiance Christians have to existing civil law. With specific reference to the practice of bribery, North says that Christians may need to break civil law. To make this argument, he first needs to make a case against (Babelian) universals in law and language. He writes, "There can be no universal application of a word like 'bribery,' for, to make such a universal definition, we would have to assume the existence of some universal, neutral, and completely accepted legal code. That is the basic presupposition of humanism, but Christianity denies such neutrality. Neutrality does not exist" (1973, 843). He continues, "Everything must be interpreted in terms of what God has revealed. The humanistic goal of neutral language (and therefore neutral law) was overturned at the Tower of Babel. Our definitions must be in terms of biblical revelation. Resistance to unjust laws is not anarchy" (843).

The equivocation between unity and multiplicity is clearly evident in these statements. Too much individual agency would be anarchy, but the resistance that North envisions is grounded in the unifying higher principles expounded in the Bible.

With respect to bribery, for North, this means that the Bible indicates that Christians do not necessarily have to follow civil laws about bribery. He indicates that though "a bribe may not be accepted . . . the Bible nowhere condemns the giving of bribes in order to impede the progress of apostate governments" (1973, 842). He takes as an example Jesus's instructions to give a person suing for a tunic not only the tunic but also a cloak (Mt 5:40). This additional gift is understood as a kind of bribe, "a gift that will encourage the offending party to leave the Christian and the church in peace" (845). If it will help the church in the face of an ungodly government, a Christian may break civil laws to bribe someone.

North sounds much like Schmitt and Kristol in arguing against neutrality, or a kind of unified liberal position, though he is interested in individual (local) political action in a way that Schmitt and Kristol are not. North goes further than Kristol in emphasizing a kind of Schmittian need for moral decision based on knowing the difference between good and evil, implying that the result of Babel's fall is a world in which Christian decision on the law is both permissible and necessary. Christians must decide what laws should be kept and what should be broken on the basis of biblical revelation. On the basis of a higher authority, Christians can and must make exceptions to unrighteous civil law.

The Babel of Humanism and the Multiplicity of Conflict

A similar dynamic emerges in the extended neoconservative meditation on the Babel myth by Leon Kass, a leading neoconservative bioethicist, and the one-time president of Bush's President's Council on Bioethethics (2002–5). Though Kass does not directly advocate exception to law in his reading of Babel, his thinking closely corresponds to that of Schmitt, in the way that he advocates for problematically autonomous difference (called unity) to be contested and bypassed by decisive leaders, through conflict. In many ways, his reading of Babel develops themes that appear in Kristol's text, especially in giving a philosophical rationale for securing national interest, though Kass emphasizes bellicosity where Kristol emphasizes executive power. The main lines of Kass's reading are also strikingly similar to the religiously motivated readings of the theonomists, though his approach to the Bible is different. For Kass the remedy for the immoral, neutralized secularism of Babel comes through reestablishing patriarchal heteronormativity at the grassroots level.[15]

Trained in philosophy and science, with a secular Straussian and neoconservative bent, Kass nonetheless turns back to the Bible as a source of moral wisdom (2003, xi–xiv). His book *The Beginning of Wisdom: Reading Genesis* (2003), "offers a philosophic reading of the book of Genesis" (1). Kass understands Genesis as a text that says much about human realities and truth, even if it is not understood as the revealed word of God. "The truth of the Bible's assertion does not rest on biblical authority," he asserts, but rather on humans' discovery of their ability to imitate the divine in matters of law and virtue (185). Kass follows a Straussian return to classical philosophy's understanding of moral virtue as the highest good, available to humans through philosophical contemplation. He is aided by contemplation of the text of Genesis. To this end, a chapter is devoted to unpacking the truths of the story of Babel regarding "the failures of civilization" (217).

One might expect that, for a conservative bioethicist, a main object with the Babel story would be to take up the fear of technology that the story is often used to elaborate, and Kass does not disappoint his readers on this front; however, his concerns over technology are subsumed into larger questions of governance and political organization as they relate to questions of (philosophic) truth. He is especially concerned with criticizing a "revived Babylonian vision" in the contemporary world (2003, 243), in which "science and technology are again in the ascendancy, defying political boundaries en route to a projected human imperium over nature" (242). Although true to his professional profile in worrying about technology, his reference to political boundaries indicates that he has other interests (e.g., governance, control) in retelling the story of Babel. Kass's reading of Babel

15. For more on the patriarchal affinities between theonomists and neoconservatives, see Runions 2007.

reflects the neoconservative view that politics must be oriented through *virtue* and philosophic contemplation of that virtue (as best exemplified by classical Greek philosophy). As a cautionary counterpoint to this view of governance, Babel/Babylon represents a place where astrologers and priests observed the stars not for the "restful and disinterested contemplation celebrated by Greek philosophers" (as per the neoconservative approach to politics) but rather "in the service of calculation, prediction and control" (220).

Babel represents, for Kass, the controlling and calculating humanist dream of self-sufficiency—the dream of "humankind united, living together in peace and freedom" (2003, 219). He focuses his reading of Genesis 11 on the ways in which language and the city try to reach unity. Language is the invention by which humans attempt "to be of one mind about the most fundamental things" (223). The story's central philosophical insight is in understanding "man as a rational and political animal" (217); but it shows that the "universal city" is the wrong way to enact governance, as it is incorrectly privileges reason and does not look beyond reason to truth. Humanism incorrectly assumes that reason can produce moral and political standards (233–35).

The remedy for the arrogance and control of the humanist universal city, for Kass, is precisely the solution that God supplies in Genesis 11: multiplicity and the contention and conflict it brings. Here, he reflects both a classically neoconservative and a Schmittian desire for conflict and war—that is, for the enemy who can be killed—in the production of moral or political authenticity (Schmitt [1923] 1996, 34–37). Kass writes: "It is easy to see how linguistic and cultural multiplicity, contention, and the threat of destruction through war fit, as remedies of opposition, the aspirations to unity, harmony, and prideful self-sufficiency. . . . The emergence of multiple nations, with their divergent customs and competing interests challenges the view of self-sufficiency" (2003, 237). Conflict is not only a corrective to self-sufficiency, however; it also pushes people toward philosophic contemplation of truth. War is valorized as a time in which people are forced to think about truth: "The prospect of war and, even more, its actual horrors prevent forgetfulness of mortality, vulnerability, and insufficiency. Such times of crisis are often times that open men most to think about the eternal and the divine" (237).

Kass's retelling of Babel falls into line with other neoconservative thinking that understands war as necessary for securing national interest—in other words, for maintaining U.S. primacy in the world. For instance, his heroization of conflict and war as a route to the production of virtue brings to mind Harvey Mansfield's celebration of manly courage and risk (i.e., *thumos*)—that is, the willingness to fight and to sacrifice one's own life in the service of truth (Mansfield 2006, 206–7, 220–21). Likewise, the Hegelian fashion in which Kass pits the "mass consciousness" of unity against "true self-consciousness" and the "face-to-face" (2003, 235) echoes Kristol's disdain for an un(in)formed public. It strongly resembles Francis Fukuyama's assessment, in *The End of History and the Last Man* (1992), of "the way in which struggle and risk are constituent parts of the human soul" (313), as well as his argument that liberal democracies may want to fight periodic wars in order to maintain superiority, virtue, and ambition (328–29).[16] In this view, multiplicity and conflict push humans to seek out *superior* truths and virtues. "The discovery of multiple human ways invites an interest in the *best* possible way" (Kass 2003, 238). Difference is managed by searching for superiority.

In contrast to the unity of Babel, Kass proposes a decentralized patriarchal political order. The story of Abraham provides a patriarchal model for governance. The family, formed through marriage and "properly understood" patriarchy, is the form of political organization that will most easily allow contemplation of the divine and cultivation of virtue (2003, 249–50, 348–51). Abraham is the perfect father (of his family and of the people). In terms consistent with other conservative culture warriors, patriarchy is Kass's answer to post-Enlightenment politics and the supposed degenerate sexuality that these politics have produced.

In fact, sexuality is one of the central concerns of *The Beginning of Wisdom*. Space does not permit a thorough examination of the permutations of this theme, but I would like to at least notice the way in which Kass links Babel, and cities in general, to "Sodom, babbling and dissipating away" (2003, 243). Kass finds the story of Sodom to be exemplary for building the case that cities in Genesis (for which Babel is the archetype) are "linked . . .

---

16. See Runions 2005.

with violence lewdness, and corruption." He goes on to make the connection between these vices and the universal city, even as he admits there is no link to Babel: "But none of those features appear tied to the city of Babel—at least not yet—which proceeds through peaceful cooperation under the rule of reason" (2003, 227). Nonetheless, Babel embodies "idolatry, the denial of mortality, the lack of standards . . . and the lack of self-examination" (237). His implication is clear: reliance on reason (as in the universal city of Babel) leads to the destruction of morality in general, and to sexual immorality in particular.

Recalling the fear of democracy discussed in chapter 1, Kass follows the Platonic view that democracy and indulgence are closely associated. In a footnote to a discussion on paternity and piety, Kass compares the habits of "democratic man" to the biblical Ham's lack of filial piety for Noah in "looking on his father's nakedness" (Gn 9:20–27). Kass writes, "Modern times have produced a new human type . . . who seems also to be deaf to authority and who knows neither reverence nor awe: democratic man. . . . Democratic fathers find it easier not to exercise authority; democratic sons find it easier not to recognize it. Sex, utterly demystified, is now sport and chatter; nakedness is no big deal" (2003, 215n21). In this view, righteousness, patriarchal authority, and (hetero)sexual propriety line up, whereas democracy is considered antiauthoritarian and is equated with immoral (nonheteronormative) sexuality. Given the racialization of Ham (and his grandson Nimrod) discussed in chapter 1, the comparison between Ham and the unruly democratic man has troubling implications.

If Babel and Sodom are democratically dissolute, the opposite of moral uprightness, perhaps they are not as unified as Kass insists. In fact, the connection Kass draws between Babel and Sodom reveals precisely the odd interchangeability between multiplicity and unity that I have been noting. When he comes to contemplate Sodom in detail, Kass returns to the comparison with Babel: "As with Babel, [Sodom] as a city strives for a certain unity and homogeneity" (2003, 329). The hostility toward Lot and his guests displayed by the men of Sodom indicates to Kass that they are interested only in unity, including the "unity" of moral relativity. Reading the story as a story about lust and rape, Kass finds the men of Sodom likely to "hold themselves beyond good and evil, bound only by their own habitual selfish ways" (328). The archetypal city (now Sodom), is problematic in that its "drive for one-ness creates *opposition* not only to outsiders but even to the small groupings that comprise it: the archetypal city [Babel and Sodom] . . . looks with suspicion on the family and the household" (329, emphasis mine). In this case, *opposition* does not produce the usual positive results for Kass. Rather, he argues that this opposition is problematic in that it is derived from homogeneity. He explains as follows: "The Sodomites thus endorse not only xenophobia and sodomy, but also moral relativism—all exaggerated expressions of the 'love of the same'" (328).[17] In a whirling set of rhetorical moves, Kass equates homophilia and xenophobia with the problematic unity of moral relativism. Conversely, he equates the love and inclusion of the other with multiplicity rather than with unity. Kass seems to forget his approval of the competing interests of multiple nations that arise in the wake of Babel's destruction, which also requires a sort of xenophobia (and presumably homophilia). For some reason, the story of Sodom does not become a story about the value of conflict or the threat of "mortality, vulnerability, and insufficiency" in a time of war that would inspire contemplation of truth (237). Further, what many might think of as diversity (in the colloquial way that Sodom is used to represent homosexuality)[18] becomes a vilified unity, whereas the multiplicity of a society built on families (one kind of family, it might be noted) points the way to a superior truth.

Kass's stated commitment to multiplicity and decentralization may seem surprising given the overall imperialist impulse of neoconservative planning and the focus on the executive branch (as advocated by Kristol). Simon Critchley has called the neoconservative agenda crypto-Schmittian, in that it relies on the friend/enemy distinction, but uses it in the service of an "utterly moralizing, universalist, indeed millennial, ideology whose key signifier is freedom" (2006). But Kass's reading of Babel/Sodom shows just how slippery conceptions of unity and diversity are in this discourse, perhaps caused, in part, by the overlap between conservatism and liberalism at work in the commitment to a strong nation and a decentralized and individualized patriarchal family—both kept in check by a higher moral order. These

17. Kass problematically conflates "love of the same," sodomy, lust, and rape in his interpretation of the story.
18. For a helpful discussion of why the Sodom story should not be read as referring to gay sex and might rather be understood as the threat of male rape as a form of homophobic and heterosexist violence, see Carden 1999.

rhetorical moves are symptomatic of the biopolitical tension between sovereignty and the subject of interest. Each constantly feeds, weakens, and then reinforces each other, like some kind of retro/peristaltic digestive loop or Möbius strip.

Significantly, although Kass understands language as a "strictly human creation" (2003, 223), he does not see any incongruity in raising text to the rank of moral authority. Even as he derogates the unifying function of language and calculating reason, he uses the disparate narratives of Genesis allegorically to contemplate a higher truth that dictates not only a national belligerence amenable to U.S. superiority on the world stage but also a morality that seeks to curtail diverse forms of sexual expression and kinship arrangements.

Imperialism versus God's Kingdom

I turn now to three texts that are illustrative of frequent theonomist recourse to Babylon in negotiating the potential conflict between a theological commitment to God's law and a political libertarianism and individualism.[19] The texts to be discussed here are authored by R. Rushdoony's son, Mark Rushdoony (2006), Tom Rose (2006), and Lee Grady (posted online in 2008, but dated by its many references to the 1980s).[20] In these texts, political unities, such as empires and international peace processes, pose a problem for keeping the individual's relationship to Christ as the central focus for political action and decision making. But although the response to political unity relies on individualism, it does not celebrate the diversity that might accompany it, since individual autonomy must be submitted to God's law. All of these texts advocate resistance to existing legal structures on the part of the individual believer. The combination of political and theological leanings found in these texts emphasizes both the scripturalized and imperialist structure of the exceptions to law that they envision:

19. For more on the libertarian impulse of theonomy, see McVicar 2007.
20. These texts are all published online by the Chalcedon Foundation, a theonomist think tank started by Rousas Rushdoony and now directed by his son, Mark Rushdoony, and by the Forerunner, a theonomist website devoted to "the training of student interns to produce [Christian evangelical] media."

secular laws are disdained in favor of God's law; libertarian views are raised to the status of God's law, which must be imposed internationally to correct the wrongs of other political unities. As will become clear, it is not political unity per se but how it is constructed and wherein sovereignty lies that is the problem.

Babel and Babylon are allegorized in these texts in a way that is consistent with other theonomist teaching in which Babel stands in for the evil of the state or, worse, any vision of a one-world government. M. Rushdoony explains that "God's Word uses the term Babylon as a euphemism for all the statist regimes of history that have sought to play god" (2006, 12). Grady is more specific in using Babel to metaphorize the sinful aims of humanist peace-making processes (2008, 1–2, 5). For Rose, even U.S. imperialism is considered Babylonian. He singles out several practices of U.S. governance for critique: perceived heavy taxes, monetary inflation, the war on drugs, government secrecy, fear mongering, and repressive federal agencies such as the Department of Homeland Security (2006, 28).

These texts display a robust skepticism about peace processes, because such processes are thought to impose a non-Christian, universalist order on individuals and nations. International treaties are evaluated less on their political merits than on their pretensions to humanist unity. Rose writes, "To be Biblical, America should abhor foreign possessions and international entanglements like the United Nations, NAFTA, etc." (2006, 24). As in other rightist thought, the United Nations is singled out as particularly humanistic and therefore problematic in seeking a world order. M. Rushdoony explains: The U.N. does not seek a moral order "in any Biblical sense. . . . The world at peace it seeks must be a world under its rule and law, a new version of *Pax Romana* or 'peace of Islam.' It is thus, perhaps, the very worst manifestation of the dream of Babylon, for it seeks a *world* law and a *world* state" (2006, 14). Though the stated fear is of humanism and a one-world order, another fear emerges, of a peace ("the peace of Islam") that might involve worship of a different God than the Christian God or that would prioritize another kind of law than that found in the Bible.

Grady elaborates M. Rushdoony's fears, worrying about the imposition of humanist "value-free" peace rather than the peace found in the unified set of values that must be (perhaps violently) imposed across cultures to establish the kingdom of God. True peace, says Grady, "is a state in which there is *no conflict of values or morals.* . . . True peace must require surrender on the part of all opposing parties. Only then will there be an absence of moral conflict" (2008, 2, emphasis mine). Until then, "We are in a battle for ownership of the world. . . . The atheists, the communists, the humanists, and adherents of Islam, and the Christians are all vying for the title of world leader. . . . To deny that we are in ideological war is to capitulate to the enemy" (3). In seeking a different kind of world political unity, Grady is consistent with the theonomist doctrine of dominion, where the battle for God's law must be fought worldwide, through evangelism and action against ungodly civil laws. As Julie Ingersoll puts it, for theonomists "there can be no religiously neutral legal systems or economic systems" (2009, 184). To quote North, "God's requirement for men is that they subdue the earth in terms of His revealed law structure, and that they do it to his glory" (1973, 843). There is a bellicosity here that resonates with Kass's valorization of conflict in the quest for truth.

Again, much like Kass's statements, theonomist responses to statism, imperialism, and humanist efforts at world peace turn to the Bible to explicate recommendations on decentralized government. So, for instance, Rose finds a model for decentralized government after Babel in Jethro's instructions to Moses, found in Exodus 18, to train men from the people of Israel to act as judges for the people.

> Building empires, either domestic or foreign, is completely contrary to God's Word. In man's first world-empire-building attempt, the Tower of Babel, God confused the language and dispersed the people. . . . God's clear plan for civil government is for the establishment of small, democratic-republic civil units, not large, unitary dictator-type units (Ex 18:13–26). (Rose 2006, 24)

Along similar lines, M. Rushdoony argues that Christians must resist Babylon in all its forms and instead participate in the kingdom of God at a localized level, which "exists wherever Christ rules, in church, in family, or school" (2006, 12). Church, family, and school (particularly home schooling) are the chief modes of organizing for theonomists, and evangelism is understood to be central within these structures. Grady imagines that "world peace will envelope the globe as more individuals, families, institutions, and nations submit to the gospel of Jesus Christ and embrace Christianity" (2008, 4). It is within the context of resisting Babylon in all its forms so that

God's kingdom might be established that theonomists, like North, advocate breaking ungodly civil laws.[21]

Even as these authors reject a certain kind of U.S. hegemony as ambition to Babelian unity, they also affirm it in some aspects. One of the ways this happens is through the vilification of the "enemies" of the United States as somehow even more dangerously Babylonian than the nation itself. Take, for example, M. Rushdoony's assessment of the "peace of Islam" as Babylonian. Similarly, Rose criticizes U.S. imperialism by associating it with empires in the ancient Near East, giving a strongly orientalist history of imperialist regimes, from the Hyksos and the Hittites through to Britain and the United States. The ancient Near East becomes the birthplace of empire, best symbolized by Babylon. By extension, Christians in the United States must take a stand against anything that might bear resemblance to foreign influences and return to proper principles of biblical law and governance, as exemplified in the early days of U.S. republican democracy.

Theonomist thought shifts seamlessly between a commitment to individualism (in the sense of personal relationship with God, patriarchal leadership in the family, and individual ability to make moral judgments and resist the laws of "Babylon") and a commitment to political unity (of the Christian nation and of God's kingdom on earth), without being troubled by any apparent contradiction. But the logic is fairly persuasive when read in biblical terms: the (peaceful) unity to which Babel strives was a sin and must be replaced by the individual agency of commitment to Christ. Human attempts at sovereignty are replaced by God's sovereignty. According to this reasoning, the Christian becomes vicariously sovereign with respect to civil law, individually acting on behalf of God—which will necessarily involve spiritual, and perhaps physical, battle to establish a superior form of truth on the political level. As with Kass, truth is not conceived as social unity, since it must always battle to demonstrate superiority; still, it clearly requires some homogeneity in thought.

---

21. Other movement spokespeople espouse similar views in the video production *God's Law and Society* (Alliance for Revival and Reformation, 1999).

Scripturalizing

The kind of Schmittian impulse for decisionism, conflict, and political dominion advocated in these conservative texts is deeply entwined with often disavowed liberal commitments, producing a profound equivocation between desire for social agreement or disagreement. As I have been arguing, these retellings of the Babel story try to keep hold of some kind of (theo)democratic notion of individual agency while using it as a vehicle to reach the truth, hence revealing a kind of scripturalized dynamic. A particular (patriarchal, familial) version of multiplicity is posited insofar as it points to a higher truth that regulates allowable forms of individual autonomy. The ease with which one kind of unity or one kind of multiplicity can be rejected and replaced with another is striking, but the process of allegorizing through the biblical story allows and occludes these shifts (for more on allegorizing, see chapter 4). The explicit problem in these readings of the biblical text is not actually political unity per se—it is political unity motivated by human rather than godly (or philosophically true) desire. Yet these readings tend to ignore the fact that the Babel story itself does not reestablish any new and more righteous political or moral unity after the fall of the tower.[22] Rather, other biblical narratives and texts supply examples of the moral unity assumed to be necessary for conservative models of governance (e.g., as found in biblical law) or the grassroots political organizing that will lead to that unity (e.g., Abraham's patriarchy, or Moses's and Jethro's trained judges). This garden-variety mode of reading the biblical canon as a singular text seems prototypical of the slip between multiplicity and unity.

The relation between the exception and the authority used to motivate it is, not surprisingly, much like the relation between text and truth on which these readings rely. Because the Bible is assumed to make transcendent truth claims (even by Kass, who rejects a notion of biblical authority), particular elements of the biblical text—and, for the neocons, Greek philosophy plus the Bible—can be raised to the status of authoritative and unified truth. Truth is understood to be autonomous, but it is accessed through the text.

---

22. For the excellently argued reading that the central concern of Genesis 11 is not empire, unity, or prideful self-sufficiency but rather cultural solidarity and cultural difference, see Hiebert 2007.

This authority is then read back onto the text, affecting which forms of diverse opinion and action are accepted and which rejected. Individual action and the multiplicity of conflict are valorized, but only insofar as they submit to this textually produced unity of truth and authority. The authority to bypass civil law depends on this truth.

The tension between social cohesion and social division is also at work when laws (manifestations of social unity) are suspended (through independent actions) in order to serve another (unified) higher purpose. Those who make decisions to go beyond the law step outside of a vilified unity, but, at the same time, such decisions are understood to be constrained by a higher authority. Independent action to break ungodly or humanist civil law is highly valued if it is in the service of truth.

It seems reasonable to suppose that this relation between truth and text, or law, is one that comes out of a particularly Protestant tradition of reading the Bible, a mode that is exemplified in the Reformed tradition in which the theonomists are based. Like many other Protestant readers of the Bible, theonomists follow Luther's insistence on *sola scriptura*, understanding the biblical text and its reader—already a multiplicity—to be (almost) sufficient for understanding. At the same time, they require the external unifying authority of the divine; in good Reformed fashion, it is the Holy Spirit who informs reading. As the theonomist Coalition on Revival puts it: "We affirm that man's understanding of God's Law and its application to civil law can be enlightened and enlivened constantly by the work of the Holy Spirit in the world today" (Grimstead and Beisner 2000, 12). The Spirit acts as an exception to the final authority of the Bible. The Spirit helps humans decide where and how to apply the Bible to civil law. So although the Bible is seen to be the final authority by which actions and ideas are judged, the Spirit's authority is also required. But how is the Spirit's work to be judged? Presumably, through the Bible. The Spirit has no authority apart from the Bible. So, in theonomists' attempts to make civil law scriptural, the scripture cannot fully be understood without recourse to the external authority of the Spirit, which, as it turns out, is also internally produced. Neoconservatives are certainly not working within the logic of the Holy Spirit's inspiration, but it might be said that their understanding of truth and virtue—taken from classical philosophical sources—also looks to ancient texts to speak the truth that grants the reader moral authority. It is not surprising, given this interpretive structure, that the truth produced in the reading of biblical and philosophical texts also authorizes exceptional interpretation of civil law.

Scripturalized Law

There are other scripturalizing dynamics between truth, text, and law in these texts, as well—dynamics that reveal the exception's dependence on a liberal democratic view of law. In much neoconservative and theonomist discussion about resisting civil law, the authority to break the law also comes from the law itself. Thus, authority is produced on two fronts: from the ancient text and from contemporary law. The impetus to contravene the law in the name of truth has the double force of ancient text and the contemporary liberal legal tradition. Though the latter source of authority is ostensibly given less weight than is the Bible, it turns out to be equally operative.

These two sources of authority gave weight to the on-the-ground working of the neocon's valorization of decisionism evident in the George W. Bush administration and especially Bush's willingness to go beyond the law.[23] Like other U.S. presidents but far more prolifically, Bush used signing statements to override bills being signed into law, a power that he based on some notion of a constitutionally based presidential authority (Cooper 2005; Kinkopf and Shane 2007; Savage 2006a, 2006b). Most notoriously, Bush instituted a signing statement (2005b) accompanying the ban on torture (part of the Department of Defense Appropriations Bill, H.R. 2863, 109th Cong. [2006]), in which he stated that he would interpret (i.e., bypass) that section of the bill dealing with torture on the basis of his constitutional authority to protect the people of the United States.[24] The

23. One of the most obvious symptoms of this prevailing right-wing decisionism was George W. Bush's celebrated statement of April 18, 2006, "I'm the decider and I decide what's best" (2006). He made this statement when challenged by a reporter about whether he was listening to the advice of military commanders and retired generals about Rumsfeld's poor leadership in the Iraq war.

24. The ban on torture was proposed as an amendment to the bill by Senator John McCain (R-Ariz.). For the text of the amendment limiting interrogation see the records of 109th congress, H.R. 2863, amendment 1977, which became Public Law 109–48. Bush's statement reads, "The executive branch shall construe Title X in Division A of the Act, relating to de-

"sovereign's" authority to bypass statutory law is generated from constitutional law. But, in the case of Bush, decisions to make exception to law were also motivated through reference to the struggle between good and evil, as well as the moral virtues of goodness and freedom. These values, Bush's speechwriters signaled, often in coded language, are biblical.[25] Thus the Bush administration appealed to both textual-transcendent authority (the Bible) and legal-transcendent authority (the Constitution) in making decisions to make exceptions to law.

Likewise, this double textual and legal origin for moral authority may explain why theonomists think that the biblical laws to be put in place should be structured by some form of U.S. American democracy. The biblical laws they envision will not resemble, as they take great pains to say, Islamic law, totalitarian law, or centralized church (read Catholic) law. The external power of biblical law—to which theonomists appeal when they argue against a particular civil law or when they decide to break a law—is already inscribed in and dictated by their understanding of a true principle to be found already existing in U.S. law. In looking for appropriate U.S. models (since present forms of U.S. law are thought to be morally deficient), they romanticize the original U.S. Constitution and its vision of democracy as somehow exemplifying God's law. So, for instance, Rose suggests in his critique of U.S. imperialism that following the Bible would move away from Babylonian imperialism by "restoring our Constitutional Republic and eliminating the unitary aspect of our national government" (2006, 29). It is this almost paradoxical, decentered view of God-centered civil law that theonomists feel has been lost and to which they wish U.S. American civil law would return.

Both theonomists and the neoconservatively shaped Bush administration idealized U.S. liberal democratic law to the extent that this very law appears as a form of external power that allows for exceptions to the law. This idealized power is confirmed by religious and philosophical texts.

---

tainees, in a manner consistent with the constitutional authority of the President to supervise the unitary executive branch and as Commander in Chief and consistent with the constitutional limitations on the judicial power, which will assist in achieving the shared objective of the Congress and the President, evidenced in Title X, of protecting the American people from further terrorist attacks" (Bush 2005b).

25. See Runions 2004, 2005.

The double textual authority (Bible and law) makes the production of power invisible. Moreover, the focus on biblical authority hides the scripturalized functioning of law within liberal democracy. Like the biblical text, the law is also raised to the status of truth and then read back onto itself.

Agamben suggests that a homologous logic operates in Schmitt's conceptualization of the sovereign exception. As mentioned at the outset of this chapter, Agamben is interested in the process in Schmitt's thought whereby sovereign authority, which comes from outside the law to make the exacting moral decision on the exception (and on the enemy), is also inscribed within the law. The sovereign has to be above the law in order to suspend it, but the sovereign's power comes from within the law. Agamben describes the relation between authority and law as "indeterminacy between inside and outside," whereby the law "is applied in disapplying itself" ([2003] 2005, 105). As Schmitt expresses it in *Political Theology*, "The exception remains, nevertheless, accessible to jurisprudence because both elements, the norm as well as the decision, remain within the framework of the juristic" ([1922] 2005, 13). In other words, there is room within the law for the exception to it. Agamben argues that this process is totalizing, precisely because of the indeterminacy it creates between inside and outside of the law. In effect, authority generated from within the law is implemented as if it were authority that comes from outside the law.

The interior exteriority of the authority produced by the law within liberal democracy operates in the same fashion as scripture in authorizing the exception. Although theonomist and neoconservative thought requires truth produced from ancient text, both additionally depend on truth produced by law. Scripture and civil law (i.e., secular law)[26] are raised to the status of truth in motivating the exception. The fact that these readings need to find authority in the law itself suggests that scriptural justification is not sufficient. Law in liberal democracy also contains its own scripturalizing impulse.

---

26. I am using "civil law" here in the sense that the theonomists use it, to mean secular law (not God's law), without getting into the technical distinction between constitutional law and civil law. With respect to that distinction, clearly (original) constitutional law is seen to be on a higher order than regular civil laws.

Miracles, Scripture, and the Exception

Schmitt offers a reason in *Political Theology* for the scripturalized structure of the exception, and for the scriptural functioning of law within liberal democracy. In chapter 3 of *Political Theology*, he indicates that a return to hierarchy and the decision would be merely the replenishing of a theological structure that has persisted in liberalism through the process of secularization. In this genealogy, he famously claims, "The exception in jurisprudence is analogous to the miracle in theology" ([1922] 2005, 36). What is interesting for the purposes of my argument here is that the miracle, God, exception to law, and scripture are homologous in the theological history of the exception that Schmitt presents. Not only does his genealogy makes sense of the scripturalizing structure of the exception to law, but it also further explains the acceptance of liberal democratic principles by conservatives who eschew post-Enlightenment thought. Schmitt wants to reclaim an older theological conception of jurisprudence, on the model of a transcendent *and* immanent God. Before the Enlightenment, belief in the transcendent God who could also immanently intervene in the world allowed for belief in both miracles and sovereign exceptions (48). The miracle, like the exception, requires that the immanent order be affected by transcendence. In other words, for Schmitt, proper secular juridical thinking has the structure of the miracle (transcendent yet immanent, exterior yet interior) and therefore allows for the possibility of the exception.

Enter scripturalization. Schmitt explains approvingly, via Leibniz, that this secularized conception of jurisprudence, like theology, has "a double principle, *reason* (hence there is a natural theology and natural jurisprudence) *and scripture*, which means a book with positive revelations and directives" ([1922] 2005, 37–38, emphasis mine).[27] Though he does not fully explain this formulation, it seems that he follows Leibniz in saying that reason (which apprehends natural law) remains in the structural place of

---

27. In general, Schmitt does not appreciate Leibniz's move away from a conception of a transcendent immanent relationship between God and law to one in which—in Schmitt's reading of Leibniz—"God enunciates only general and not particular declarations of will" ([1922] 2005, 48). Nonetheless, it seems that Leibniz is useful to Schmitt in his argument that even a concept of natural law cannot escape its theological foundations.

the transcendent, whereas scripture (positive law) is immanent.[28] Even in the Enlightenment, reason was seen as apprehending the higher principle of the law and was enacted on positive law by the sovereign. In this vein, for Schmitt, "the best constitutions [i.e., scriptures] are the work of a sole wise legislator [reason]" who fills in the structural place formerly belonging to God (47; cf. Norris 2000). In this double principle, scripture ("a book with positive revelations and directives"), that is, positive law, still requires a higher outside element, reason, for its interpretation; but reason also follows scripture. Post-Enlightenment transcendence can still be filled, for Schmitt, through the reason of the wise sovereign, or even the state. Like the transcendent God, "The state intervenes everywhere. At times it does so as a *deus ex machina* [reason], to decide according to positive statute [scripture] a controversy that the independent act of juristic perception failed to bring to a generally plausible solution; at other times it does so as the graceful and merciful lord who proves by pardons and amnesties his supremacy over his own laws" (38). The indeterminacy between the inside and the outside of the law becomes evident here: The state acts like God, either raising legal statutes to act as if from the outside or more directly making exception to its own laws.

If Schmitt is right that theological conceptions have persisted in liberal democracy in this double principle of reason and scripture, then it is not surprising to find a comparable dynamic existing between text and truth, law and exception. The interior exteriority in the structure of law described by Agamben is enabled by an inherited conception of an exterior-interior, transcendent-immanent, miracle-working God who moves fluidly between transcendence and immanence. The double principle of reason and scripture that Schmitt references marks a point of slippage between the interiority and exteriority of the law that seems to have become of feature of liberal democracy.

Schmitt's genealogy also draws to the fore the need for transcendence in securing the authority required for conservatives' decision to make exception to law. With transcendence comes both a hierarchical structure and a

---

28. Leibniz's *Nova Methodus Discendae Docendaeque Jurisprudentiae* (1667), which Schmitt cites, is not readily available in translation at the time of writing. For a helpful exposition of Leibniz's view of natural law, see Cairns 1946.

higher authority by which to guarantee these hierarchies. Thus, the right to leadership and decision making for fathers and the president is secured through reference to the structural place of God. Patriarchal leaders act on the authority of a higher sovereignty. And yet, as I have been arguing, this authority is also produced via the immanent domain of law.

Babylonian Longing

Guided by allusions to Babylon in theonomist and neoconservative writings, I have tried to plot out the complex constellation of a theopolitics in which tensions over homogeneity and heterogeneity in U.S. liberal democracy are tied up with a scripturalized approach to law and exception to it. These dynamics become particularly visible in conservative discourses that do not hide their longing for authority, or the ways in which they see truth, decisionism, and political dominion to be mutually implicated, even as they decry empire. Yet the configuration of liberalism—produced in the overlap between pre- and post-Enlightenment thought that creates ambivalence over unity and diversity—itself facilitates the scripturalization of law that allows for the exception. Moreover, the structural remnants of transcendence within U.S. liberal democracy make it amenable not only to conservative reaffirmations of patriarchy and heteronormativity but also to ambitions of world dominance.

Although this theopolitics is neither strictly secular nor strictly religious in its final form, it appears that what may be distinctive for the U.S. form of liberal democracy is the theological inheritance of a particularly Protestant mode of reading scripture and law. As these conservative texts show, this is a mode of decisionism that enhances the authority by which the exception can be enacted, by grafting spiritual authority onto legal authority. The close resemblance of the exception to Protestant reading practices, including indeterminacy between multiplicity and unity, inside and outside, text and spirit, suggests that it may be precisely this Protestant reading practice that is foundational for the structure of law within liberal democracy. Immanent law becomes the transcendent principle by which it can be suspended or transgressed. The exacting moral decision simply reclaims and repeats the role of the transcendent, immanent God, as revealed through scripture and again by the Spirit. Conservative claims that America is a Christian nation may be on to something, at least in this respect.

Ultimately, conservative readings of Babylon and Babel are symptomatic of both a sometimes disavowed longing for empire and the larger scripturalizing impulse central to liberal democracy whereby immanence is always both guaranteed and trumped by transcendence. Sovereignty is produced in the interstices of scripture and law, in a continual bid for the authority needed to make exception to law. The indeterminate double textual sources of moral authority (the Bible and the tradition of democratic law)—along with their supratextual sources of truth—make longings for empire and unity easy to deny. Law can be upheld and surpassed at the same time, often in the service of war. The result is an imagined religious community (of the theonomists) and an actual nation-state (shaped by neoconservatives) that can maintain a notion of juridical sovereignty (God's law, constitutional law) while surpassing actual law. These imagined and real sovereignties end up acting like the subject of interest, not compelled by so-called neutralizing social contracts. But when, in this blurring between economic and juridical logics, the *nation* of interest operates on higher (messianic) orders, not bound by domestic laws or international agreements, as we will see in chapters 4–5, it risks becoming the tyrant it abhors.

Tolerating Babel: Biopolitics, Film, and Family

The previous two chapters have shown how Babylon has come to represent a variety of perceived political ills: economic equality, state control, foreign empires, and the wrong kind of heterogeneity. Babelian fears are often countered by the proposed security and transcendent mandate of the heteropatriarchal nuclear family and strong (male) political leadership and decisionism. Against Babel, the United States is hailed as a better, hierarchically stratified kind of unified empire, promoting truth, universal values, freedom, and a certain limited kind of diversity. This chapter changes gears to match the terrain of another Babylonian fantasy, in which a new Babylon becomes a place of enviable tolerance. If security, hierarchy, and the market are the bywords of U.S. conservatism, then tolerance might be considered a chief value of U.S. liberalism. No less than conservative ideals, however, tolerance feeds the biopolitical regularization of populations, hierarchized and graduated through the family.

To see tolerance in action, I turn to the prominent U.S. art form of film. Two important and innovative films connect cinema with Babylon: D. W. Griffith's *Intolerance: Love's Struggle through the Ages* (1916) and Alejandro González Iñárritu's *Babel* (2006). These films wish to rebuild Babel: They propose cinema as a universal language able to reverse the damages incurred by God's disruption, bridge communicative divides, and remedy the violence and social control of intolerant empire. Both have tolerance as their central message. Yet their push for tolerance ends up being somewhat parochial in that they both ultimately prioritize the traditional family. A closer look at this dynamic highlights how these films exhibit what others have argued are the *limits* of tolerance as well as its participation in the biopolitical (Brown 2006; Jakobsen and Pellegrini 2003); in these films, tolerance connects to the constellations of capital, political subjectivity, families, and populations that characterize the biopolitical. Babylon and Babel are used in film to promote the subject of interest, but to curtail it as well, containing it within families that are properly arranged within and across nation-states in graduated forms of *capital-ability* (Foucault 2008, 225; see also Ong 2006). The value placed on film and family facilitates a biopolitics that reinforces (white) U.S. dominance.

The scriptural bid for cinema's constructive potential exhibits a marked ambivalence toward political unity and empire that is grounded in the biblical text itself. Both films concur with traditional assessments of Genesis 11 as a critique of Babylon's political domination; at the same time, they want to rebuild Babel. Cinema is envisioned as that which can mend the rifts of culture, miscommunication, intolerance, and militarization, in order to return to some semblance of unity. But like the Babel story within the larger context of the book of Genesis, where the narrative continues with the family of Abraham, healing is worked out in both films in the very localized site of the family. One particular cultural form—the nuclear family—is imagined to hold the weight of human unity, societal tolerance, moral health, and sexual normativity, even as both films place value on cultural diversity. Thus, these films exhibit the reversibility between diversity and unity that I have been tracing, which also manifests in an overlap between tolerance and control. As ever, such slippages are facilitated by the Babylon symbol.

The fluctuating appreciation of these films for their central metaphor also maps onto the vacillation we have been following between centralized sites of political power (traditional empires and nation-states) and dispersed forms of biopolitical power in an increasingly globalized world. As noted in the introduction, biopolitics extends from older disciplinary forms of power focused on the regulation of individual bodies to management of populations through the regularization of birthrates, mortality rates, and longevity. This extension from the disciplinary management of individuals to the management of populations aggravates the tensions between social cohesion and social difference, inclusion and exclusion, that are apparent in calls for tolerance. The ambivalence toward Babel/Babylon and tolerance in *Intolerance* and *Babel* stands at the center of these overlapping techniques of power. Together, these two films reveal how the medium of film, the Bible, the figure of Babylon, the social institution of family, and the discourse of tolerance are all woven together—on the warp of shifting modes of power—to form symbols, practices, and attitudes that domesticate and normalize U.S. sovereignty, even as empire is disparaged. Both films want to criticize empire, but their approaches to tolerance ultimately shore up the biopolitical—and U.S. dominance with it. I take as instructive Amy Kaplan's argument (2002) that the success of U.S. empire is a result not only of foreign policy and international relations but also of domestic debates, policies, beliefs, domesticities, literary genres, and art forms—including film—that conditioned acceptance of imperialism.[1] In a time after national sovereignty, this empire is a biopolitical empire, seeking to hold the highest cards for global capital, one of which is a properly shaped and striated population.

Much has been written about *Intolerance*, both with respect to its influence on cinema, its treatment of the family, sex, and gender, and its connection to Griffith's racializing project—on which analyses I draw (Hansen 1989, 1991; L. Jacobs [1939] 1968; Lennig 2005; May 1980; Rogin 1989); but to my knowledge no one has explored its relation to the biopolitical or to U.S. empire. *Babel* has been the subject of less analysis. Although in need of trenchant critique, it is more genuinely open to other cultures than is *Intolerance*, doubtless reflecting Iñárritu's own experience as an immigrant in the United States, as well as his own lifelong desire to travel (2006a, 183).

---

1. Elizabeth Povinelli has shown how this works with respect to intimacy—which may seem very local but cannot be separated from transnationally conditioned "dynamic[s] of individual freedom and social constraint" (2006, 17–19).

Iñárritu's thoughts, struggles, and respect for the cultures he films—which includes democratizing film making by working with untrained actors— are documented in his book about the film (2006b). Still, the film is limited by the concepts of tolerance, universalism, and the family that it tries to rework, all of which are implicated in a structure of graduated global sovereignty, capital-ability, and control.

I show in stages that these films' shifting valuation of Babylon and Babel mirrors the tension between unity and diversity already present in the biblical text and that it maps onto a pursued and detested biopolitical U.S. empire. I explore the films' understanding of cinema and their use of cinematic techniques, their view of the family and corresponding norms of gender and sexuality, their discourse of tolerance, and the kinds of subjectivity they imagine.

Rebuilding Babel

Griffith famously envisioned film as a universal language that could rebuild the biblical Tower of Babel. Lillian Gish, Griffith's favored actress, reports that he called film "a great power that had been predicted in the Bible as the universal language . . . [that] was going to end wars and bring about the millennium" (quoted in May 1980, 73). In her autobiography, Gish recalls that, when Griffith began filming *Intolerance*, he said, "I've always said I would rebuild Babylon for you. Now I'm going to do it" (1969, 165). *Intolerance*'s Babylon story line—the most extravagant of the film's four story lines with its hugely elaborate set, costume design, and choreography—celebrates the medium of film. It depicts Babylon as an ideal place of luxury, joy, and tolerance. It also alludes to the Tower of Babel. As the film scholar Miriam Hansen has pointed out, one of the intertitles at the beginning of act 2 states (inaccurately) that with the destruction of Babylon, "a universal written language (the cuneiform) was made to become an unknown cypher upon the face of the earth." Hansen suggests that this intertitle makes the connection between the lost universal language of Babylon and Griffith's aspiration for film (1991, 183–84). Babylon and Babel—place and symbol combined—is a site of nostalgia for Griffith, a beautiful universal before the division of language, to which film can return.

Exactly fifty years later, Iñárritu's *Babel* makes a similar bid for understanding film as a universal language. The film explores the breakdown of communication and the pain it causes within families and across borders and cultures. Reflecting on the film's title, Iñárritu says that the metaphor of God punishing humans by creating different languages was "a simple way to define what this film is about" (Iñárritu 2007a, 21). The film represents the aftermath of the fall of the Tower of Babel. In contrast, the universals of listening and hope are offered as a way of rebuilding after the disorientation, pain, and intolerance of Babel's legacy of miscommunication. Tag lines for the film include "If you want to be understood, listen" and "Pain is universal . . . but so is hope." Like Griffith, Iñárritu imagines the medium of film to be central to this project. As he tells one reporter, "The beauty of cinema is that it is the universal language" (O'Keeffe 2007, 38). Elsewhere, he suggests that the cinematic image is like God, more powerful than words and scripts (Iñárritu 2006a, 189). *Babel* signifies this argument diegetically, too; as reviewer Ashley Barrera notices, viewers "see how words often fail to help us communicate with those closest to us" (2007, 82). Filmic images are purported to transcend words.

These two films bear other resemblances as well. Jim Ridley of the *Village Voice* has called *Babel* "an apparent bid to out-intolerate *Intolerance*" (2006). Ridley's sarcasm is marked, but he is onto something when he implies that Iñárritu is drawing on the earlier film so important to film history. *Babel* does seem to share themes and structures with *Intolerance*. In addition to making pleas for film as a universal language, both films have four story lines, both tint or color each story differently,[2] both cut between the stories for dramatic effect, and both use cinematic techniques deliberately to work on the level of emotions.[3] On the levels of technical skill and

2. The Babylon story is tinted grey green; the French story, sepia; the Judean story, blue; and the modern story, amber (Dirks 2008). For *Babel*, "Art designer Brigitte Broch suggested . . . a gamut of reds: burgundy for Morocco, bright-red for Mexico, and violet for Japan. Morocco was shot in 16mm with faded colors, Mexico in 35mm with vivid colors, and . . . Japan in Panavision with anamorphic lenses" (Iñárritu 2006b, 259).

3. Andrew Sarris writes, "Griffith devised a grammar of emotions through his expressive editing. The focal length of his lens became a function of feeling. Close-ups not only intensified an emotion; they shifted characters from the republic of prose to the kingdom of poetry" ([1968] 1996, 52). Iñárritu uses similar techniques. He comments, "It's emotion and humanity that make the connection in our global community" (2007b, 7).

innovation, there is much to be admired in both films. Griffith's camera and editing work was highly influential in the development of film. Likewise, *Babel* is remarkable for the beauty of its shots and cutting, as well as for its ability to stage emotion and evoke feeling.

Setting the directors' skill aside, it is important to notice that the project of imagining film as a universal language participates in Hollywood's complicity with the violent expansionist impulses of U.S. nation making.[4] Guy Vanderhaeghe makes this argument about early film in his brilliant novel, *The Englishman's Boy*. In the novel, Ira Chance, a director who seeks to emulate Griffith, excitedly pontificates:

> Griffith marks the birth of spiritual Americanism. . . . The American spirit is a frontier spirit, restless, impatient of constraint, eager for a look over the next hill, the next peek around the bend in the river. The American destiny is forward momentum. What the old frontiersman called westering. What the American spirit required was an art form of forward momentum, an art form as bold and unbounded as the American spirit. A westering art form! It had to wait for motion pictures. The art form of motion! (1996, 107–8)

Film is the new-world imperial art form, intent on the colonizing impulses of exploration, "westering," and forward motion. Miriam Hansen's discussion of early film's universalizing aspirations, on which Griffith drew, corroborates Vanderhaeghe's suggestions. She cites (markedly imperial) images used in advertising by Carl Laemmle, founder of Universal Pictures.

> The globe (the Universal logo), the lighthouse, a map of the United States, Uncle Sam among representatives of world nations, a Roman legionnaire with the logo on his shield; finally (possibly as late as 1916) the silhouette of a Westerner with a gun and the caption, "UNIVERSAL Moving Pictures Are Mightier Than PEN or SWORD." (1985, 330–31)

The emerging art form promotes itself as warring for universalism; the United States is dominant among nations. Along these lines, Kaplan shows how Griffith's influential *Birth of a Nation* (1915) depicts the ride of the Klan to "save" the nation in terms that also evoke an international context in

---

4. See also Kaplan on early film and empire (2002, 146–70). For film's more recent imperial implications, see Hall (1991) 1997; Prince 1992; Rogin 1990.

which the United States rides to the rescue (the Cuban War of Independence, the Spanish-American War, and World War I; 2002, 162–63). U.S. messianism is endemic to the mission of U.S. film.

The film form, and the use of Babylon to represent it, is also very well suited to the emerging biopolitical formulation of U.S. empire. As a symbol both for an imperializing medium and an anti-imperialist message, Babylon is able to convey both love and hate of empire. Its malleability as a symbol should by now be evident: It can be read as placing value on both unity and diversity, or on neither. As such, it is useful in negotiating the dominant position of the United States within biopolitics; at the same time, it occludes that negotiation by protesting against empire. Babylon ultimately symbolizes a set of contradictions that facilitate the biopolitical and secure a sense of U.S. superiority.

Montage Babel

Even the structure of these films reveals their ambivalence toward Babylon. Neither film seems able to achieve the unity across its story lines that one might expect given its belief in the power of the cinematic image. Neither is able to rebuild the Tower of Babel with the diversity of their material, a diversity that they both try to celebrate. Critics decried the films' inability to make a convincing unified whole from the fragmented images and stories that they try to stitch together.

After the enormous success of Griffith's earlier *Birth, Intolerance* was "Griffith's first critical and financial failure" (May 1980, 86). Hansen summarizes reviewers' frustration with the film's form: "While many reviewers admired the film, some noted that popular reception might be impeded by its experimental narration, the systematic intercutting of four different stories set in different periods of history and geographic locations" (1989, 28). The most famous critique of *Intolerance* is that of Sergei Eisenstein, who acknowledges his debt to Griffith's cutting style in developing his own distinctive Soviet technique of montage. Eisenstein felt that *Intolerance* failed to achieve its unifying metaphor. In his view, montage should create a dialectical "unity, which in the inner stress of contradictions [between juxtaposed disparate shots] is halved in order to be re-assembled in a new unity on a new plane, qualitatively higher, its imagery newly perceived" ([1944] 1977, 235–36). In other words, montage produces a set of contradictions that are sublated into metaphor rather than remaining in the realm of representation (241). In Eisenstein's judgment, Griffith was not able to make the historical parallels work together metaphorically: He "made no attempt at a genuinely thoughtful abstraction of phenomena—at an extraction of generalized conclusions on historical phenomena from a wide variety of historical data" (244).[5] For Eisenstein, Griffith's work does not depart from the bourgeois structure of the Dickens narratives that he emulated. Rather, "the montage concept of Griffith, as a primarily parallel montage, appears to be a copy of [Dickens's] dualistic picture of the world, running in two parallel lines of poor and rich toward some hypothetical [and never realized] 'reconciliation'" (235).

Eisenstein's critique of *Intolerance* might also be applied to *Babel*, which also does not quite manage to bring the diversity it celebrates cinematically into a unified metaphor. The film was met with mixed, but mostly negative, reception.[6] Critics did notice the film's "unusual aesthetic force" (Scott 2006), with "beauty in its lapidary details, which sparkle with feeling and surprise" (Chocano 2006). Nonetheless, many accused the film of using the "gimmick" of parallel stories (Hunter 2006), of "play[ing] pointlessly with time sequences" (Kaufman 2006), and of "jarringly abrupt cuts and shifts of tone" (Scott 2006). Others disliked the film's central project. Leslie Felperin notes that the film's title "declaims grand ambition, if not a little self-importance" (2007, 41). Some turned to (Josephan-influenced) biblical language to find fault. Andrew Sarris condemns *Babel*'s pretension to universality, which he called "the excessive pride and presumption of filmmakers who attempt to succeed where their predecessors failed—in the crossing of ethnic and linguistic boundaries—through their use of the latest technology" (2006). A. O. Scott highlights the slipperiness of the metaphor: "In the end 'Babel,' like that tower in the book of Genesis, is a grand wreck, an incomplete monument to its own limitless ambition. . . . It's a folly, and also,

---

5. Eisenstein finds the recurring cradle shot to be symptomatic of the disconnectedness of Griffith's montage; for disagreement with this analysis, see Hansen (1991, 199–217), who finds it to be complexly connected to other gendered elements in the film.

6. *Babel* grossed only $34 million domestically and $101 million internationally.

perversely, a wonder" (2006). Likewise, Andrew O'Hehir writes, "It felt like a transformative experience, the kind of movie that reaches for the ineffable, combining prodigious cinematic technique with impressive human range. Then . . . the energy gradually dissipates, leaving me asking . . . : What is this movie, shot on three continents in at least seven languages, actually about?" (2006). In a film about the unity of human experience via a new universal language, one might expect this question to be answered more easily.

Ambiguous Babel

A conflicting attitude about Babylon emerges in *Intolerance*'s narratives. As the title suggests, *Intolerance* tells four parallel stories about intolerance through the ages and about love's capacity to overcome it. The Babylon story line parallels three others: the persecution of Jesus by the Pharisees, the persecution of the Huguenots by the Medicis, and a modern love story in the face of corporate control. The Babylonian story is the most elaborate in terms of cinematic spectacle, whereas the modern story carries the bulk of Griffith's political message—a critique of censorship. All four stories seem to work together to argue against the control of individuals, against war, and against the violent suppression of populations. Imperializing tactics are negatively assessed. The film's final scene is of a millennial peace in which war and killing are ended and love triumphs. In all but the modern romance, however, love does not actually overcome intolerance but is thwarted by it. The modern story, prioritizing the nuclear family, is therefore designed to give the last word.

The Babylon story depicts the great city as a wondrous place of religious tolerance, aesthetic luxury, and sexual openness. The city tragically falls because of religious intolerance. Belshazzar (Alfred Paget), the religiously inclusive ruler of Babylon, is betrayed to Cyrus of Persia (George Siegmann) from the inside. Upset over Belshazzar's worship of Ishtar, the goddess of love and war, the high priest of Bel (Tully Marshall) opens the city gates in the wee hours of the morning after the city has spent itself celebrating success in repelling Cyrus's first siege. Griffith's portrayal of Babylon runs contrary to the biblical text, where Belshazzar is depicted as an arrogant and blasphemous enemy of Yahweh (Dn 5) and Cyrus the great liberator of the Israelites from Babylon (Ezr 1; Is 45). In *Intolerance*, Belshazzar is the hero, and Cyrus the villain. Belshazzar is tolerant—to quote an intertitle, an "apostle of religious freedom" trying to establish a universal religion. Cyrus, by contrast, was loyal to one local god, Shamash, the Sun God.[7] Griffith idealized Babylon as a lost space of religious universalism and tolerance because he felt that with demands for censorship, film—like Babylonian language and the Babylonian vision for universal religion—was under attack (more on this point further on). Griffith understood the idea of a universal religion to be more tolerant than the recognition and acceptance of local religious traditions.

Freedom to pursue a more tolerant universal religion is associated, in Griffith's Babylon, with the pursuit of pleasure and sexual freedom. The worship of Ishtar is visualized in extended (orientalizing) scenes of scantily clad women dancing and languishing in the "Temple of Love." In Griffith's idyllic world of Babylon, people are not controlled by laws. They are allowed to pursue their own pleasures and interests, sexually and religiously. Access to pleasure was central to Griffith's imagination of cinema, and he paired it with religious and sexual openness as a way of arguing against the censorship of film. Griffith appears to be advocating for a world in which pleasure and access to sex are easily available—in other words, not curtailed by law.

The film's modern story negatively portrays old-maid social reformers as parallel to Babylon's anti-Ishtar (antipleasure) Babylonian high priest of Bel. Against a backdrop of social unrest caused by capitalist exploitation of workers,[8] these social reformers try to legislate away pleasure, including dancing, prostitution, and alcohol. Ms. Jenkins (Vera Lewis), whose villainy is partly cued by the fact that she is the daughter of the exploitative

7. As William Drew points out, Griffith was making (loose) use of scholarship on Babylonian religion. For instance, A. H. Sayce and Morris Jastrow suggested that Belshazzar's father, Nabodinus, had tried to create a universal and centralized religion of Marduk, which was opposed by many within Babylon who preferred a system of local deities, as did Cyrus (Drew 1986, 43; Jastrow 1915, 183–85; Sayce 1897, 85–91). It was for this reason, Sayce argues, that Babylon was betrayed from the inside. Griffith embellished this historical hypothesis, substituting Belshazzar for Nabodinus and Ishtar for Marduk, and regarding Cyrus as a villain.

8. For the film's critique of capitalism, and especially the Rockefellers, see Lennig 2005.

factory owner, works with a team of Vestal Virgins to advocate laws for social reforms. Their reforms interfere with the lives of the other characters, including the two central characters, the Boy (Robert Harron) and the Dear One (Mae Marsh), who meet, fall in love, are married, and have a child. Until the very end, the Boy and the Dear One are continually separated by various plot twists, many caused by the reformers' meddling. Critics have noticed the way in which the modern story prioritizes the nuclear family form, idealized in the successful heterosexual pairing of the Boy and the Dear One (Hansen 1989, 1991; Rogin 1989). Like the Babylon story, the modern story prioritizes access to pleasure, but it offers the family as the most fulfilling way to pursue pleasure.

Nonetheless, there is also an unfavorable moral appraisal of Babylon in *Intolerance* that serves to orient the viewer to appreciate the modern story's outcome. As the film critic Russell Merritt points out, even though ancient Babylon is portrayed positively, its pleasures are what cause the city's downfall, since its night of revelry and feasting means that there is no one available or sober to protect the city when it is betrayed. Merritt writes, "The spectacle of this city has a divided purpose: to reveal the pleasures of glittering sumptuousness and to repeat one all-powerful commandment: 'Don't'" (1979, 20). The pursuit of pleasure is both desired and judged. Babylon does not censor pleasure but comes to harm because of it. The world of Babylon is, ultimately, not to be emulated. In contrast, the happy ending of the modern story suggests that contemporary society may have at its disposal resources to right Babylon's error. It appears that those resources are film and the family. Both allow the viewing public the safe pleasures of titillation and scopic gratification without actual participation in decadence.

Babel likewise displays an uncertain assessment of its titular metaphor, which is far less visually present than it is conceptually. The film also tells four stories, separated geographically rather than historically and interconnected through an overlapping series of events. All of the stories deal with the pain of failed communication within families and across cultures. The distance, yet interconnection, of the stories symbolizes a universal human connection that is disrupted by miscommunication. In the Moroccan desert, two boys practice shooting with their father's newly acquired rifle. Yussef (Boubker Ait El Caid), the favored younger of the two boys, makes a series of bad judgments that end up getting his brother killed in a shootout with Moroccan police. The first of Yussef's mistakes is to take a shot that finds its mark in a tour bus below, hitting U.S. citizen Susan Jones (Cate Blanchett) in the neck. This event begins the second story. The wounded Susan and her distraught husband Richard (Brad Pitt) are stranded in a small Moroccan village as they await help and have to rely on the kindness of strangers. Help is delayed because of security measures enacted by the United States in response to the shooting, which is considered a threat of terror. When they eventually get to a hospital, Richard calls home to their nanny, Amelia (Adriana Barraza), and tells her she will not be able to take the day off to go to her son's wedding in Mexico (thus beginning the third story). Unable to find another sitter, Amelia decides to take the children with her to Mexico, which causes trouble at the border when they try to return to the United States. Amelia is ultimately deported as a result of their misadventure. In these three stories, the film criticizes U.S. empire and its effects, including its easy assumption and accusation of terrorism in Morocco and the militarization of the U.S.-Mexico border.

The fourth story is tangentially related to the others yet still vital to the film. It is the story of the deaf high school girl, Chieko (Rinko Kikuchi). She is the daughter of the Japanese businessman who has left his gun in Morocco—the same gun that is sold to the father of Yussef. Chieko is angry, confused, rejected by boys, and highly libidinous. Chieko's anger and confusion, we learn, is due to the shooting suicide of her mother. Although initially alienated from her father, Chieko is reconciled with him at the end of the film.

Although the Japanese story seems less integrated into the film than the other story lines, it contains the only visual reference to the Tower of Babel, marking it as central. Not incidentally, the sequence in which the allusion occurs marks the exact temporal center point of the film (in chapter 12 of 24; 1:11:58–1:12:18 of a total 2:23:22). In a scene commented on by critics for its aesthetic power, Chieko goes clubbing, on ecstasy, with her friends and some young men they have met. The camera focuses on her face, which brilliantly expresses her anticipation of finally being loved. Haruki, the good-looking and charismatic cousin of one of her friends, has his eye on her. They pair off, beginning with flirtation on the playground where they meet and continuing on to the subway. Once in the nightclub, the camera cuts between close-ups of Chieko's experience of stimulus overload, enjoyment, and anticipation: the press of dancing, sweating bodies, and a dazzling light show. The soundtrack switches back and forth from Chieko's silence to the pounding pulse of the music. Felperin describes this club scene as "a moment that demonstrates empathy for the character, while at the same time showing off the film-makers' exquisite levels of craftsmanship" (2007, 42). Significantly, yet overlooked by critics, the club's light show projects swirling clouds onto the ceiling, seemingly alluding to Babel's attempt to reach the heavens (1:11:57–1:12:18). In one frame, a vertical bank of lights evokes a tower.

As with Griffith's ambiguous depiction of Babylon, *Babel*'s club scene suggests that the pursuit of meaning through unconstrained pleasure will not succeed. Like attempts to build the Tower of Babel, Chieko's attempt to reach happiness through casual sex goes awry. Immediately following cuts to the Babelian lightshow, Chieko's face falls as she realizes Haruki's attentions have migrated elsewhere. Via close-ups and cutting, the scene is intensely evocative of her emotion, confusion, and disappointment as she watches Haruki kissing her friend. She leaves the venue alone and dejected. As the story continues, when Chieko returns home, she invites the detective investigating the gun to her home, where she propositions him by appearing before him naked. He respectfully and politely refuses her. When her father comes home to find her naked, he develops some empathy and expresses his acceptance of her.

This story line presents an impasse in Iñárritu's various aspirations. Cinematically, Iñárritu provocatively cuts together bits of sound and image to make a whole, but narratively, the film is limited, rejecting many forms of pleasure and prioritizing the family as the sole site of meaning. Chieko is depicted as vulnerable—first in her hope for affection, then in her disappointment, and finally in her nakedness. She ends up needing the love of her father. Of the film's narrative, Iñárritu writes, "This picture is concerned precisely with how vulnerable and fragile the human being is; . . . how we love and need one another even while pissing; . . . In *Babel* it was God who created the confusion and man who now has to find the solution. God is missing in this equation" (2006b, 261). The club scene (and the rest of the story line as well) suggests that God's destructive endowment of vulnerability and isolation can be overcome only by familial love and not by other forms of distraction, entertainment, or human achievement. One wonders, therefore, where film figures in this argument. By making such moral judgments in the narrative, Iñárritu demeans the value of film even as he seeks to valorize the medium. Again, ambivalence to the Babel symbol emerges. Iñárritu's goals for film (to rebuild Babel) and his narrative (the critique of Babel) are at odds.

The Bible's Babel

Shifting attitudes toward Babylon in *Intolerance* and *Babel* reflect the biblical text's own indeterminacy. The instability of the Babel metaphor is already present in Genesis 11, where the relationship between unity and diversity is complex. A variation in contemporary scholarly interpretation of the text is indicative of its undecidability. Most frequently—from Josephus's establishing commentary on the story (*Antiquities of the Jews* 1:109–19) until now—it has been taken to be a tale of hubris and punishment and a critique of human attempts at self-sufficiency.[9] In these interpretations, both unity and diversity are disparaged: the former as having prideful intentions and the latter as the punished consequence. The influential Gerhard Von Rad, for instance, says that humans "in their striving for fame, alliance, and political development set themselves against God," for which the creation of nations is a judgment and a punishment (1972, 147–48). More recently, scholars take up the opposite view, initially suggested by Ibn Ezra in the twelfth century but apparently forgotten (Hiebert 2007, 31): The dispersal of peoples and languages is not read as punishment, but rather as a completion of creation, filling the earth as per God's command in Genesis 1:28, and valuing the diversity of language and culture (B. Anderson 1978; Brueggemann 1982; Fernandez 2002, 2009; Hiebert 2007; Houck-Loomis 2009; Ibn Ezra 1988, 143; Van Wolde 1994). Diversity is claimed as the intended goal of God's creation. Others acknowledge the text's tensions (Fewell 2001; Van Wolde 1994). Walter Brueggemann considers the text to value both diversity and unity, presenting a "dialectic of unity and scattering,"

9. For examples see Blenkinsopp 1992, 91; Fokkelman 1975; Sasson 1980; Strong 2008; Walton 1995; Wenham 1987.

whereby scattering is not punishment, but rather creates the conditions by which "all of humankind shall be in covenant with [God] . . . and with him only" (1982, 98–99). With corresponding structural indeterminacy, this text about scattering showcases literary unity, despite its demand for dispersal. As Hiebert notes, scholars of the literary structure of the text have shown it to be "a beautifully crafted whole" (2007, 32).[10]

The mythological subtext of Genesis 11 further adds to the variable value of unity and diversity. As discussed in the introduction, the text clearly alludes to the Babylonian creation myth, the Enuma Elish, in which Marduk, the patron god of Babylon, allows the gods to build the ziggurat Esagila with mud bricks, as a sanctuary for himself and as a place for the gods to gather and feast in times of assembly (Tablets V and VI; Coote and Ord 1989, 90–91; Sarna 1989; Speiser 1964, 75–76; Walton 1995). Scholars have emphasized how the biblical text parodies this myth as a critique of the Babylonian empire (Croatto 1998; Fewell 2001, 8–10; Van Seters 1992, 183–84; Wenham 1987, 244–45). Ironically, though, the biblical writer's critique of the unity and homogeneity of the Babylonian empire (via the imagery of one language) also carries with it a critique of the Babylonian pantheon, which happens to be rather diverse.

Indeed, in view of the text's placement in Genesis, the tension between diversity and unity seems to come down on the side of a new homogeneous social formation.[11] While making a critique of oneness and empire in favor of diversity, the tale ends up buying into oneness. Many readers of the text have noticed that Genesis 11 sets the stage for the story of Abraham, the father of the people of Israel, which begins in Genesis 12 (Dershowitz 1994; Hamilton 1990, 372–73; Sarna 1989; Sasson 1980, 219). Von Rad, in his salvation-historical reading, calls the Abraham cycle the beginning of sacred history (1972, 149). As a preface to the story of Abraham and monotheism, the story of Babel seems to prioritize one God, not many. (Although even there the text is ambiguous: The deity speaks in plural forms in 11:7, "Let us go down and there let us confuse their lan-

---

10. See Fokkelman 1975; Kikawada 1974.
11. This dynamic is extended in later texts. In the prophetic tradition, the mountain of Yahweh is imagined to encompass the whole earth, effectively rebuilding the Tower of Babel (Is 56:4–8, 60:10–14; Zep 3:9–11); see Cassuto 1964, 230–31; Pinker 2000. Griffith, certainly, was aware of this tradition as it came into U.S. millennial thought.

guage," which are perhaps a throwback to its pantheistic origins.) Still, the story of Babel creates the context in which the one chosen family and people can emerge to follow the one God. Dispersal is followed by consolidation and exclusion of difference. After Abraham's call, the text gives clear etiologies for why certain peoples are considered Israel's enemies and are not included in the promises and blessing of Yahweh (for instance, Lot's daughters, forebears of Moab and Ammon, are said to have sex with their father to ensure offspring).

Thus, even if Genesis 11 is read as presenting diversity as part of God's creation, it is set into a final form that prioritizes one family and vilifies those excluded by showing them as somehow perverse. The credibility of the family line—established from the creation of the heavens and earth to the people of Israel, via Adam, Noah, Shem, Abraham, Isaac, and Jacob—explicitly relies on the perversity of the other brother (e.g., Cain murders his brother Abel and becomes an outcast; Shem's brother Ham looks on his father's nakedness and is cursed).[12] This pattern of exclusion from the family tree because of some sexual or moral anomaly continues throughout the book (Abraham's first son Ishmael is excluded for being a less legitimate son of the Egyptian concubine Hagar; Isaac's oldest son, Esau, is excluded for selling his birthright, and so forth). Difference is used to set off a particular group for the new unity.

Perverse Babel

Perhaps unconsciously, both films imitate the pattern in Genesis of prioritizing one kind of family within the diversity they try to celebrate. While the films try to rebuild Babel by stitching together a valued diversity, they also paint some kinds of diversity negatively. In so doing, they end up affirming a moral structure that is racialized and sexualized. Both prioritize the white Western nuclear family (and corresponding gender norms) over and against a too-free or deviant sexuality that is nonetheless made available for viewers' pleasure.

12. Japheth is an odd exception to this story. He does not become part of the chosen people, but he has done nothing objectionable either.

Griffith's universalizing and racializing projects are tied together. The racial politics of *Intolerance* can be seen as consistent with those in *Birth of a Nation*—that deeply racist yet very popular film that reinvigorated the Ku Klux Klan. As many have noticed, *Intolerance* as a whole, and the modern story especially, offers Griffith's defensive reaction to the demands for censorship of *Birth* (Gish 1969, 161–65; Hansen 1991, 164; L. Jacobs [1939] 1968, 178; Rogin 1989, 518–20). These analyses point to the pamphlet Griffith published in response to the criticism of *Birth*, titled *The Rise and Fall of Free Speech in America* (Griffith 1916). Not only does the pamphlet defend *Birth*; it connects intolerance to censorship throughout, with the heading "Intolerance: The Root of All Censorship" appearing on almost every other page. Censorship is a far worse national ill, in Griffith's mind, than are slavery and racism. He writes, "Curtailment of individual liberty is the curse of the nation." So even though the film seems to argue against the violent suppression of populations, its largest argument, against censorship, is clearly meant to participate in the racializing work of Griffith's earlier film.

The pamphlet makes grand universalizing claims about cinema, including "The motion picture is war's greatest antidote," "The world-wide acceptance of moving pictures means the introduction of the most popular and far-reaching form of education the world has ever known," and "The moving picture is a powerful and growing factor in the uplift of humanity." With respect to censorship, Griffith suggests that the United States should differentiate itself from Russia, "the most autocratic and tyrannical of all civilized nations." Although the argument against censorship might seem to allow for diversity, it is limited by Griffith's exclusionary racial politics. Further, the conception of film as a "far-reaching" universal language that will further the (democratic, nontotalitarian) nationalist project of the "uplift of humanity" participates in the imperializing ambitions of U.S. film discussed at the outset. The narrow tolerance that this pamphlet and *Intolerance* promote is already subtly present in *Birth* and central to the logic of imperialism: As Kaplan suggests, *Birth* indicates that "the domestic unity for the nation depends on the violent subordination of blacks at home to forge a whiteness capacious enough to include immigrants" (2002, 164).

Within this political project, *Intolerance* prioritizes white heteronormativity—as exemplified in the relationship of the Dear One and the Boy.

Despite the proclamation of its title, the film is not tolerant of nonnormative gender or sexual expression. As already noted, the modern story is seen as the crowning moment in the history of progress toward tolerance; in it, the nuclear family is figured as the solution to the kinds of perverse (yet visually pleasurable) excesses of Babylon, including the orientalist depictions of sexually available Eastern women in the cult of Ishtar. The project of social reform, which frequently separates the heteronormative couple, is carried out by reformers who are neither married nor gender normative. In one much noticed scene, Ms. Jenkins and her Vestal Virgins stand watching while intolerant police raid a brothel at their behest. Unflattering camera close-ups portray them as scheming, judgmental, unattractive, and "mannish." An intertitle explains, "When women cease to be attractive to men they often turn to reform as a second choice." As Michael Rogin analyzes it, "Griffith discredited female independence by (homo)sexualizing it," thus depicting a "fear of lesbianism [that] expressed anxiety over the sexual turn of women away from men" (1989, 543). In that same scene, as Arthur Lennig has noticed, several leering men (thus cued as morally suspect) watch approvingly as the prostitutes are led away, as if this event will provide more same-sex activity for them (2005, 417). The lack of (market) access to heterosexual sex is indicated as an opening for perversity.

Clearly, some forms of gender and sexual expression are not approved. For Griffith, free sexuality seems to mean men's easy access to multiple women (as in prostitution or the scenes of the temple of Ishtar). Yet female independence is rejected in the service of building families. The modern story indicates that the nuclear family form is the ideal way to meet sexual desire. As Rogin (1989) persuasively argues, Griffith tries to integrate urban life and sexual pleasure into the family to give it a stronger foundation than it had in the repressed Victorian era.

Babel likewise positions perverse sexuality centrally. Part of the need for reconciliation and hope in many of the stories is caused by racialized sexual dysfunction. In the Moroccan and Japanese story lines, Iñárritu draws on othering sexual stereotypes, showing the characters' behaviors to be misguided and outside the proper order of the family. In Morocco, Yussef spies on his sister while she undresses; he masturbates later while tending the sheep. His brother tells their father about Yussef and his sister as the crisis heats up, which, in combination with the news about the gunshot, undoes the father with grief and anger. Iñárritu calls it "the moment of a Muslim family's moral collapse" (2006b, 88). The tragic outcome of the Moroccan story links sexual transgression with "Muslim moral collapse," rural shepherding, violence, and death; the specter of incest is linked with the fear of terrorism. In Japan, Chieko, the hyperbolic fetishized Asian schoolgirl, comes on to men in somewhat inappropriate ways. For instance, in the arcade-cafeteria where she has gone with friends, she defiantly takes off her underwear in the restroom and later exposes herself to some boys sitting nearby. In another scene, pent up with unfulfilled desire, she tries to kiss the much older dentist working on her teeth. As discussed above, the allusion to Babel clearly marks Chieko's attempts at sexual gratification as a misguided pursuit of meaning.[13]

What seems to be the film's healthiest expression of sexuality is at the marriage celebration in Mexico. In an extended scene, the film celebrates the ritual inception of the heterosexual nuclear family. Yet the marriage celebration, while surely delightful for anyone enamored of heteronormativity, cannot be retained as a pleasurable moment by viewers since events progress to undermine any sense of normalcy. The story does not end well. Under the duress of employment demands and intimidation by the border guards, Amelia and her nephew Santiago (Gael García Bernal) make a series of bad decisions on the way back to the United States (rivaling only the bad decisions of the two Moroccan boys); these culminate with Santiago leaving Amelia and the children behind in the desert to wander lost in the hopes of escape and help.

The story of the white Americans is the most sexually neutral. Susan and Richard are clearly nowhere near the level of physical intimacy at the beginning of their trip to Morocco. This disconnect is a result of the death of their newborn. Interestingly, the details of this plot line were changed at the last minute. As Iñárritu explains, "In the original screenplay, the conflict between Richard and Susan arose from a past infidelity of his. Some weeks before the shoot, I suggested taking the drama to a more profound

---

13. Iñárritu says Chieko's story "is not about pathological sex but about the need for affection. When words are not an alternative, and one can't touch or be touched by them, the body is transformed into our only tool of expression" (2006b, 239). In thus characterizing Chieko's search for affection, he implicitly associates the deaf body with excessive sexuality.

level" (2006b, 50). While possibly adding depth, this change effectively lessened the sexual dysfunction of the white characters and made it easier for reconciliation to take place. Neither character defect nor state intervention is enough to deter their reconciliation, which takes place as Susan lies wounded. Their family pulls together rather than falls apart. The happy ending of the U.S. family's story is consistent with what Barrera identifies as the Western values and gender ideals that pervade the film's gaze, including the "Westernized ideal of the female form (thin equals beautiful)" and "Western-based stereotypic gender behavior" (2007, 80–81).

Each film criticizes larger political systems and machinations of empires, positing solutions on the level of the individual and the family, yet recalling the dynamics of Genesis, the success of the family is set against racialized sexual deviance. In both films, the white U.S. nuclear family is depicted as most whole. Both seem to shun and stigmatize diversity, thereby undermining the principle of universal inclusion on which they stake their claims for cinema.

Tolerant Babel

How then, do we make sense of these films' demand for tolerance, listening, and inclusion as political solutions in the face of their simultaneous othering strategies? In depicting excessive and perverse sexuality, they enter into a logic that ultimately shores up the intolerance they seek to denounce. They ask for tolerance but are unable to grant it. Tolerance in these films is limited by family. Both films mark sexually and racially diverse subjects as other but can only incorporate them into their universalizing impulse via the traditional family. They bring diverse narrative and formal elements together as a means of establishing cinema's ability to speak across these divides. But diversity of race and sexuality is contained by the private and depolitical space of the family, which these films mark as the place in which intolerance can be overcome. Those who do not fit into the family are depicted as a threat to the social order.

Perhaps the problem is with tolerance discourse, which has been shown by cultural critics to be less benign than it purports, feeding into biopolitical systems of hierarchization and control. As Janet Jakobsen and Ann

Pellegrini have argued in their discussion of social and legal responses to same-sex relationships, "Tolerance doesn't really fight the problem of hatred; it maintains the very structures of hierarchy and discrimination on which hatred is based. . . . Tolerance sets up an us-them relation in which 'we' tolerate 'them'" (2003, 50). Tolerance further requires assimilation. The "us-them dynamic establishes the 'general public' as that with which 'minorities' should identify and aspire" (66).

Wendy Brown likewise explicates the assimilationist logic of tolerance, suggesting that it operates "as a mode of incorporating and regulating the presence of the threatening Other within" (2006, 27). "Tolerance . . . produces, organizes, and marks its subjects" (29). At the same time, she argues, it serves "to manage eruptions of the particular against the imagined universal," a universal that tolerance reinforces and relegitimates (86). Brown is interested in how tolerance works to shore up the power of the nation-state, especially in the face of the "growing number of transnational affiliations . . . and dramatic international population migration" (95). She further recognizes the "imperial aims" of tolerance (205) that emerge as the discourse is deployed between nations and across cultures (176–205). The logic that strengthens the nation in response to globalization is that which allows it to succeed as empire.

Tolerance is about the sublation of difference into unity. Otherness is permitted and incorporated as long as it is privatized and depoliticized (Brown 2006, 88–93; Jakobsen and Pellegrini 2003, 58–60). Tolerance both particularizes the other and universalizes the system into which the other is incorporated. The other helps define the norms of inclusion and liberty on which the United States prides itself; at the same time, the threat of difference is neutralized through incorporation.[14]

Along these lines, Brown argues that the vacillation of the particular and the universal in tolerance discourse participates in biopolitics precisely in the way it requires the particular yet assimilates it into the whole. She writes, "Simultaneously totalizing and individualizing, amassing and distinguishing, and achieving each effect through its seeming opposite, tolerance emerges as one technique in an arsenal for organizing and managing

---

14. For an analysis of tolerance as a particularly Protestant notion, and the limits to that tolerance, see Fessenden 2007.

large and potentially unruly populations. As such, it is a strand of bio-power" (2006, 79). Notably, in this account, tolerance and biopolitics both operate through the same oscillation between unity and diversity that we have seen in both the biblical text and in these films. Diversity is required in order to establish hegemony.

Recall that for Foucault biopolitics broadens the operations of power in modernity from tactics that were initially focused on preparing individuals—via bodily disciplines—to take their place in local systems of capital. Over time, biopolitical tactics proliferated to stratify, cultivate, and regularize entire populations as capital. Biopolitical operations produce geographic hierarchies of domination within and between nations (see Ong 2006). In this global context, workers' skill becomes a form of capital to be moved around (Foucault 2008, 224). Migration becomes a tightly managed biopolitical investment. As corollaries to mobility, securitization and racialization maintain control. Political decisions are made about which populations are of most worth (Foucault 2003, 254–63). Territories are securitized through war or alternate forms of militarized violence keeping other populations at bay.

Gilles Deleuze (1992) elaborates Foucault's genealogy of power by naming a shift from disciplinary societies to "societies of control;" he does so in a way that highlights the spatial and conceptual slipperiness of the operation. Deleuze suggests that enclosed spaces such as the family, prison, hospital, factory, school (and, I would add, nation) that inculcate bodily disciplines are gradually being replaced by a system of corporate control (and globalization), which is more overarching and at the same time more ephemeral. The focus on the individual becomes the focus on the mass. Enclosure, repetition, habit, and surveillance are replaced with speed, flexibility, variance, and securitization. Paradoxically, "societies of control" seem open and, at the same time, controlled; the point that both Deleuze and Foucault want to make is that this openness facilitates very particular movements of human capital. Deleuze indicates how openness and mobility (creating diversity) work together with enforced closure (securitizing unity) in biopolitics.

As readers of Foucault will know, he does not suggest that, as biopolitics develops, one kind of technology of power completely supplants the other; rather they work together. The disciplines continue to be articulated together with the regularization of the population (Foucault 2008, 67). It may be the case that the subject of interest is no longer motivated by adherence to a social contract (see the introduction and chapter 1) and that freedom is lived out by individuals motivated by economic interests. Still, subjects of interest may temporarily become subjects of right, if it is in their interest (274). Paradoxically, though, freedom is increased through "additional control and intervention"; control becomes the "mainspring" of freedom. The subject of interest is not truly free.

The family is central to both systems and to maintaining tractability. Foucault has argued throughout his oeuvre that the family is an especially important site for instilling disciplines. The family disciplines the body and surveils sexuality; at the same time, it participates in biopolitics by regularizing the body as part of the population's health and longevity—sexuality is related to procreation and birthrates (2008, 251–52). Further, the family becomes the place in which humans are formed as capital. Parents teach their children how to become skilled capital machines (225–30). So disciplines are mixed up with biopolitics. The discipline and enclosure of the family obscure the work that families do in biopolitics' global management of human resources. These two modes of power are sometimes contradictory, and yet their interarticulation facilitates control.

In these two films, families are the place that tolerance is best enacted. Families manage the vacillation between unity and diversity that I have been tracing—a tension that is symptomatic of the larger discourse of tolerance. The close connection of tolerance to the family in these films indicates the limits of the their universalism. Moreover, families become petri dishes for producing and controlling biopolitical U.S. subjects of interest. They are social units that are portrayed as having significant mobility and freedoms unhindered by oppressive social contracts, and yet they are constrained by (racial and hetero) norms of sexual behavior.

Hollywood Babel

The use of Babylon in *Intolerance* and *Babel* exhibits the contradictory push and pull between disciplines and regularization, individual bodies and populations, rights and interests, that is typical of biopolitics. Both films find fault with societies of control. Both want to argue against control and regularization of populations, against violent forms of securitization and war. I turn now to the ways that both contribute to the dynamics that they criticize—through their treatment of sexuality and the family, the kind of subjectivity that they advance, and their attitudes toward movement and control of populations. The result is the promotion of a mobile and unconstrained subject of interest who is nonetheless controlled by integration into a narrowly conceived universal and thus prepared for a specific placement in the hierarchies of global capital.

In Griffith's idyllic world of Babylon, people are not controlled by laws or Foucauldian disciplines. They are allowed to pursue their own pleasures and interests, sexually and religiously. Babylon becomes, rather anachronistically, a world that caters to subjects who are motivated by their own interests rather than those who are defined by a social contract that bestows rights upon them. Yet even though Babylon does not censor pleasure and caters to the subject of interest, ultimately it comes to harm because of its love of pleasure. The film seems to support and decry the operations of power that allow for the emergence of biopolitical subjectivity.

The contradiction between subject of right and subject of interest comes through clearly in a subplot of the Babylon story. In it, the fiercely independent Mountain Girl (Constance Talmadge) is condemned by law to the marriage market. When she is taken by her brother to the courts to decide her fate, an intertitle lauds Babylon's social contract: "The first known court of justice in the world. NOTE—Babylonian justice, according to the code of Hammurabi, protecting the weak from the strong." Babylon is thus shown to be worthy of Griffith's nostalgia, but the system of law is also immediately shown to be flawed because it forces the Mountain Girl into a relationship she does not want. Fortunately for her, Belshazzar happens to be passing by, sees her plight, and grants her freedom (privileging the biopolitical subject of interest and making exception to law). But her freedom from the law is trumped by Griffith's adherence to the disciplining work of gender norms: while she is by far the most likable of the film's independent women, ultimately her autonomy is not permitted; she dies defending Belshazzar, without his knowledge.

In the modern story too, the film is uncertain about whether it prefers older or newer techniques of power. Certainly it argues against a notion of social contract and for individual freedom. It portrays the reformers' demand for a social contract as destroying access to pleasure, thus very much championing the subject of interest. Yet in arguing for the gender and sexual norms of the nuclear family and against what it deems to be perverse nonheteronormative desires and gender expression, the film operates in the mode of the individual bodily disciplines that Foucault and Deleuze suggest more fully characterizes the era of the subject of right and societies of discipline. Similarly ambiguous, even though the film's largest argument is against war, securitization, and the violent suppression of populations (i.e., against the securitization of biopolitics), the modern story's argument against censorship, as discussed above, cannot be separated from Griffith's desire for the biopolitical regulation of African Americans as a particular kind of human capital. In contrast, the film's depiction of marriage and procreation regularizes and reinforces the white population (which the reformers also threaten when they take away the Dear One's child).

The overlap between disciplines and regularization is precisely the dynamic that sustains the biopolitical, and, as we might expect, the family and sexuality stand as the hinge. It seems that *Intolerance* ends up on the side of biopolitics even as it ostensibly argues against securitization. The subject of interest is prioritized over the subject of right, and yet there is still a longing for the social contract and the disciplines. The film seems to suggest that the subject of interest ought to be able to buy in (rather literally) to the film's proposed social contract of universal love and the nuclear family.

In contrast, *Babel* clearly criticizes the operations of biopolitics and accompanying systems of control; it seems to want to return to a rights-based social contract. Where *Intolerance* wanted to promote the subject of interest, *Babel* rejects the atomistic pursuit of pleasure. But both films turn to the smaller space of family as the ideal unit for political subjectivity. In *Babel*, familial love is the solution to the vulnerability of humanity, especially in a globalized world; meaning is not made by the wrongheaded pursuit of sexual pleasure.

At the same time, Iñárritu's film shows awareness that the social contract can turn into biopolitical control through a militaristic securitization of the rule of law against terror and through the criminalization of immigration. Although lack of listening is identified as a key cause of distress, many of the problems that the main characters encounter are caused by hegemonic structures of securitization. The film launches a fairly trenchant critique of U.S. securitizing policies, which not only delay help for Susan and Richard in Morocco but have dangerous consequences for Amelia and the children trying to regain entry into the United States from Mexico. The camera poignantly cuts between U.S. border guards and their dogs, the miles of hideously imposing metal wall along the border, the crosses memorializing missing persons, and the desert on either side. In speaking of the wall, Iñárritu says, "Thousands of crosses hang from it with the names of men, women, and children who were swallowed up by the desert or disappeared at the Mexico–United States border, the busiest in the world. When completed it will be the *greatest monument to intolerance* in human history" (2006b, 114, emphasis mine).

In employing the language of tolerance, however, Iñárritu subtly indicates how the film—and the project of a universal film language—is aligned with the kind of (neo)liberalism that produces and contains difference as it privatizes and depoliticizes political action.[15] Difference is judged by the standard of the white family, which is the successful site of social contract. The critique of securitization and the idealization of the family might signal a wish to return to an older form of power, yet, at the film's conclusion, familial health corresponds to the geopolitical relations of capital. The white American nuclear family is restored (against the odds); the Japanese family is a close but hurting second (lacking the mother); the Moroccan family is seriously wounded, with one son dead and another in custody; and the Mexican family's fate depends on the border. Dolores Tierney calls this ending "politically and radically conservative. . . . The privileged (white) family is saved/rescued . . . and the (dark-skinned) inhabitants of Third World . . . suffer or die"; it presents and confirms "a stratified social and racial World order" (2007, 14). Tierney correctly assesses it as both a critique of political reality and a failure of imagination.

This racial division across a securitized border can be read as an acceptance of the order of biopolitics. *Babel* does not take up its reconciliatory impulse to imagine families constructed in another way. If Richard and

15. For neoliberalism's push to privatization and depoliticization, see Duggan 2003.

Susan are so easily reconciled, why isn't Amelia's vulnerability as an immigrant worker ameliorated in some way, and her status as a servant changed to one of fully participating family member? (After all, she protests to immigration officials that the children are like her own.) To be sure, such an ending would be unrealistic within the globalized circuits of biopolitics and the power dynamics of domestic help—but possible in a film wishing to think against securitization and to remedy vulnerability through the family. By returning the family to its strict, racially separated, nuclear form, the film ends up being consistent with the biopolitical project of militarized borders that it protests. Inadvertently perhaps, *Babel* brilliantly shows how the family is central to both disciplinary and biopolitical modes of power.

Further, Iñárritu's wish for film to be a universal language must be interrogated in the light of the form of his film. He, like Griffith, thinks that film can heal the wounds of empire. Iñárritu imagines his film as being able to cross national and cultural borders, where some people, clearly, cannot. In working to this end, Iñárritu cannot help but promote mobility. Although the film depicts tourists in a highly negative way, it cannot resist the scopic pleasures of tourism. In shooting the film, Iñárritu traveled from the United States to Mexico, Morocco, and Japan. The film is a form of tourism, interpellating viewers into the desire to travel. Yet who is able to be a tourist? Those populations who are capitalized as investors, not commodities. Mobility is essential for globalized markets and the subject of interest. So even as the film advocates a return to the family and the disciplines, it pushes toward the biopolitical; it teaches its viewers the appropriate desires and skills of mobility and *capital-ability* (Foucault 2008, 225).

Indeed, the medium of film and the film grammar of cutting, as pioneered by Griffith and carried on by Iñárritu, promotes mobility and flexibility in its viewers. Both filmmakers play with cutting styles in ways that challenge their viewers (as evidenced in reviews of the films). Further, the film language they create works to shape viewers' subjectivity via emotion. Iñárritu wants his films to speak to viewers through their emotions. He goes so far as to say, "I don't want that the [audience's] rational process affects the emotional process" (2006a, 190). For him the (universal) understanding of the film is at the emotional level. There is no doubt that both films are masterly in portraying and evoking emotion via color, speed of cutting, and facial close-ups. Affectively trained in this film grammar, viewers come to desire speed and flexibility. The film form helps viewers to become good, capital-able, biopolitical subjects without thinking too much about it.

A universal language that allows for mobility could be a metaphor for the market. Such biopolitical logics are corroborated by the humorous and cinematically stunning Nike advertisement directed by Iñárritu to air at the time of the 2010 World Cup. In the ad, titled "Write the Future," film, soccer, and Nike (all of them with significant markets) are pitched as global universals that bridge cultural and geographic divides. Mobility—athletic, filmic, geographic—stimulates consumption, competition, and the market. Gradations of capital-ability are clear in the ad, which also stimulates longing for something more in the future (success, fame, fitness, soccer, film, consumption, Nike). Representing it all is film, the kingpin of universals, and perhaps the art form of the biopolitical.[16]

As if to clinch the nomination for best market-stimulating media, Hollywood Babylon's titillating reputation was transformed into a nonfilmic capitalist venture with the opening of the Hollywood and Highland Center in Los Angeles in November of 2001. The mall, which has become a major tourist destination, is also home of the Kodak Theatre, where the Academy Awards take place. The mall's "Babylon Court" reproduces parts of Griffith's set (discussed in the introduction). A huge archway, replicating just one of Griffith's double arches, frames the Hollywood sign in the L.A. hills behind. The walls and floors of the courtyard are adorned with the faux Babylonian reliefs used by Griffith: a stylized tree of life; winged, human-headed deities; and eagle-headed winged figures. Four pillars around the courtyard are topped by statues of elephants (only half the number used in Griffith's set). Babylon Court celebrates Hollywood glamour and spectacle. More importantly, it celebrates the consumerism that Hollywood generates and the mobility of those who can afford to participate.[17]

16. I am indebted to my former student Zev Gurman for pointing me to this advertisement. For the ad, see the YouTube video, 3:02, posted by Cinnamon, May 4, 2012, http://www.youtube.com/watch?v=B5FyAXgiTvE. For a narrative description and uncritical praise of it, see Stevenson 2010.

17. Beyond attracting travel to Babylon Court, the construction of the mall was part of a gentrification of the area that displaced residents (Curti, Davenport, and Jackiewicz 2007).

Containing Babel

Film, the art form of the U.S. imperial spirit, integrates older and newer techniques of power in the biopolitical. Film caters to the subject of interest but promotes the ideal of the social contract. It prescribes openness and flexibility, but it reassures viewers of the more familiar world of disciplines, morals, and heterosexual families. It accomplishes these transitions through a form that teaches mobility and capital-ability. As a form of cultural reasoning, it can be seen as an attempt to negotiate the contradictory space between disciplines and biopolitics.

In associating the family with film (as a universal language), *Intolerance* and *Babel* show how biopolitics thrives precisely within the contradictions that the Babel story models; biopolitics requires diversity and difference yet elevates one particular social form to the level of the universal, demanding that diversity be integrated into it. The family is the norm through which otherness is recognized and tolerance practiced. White families are seen as safe, localized, and enclosed, the antithesis of the reaching desire of Babylon and biopolitics, and yet they participate in the sometimes muted desire for the same, thus smoothing the transition and overlap into the new technology of power. U.S. biopolitical empire is domesticated through family in film and made palatable to viewers.

It is almost as if these filmmakers, having promoted all kinds of scopic pleasures, treat their characters and their viewers in the same way that Josephus treats the people who follow Nimrod in his retelling of the Babel story: Their pleasure must be contained. Too much pleasure will be unruly, perhaps ungovernable, and must be contained and hierarchized in families. As we have seen in chapter 1, family lineages help regulate the distribution of profit opened up by the participation of subjects of interest in markets; in biopolitics, families can control the subjects of interest that the films promote.

The films' use of the biblical metaphor of the Tower of Babel is not, therefore, incidental. *Intolerance* and *Babel* go to the Bible for their central authorizing symbol both to criticize empire and to make a name for the medium of cinema as universal. They end up, however, being equally ambivalent about the project of name building as the biblical text is itself. Just as the text raises the particular of Abraham's family to the status of the (monotheistic) universal, these films raise the U.S. film industry and racialized U.S. norms for culture and family to the status of the universal. The Bible's own divided attraction to the logic of empire matches that of the United States; this ambivalence cannot help but be translated into film. The Bible and film work together as media for the production of biopolitical U.S. empire.

Revenge on Babylon: Literalist Allegory, Scripture, Torture

As much as the fictional Babylon might generate markets, sensual aspirations, cinematic ambition, and overall consumption, the actual place has been subjected to brutal violence. Less than two years after Hollywood Babylon was celebrated as a modern marketplace in the opening of the Hollywood and Highland Center in Los Angeles with its Babylon Court, the ancient city of Babylon was being destroyed in the war on Iraq. As noted in the introduction, troops occupied and seriously damaged the ancient city, beginning in 2003. The war on Iraq makes patently clear that an admired Babylon is only a place of fantasy. The actual ancient Babylon is treated as though it is of no real worth. Worse, ancient Babylon becomes a symbol of all that threatens the Western market—it becomes the birthplace of terrorism. The disparity between Babylon Court in the L.A. mall and ancient Babylon in the Iraq war betrays an underlying orientalism. Fantasy Babylon is to be desired only insofar as it stimulates consumption that favors U.S. markets. Babylon is to be desired but not actually valued. Its main role is as a foil in the project of producing U.S. superiority.

In fact, Babylon makes an appearance in relation to U.S. torture of Iraqi prisoners. Haj Ali Shalal—the Iraqi prisoner whose testimony matches the now-iconic photo of the hooded man on a box—told a conference on war crimes in Kuala Lumpur that, among many other cruelties at Abu Ghraib, he was forced to listen to loud and constant repetitions of Boney M's version of the song "Rivers of Babylon" (Blasberg and Blasberg 2005; Kent 2007; Shalal 2009). The lyrics of "Rivers of Babylon" are biblical: They repeat the first part of Psalm 137, in which the psalmist expresses agony over the Babylonian exile of the Judean elite in 597 and 586 B.C.E.

> By the rivers of Babylon
> There we sat down
> Yeah we wept
> When we remembered Zion
> When the wicked carried us away in captivity
> Required from us a song
> Now how shall we sing the lord's song in a strange land.

A refrain from Psalm 19 is added: "Let the words of our mouth and the meditations of our heart / Be acceptable in thy sight here tonight." No cries of sacrilege have gone up over this use of the Bible at Abu Ghraib. No one has asked how torture might be acceptable in God's sight. This use of scripture has gone unnoticed.

Then again, the torture at Abu Ghraib has been all but forgotten. I am shocked each time I hear that my students have not heard about it. There is no active cultural memory of U.S. torture of prisoners at the prison in Iraq, or elsewhere. Among its other aims, this chapter seeks to recall that the biopolitical success of the United States relies on tactics such as torture. It would be satisfying to be able to say that this incident at Abu Ghraib and torture in general are particular to a certain political party, philosophy, or administration, but that would be to engage in a denialist fantasy. Although the G. W. Bush regime was egregious in its solicitation and facilitation of torture, President Obama has not held to a strong stance against torture, despite initially signing an executive order to ban it.[1] It has become clear that torture is not the surprising exception to law, the outworkings of a particular administrative regime, but rather the routine exception to law on which empire depends.[2] Torture is considered a necessary and justifiable practice. But it is not admitted to be unexceptional.

Loud music was but one tactic among many used to inflict harm on prisoners at Abu Ghraib. In 2004, the scandal of torture at Abu Ghraib broke with the release of incriminating photos of prisoners being sexually humiliated, hooded, and threatened with electrocution by U.S. soldiers. As Seymour Hersh (2004) reported shortly following the release of the photos, an internal military report by Major General Antonio Taguba further confirmed that soldiers had beaten, threatened, sodomized, and used other violent and demeaning tactics on prisoners at Abu Ghraib.[3]

Central to my concern in this chapter is how the Bible comes to be used as torture, and how biblical interpretations circling around Babylon come to make torture unexceptional. It is remarkable that, of all the biblical songs that could be played as torture, the one chosen alludes to one of the most troubling passages of scripture. In the last few verses of the psalm, the psalmist entertains a potent and disquieting revenge fantasy: "O Daughter of Babylon . . . happy is the one who repays you for what you have done to us; happy is the one who seizes your infants and dashes them against the rocks." These lines were not explicitly voiced at Abu Ghraib because the song "Rivers of Babylon" itself excises them, focusing instead on the reggae desire for future freedom. But for anyone versed in scripture, these violent sentiments haunt any citation of the psalm. The use of this particular psalm as a form of torture—ending with revenge as it does—suggests we might well interrogate the relationship of revenge to torture.

---

1. See "Scorecard on Torture: The Obama Administration's First Year," North Carolina Stop Torture Now, accessed May 17, 2010, http://www.ncstoptorturenow.org/PDF_Archives/ ScorecardOnTorture20100201.pdf.

   Not only has Guantánamo not been shut down, as promised, and the trials of detainees not become more transparent but detention and abuse has also continued at Bagram prison in Afghanistan. In 2010, the BBC confirmed the presence of a second, secret prison at Bagram, where prisoners are taken and often abused (Andersson 2010). Tina Foster, an attorney who represents a number of the detainees at Bagram, has said that there is no discernible difference between the Bush and Obama administrations (Gebauer, Goetz, and Sandberg 2009).

2. See Crocker 2008; Rejali 2007.

3. For what happened following the filing of Taguba's report in March of 2004, see Hersh 2007.

My argument in this chapter is that there are strong temporal and structural homologies between torture, the revenge that Psalm 137 evokes, the structure of the psalm itself, apocalyptic allegorical interpretation of Babylon, and the process of scripturalization, whereby ancient text becomes truth. As I will argue, the mode of biblical interpretation at work in bringing this psalm to Abu Ghraib is built on a tradition of prophetic and apocalyptic biblical texts that dream of revenge on Babylon. This kind of apocalypticism produces what I am calling literalist allegory, or the allegorization of present events by way of the text; it is different from traditional allegorical reading, as I will discuss. Drawing on the work of the literary theorists Angus Fletcher and Gordon Teskey on the violence of allegory, I show that scripture, literalist allegory, torture, and revenge similarly wreak violence in the process of making the world for the self; they all discharge interiority and excise difference in the name of a certain future, thereby transvaluing a hatred of Babylon into an imitation of it.

What Were the Soldiers Thinking?

One of the difficulties of talking about the use of "Rivers of Babylon" at Abu Ghraib is the impossibility of knowing the soldiers' intent. To whom do the song's captives refer—weeping by the rivers of Babylon and refusing to sing in a foreign land? U.S. military in Iraq? The detained Iraqis? Depending on whom one imagines the song addressing, it can be understood as a prayer on the part of soldiers or a taunt against Iraqis for being imprisoned in their homeland, for having become Babylon imprisoned.

Did soldiers think through the implications of playing this particular incarnation of Psalm 137? I cannot know, but certainly the U.S. military did think through the implications of playing unbearably loud music as a form of psychological stress (Cusick 2006; DeGregory 2004; Pieslak 2009; Sharrock 2008a, 2008b). Moreover, the use of the Bible in the war on terror has been well documented (Associated Press 2009; Draper 2009), revealing a particular mode of literalist biblical interpretation. Soldiers' decisions to play the biblical "Rivers of Babylon" at top volume to prisoners in Abu Ghraib are consistent with general strategic and theological elements that have surfaced in the war on Iraq.

The tactic of playing deafening music has become commonplace in U.S. warfare, both to psych up soldiers on the battlefield and to break opponents either before or after capture (Peisner 2006). The most famous uses were at the 1989 capture of Noriega in Panama; the first siege on Fallujah, Iraq, in 2004, which soldiers came to call LalaFallujah (Cusick 2006; DeGregory 2004; Pieslak 2009, 81–86); and Abu Ghraib and Guantánamo Bay prisons. Psychological operations (PSYOP) experts claim that the purpose of this tactic is to disorient and upset the enemy, and to break them in interrogation. A spokesperson for the army's PSYOP command center at Fort Bragg, Ben Abel, comments approvingly that soldiers get "really creative in finding sounds they think would make the enemy upset" (DeGregory 2004). Songs are chosen for the quality of the sound to irritate or disorient, but, as Justine Sharrock explains in her commentary on *Mother Jones*, the torture lyrics were also chosen for their imagined semantic potential to upset and taunt detainees (the degree to which prisoners' capacity with English was a consideration is unclear); for instance, songs were chosen for their sexual content, or for words that give expression to U.S. superiority or the soldiers' aggressive sentiments (2008b). The torture playlist at Abu Ghraib and Guantánamo included the theme song to Barney (the purple dinosaur), songs with "America" in their titles (including Enimem's "White America" and Neil Diamond's "Coming to America"), songs with Babylon in their titles (including David Gray's "Babylon"),[4] and various hard-rock tunes (including selections from Rage Against the Machine and Metallica; Sharrock 2008b).

Significantly, the tactic of playing loud music is given authorization by the Bible. Military PSYOP experts cite the biblical story of Joshua bringing down the walls of Jericho with trumpets (Jo 6) as precedent and moral authority for this tactic. According to Air Force Lt. Col. Dan Kuehl, professor of information operations at Fort McNair's National Defense University in Washington, D.C., "Joshua's army used horns to strike fear into the hearts of the people of Jericho. . . . His men might not have been able to break down literal walls with their trumpets. But . . . the noise eroded the ene-

---

4. Some musicians were upset about the use of their music in this way. See Peisner 2006; "Gray's Warning on 'Torture' Music," BBC News, July 4, 2008, http://news.bbc.co.uk/2/hi /entertainment/7488498.stm. See also a musicians' open letter on this issue at New Security Action, "Musicians Standing Against Torture," accessed November 16, 2012. http://new securityaction.org/pages/music-used-to-torture.

mies' courage. Maybe those psychological walls were what really crumbled" (DeGregory 2004).[5] The Bible is, therefore, already part of the military tactic before any particular use of it.

Lt. Col. Dan Kuehl acknowledges that music can have more than one meaning, so that a song might encourage a U.S. soldier while bothering a combatant. Kuehl instructs soldiers to be careful because the range of meanings produced might also be unpredictable and have the opposite of the expected effect (DeGregory 2004).[6] Thus "Rivers of Babylon" might have been chosen both to disturb detainees aurally and cognitively—to break down psychological walls—and, at the same time, to pump up service people. The song may have been chosen for its quickly maddening disco beat and repetitive tune, for its reference to captivity in Babylon, and for the longing for freedom that is emphasized by the song's reggae origins. There may be, in the choice of this song, inconsonant and contradictory elements of taunting and making fun of the enemy, and also encouraging the soldiers. "Rivers of Babylon" might well be meant to voice the lament of embattled service people and, at the same time, laugh at, upset, and disorient Iraqi detainees.

In soldiers' use of songs referring to Babylon it seems clear that ancient Babylon is grafted onto its contemporary counterpart, Iraq. Certainly soldiers knew that a military camp sat on the ancient city of Babylon. Further, soldiers may have received biblical teaching about Babylon from military chaplains. One such example is documented in a YouTube video with the description "Chaplain Missick and Chaplain Seabolt drive by the rivers of Babylon in Baghdad, Iraq, and discuss their Biblical significance."[7] Filmed from a moving vehicle, the video focuses on a river, ensconced in concrete and barbed wire. A voice indicates, "Rivers of Babylon," to which a second voice assents by expressing the need for "a song," like the one Daniel needed when he was "on the staff of Saddam Hussein." The first voice

5. See also Friedman 2013.
6. As Clive Stafford Smith writes in the *Guardian*, there can be unintended ironies in the use of the particular songs, so that they "unwittingly give voice to what could well be the prisoners' inner thoughts," as for instance with Rage Against the Machine's lyrics: "Fuck you, I won't do what you tell me!" (2008).
7. "By the Rivers of Babylon," YouTube video, 1:09, posted by Aramaic12, July 31, 2010, http://www.youtube.com/watch?v=HxIGihkL-As.

jumps in to unpack this statement and the conflation made between the present and the biblical text. He explains that Saddam was like the ancient king of Babylon, Nebuchadnezzar. The song in question is unspecified (Daniel is not particularly known for singing, although he does utter a psalm-like statement in Daniel 2:20–23); but the reference to the rivers of Babylon suggests that Psalm 137 is in mind.

The chaplains' mode of biblical interpretation is not atypical. In it, the historical events referenced by the book of Daniel and Psalm 137 are projected onto a situation in the present. The only way this can happen is if the biblical texts are thought to be prophetic of the present in some way. Apocalypticism, which since the late nineteenth century has pervaded much biblical interpretation in the United States, focuses on prophecy, but calls its mode of reading "literal."[8] In its most extreme form, present events become signs of the end times, to which all biblical texts are thought to point, whether they are explicitly apocalyptic or not. In its milder form, biblical texts are still thought to reference the future, which may well be the reader's present. As Stephen O'Leary points out in *Arguing the Apocalypse*, drawing on Hans Frei (1974), this tradition's self-understanding as "literal" grew out of the Reformation's departure from allegorical reading of scripture to a mode influenced by the Enlightenment, in which "interpreters sought concrete historical and scientific fulfillments of prophecy that would provide objective demonstrations of the veracity of Scripture" (1994, 59).[9] Thus, in the nineteenth and twentieth centuries, a systematized apocalyptic narrative about the sweep and culmination of human history has merged with an increasing desire for prophecy to be empirically confirmed, especially in England and the United States. "Literal" interpretations began to be about

8. Certainly the practice of reading apocalyptic imagery onto contemporary events did not begin in the nineteenth century, but it became a more prevalent practice. Because apocalyptic texts are written as allegories, cryptically pointing to real life situations, they were more likely to be read literally (and therefore politically) than allegorically. For instance, the obvious connection between the Whore of Babylon and the literal Rome (via the seven hills referenced in Revelation 17:9) has not been not lost on interpreters throughout the centuries.
9. As Frei points out, in the eighteenth century, the historical and literal began to be separated. Scholars began to suggest that the narratives of the Bible may not have occurred literally as written, creating "distance between the stories and the 'reality' they depict" (1974, 5). This split between text and reality results in the development of historical criticism but also, in response to it, a reassertion of a strict literalism, such as the kind that insists that the world was created in seven days and that apocalypse is predictive of literal future events.

the literal present and future. This literalism fundamentally relies on a larger cosmic myth, told in apocalyptic terms. Put another way, it is a literalism that relies on apocalyptic allegory (more on this point below).

Literalist-allegorical biblical interpretation of this type has been rather prevalent in the war on terror. An egregious example took place in the G. W. Bush administration, during which biblical verses made frequent appearances alongside images of the war on the cover page of the secretary of defense's daily "Worldwide Intelligence Update" report to the president (Draper 2009). On April 3, 2003, God's command to Joshua at the beginning of the conquest of Canaan was printed above images of tanks near Baghdad. "Have I not commanded you? Be strong and courageous. Do not be terrified; do not be discouraged; for the Lord your God will be with you wherever you go" (Jo 1:9). The myth of the conquering chosen people was projected onto the present. Another such exhortation explicitly aligned Iraq and Babylon, citing the writing on the wall that appeared before Belshazzer: "God has numbered the days of your reign and brought it to an end" (Dn 5:5–8).[10]

Within this context, the song "Rivers of Babylon" calls to mind all that attaches to Babylon in the biblical tradition and the national myth (as described in the introduction). The story of Babylon conquering ancient Judah referenced in Psalm 137 is read as one moment within an ancient mythical and spiritual struggle that continues into the present. In literalist allegorical interpretation, events that take place in Iraq, the site of ancient Babylon, are understood as referencing this larger eschatological narrative about Babylon.

The war efforts of the United States, and the soldiers' use of scripture within them, must also be understood within the biopolitical project of cultivating life. As contradictory as it might seem, the belief that the United States will bring peace and prosperity to the entire world is foundational to its project of war, as official security strategies and reports make clear (Kagan, Schmitt, and Donnelly 2000; White House 2002, 2010). The U.S. mission in the world is consistent with what Michael Dillon and Julian Reid have called the liberal project of killing to make life live (2009). As they argue, within liberalism, war is imagined to protect the entire species. War is

---

10. Dereck Daschke also draws on this material to suggest that Bush may have understood himself as "facing down a 'Babylonian' enemy" (2010, 166).

used to further and cultivate the best forms of species life, shaping and transforming species life into what it "might become in the future" (44). The U.S. messianism that aligns itself with Israel against Babylon takes this project on board and reinforces it with righteousness.[11]

Specific tactics of war, like torture, are seen as aiding in this biopolitical mission for the species. The information extracted through torture is promised to protect people in the United States from further damage (as I will discuss presently). If the United States is protected, so is the rest of the world. Playing loud music or engaging in torture tactics aggressively intensifies "life-forms" deemed dangerous. If, as Eric Santner (2011) suggests, there is a kind of excess that haunts the fleshiness of the transfer of power from the king's body to the people's body in democracy, some of that excess is routed outside of zones of sovereignty and enacted as pain on the bodies of "less-than-good" life. As will be argued in chapter 5, these zones of pain act as the constituent outside not only to sovereignty, but also to the very notion of the human. Not only does war protect the human species, then, it also helps define it.[12] Apparently the Bible is recruited to participate in this process.

Literalist Allegory and Scripture

It is worth pausing to reflect on the mechanisms of the literalist-allegorical interpretation that lays the foundation for the use of Psalm 137 at Abu Ghraib. In literalist allegory, both ancient texts and contemporary events gain religious significance and authority in the process of being related to truth and the future. Texts, geographical locations, and events described in the Bible are understood as saying something about contemporary events

---

11. Against my argument in chapter 2, Dillon and Reid suggest that the liberal way of war does not rely on an easily defined Schmittian enemy, but rather has to continuously ascertain what is dangerous (2009, 44). Certainly it is true that the enemy of the United States is continually shifting, but a theopolitical overlay gives the concept of the enemy a certain degree of epistemic stability.

12. Dillon and Reid suggest that liberal governance shapes the definition of the human by "informationalizing" and digitizing life and relationality; war draws on this knowledge. See Dillon and Reid 2009, 55–75.

in the light of ultimate truths. The present is given meaning by the "truth" attached to sometimes obscure or confusing ancient texts, and at the same time to a sense that the truth matters for the future.

Reading scripture through allegory is one of the most common and banal forms of scripturalization, in which texts are given the meaning and status of "scripture." The literary theorist Angus Fletcher comments that allegorical interpretation is as old "as the desire to convert speech and writing into 'scripture' where sacred writ is accorded an authoritative status" (2010, 12). One might say that allegory is one of the chief mechanisms of scripturalization—that is, of uncovering in ancient text something meaningful for the present. It is a pervasive Christian mode of reading, certainly not one that is limited to conservative practitioners; theological orientation is marked only by degree of literalism in the allegorical mapping. From its earliest uses, allegorical interpretation is what Rita Copeland and Peter Struck call "a search for esoteric truths, for meaning that is concealed but ultimately interpretable" (2010, 3).[13] The early Greek search for "transcendental meaning that is at once immediate and remote" (3) is one that carries over into the assumptions about ancient texts that continue to establish them as authoritative scripture.

Christian exegetes from Origen on have established the practice of allegorical reading, whereby biblical texts are read as indicative of these universal truths and essences to which the believer ought to conform and shape his or her actions and spiritual life. Origen, for instance, read the creation story not as about the actual order of events but as about the relation of the soul to Christ.[14] Augustine interpreted Psalm 137's violent ending as instruction for how the Christian should resist temptation.[15] Texts had significance for the present insofar as they shaped believers' understanding of their spiritual life and its ultimate purpose, as well as moral action. Orienting readers to their final ends or purposes is always important in

13. Copeland and Struck (2010) date the earliest extant example of this kind of interpretation to the Greek Derveni papyrus (4th century B.C.E.), which interprets an Orphic poem religiously and cosmologically (2). They point out that allegorical interpretation precedes the literary form of allegory, which deliberately tries to encode hidden meanings.
14. Origen, *Homilies on Genesis* 1.
15. Augustine, "Exposition on Psalm 137"; for more on Augustine's interpretation of this psalm, see Kirschner 1990.

allegorical interpretation. Fletcher points out that early and medieval Christian allegorical interpretation understood texts as pointing toward universal essences, which were "presided over by an ultimate unchanging essence, the final cause . . . of Christian destiny" (2010, 15).[16] The well-known medieval four-part schema for allegorical interpretation—literal, allegorical, moral, and anagogic—ends with an emphasis on final purpose (spiritual elevation). In the words of the mnemonic verse, "whither you are leaning is the anagogy" (13).

How then does the contemporary form of allegorical reading differ from past allegorical reading? Literalist allegory is allegorical in that it searches for higher meanings that only astute interpreters can ascertain, such as affiliations with cosmic evil; but it is different from either traditional literal interpretation or allegorical reading in that it searches present events for their transcendent meanings. For Christians of late antiquity and the middle ages, the text oriented believers and their actions with respect to higher truth and ultimate purpose. By contrast, in the contemporary moment, the present is thought to point to the truth of a systematized apocalyptic narrative, not the other way around. The literal futurity of final purpose is emphasized. Literalist allegory requires the same allegorical and scripturalizing process of interpretation by higher truths, but now it is politics, present events, and people that are allegorized by texts, which are also used to predict the future. Formerly, allegorical reading was meant to inform the believer's spiritual life; now, life is the marker of future cosmological truths. In literalist-allegorical readings, apocalyptic imagery provides the allegory itself, understood as the "literal" prophetic meaning of the present. The postbiblical apocalyptic narrative—stitched together from a variety of discontinuous biblical texts—becomes the allegorical referent to which present events refer; paradoxically, this fantasy futuristic language of apocalypse is understood as "literal."

This mode of reading is scripturalizing par excellence: Scripture, the future, truth, life, and interpretation are of a piece, inseparable. Literalist allegory requires the same allegorical and scripturalizing process of interpreting ancient text by higher truths and the future, but the text is now

---

16. Fletcher wants to theorize "allegory without ideas" (2010, 16–32).

aligned with present events via a larger eschatological story. The future is always realized in the present and also deferred. Literalist allegory is therefore more tautological than earlier allegory; here past, present, and future are collapsed into one. Paradoxically, this form of scripturalizing both augments and diminishes the importance of the present in and of itself; the present becomes a mediator between past/text and future. Actions in the present are judged in future terms, as we will see presently, thus mitigating the need to take responsibility for their effects in the present.

The Biblical Tradition of Revenge on Babylon

The use of Psalm 137 at Abu Ghraib is somewhat perplexing, given the way it been cited by diasporic peoples who feel oppressed in their separation from their homelands (Black 2012). As Fiona Black puts it in her reflection on a Caribbean diaspora, the psalm supplies a vocabulary for displaced peoples: "It provides a means of articulating grief and loss . . . a means to hope for reparation" (260). So how does this psalm get taken up into the kind of literalist allegory that evokes an apocalyptic future and provokes torture? Although not itself apocalyptic, it contains some disturbing sentiments that feed into a tradition that culminates with desire for revenge on the Whore of Babylon. As mentioned, Psalm 137 infamously ends with the proclamation: "Happy is the one who repays you for what you have done to us. Happy is the one who seizes your infants and dashes them against the rocks" (vv. 8–9). With these words, it takes up a tradition of revenge on Babylon that is completely naturalized in the biblical prophetic literature and in the later apocalyptic tradition. Revenge is simultaneously abhorrent and acceptable. Noting the psalm's competing impulses of reverie, grief, and violence, Black writes, "The language is affective, surely. It generates the same remorse, the same visceral hatred and desire for revenge, that the speaker himself expresses" (2012, 259). As we will see, the psalm's advocacy for revenge becomes palatable for literal mimicry, somewhat paradoxically, through allegorization. Although I do not want to diminish the role of the psalm in giving hope to oppressed people, the implications of the revenge it imagines ought also to be taken seriously, especially when voiced by a powerful occupying military force.

Psalm 137 puts revenge into the hands of humans in a way that is atypical in the larger biblical corpus, which is adamant that "vengeance is the Lord's." This psalm is part of a subgenre that scholars have called complaint or lament psalms, which typically depict a situation of embattlement and pray for a reversal of fortunes through God's intervention. As Adele Berlin points out, the ending of Psalm 137 reflects "thoughts of retaliation that typify complaints" (2005, 69). The other "imprecatory" psalms, however—in which the poet prays specifically for the destruction of enemies—leave defeat of enemies in the hands of God.[17] In Psalm 137, revenge is not imagined in the hands of God but rather in the hands of the once victimized. The phrasing, which I will discuss in more detail further on, is unique in suggesting that God will reward the person who violently repays the enemy—in this case, Babylon.[18] Although perhaps a matter of semantics—since humans are frequently the vehicle of God's vengeance in the Psalms—the authorization of direct human revenge is unusual, and so significant.

It is perhaps precisely because of the unusual authorization of human agency that the psalm's ending has always posed an ethical problem for readers of the Bible, compounded by its injunction to destroy innocent children. As William Lyons (2005) and Siegfried Risse (2006) point out, throughout its reception history, the psalm's ending has been downplayed either as spiritual allegory or as an understandable response to the violence of war. Along these lines, many scholars think that the psalm simply reflects the cruelty of warfare, citing other biblical passages where similar language occurs (Bar-Efrat 1997, 9; Dahood 1970, 273; Kidner 1975, 460; Kraus 1988, 504; McCann 1996, 1228).[19] A number of scholars cite or allude to the Holocaust as a literal scenario through which one could possibly understand the psalmist's grief and rage (e.g., Ahn 2008, 268n5; Brueggemann 1984, 75; Kidner 1975, 460n3; McCann 1996, 1229; Plank 2008).

---

17. For examples of particularly violent demands for retribution, see Psalms 28, 35, 52, 58, 83, 109, 140.

18. Psalm 58:10–11 comes close to authorizing human revenge when the poet says, "The righteous will rejoice when he sees vengeance, he will wash his feet in the blood of the wicked. People will say, 'Surely this is the fruit of the righteous; surely there is a God who judges the earth.'" Ultimately though, revenge is attributed to God, even if the righteous are close enough to dip their feet into it.

19. 2 Kgs 8:12; Is 13:16; Hos 10:14, 13:16; Na 3:10.

Psalm 137 may be unique in assigning a human agent of revenge, but it is not alone in the biblical tradition in its longing for revenge on Babylon. Violent retribution by God is normalized in the prophetic tradition of revenge toward Babylon. Scholars have noted that the ending of Psalm 137 has close affinities with the oracles against Babylon in Jeremiah 50–51, notorious as those oracles are both for praising Babylon as God's instrument and imagining the violent destruction of Babylon (Savran 2000, 57). As noted in the introduction, the destruction of Babylon is described in Jeremiah 50–51 as God's repayment on it for destroying Jerusalem. Jeremiah describes Babylon as "a gold cup in the Lord's hand, she made the whole earth drunk," yet "Babylon will suddenly fall and be broken" (51:7–8). Babylon is described as both the agent of God, bringing God's judgment on the people of Israel for their sins, and also as deserving punishment.[20] Psalm 137 shares Jeremiah's desire for violent repayment of Babylon. Jeremiah speaks the words of Yahweh, who says, "Before your eyes I will repay Babylon and all who live in Babylonia for all the evil that they did in Zion, declares the Lord" (51:24).[21] Despite the close connections between the two passages, the language of revenge is more palatable to readers and interpreters of Jeremiah than of Psalm 137, however, because the agents of revenge are not

20. These oracles may indicate the historical events of Babylon's conquest by Cyrus of Persia, turning them into predictions of God's punishment on Babylon; or they may simply be revenge fantasies for the destruction of Jerusalem. Vanderhooft suggests that historical events are indicated by the prophet's accurate descriptions and occasional slips into present tense. He argues that the text of Jeremiah 50–51 depicts the architecture (walls, towers, and water defenses) of Babylon, as well as the events of the siege (1999, 194–201). For instance, 51:30–32 uses perfect verb forms (roughly present tense) and passive stems when it reports that Babylon's "dwellings are burned; its bars are smashed. . . . The fords are seized and they have burned the reed marshes" (200). Because Cyrus did not actually destroy Babylon in his conquest, however, others have suggested an earlier, pre-Cyrus dating for the oracles (Kessler 2003, 206; Smelik 2004, 96).

21. The verb *repay* (*šlm*) in Jeremiah 51:24 is the same as used in Psalm 137:8 ("Happy is the one who repays you"). In fact, all three verbs of Psalm 137:8 are repeated more than once each in Jeremiah 50–51. For instance, Jeremiah 51:56 echoes the specific language of Babylon destroyed (*šdd*) and repaid (*šlm*) for her deeds (*nmlwt*). Likewise, the verb "to smash in pieces" (*npṣ*) of 137:9 is repeated nine times in Jeremiah 51:20–23, though, as noted in the introduction, the addressee of this passage is unclear; either way, the result is the same: Babylon will be repaid *for* or *by* smashing. These overlaps in vocabulary and concept suggest that, at the very least, there is knowledge of one of these texts by the author of the other. Freedman calls the passages "contemporary or nearly contemporary" of each other (1971, 202).

the text's addressees. Revenge is put into the mouth of Yahweh, and it is carried out by another imperial power.

Revenge on Babylon is pushed into the future in the book of Revelation's description of the Whore of Babylon, who signifies the evil, oppressive imperial power of Rome that is ultimately overcome by God. In the hyperbole of the apocalypse, Babylon is to be paid twice what she deserves. The seer says, "Give back to her as she has given, pay her back double for what she has done" (18:6–7). Bringing the idea of torture as revenge into the mix, the text continues: *"Give her as much torture* and grief as the glory and luxury she gave herself."[22] Although this may be a legitimate expression of anger for early Christians in Rome, there is an opening here for the text to be literalized in later contexts, when Babylon is read onto a present entity. Because of Revelation's mythic language, Babylon is elevated beyond an imperial power to become a symbol of cosmic evil that must be stopped at all costs.

So when Psalm 137, a psalm about revenge, is used as torture in a region that corresponds to ancient Babylon, it is accompanied by the weight of the biblical tradition of revenge toward Babylon. Its use as torture may be authorized by that tradition. Apocalyptic violence can be literalized in the present and understood as protecting not only a national future but also a cosmic future. The lines between ancient, present, and future Babylon are blurred. It is telling that the biblical passage chosen for the torture playlist is the one clear place in the biblical tradition where revenge on Babylon—or revenge at all—is put into the hands of human agents. The cosmic nature of the literalist-allegorical mode makes it palatable because human action is construed only as part of a larger eschatological drama.

One of the most troubling elements of the torture-by-Bible soundscape at Abu Ghraib, then, is that it makes use of a psalm that models a scriptural—and so for many instructive and empowering—authority for revenge. The heinous abuse of men, women, and teenagers at Abu

---

22. Although sometimes translated with the less specific term "torment," the term *basanismos* used in Revelation 18:7 refers elsewhere to physical, bodily torture (4 Mc 9:6, 11:2; Rv 9:5). Notably, the addressee in 18:7 is vague. It is unclear whether it is God or the listener who is being addressed by the imperative "Give her as much torture."

Ghraib[23] seems perilously close to the biblical depiction of revenge. The use of this particular psalm at Abu Ghraib raises the specter of revenge as torture; it suggests the possibility that torture is used for more than extracting information. Certainly this way of thinking about torture is not acknowledged in official public discourse.

Revenge on the Whore and bin Laden

Revenge, Babylon, Psalm 137, and literalist allegory appear together elsewhere in the war on terror: when Osama bin Laden was captured and killed. On the day of bin Laden's death President Obama gave a speech justifying the action by retelling the events of September 11, 2011, and insisting that "justice has been done." The context for his unilateral decision, he notes, is the fact that al Qaeda had "openly declared war on the United States and was committed to killing innocents in our country and around the globe." The U.S. response to al Qaeda was messianically proclaimed to be about justice and protection for the world, for species life, and for the future. But in a nonconventional war, and outside of any legal structures, this justice can also be called revenge. If the war on terror was the secular means by which this seemingly vengeful action was turned into justice, apocalyptic literalist allegory provided another context for believers. Hardly surprisingly, Babylon makes several appearances.

While fireworks went off and people partied in the streets at bin Laden's death, a flurry of blog and Facebook messages used the Bible to weigh in on the appropriateness of this celebration. Many contributors were measured and argued against celebrating a death. Others wondered whether or not to be elated at the "justice" served. A number cited Psalm 137 in this deliberation. Some used it as an example of biblical vengeful feelings, which ought to be tempered by forgiveness or humility (e.g., Lowry 2011; Strauss 2011). The blogger Randy Pope was less circumspect: "In one sense *the Christian can be happy over the destruction of an evil man (Psalm 137:7–9).* There is no

---

23. As reported by General Taguba, who conducted an inquiry on military misconduct in 2004 at the behest of Donald Rumsfeld. See Hersh 2007.

doubt that Osama Bin Laden was an evil man, and his desire was the destruction of the people of the one true living God" (2011, emphasis mine).[24] Others cited Revelation 18:20 (e.g., Burk 2011; Zenor 2011), which scripts a response to the Whore of Babylon's doom: "Rejoice over her O heavens. Rejoice saints and apostles and prophets. God has judged her for the way she has treated you." In these citations, bin Laden becomes the Whore, and the readers become saints, apostles, and prophets who have been mistreated by her.

The "saints'" rejoicing, however, is tempered by their own possible proximity to bin Laden's ultimate spiritual fate. In an attempt to dampen outright jubilation, Denny Burk, a blogger and associate professor of biblical studies at Southern Baptist Theological Seminary in Louisville, Kentucky, wrote, "I shudder to think of what bin Laden is facing right now. I do not question the justice of it." Burk was not alone in evoking the image of bin Laden's ultimate end in "the consuming fire"—a CNN poll reported that 61 percent of the U.S. population thought bin Laden would burn in hell.[25] "But," Burke continues, not wanting to celebrate inappropriately, "the day will come when God will command me to rejoice in His justice in the damnation of the wicked (Revelation 18:20). Until then, the horror should serve as a motivation to warn people to flee the wrath to come" (2011).

The association between bin Laden and the Whore of Babylon was not new. For example, in a sermon preached two years earlier (published online), Reverend Adrian Dieleman of Trinity United Reformed Church in Visalia, California, refers to bin Laden while explaining to his congregation how they might accept the violence of Revelation 18 and the jubilation at Babylon's destruction.

> At stake is this: do we recognize evil when we see it, do we know evil is
> rebellion against God and deserves punishment? Unless that is your starting
> point, you will not appreciate Babylon's funeral as it further unfolds for us this

24. This blog post had some circulation; it was reposted on Theonomy Resources, Christian Liberty News, and ezinearticles.com.
25. CNN Political Unit, "CNN Poll: Majority in U.S. Say bin Laden in Hell," CNN Politics, May 4, 2011, http://politicalticker.blogs.cnn.com/2011/05/04/cnn-poll-majority-in-u-s-say-bin-laden-in-hell/.

morning. Do you remember the joy when Saddam Hussein was caught and, later, when he was executed? Can you imagine the joy if Osama bin Laden is caught and executed? Well, multiply this joy many times over. That's what we have in front of us.[26]

The scripture is explained by the present. "At stake" is whether believers can recognize rebellion against God and its deserved punishment. As it turned out, when bin Laden was caught and killed many believers *could* recognize his evil and *God's* righteous vengeance in the situation. These examples show how, in the literalist-allegorical mode of interpreting, the future eschatological narrative allows Babylon to extend beyond any literal geographic referents to other present-day referents.

Revenge and Torture

Revenge may be imaginable in war, but that it might be a reason for torture is almost unthinkable in liberal democracies. The standard understanding of torture within liberalism, as the legal scholar David Luban argues (2005), has been to allow it "only" if it will produce intelligence within the "ticking bomb" scenario. Then it becomes permissible and necessary as part of defending democracy. The fiction of emergency is what makes torture thinkable for U.S. citizens within liberalism. Historically, as Luban outlines, torture has been practiced for a variety of reasons: punishment, serving the victor's pleasure and entertainment, producing terror, and extracting confessions. As he argues, cruelty has been rejected in liberalism because it is associated with tyranny and the willful subjugation of others in order to humiliate, punish, or otherwise prove superiority. In the liberal imagination, the only conceivable reason for cruelty is intelligence gathering in an urgent situation, because it will presumably save lives in the future and prevent suffering. Luban writes, "The liberal ideology insists that the sole purpose of torture must be intelligence gathering to prevent a catastrophe; that torture is necessary to

26. Adrian Dieleman, "Sermon on Revelation 18:20–19:10," Trinity United Reformed Church, August 30, 2009, http://www.trinityurcvisalia.com/sermons/rev18v20-rev19v10 .html.

prevent the catastrophe; that torturing is the exception, not the rule, so that it has nothing to do with state tyranny; that those who inflict the torture are motivated solely by the looming catastrophe, with no tincture of cruelty" (1439).

But recently, psychologists have suggested that desire for retribution and punishment plays a significant role in the way the U.S. population thinks about war and torture (Carlsmith and Sood 2009; Janoff-Bulman 2007; Liberman 2006). In general, people are more willing to accept the idea of harsh interrogation practices if they think the person interrogated is guilty. This way of thinking about torture can be observed anecdotally, as well, in online discussions about harsh interrogation tactics. Almost inevitably, the Iraqi beheadings of U.S. citizens are referenced. Those arguing in favor of harsh interrogation practices suggest that they are "not as bad" as beheading; the inference is that those tortured deserve it because what they are doing or planning is worse. To give just one example among many, a commenter responding to the posting of Abu Ghraib pictures on the Bay Area Indy Media goes as far as to say, "All of you whiners should watch the beheading videos. Who cares how we have to get information from these people."[27] The assumption of information retrieval is present, but there is also a sense of "just deserts" in this line of reasoning. Yet outside of a legal framework, what is retribution, if not revenge? The use of Psalm 137 at Abu Ghraib hints that this way of thinking may be present in the minds of military prison guards as well.

The combination of torturing for revenge and torturing for the extraction of truth to prevent future harm—the unofficial and official reasons for U.S. torture—links memory with the future. Here the reflections of Berel Lang in his work on Holocaust memory and revenge are instructive (1996). Lang argues that revenge was not a dominant response to the suffering of the Shoah. Indeed, violent retribution is more likely performed (or imagined) by those who were not directly involved.[28] Lang

---

27. "Photos of US Torture of Iraqi Prisoners at the Abu Ghraib Prison in Iraq," Indybay, April 30, 2004, http://www.indybay.org/newsitems/2004/04/30/16790301.
28. One might think of Alan Dershowitz's novel *Just Revenge* or Quentin Tarantino's film *Inglourious Basterds* (2009).

suggests that because revenge is not usually an immediate response to violence (and is therefore different from resistance), it requires memory— indeed, he says it "motivates memory," drawing on Nietzsche's idea that what is painful is more memorable. More important, revenge rouses "the sense of personal or communal identity for which memory is a necessary condition" (16).

Lang points out that retribution can take on the role of guarding the future. Revenge fantasies are always about something that will happen in the future to compensate for the past. Thus he suggests that revenge can easily be displaced (in the Freudian sense) and reconfigured. Pushed into the future, violence can be transformed into something that no longer seems like revenge. As Lang points out, "Virtually any reaction in the present against an act in the past can also be interpreted as directed against a future recurrence of the same act" (1996, 10). Prevention of a future recurrence hardly looks like revenge, but it might simply be displaced. Lang's argument is suggestive: Perhaps the official reason for U.S. torture (the extraction of information to protect the future) is a kind of displaced revenge. In this case, the use of the song "Rivers of Babylon" as torture would indicate a covert agenda of torture within liberalism— torture as unacknowledged revenge in the name of future freedom. As in the process of literalist-allegorical scripturalization, the imagined future eclipses the present and forcibly demands particular interpretations of past events.

Memory, Futurity, and Revenge in Psalm 137

Remarkably, the temporal dynamics of Psalm 137 resemble the logic of torture as revenge: it remembers the past for the sake of an idealized future. The revenge of the psalm is motivated by memory, by the need to produce memory, which ends up looking like a longing for the future. The psalm's struggles with lament, memory, futurity, and revenge are tied together into a proto-allegorical structure.

A careful look at the psalm suggests that it is also deeply ambivalent toward Babylon, which may be part of its drive to violence. The psalmist glorifies the past and Zion, even as we might suspect the present moment and Babylon are becoming quite seductive. By raising an idealized Zion over and against Babylon, the psalmist fends off the possibility of forgetting Zion. The famous opening lines "by the rivers of Babylon, there we sat down and wept when we remembered Zion" can be read as a kind of resignation to living in Babylon. "There we lived," the verb *yšb* might imply, "even though we wept when we remembered Zion." In this light, the lament over Zion may be motivated not so much by loss as by the attractions of Babylon.[29] One might imagine Judeans who stayed on after the Babylonian empire fell to Persia when many exiles returned to Jerusalem. The sense of having lived in Babylon for some time is supported by the fact that, throughout the psalm, the poet works very hard not to forget the beloved Jerusalem. The psalmist worries about forgetting Jerusalem, threatening himself with curses to compel memory: "If I forget you, O Jerusalem, let my right hand forget" (v. 5).[30] The double forgetting is odd, "if I forget . . . then let . . . me forget." Does the psalmist want to forget? Living by the rivers of Babylon, perhaps the psalmist is in danger of forgetting. The poet continues, "Let my tongue cleave to the roof of my mouth, if I do not remember, if I do not raise Jerusalem above my highest song of joy" (v. 6).[31] Jerusalem is raised, somewhat forcibly—via threat to the speaker's own body—to the Jerusalem of "my highest song of joy."

29. Bar-Efrat comments on the possible ambivalence toward Babylon when he says, "From a material point of view, the exiles' condition had improved. They had settled in a country richer in water and more fertile than their own, they could build houses and plant fruit trees (Jer 29:5) and start a new life. . . . Alongside the abundance of water was the memory of Zion, and it weighed more heavily" (1997, 5).

30. I have chosen to read with the most frequent and straightforward meaning of the verb. Many translations read "let my right hand wither" instead of the more ambiguous "let my right hand forget," which seems to lack an object. David Noel Freedman points out that this solution to the otherwise strange repetition of the verb *škḥ* ("to forget") was posed by W. F. Albright in 1941; based on an Ugaritic root (*ṯkḥ*), he suggested the meaning "to wither" (Freedman 1971, 195–96). This reading has been adopted by commentators (e.g., Allen 1983; Anderson 1981; Renfroe 1988) and creates parallelism in verses 5–6. Nonetheless, it is somewhat tenuous to propose such a cognate verb. Leslie Allen says, "There is no certainty as to the meaning" of the proposed Ugaritic root, "but it is commonly rendered as 'be hot, passionate' . . . whence a derived meaning 'wither (from heat)' is plausible" (1983, 236n5.a). The weak connection indicates that perhaps a desired parallelism drives the translation. Others suggest that a scribal error mixed up the letters of *kḥš* (to grow lean; also read as "wither"; e.g., Bar-Efrat 1997; Kraus 1988; Weiser 1962).

31. For a similar translation of verse 6, see Allen 1983, 235; Kraus 1988, 500. Bar-Efrat also suggests "'if I do not bring up [bring to mind] Jerusalem at [the time of] my highest joy'"

In the possibility of forgetting, Zion is idealized while expressing joy in Babylon becomes unthinkable. Throughout the psalm, the present is displaced by the past and the future. The description of Jerusalem as the highest joy is, paradoxically, a song (*śmḥ*) that calls itself a refusal to sing. The psalm's opening complaint uses the same term: "Our captors asked us for a *song of joy (śmḥ)*" (v. 3), but "we hung up our harps" (v. 2); "how shall we sing in a foreign land?" (v. 4). Life, joy, and music are said to be delayed until Jerusalem is restored to a place of honor. The poet sings in self-contradiction. In the gap between remembering and forgetting, singing and not singing, Jerusalem shines like the sun, over a horizon that is not Zion, a horizon that looks like the banks of the Rivers of Babylon. The present is deferred to the future by way of memory. These displacements of the present by way of an idealized figure make the psalm proto-allegorical. Zion becomes an allegory for the longing of the psalmist, which is, in fact, a longing not to forget.

Another temporal and spatial dislocation emerges at the beginning of the psalm to eclipse the psalmist's present. Clearly the speaker is not in Jerusalem. Yet as Karl Plank has noted, the poet may not be in Babylon either. Babylon is referred to as "there" (*śm*): "There we sat down (or dwelt)" (v. 1), "There our captors asked us for a song" (v. 3). As he puts it, "'Not-there' marks a site somewhere else that, in light of the rest of the psalm, looms as a place accessible only in memory: Zion (v. 1) or Jerusalem (vv. 5–6)" (2008, 182). Even further scrambling temporal orientation, Babylon is described at the end of the psalm (v.8) as already destroyed, with the passive participle "the one destroyed" (*hšdwdh*).[32] Since the city was not destroyed until much later than the psalm is usually thought to have been written, this may be a rhetorical destruction, or a celebration of the end of the Babylonian empire.[33] Or perhaps the psalm was written

---

(1997, 8). Renfroe (1988, 517) and Freedman (1971, 193, 197–98) translate, "Surely I will ascend Jerusalem with joy upon my head." As Freedman points out, the issue is with the hiphil of the verb *'lh* (to raise), which is not elsewhere applied to geographical figures (1971, 197). But if this is a figural Jerusalem, such a use does not pose a problem—it can be metaphorically raised up.

32. As A. A. Anderson points out, reading with the passive participle raises a question about dating, since the city of Babylon was not destroyed by Cyrus (1981, 900). Most translators have smoothed out this issue, making it consistent with the rest of the psalm by placing it into the future, "Daughter of Babylon, *one doomed* to destruction."

33. An example of anger directed toward the neo-Babylonians long after their demise occurs in the Babylonian Talmud b. Ber. 57b, which blesses the destruction of Nebuchadnezzar's Babylon.

at an even later date, when Babylon is already the allegory for another diasporic location.

Whatever the location of writing, the poet's lament is energized by remembering a new, nostalgic-yet-future Jerusalem that triggers revenge. As Harris Lenowitz and George Savran have persuasively argued, the last three verses could represent the song (*śmḥ*) tauntingly demanded by the captors in verse 3 (Lenowitz 1987; Savran 2000). They contend that the same term (*śmḥ*) can also mean a jeering victory song, to which the vengeful sentiments of verses 7–9 might give voice. If so, the ending of the psalm would be a victory song responding to the oppression described at the outset. Likewise, the mid-strophe yearning to raise Jerusalem over "my highest *song* of joy" (also *śmḥ*), may be aiming for a final victory to sing about.[34] In this way, the violent revenge fantasy against Babylon grounds the renewal of an ever-fading memory of Zion, which the poet tries to elevate to the promise of a brighter future. The lament of the psalm is tied into revenge; it is no longer innocent.

Past and future are further joined in this final victory song of vengeance. These verses are a call to reward those who repay Babylon's past wrongs. The song (within the song), when it is finally sung, is marked by a traditional psalmic imperative: "Remember O Yahweh" (v. 7). The psalmist asks Yahweh to *remember* the past, to remember the day on which Jerusalem was destroyed. But there is future reward in the violent destruction of enemies. The phrase "Happy is the one who" (*'šry*) recurs twice: "Happy is the one who *repays you* for what you have done to us. Happy is the one who seizes your children and dashes them against the rocks" (vv. 8–9). This formulation—sometimes also translated "Blessed is the one"—is familiar in the wisdom psalms as part of a retributive worldview, in which blessing is the result of following God's path.[35] There is a futurity to this retributive structure: Blessing is future reward. In the more vindictive than

34. Lenowitz 1987, Savran 2000, and also Renfroe 1988 imagine the psalm's violent ending to be composed under duress at the time of captivity and sung in Hebrew so the captors could not understand that they were being mocked. Although that scenario is compelling in many ways the psalm contains strong indicators of a more conflicted attitude toward Babylon and another temporality, as I have been suggesting.

35. E.g., Psalm 119:1, "Happy are they whose ways are blameless, who walk according to the law of the Lord."

usual use of this phrase in Psalm 137:8–9, *blessing is revenge*; it is the destruction of children (and thereby, presumably, a Babylonian future) in the name of Zion.

Recalling Lang's assertion that revenge motivates memory and is displaced to the future, the memory of captivity in this psalm may be motivated by an attempt not to forget, an attempt that becomes a longing and an urge to protect violently what is perceived as a threatened future. The relationship between revenge, memory, and the future are part of the psalm's proto-allegorical structure, a structure that also finds its way, through the allegorical apocalyptic tradition of violence against Babylon, into contemporary feelings about torture. The structure of this psalm, when read as literalist-allegorical scripture, allows torture—as a form of revenge—to become thinkable.

Allegory, Futurity, Truth, and Torture

When the psalm is taken up into literalist allegory about the enemies of the United States, the relation of the structure of literalist allegory to torture ought also to be considered. Allegory—and perhaps also the scripturalization it engenders—is in itself a violent form of making meaning but disavows itself as such. Some literary theorists note the way that allegory relates to violence and power (Machosky 2010), in part by forcing a hierarchical order of meaning that centers on localized values and experience, which are then rendered universal by virtue of being associated with the transcendent (Fletcher 2010; Teskey 1996). Although these theorists treat allegory as a literary form rather than as a mode of interpretation, their insights can be applied to the literalist-allegorical interpretation I am discussing here. Perhaps not surprisingly, the purposes of literalist allegory resemble those for torture within liberalism—both intend to extract truth for the sake of the interpreter's future.

Teskey compellingly argues that the coupling of the mundane with the universal in allegory is inherently violent. Objects or signs are forcibly "raised to the position of the transcendental 'other'" (1996, 6). Allegory "captures" incoherent elements, narratives, signs, or objects and "reinterprets the noise beneath the things we can see as the inner desire of those things to return to their origin in the One" (6). Allegory devours the other (8): "The more powerful the allegory, the more openly violent the moments in which the materials of narrative are shown being actively subdued for the purpose of raising a structure of meaning" (23). Allegory disavows this rift, however, and seeks to secure truth so that "every opposition arising from the contrast of meaning and life is redistributed hierarchically such that one term is placed over the other. . . . Anything that appears to escape or to resist the project of meaning—passion, body, irony—is interpreted as a further extension of meaning" (30). This process is even more pronounced in literalist allegory because it captures the meaning not only of the text but also of literal events.

Fletcher and Teskey both draw out the self-centeredness of this operation. Teskey argues that allegory tries to seal the "rift between the chaotic otherness of the world and the transcendental otherness that we situate above the world in order to make that world, as the macrocosm, *coincide with the self*" (1996, 7, emphasis mine). As Fletcher notes, allegory "tends always to ruminate on its own levels of meaning, its own hermeneutic imperative" (2010, 10). A self-reflexive mode of interpretation, allegory makes meaning for the self but universalizes it. This kind of self-centeredness is evident in the assumption, seen earlier, that the United States is on the side of God. Literalist allegory secures the truthfulness of the actions of the allegorizer in the cultural-political present and promises a favorable outcome. As we saw with the production of sovereignty and scripture in chapter 2, here too we find authority garnered from within the self, the present moment, and scripture applied as though situated outside in the realm of transcendent truth. Allegory allows for this movement, projecting what is internal as external truth, in order to authorize annihilation of what is actually exterior to it. As argued in chapter 2, this is the very structure of scripture and a Schmittian exception to law that seeks to battle an enemy.

The violent devouring of the other for the purpose of making the world for the self—structured through a hierarchical ordering of meaning and truth—is reminiscent of the violence performed on the body of the other in torture to establish truth (including the truth of freedom and democracy). Although Teskey does not analyze it in these terms, it can be said to model a kind of colonial relation. The hierarchical and violent "world making" of allegory—to borrow a line from Jacqueline Hidalgo's analysis of the scripturalizing function of utopia (2010)—produces a sense of self-righteousness and models violent interactions with others.

Teskey points to the fact that the relation of individual persons and bodies to the *agora* (the political collective, or, assembly) has often been described in allegorical terms. He takes as an example the frontispiece of Hobbes's *Leviathan*, in which many bodies make up the body of the monarch looming over the countryside (1996, 127–29). He points out that the "image of one body incorporating others is the goal, so to speak, of allegorical expression, *its anagogical fulfillment*" (126, emphasis mine). Allegory and the sovereign incorporation of the people operate homologously: Both discharge interiority to make a whole. Allegory seeks to reveal the interiority (the hidden truths) of signs, which point to a larger essence or truth. Likewise, the agora forms a unit: "As a gathering of bodies with interiors the agora is a corporeal manifold, a space containing spaces that are nevertheless external to it" (124). The agora makes individual interiority and difference accede to its demands, and the diverse parts of the nation are ostensibly unified in this maneuver. Arguably then, allegory and U.S. national sovereignty are structurally similar. The somewhat paradoxical neutralizing of exteriority through the discharge of interiority is to secure the destined future of national sovereignty for a universalized truth.

As in allegory and national sovereignty, a discharge of interiority in the name of the future is demanded by torture. Teskey suggests that there is, in fact, a close connection between the formation of the sovereign political whole and the forcible discharge of interiority in torture. Interiority comes to be seen as counter to the agora, so that, in the Inquisition for instance, torture is used to root out interiority as heresy (1996, 126–27). The demand to discharge hidden "truth" or information—which is also the purpose of allegorical reading and scriptural interpretation—is a demand to accede to the truth of an imposed social order; it is a demand to destroy difference.[36]

---

36. In Teskey's view, voice is what signifies interiority, difference, and freedom within a social order; once voice is lost, so is a sense of interiority. Teskey writes, "The destruction of the sanctuary of the mind is the true object of torture, which reduces the voice, the index of the mind, to a scream" (1996, 130). He goes onto say that the scream is the last expiring moment of freedom and voice. I do not want to use Teskey to argue that there is a strict division between interiority and exteriority or that what is extracted in torture or allegory is somehow a true interiority.

Thus, if a discharge of interiority and difference is important for the formation of the sovereign whole, it is also operative in protecting it, as in the case of searching for, torturing, or killing an enemy combatant. The lengthy search for bin Laden resonates strongly with this need to discharge dangerous difference that threatens the security of the nation.

Teskey's formulations, therefore, help conceptualize the way allegory, scripture, torture, revenge, and national sovereignty all function homologously in the contemporary moment. It is precisely the uncovering of a hidden or interior truth for an ultimate future that makes compelling allegories and scripturalization, particularly those of the apocalyptic literalist variety, in which the "interiority" of cosmic truth is made plain and visible in its mapping onto political events. It is this same demand of national sovereignty for the homogenous and visible truth in the present, to protect the idealized future, that compels torture and torture as revenge. The so-called terrorist detainee in Iraq, external to the United States, is thought to be a stumbling block to U.S. sovereignty. The practice of torture seeks to discharge hidden meaning in order to neutralize the difference of those external to the United States.

Conflicted Allegories

It would seem that any literalist-allegorical scripturalizing of ancient text is impossible to oppose, as any literal discrepancies can be explained in terms of allegory and as allegorical discrepancies are violently subsumed into the notion of truth. Yet even though allegory and scripture create the illusion of totality, oneness, and truth, they cannot ever fully achieve the capture of meaning, even though they continually try.[37] As Fletcher puts it, the futurity of allegory (i.e., anagogy) "implies an openness to change" that is always contradicted by its authoritarian structure and its insistence on universals. He flags this contradiction as "a deep internal conflict, or evasion, at the heart of an ambivalent allegorical procedure" (2010, 20). Likewise, Teskey notes that the difference—the noise beneath material signifiers—that alle-

---

37. Both Teskey and Fletcher favor a deconstructive approach—strongly influenced by Paul de Man's writing on allegory and Derrida's emphasis on allegory's supplementarity.

gory tries to suture over "continues to subvert every imposed structure of meaning, it creates a background of resonant noise. Any logocentric reencoding of that noise can never be wholly persuasive because the struggle at the rift can never be wholly concealed" (1996, 23).[38]

One might hope for such a reading here, but literalist allegory does not let this happen very easily. (The kind of destabilization that Fletcher and Teskey assert might be possible will take a more radical approach, as imagined in chapter 6.) A literalist-allegorical reading practice assumes what Fletcher calls a "deep essentialism" about the production of meaning, which makes change and contradiction manageable as they are subordinated to a fixed "eternal" set of coordinates (2010, 15). It is a reading practice that is violent in the connections it forces, the military actions it authorizes, and the sovereignty it seeks to secure. Its temporal structuring diminishes the importance of the present, deferring judgment on present policy to the cosmic future via memory of the past. The production and recuperation of excessive, transcendental meaning in literalist allegory works to normalize revenge as a form of justice. In this sense, revenge can draw on the "mythic memory" that is provided by the appropriation and apocalyptic allegorizing of the historical conflict between Israel and Babylon. In the course of producing a mythic memory of longing for freedom from innocent captivity, cruel imperial policies become permissible, necessary, and inevitable.

Nonetheless, the literalist-allegorical reading of "Rivers of Babylon" at Abu Ghraib does run into this very problem of multiple and contradictory meanings. None of the possible meanings for the allegory fits very neatly; the excess produces strange results. Although the U.S. national myth normally aligns itself with the exiled Israelites, a strange cross-identification appears in this use of scripture at Abu Ghraib whereby the United States unexpectedly also ends up in alliance with the usually vilified ancient Babylon. This reversal inadvertently points out U.S. imperial ambitions and shows that in its portability literalist allegory is not actually effective as a moral compass; indeed, it is morally obstructionist. That is to say, when the psalm's

---

38. Influenced by Walter Benjamin's reading of German tragedy as allegory ([1928] 1998), both Fletcher and Teskey see the materiality of signs as impossible to destroy, even in their capture and elevation into universalist truths. In some ways, they both want to hold onto Benjamin's famous notion of allegory as ruin. For a reading of Benjamin's view of allegory and its potential for critiquing religious systems, see Plate 2005.

vengeful affect is raised to the status of cosmic truth through the literalist-allegorical interpretive tradition around Babylon, it effectively creates a set of allegorical cross-identifications that obscures responsibility for unethical behavior.

The possible meanings for the song produce ironies and contradictory resonances that surely go beyond the straightforward intent of the soldiers. If playing "Rivers of Babylon" was cruelly meant to remind detained Iraqis of their captivity, U.S. military personnel would be placed in the position of the ancient Babylonian oppressors. This scenario runs contrary to the national mythic identification with ancient Israel but is indicative of actual power relations. However, if the song was meant to pump up the soldiers, the ancient Israelite captives would represent the United States under threat by Babylon, suggesting that U.S. military forces were somehow captive. Clearly they were not, although some reports have indicated that U.S. soldiers in Iraq *felt* trapped, meaningless, and unsupported (see Blasberg and Blasberg 2005; Sharrock 2008a).

The feeling of being trapped might explain the choice of a Rastafarian (Melodians) cover tune, which further adds to the dissonance of the allegory. In Boney M's hit cover (1978) of the Melodians' original tune (1972), Babylon is a symbol for tyranny. With its reggae-disco beat and Jamaican origin, the song takes up Rastafarianism's critique of Babylon as colonial power that enslaves and oppresses. Boney M's music video reverses scenes of slavery, depicting boats filled with free black people propelling themselves toward their own destiny. The irony in the song's use at Abu Ghraib is staggering. What can it mean when a country that likes to proclaim itself as beyond slavery plays a song about freedom to people it is torturing? Even if soldiers felt that they were in a similar position to the song's embattled protagonists, or even if they believed what they were told—that they were bringing freedom to Iraq—how can a comparison of the United States with colonial Babylon be avoided? In its exceptionalism, the United States likes to think of itself in the mode of Rasta yet behaves like Babylon. It critiques the regime that it reflects.

Despite any identification with ancient Israel or the Rastafarian freedom movement, as noted, the soldiers' violence toward prisoners at Abu Ghraib seemed to imitate the troubling ending of Psalm 137, which calls for mimicry of Babylon's violence. Perhaps U.S. soldiers, versed in scripture, were using the song only as a cynical reminder of the reversal of fortune whereby the Babylonians eventually met the same fate as the Judeans. Yet, if soldiers were imitating a vengeful Judah *repaying* Babylon's violence, they would end up, again, imitating Babylon. This double or triple identification—with Israel, with Babylon, with Israel imitating Babylon—points to a longing for dominance. The United States wants to repay Babylon by imitating it. It wants to be like Babylon; and it is.

This kind of cross-identification is one of the things that allows torture to be acceptable while being decried. The muddiness that emerges between victim and victor, colonized and colonizer is precisely what allows torture to proceed as an exception to democractic self-conceptions of freedom, human rights, and lawfulness. The structure of double identification (as victim and oppressor) facilitated by the constellation of literalist-allegorical interpretations that cluster around the psalm effectively masks the vengeful aims of torture. Although none of the literalist-allegorical readings quite fit, taken together, the possibilities they open up establish the moral universe in which the United States can torture in Iraq.

Because the biblical text is so distant from the present, and because it is routed through fixed notions of truth (about God, evil, or God's relation to the world), the referents in the present are quite movable. The mythic evil, or allure, of Babylon can be applied to more than one target in the present (e.g., Iraq or bin Laden). The portability of a kind of apocalyptic literalist allegory means that the United States can, without contradiction, be understood as the imprisoned Judeans (Israel), the conquering Babylon, and the vengeful Israel. Allegorical mobility amplifies a sense of necessity and justification for torture. These multiple identifications that a portable biblical allegory makes possible allow interrogators and policy makers to feel righteous in taking mythic and literal revenge, all the while doing horrible things that might otherwise be unthinkable.

This mode of scripturalization is crucial to the co-optation of this psalm at Abu Ghraib and at the death of bin Laden; but the structure of role reversal is already present in the psalm, which significantly contributes to the conflicting meanings produced by the literalist-allegorical reading of it. The reversals that we see in the use of the psalm at Abu Ghraib are related to the ambivalent structure of the lament. The psalmist moves from weeping in captivity to promising reward to the one who destroys Babylon and her children. Those conquered become the conqueror. The imperial impulses of an identification with Babylon become attached to the embattled position created through a counteridentification with the captive Israelites. These shifts occlude the troublesome fact of the biblical text's vengefulness and, with it, the possibility of recognizing revenge as a motivator in contemporary torture.

Who Lives in Babylon? The Gay Antichrist as Political Enemy

If, in the biopolitical gradation of populations, "good life" (life worth protecting) is controlled and arranged within the nation by means of the virtuous non-Babelian family, then outside of the nation, in the war on terror,
"less-good" Babylonian life is shaped through pain. In the last chapter we
saw how U.S. sovereignty violently extracts truth from enemy combatants—
for the sake of the future of the nation and also the species—in a mode
homologous to literalist-allegorical interpretation of biblical text. In this
chapter, serious and nonserious renderings of Babylon's prince, the antichrist, point to a heteroteleological national eschatology that encompasses
and hierarchizes life within and outside the boundaries of the human in
ways that affect the relative value of law. As in chapter 2, here again we see
Babylonian fantasies reinforcing the securitizing tactic of bypassing law for
the sake of national interest.

In a disquieting manifestation of contemporary U.S. anxieties about
security, sexuality, and the end of the world, a politically malicious,

homosexualized antichrist emerges from the mystic realm of Babylon in pop culture, political humor, and internet religious reflection. After 9/11, the "enemy" of the United States, that potential harbinger of apocalyptic chaos, has been named "terrorism" in general and localized for a time in the persons of Saddam Hussein and Osama bin Laden. In a culture given to apocalyptic fantasm and homophobia, Hussein and bin Laden were predictably associated with Babylon and portrayed as antichrists, as gay, and, on occasion, as both.

The pastiche apocalyptic figure that rises in the media from the sea of collective concern calls attention to the relation betweeen desire and apocalyptic temporality in U.S. delimitations of the in/human, as they relate to exception to law. I consider here images that demonstrate the religious, sexual, and political desires that are permissible in the realm of the redeemable human, and those that tip over into fear of the irredeemable, inhuman, antichristic, beastly, homosexual, and Babylonian. These visual and discursive images make apparent theologically and apocalyptically informed social and legal constraints on desire, which serve to establish the limit between the human and the inhuman, between those whose lives are bound up with the imperialist eschatology of the nation and those whose lives and desires are seen to flout that eschatology.

References to an apocalyptically constructed antichrist are particularly instructive for decoding a continuous logic that held together the George W. Bush administration's seemingly disparate projects of trying to legally enforce a "culture of life" at home, while refusing any legal restriction in fighting the war on terror abroad. Specifically, the attempted proliferation of federal and state law prohibiting gay marriage markedly contrasted with the refusal of legal regulations for interrogation at war (i.e., torture). In other words, attempts to write gay marriage out of the U.S. Constitution were more than simply a ploy in garnering support for the Bush administration's tactics in its war on terror. I suggest that these contradictory legal strategies on domestic and foreign fronts were jointly governed by the desires, fears, and apocalyptic temporalities represented in the images under examination and their precursors, and by the limit between human and inhuman that they mark. This apocalyptic logic makes clear why the rule of law is valorized for U.S. citizens whereas the exception to law becomes the norm in the war on terror; it is the same logic that holds homophobia in

Figure 1. Saddam pesters Satan for sex in *South Park: Bigger, Longer, and Uncut*, directed by Trey Parker, produced by Trey Parker and Matt Stone. Paramount Pictures and Warner Bros.

the United States together with the unconscionable and dehumanizing tactics of imperialism. Although these dynamics were accentuated during the years of the Bush administration, they helpfully allow us to see the theopolitical logics of the biopolitical investment in reproducing some populations as human and others as nonhuman.

Perhaps the clearest and most familiar depiction of the homosexualized, antichristic enemy is that of Saddam Hussein as Satan's sadistic and insensitive gay lover in the parodic film *South Park: Bigger, Longer, and Uncut*. Satan aims for a more loving relationship, while Saddam just wants to have sex, and be turned on by the possibility of taking over the world.

The humor of screenwriters Trey Parker, Matt Stone, and Pam Brady seems to be poking fun at a number of religious and cultural traditions: the long-standing designation of the political enemy as Babylonian antichrist; the more recent conservative Christian belief that the antichrist is likely to be homosexual; and the orientalist imagination about Muslim men's sexuality that is central to popular depictions of terrorists, as analyzed by Jonathan

Goldberg (1992), Jasbir Puar (2007), Junaid Rana (2011), and others. The depictions of the antichrist produced by these traditions stand somewhat independent of each other and are rarely combined quite as they are in *South Park*. Nonetheless, the fact that they can be humorously combined perhaps derives from the fact that each of these traditions relies in some way on apocalyptic eschatological orientation toward desire (including longing for the glorious future of the nation and humanity) or its byproduct, fear.

In what follows, I outline these traditions with an eye to the kinds of in/human desires and Babylonian provenance ascribed to such homosexualized antichrists and their precursors. Then, in order to unravel the relation between law, apocalyptic desire, and the in/human, I turn again to the work of Giorgio Agamben on the state of exception, this time with a focus on his conception of "bare life" (life considered to be borderline human). His work helps us see how legal attempts to ban gay marriage from U.S. polity are integral to U.S. disregard for international law (the state of exception) that allows for torture overseas. Both approaches to law draw boundaries around the human in ways that try to promote apocalyptically oriented desire. Scripture is again in the background to the way that populations are positioned with respect to sovereignty, capital, and law, demanding that some (white, citizen) bodies be invested with normalized sexuality and reproductive capacity, while assuming others to be perverse, and therefore not quite human, good for either disposable labor (at best), or demonstrations of U.S. sovereignty through torture and death (at worst).

In/Human Antichrist

It is in no way surprising that contentious political leaders such as Hussein and bin Laden have been portrayed in both spoof and serious forms as the antichrist.[1] Within U.S. apocalyptic thought, the antichrist has long been shorthand for any and every political threat. Babylon is his home turf.

---

1. Of course, these are not the only candidates for antichrist; others suggested include the pope, George Bush, a future president of the E.U., Bill Gates, and Barney the Dinosaur.

Descriptions of the antichrist throughout the ages have made clear that the threat he brings to humanity from Babylon (understood either allegorically, or literally, or both) is a result of his quasi-inhuman, beastly, and deceptive nature. It is precisely this deceptiveness that makes the humanity of the antichrist difficult to determine: Deception is evidence of the antichrist's inhumanity and possible connection to Satan, and yet it is the human form of the antichrist that allows him to be deceptive. The antichrist's potential human form allows for human religious and political leaders to be suspect, especially those who do not appear to do God's will (in the eye of the beholder). The figure has tenuous biblical foundations, however. How, then, has it come to be such a powerful symbol for a hostile political leader who occupies a position somewhere between human and inhuman?

It should be remembered that the term *antichrist* is only biblically found in the epistles of John in the context of cautioning believers against false doctrine (1 Jn 2:18, 22; 4:3; 2 Jn 7). There is no connection between the antichrist and Babylon in these Johannine texts. Indeed, it unclear whether the term designates a unique figure or if it refers to any person who teaches against Christ. So, for instance, 1 John 2:18 refers to the antichrist in both singular and plural terms: "Children, it is the last hour! As you have heard that antichrist is coming, so now many antichrists have come. From this we know that it is the last hour." Because of this possibility for multiple antichrists, Christian interpreters began to suggest that many little antichrists would precede the one final antichrist, or following the antiapocalyptic Augustine, that any heretic or hostile leader could be called an antichrist (*Tractates on the First Epistle of John* 6:12–14; McGinn 1994, 76–77; Weinrich 1985, 137). This semantic confusion in the biblical text is perhaps why nominations for antichrist can flourish as they do. It also leaves open the option that *anyone* could be an antichrist; thus possibilities for deception abound.

The need to identify the one final antichrist has led interpreters throughout the tradition to try to clarify the nature of the antichrist. To this end, other biblical texts warning of deceptive teachers have been used to illuminate the cryptic reference to the antichrist(s) in the letters of John. Through this process, the one final antichrist has come to be associated with Satan and described in bestial terms. In particular, the apocalyptic visions in the books of Daniel (chaps. 7–11) and Revelation (chaps. 13–17) that depict successive imperial powers as a series of beasts—culminating with the most frightening imperial danger—are grafted onto the notion of a deceptive and Satanic leader.[2] Both Daniel and Revelation use a bestial image of Babylon as a stand-in for the Seleucid and Roman empires against which, respectively, the writers take their stands. In later interpretation, these apocalyptic beasts become representative of the antichrist, merging empire with its feared ruler. The composite image thus drawn of the biblical antichrist is both human and inhuman; he is a leader to be feared—part human, part beast. He is worldly, with otherworldly ties to the kingdom of Satan. Any leader that can be shown to be boastful or deceitful, or opposing God's work, can be suspect.

Though use of the term *antichrist* is infrequent in the texts that form the biblical canon, the larger apocalyptic tradition in the Greco-Roman world did frequently posit an eschatological opponent. Early extrabiblical Jewish and Christian apocalypses and their later interpreters were divided on whether this eschatological opponent would be human or inhuman, whether he would be simply a human tool of greater evil forces, or whether he would be of demonic origin. On one hand, as Gregory Jenks has pointed out, many early Christian texts, such as the epistles of John, the *Apocalypse of Peter*, and the *Didache*, speak of deceivers but not of their connection to Satan (1991, 360). Such texts indicate that a lawless deceiver is expected, as a human false prophet or deceptive teacher—simply a tool of evil forces. But other texts affiliate the antichrist much more closely with Satan, or with his predecessor in Jewish literature, Beliar.[3] Some early Christian theologians suggested that the antichrist would be a kind of Satan incarnate, appearing as human but having the nature of Satan—a corollary to the incarnate God, Christ. For instance, Irenaeus (2nd century C.E.) taught that just as Christ "recapitulates" God and goodness, so the antichrist would recapitulate all

2. Indeed, the strong allegorical anti-imperial rhetoric of the book of Revelation—which might discourage invocation of its images in the service of the American empire—has been much discussed by scholars. For the debate over the extent to which the text responds to real imperialist oppression, see Boesak 1987; A. Y. Collins 1984; Kraybill 1996; Schüssler Fiorenza 1985, 1991; Thompson 1990.

3. In the 2nd century C.E. apocalypse *The Ascension of Isaiah* (of debated, but probably Jewish, origins), Beliar, the angel of lawlessness, descends in the form of a lawless king. For further discussion of this text, see Peerbolte 1996, 194–205; J. Knight 1995.

evil and apostasy (*Against Heresies* 5.29.2; McGinn 1994, 58–60). A little later in the tradition, Origen (3rd century C.E.) taught that the antichrist could do evil miracles by the powers of "his father" Satan (*Contra Celsum* 6.45).[4] As the early tradition developed, the antichrist increasingly appeared as more demonic than human.

The interpretive indeterminacy of the antichrist's humanity is further exemplified by the physical descriptions of the antichrist that began to appear in early apocalyptic texts and carried on into late antiquity. In these descriptions, the antichrist is portrayed as grotesque: often with a bald head, a leprous spot on the forehead, asymmetrical or oversized features, awful teeth, and a misproportioned body. He is sometimes depicted as a wild animal, or with an eye like a lion (Ford 1996; McGinn 1994, 68–73; Rosenstiehl 1967). So, for instance, the *Apocalypse of Elijah*, written between the first and fourth centuries C.E. describes the antichrist as follows: "He is a skinny-legged young lad, having a tuft of gray hair at the front of his bald head. His eyebrows will reach to his ears. There is a leprous bare spot on the front of his hands" (3:15–16). Likewise, the *Greek Apocalypse of Ezra*, written sometime between the second and ninth centuries C.E., describes the antichrist in monstrous terms: "The appearance of his face is as of a wild man. His right eye is like a star rising at dawn and the other is unmoving. His mouth is one cubit, his teeth are a span long, his fingers like scythes, the soles of his feet two span, and on his forehead an inscription, 'Antichrist'" (4:30–32).

Not surprisingly, given the reliance on Revelation (chaps. 13 and 17) to fill out the antichrist, descriptions of the in/human antichrist also associate him with Babylon. For instance, Irenaeus describes a beast that is likened to the statue of Babylon's king, Nebuchadnezzar, the persecuting ruler who threw Shadrach, Meshach, and Abednego into the fiery furnace (*Against Heresies* 5.29.2). Likewise, Origen suggests that study of biblical passages lamenting the tyrannical rules of Babylon (or Egypt) might provide enlightenment "concerning evil, as to the nature of its origin and generation, and as to how it derived its existence" (*Contra Celsum* 6.43).

4. For discussion of this and other passages in Origen concerning the antichrist, see Jenks 1991, 57–60.

Following Augustine's antiapocalyptic urgings, however, interpretation of these texts through the middle ages changed again to focus on the human form of the antichrist, who would lead the forces of evil.[5] Nonetheless, though appearing human, the antichrist was considered by many medieval Christians to have either Satanic parentage or protection, and more precisely, to be Jewish but born in Babylon (Emmerson 1981, 79–82). Adso of Montier-en-Der writes in his famous treatise about the antichrist for Gerberga, Queen of the West Franks, that "the antichrist will be born from the Jewish people. . . . At the very beginning of his conception the devil will enter his mother's womb" ([c. 950] 1979, 90). He continues on to say that just as Christ was born in Bethlehem, "the devil knew a place fit for that lost man who is called the Antichrist, a place from which the root of all evil (1 Tm 6:10) ought to come, namely, Babylon" (91). Increasingly, the antichrist was considered a threat to Christendom as a whole. As Robert Lerner points out, Joachim of Fiore—that famous and influential chiliastic biblical interpreter of the twelfth century—was innovative in understanding the final antichrist to "represent the embodiment of the worst imaginable Western corporate dangers—a depraved royalty and a depraved papacy" who would deceive the world (1985, 568).[6]

The Political Enemy as Antichrist

In contemporary prophecy writing, often the antichrist is depicted as a human—as evidenced by the attempts to name world leaders as antichristic—but one whose intentions for world dominance are inhuman in the extreme. The antichrist stands in for anything or anyone who appears to be hinder-

---

5. For a comprehensive study of the antichrist in the middle ages, see Emmerson 1981.
6. Joachim reads the biblical texts allegorically to determine the identity of both the little antichrists and the final one antichrist. The seven kings mentioned in Revelation 17:10 become the seven-headed dragon of Revelation 12:3, representing the various antichrists, who would take the form of evil kings. These would appear in final succession until the advent of the two last antichrists (one before and one after Satan's time in the abyss, Rv 20:1–10). Both the fifth and sixth heads of Joachim's dragon are metaphorically associated with those hypocritical Christians that Joachim calls Babylonian ([c. 1183] 1979, 136–38).

ing the prevalent set of nationalist and capitalist desires that originate in the colonies and culminate in U.S. hegemony (see Boyer 1992, 282–84, 328–30; Fuller 1995, 71–73, 136–60). The fear is that he will establish a one-world order, thus doing away with nations (including U.S. hegemony; see Corbett 1997; Froese 1997; Kjos 1997). As the prophecy writer Mark Hitchcock tells it, "The Bible explicitly links the final world ruler to the ancient city of Babylon. According to God's word, Satan's city will rise again to be ruled over by one man" (2003, 118). Representative of Babylon's unifying rule, the aims of the antichrist have been variously understood as the one-world strivings of Babel (Corbett 1997, 210, 214, 219, 222), the imperial ambitions of Rome (Froese 1997, 298), or literally rebuilding Babylon in Iraq (Hitchcock 2003). The war on terror provides prophecy writers with both the literal and metaphoric site of Babylon, as well as potential antichrists. It is in this vein that first Hussein and then bin Laden were questioned as possible candidates by conservative Christian and otherwise spiritually interested Internet sites (e.g., Renz and Renz 2005).[7]

Because prophecy writers understand that "human history is an arena in which the struggle between God and Satan is played out" (Feinberg 1997, 270), the antichrist's actions are thought to be in the service of the demonic, putting into question the provenance of his agency and his humanity (e.g., Baxley 2005; Webber 1997). Through deceptiveness, the antichrist leads human desire astray, perverts it, and makes it less than human. The antichrist, therefore, marks the limit between the human and inhuman. He appears in human form yet has inhuman desires and tools that he puts to inhuman ends, ends that seek to block the highest goals of humanity and divert desire for these goals. Indeed, the only way to ascertain the inhumanity of the antichrist is to recognize that his intentions and desires are wrongly oriented, to see that he seeks to thwart believers, political goals, and, ultimately, the human.

---

7. Jerry Falwell gave a sermon on November 4, 2001, at Thomas Road Baptist Church, called "Satan's Superman," in which he asked, "Is Saddam Hussein the Antichrist?? What about Osama bin Laden? Is the final great war developing between good and evil? Is America at war with one billion Moslems?" That sermon is no longer available; it was originally posted on the Internet at http://sermons.trbc.org/20011104.html.

The current naming of the political enemy as antichrist falls not only within the purview of evangelists; it operates in "coded" fashion in U.S. national politics as well.[8] For instance, in one speech on the war on terror (October 6, 2005), without ever mentioning the antichrist, George W. Bush was able to paint a picture of "the enemy" that is truly apocalyptic and inhuman, posing a "mortal danger to all humanity" (2005a). Bush's justification for the war on terror opened and closed with apocalyptic threats and rewards. The speech began with an apocalyptically drawn recollection of 9/11 "a great evil . . . a proud city covered in smoke and ashes, a fire across the Potomac, and passengers who spent their final moments on Earth *fighting the enemy*." It ended with the assurance that the war on terror "is also the *current expression of an ancient struggle*," and the promise that "the cause of freedom will once again prevail" (emphases mine). Within this apocalyptic frame, the enemy was described as "evil men, obsessed with ambition and unburdened by conscience," who in "their cold-blooded contempt for human life" were "the enemies of humanity." A sure sign of their antichristic intent, these men were said to be "part of global, borderless terrorist organizations." The president ingeniously named this *evil Islam*, and disavowed that he did so: "Some call this evil Islamic radicalism; others, militant Jihadism; still others, Islamo-fascism. Whatever it's called, this ideology is very different from the religion of Islam."

A spectral tower of Babelian Islam emerges—made particularly manifest in the term Islamo-fascism and in its allegedly global, borderless organization—as a fear of world dominance in the wrong key. (Even more in the shadows lurks Josephus's tyrant Babel-builder, Nimrod, who, as we saw in chapter 1, sometimes morphs into the antichrist.) The fear of the one-world leader was evoked again two election cycles after the Bush era when Republican presidential candidate Michele Bachmann spoke of Iran's "constitutional" ambitions to a *one-world caliphate*, in the December 15, 2011, candidate's debate (Eddlem 2011). Given this kind of "secular" political rhetoric, it is not at all surprising that Islamic leaders—those (correctly or incorrectly) associated with terrorism—have been crowned antichrists in certain religious communities. This kind of religious argumentation can

---

8. For discussions on G. W. Bush's religious coding, see Keller 2005; Lifton 2003; Lincoln 2004; Morford 2004; Runions 2005, Urban 2004).

be found in books like Joel Richardson's *The Islamic Antichrist: The Shocking Truth about the Real Nature of the Beast* (2009). Richardson demonstrates the "antichrist spirit of Islam" (103) by arguing, among other things, that "Islam has as one of its goals total world domination" (138) and that it encourages deceit.[9]

Alternatively, the enemy antichrist could reside *within* the nation. Along these lines, a troubling use of the antichrist occurred in John McCain's 2008 presidential campaign. In an ad that caused a small stir, McCain's campaign referred to Barack Obama as "the One." The ad so clearly referenced the ways in which the antichrist is depicted in the *Left Behind* series that Timothy LaHaye felt compelled to respond by saying that the antichrist would not, in fact, be American. Hal Lindsey also weighed in to say that Obama was not the antichrist; nonetheless, "Obama's world tour provided a foretaste of the reception [the antichrist] can expect to receive." Though the McCain ad was not successful in winning the full approval of apocalyptic leaders like LaHaye and Lindsey, or in swaying the decision making of the public as a whole, it was unmistakably meant to appeal to a certain theopolitical mode of thought.[10]

This tactic of endowing enemies with spiritual significance has several obvious effects. It implicitly aligns the audience's future with the kingdom of God (open to all humanity, if saved by Christ), while aligning its political enemies' future with the kingdom of Satan (the enemy of humanity and Christ's salvation of it). The spiritual enemy threatens all of humanity and the kingdom of God, whereas the political enemy threatens U.S. citizens and the nation's successful future. Within an apocalyptic framework, then, political threats to the nation become spiritual threats to the destiny of humanity. Moreover, this rhetoric increases the fear of political enemies among the apocalyptically inclined within the population, and, to borrow a

9. See also Massegee 2011.

10. "The One," Country First: The Official John McCain Youtube Channel, http://www.youtube.com/profile?user=JohnMcCaindotcom&view=videos; Carol Stream, "Left Behind Authors Speak Out on the McCain Ad "The One," Christian Newswire, August 8, 2008, http://www.christiannewswire.com/news/371367426.html; and Hal Lindsey, "How Obama Prepped the World for the Antichrist," WorldNetDaily, August 1, 2008, http://www.wnd.com/index.php?fa=PAGE.view&pageId=71144. I am grateful to Elizabeth Castelli for pointing me to this material.

line from George W. Bush, strengthens their resolve against such enemies of the nation.

Gay Antichrist versus the Nation

Relatively recently, in contemporary conservative Christian apocalyptic teaching, the antichrist has been interpreted as a homosexual or sodomite (two preferred terms of the homophobic). In this description of the homosexual antichrist, improperly oriented sexual desire is aligned with the in/human desire of the antichrist who has his sights set on the United States and who could ultimately destroy humanity itself. Such descriptions of the antichrist, as I will discuss, strongly indicate the connections made in this worldview between U.S. nationalism, heteronormativity, the future, and what it means to be human. At the same time, the deceptive antichrist poses the threat of contagion by nonnormative desire, desire that cannot be constrained or banished by the categories of human or inhuman, heterosexual or homosexual. The antichrist's deceptiveness means that human and inhuman cannot be told apart, nor their apparent sexualities. As I will argue in chapter 6, it is this "threat" that becomes a possibility for reclaiming the queer antichrist.

In conservative Christian discourse, the antichrist's probable sexual orientation is derived from a particular way of translating a clause in Daniel 11:37: "He [the oppressive arrogant ruler] will show no regard for the gods of his fathers or for the desire of women" (New American Standard Bible).[11] This alleged lack of attraction to women allows for the suggestion that the antichrist may be homosexual. A much-blogged-about example of this line of theological reasoning can be found in John Hagee's 2003 sermon "The Final Dictator," delivered at the Cornerstone Church in San Antonio, Texas. Hagee describes the antichrist, among other things, as "a blasphemer and a homosexual. . . . He shall regard neither the god of his fathers, nor the desire of women."[12] Notably, in this sermon Hagee also lauds Bush's efforts

---

11. See also Darby's apocalyptic translation, the English Revised Version, and prophecy writers' highly favored King James Version.

12. Hagee 2003. Transcripts of particularly offensive passages can be found at Bruce Wilson, "Source/Information Page for New John Hagee Video," Talk to Action: Reclaiming Citizenship, History, and Faith, June 1, 2008, http://www.talk2action.org/story/2008/6/1/163843/2726.

on the war on terror, linking the gay antichrist with the war on terror (more on this tendency below).

This translation of Daniel 11:37 is technically possible from the Hebrew phrase *ḥmdt nšym* ("desire of women"), because the noun *ḥmdh* could mean "desire"; it also could mean "treasure" or "desirable thing." Thus, many mainstream twentieth-century translations translate this text as: "He [the self-promoting king] will show no regard for the gods of his fathers or for *the one desired by women*, nor will he regard any god but will exalt himself above them all" (New International Version). Such translations follow biblical scholarship in understanding this verse to be about the deceitful king's attitude toward another empire's gods. As C. L. Seow notes, within this context, "the one desired by women" could possibly be the god Tammuz (the Mesopotamian version of Adonis), whose worship the Ptolemies took up in Egypt (2003, 183). John Goldingay points out, this god would have been "slighted by [the Seleucid king] Antiochus," in his aggressive interactions with the Ptolemies (1989, 304).[13] But the homosexualized translation allows for a steamier moralizing reading.

The sexuality of the antichrist appears to be produced as a response to societal changes with respect to sexuality and gender. Paul Boyer situates the origins of the homosexual antichrist in the culture wars following the increasing acceptance of homosexuality in the 1970s (1992, 234).[14] It would seem that, as sexual norms have changed, some religious interpreters have reacted by trying to restabilize the status quo through moral imperatives.

Not surprisingly, given the contemporary configuration of the ongoing culture wars, some commentators extrapolate from their understanding of the antichrist's sexual orientation a diagnosis of the problems facing marriage in the twenty-first century. So, for instance, Joseph Chambers of Paw Creek Ministries suggests in pamphlet and video forms that the spiritual prototype of heterosexual marriage, described in Revelation as the mar-

---

For other ruminations on the gay antichrist, see Benoit 1997, 313; Boston 2006; D. R. Reagan 2005; Remnant of God 1985–2000.

13. For similar readings, see also Lacocque 1976, 171; Porteous 1965, 169; Towner 1985, 162.

14. For a longer discussion of the fear (beginning in the 1970s) that homosexuality in the United States would result in apocalyptic demise, see Long 2005, 1–8. Long's important work also shows the apocalyptic history of the religious reaction to AIDS (20–28), as well as gay men's apocalyptic reappropriations in response to AIDS.

riage of the Lamb (i.e., the marriage between Christ and the church), is under threat from incredibly powerful and destructive "sodomites." He lays the blame at the feet of the antichrist.

> Satan is on a rampage to defile the family of humankind and the future family of the redeemed. . . . I do not believe that there is any question but that the Antichrist will be a homosexual. The world is literally hell-bent on making the sodomite lifestyle the order of the day. . . . Sodomites are thrilled to destroy any institution that stands in their way. Their motives and methods cannot be called anything but demonic. (Chambers 2005)

Beware the antichristic gay take-over.

Fear of a one-world order associates the gay antichrist with Babylon; it emerges in rhetoric that betrays and provokes a kind of panic that homosexuality might be forced upon everyone. For instance, Chambers invokes Babylon when he associates gay marriage with the filth of the "great whore" and a one-world religion. The antichrist "demands that she [the Whore] and all her priests promote total abominations against all Biblical truth and standards" (2005). Along similar lines, the Watchmen Bible Study Group finds the acceptance of homosexuality and gay marriage to be a sign of the first beast: the emergence of a "one-world political/religious system . . . which will make it possible for the antichrist to step in, take the reins, and assume control of most every soul on the planet." Within that Babelian one-world system, "Satan's false teachers" try to convince people of unbiblical truths, including acceptance of gay Christians and gay marriage.[15]

Gay marriage is thus associated with the demonic and the totalitarian one-world system, and so its supporters are rendered inhuman and antidemocratic (so also un-American). This discourse agonizes over what it considers to be sexual and political desire gone so terribly awry that it threatens the future. "Sodomites," like the pervert antichrist they follow, are a threat not only to redemption's final goal (the marriage of the Lamb) but also to the earthly mirror of that goal. Notably, for Chambers, that earthly goal is not marriage but the family (i.e., husband, wife, and children). The threat to the world, to the family, and to Christians' final future is the same.

---

15. Watchmen Bible Study Group, "Emergence of the First Beast," Watchmen Bible Study Group, accessed October 15, 2005, http://biblestudysite.com/beast.htm.

James Dobson, a renowned evangelical leader on the family, makes equally pressing, though less explicitly mythologized, arguments about the family, society, and the nation in is his book *Marriage under Fire: Why We Must Win This Battle* (2004). The eleven arguments he makes against same-sex marriage predict disaster: the accelerated end of the family on every continent, total collapse of the health care system on the national front, bankruptcy of social security, the end of religious freedom (2004, 45–64).[16] The threat to the family is clearly a threat to the future of the nation. His final arguments focus on the threat to the eschatological future: the impediment to spreading the gospel that unstable homes for children will create and the resulting apocalyptic crisis that acceptance of same-sex marriage might provoke. All over the globe, the lack of gospel teaching "will create millions of motherless children and fatherless kids" (62), as if in the wake of a natural disaster. Finally, in a catastrophic flourish, "The world may soon become 'as it was in the days of Noah' (Matthew 24:37)" (63). Here, as in the discourse of Bush on (antichristic) terror, the threat to the nation extends to the future of the globe and, one is clearly meant to extrapolate, to the future of humankind.[17]

With respect to gay marriage, Bush used a nationalist reasoning similar to that of Dobson when in February of 2004 he called for a constitutional amendment protecting marriage. As he opined, "Ages of experience have taught *humanity* that the commitment of a husband and wife to love and to serve one another promotes the welfare of children and the stability of society." Further, because "preservation of marriage rises to this level of *national* importance," the strongest legal action must be undertaken, so as to ensure that activist judges cannot whittle away at this fundamental national institution (emphasis mine in both quotations). Note the slippage between humanity and the nation characteristic of so many of Bush's speeches—

---

16. For further discussion of the uses of "freedom of religion" within conservative Christian discourse, see Castelli 2005, 2007c.

17. See Kintz 1997 for a much wider discussion of the way that conservative Christian preoccupations with family and nation intersect. See Burlein 2002 for the way in which the self-avowedly racist Christian right also uses a nationalistic discourse in which white children's futures "become a site onto which people project individual and cultural fears" (9), so as to manipulate "affective investments" (8). For some, then, the family/nation/human/future is explicitly white; for others, race may be assumed but not mentioned (or disavowed), though the way in which the antichrist is racialized suggests strong biases.

with its implication that the nation has an obligation to lead humanity in its universal truth. Though Bush did not mention Christianity, his tone was sermonic, and his message one of an almost prophetic access to timeless verity.

The rhetorical use of procreation, nation building, and apocalypse in homophobia and the fight against same-sex marriage is helpfully contextualized by Lee Edelman's critique of the futurity of the Child. With caustic humor, Edelman shows that, in the United States, a pervasive political appeal to the Child and the Child's future, as in "the fight for the Children" (2004, 3), "shapes the logic within which the political itself must be thought" (2). Identification of the Child with a political project aligns it with a forward-looking impulse, giving it an "about-to-be-realized identity" (13). The appeal to the Child is ubiquitous from the right and the left and comes to "every political vision as a vision of futurity" (13). Politics becomes "the politics of reproduction." Edelman points to the work of Lauren Berlant, who draws out the particularly U.S. way in which the Child, or fetus, has come to stand in for the future and for "anxieties and desires about whose citizenship—whose subjectivity, whose forms of intimacy and interest, whose bodies and identifications, whose heroic narratives—will direct America's future" (Berlant 1997, 6). The Child becomes almost synonymous with the narrative of the nation's future.

Without foregrounding it, Edelman makes reference to the apocalyptic theology behind much of this futurity. For instance, he cites Donald Wildmon of the American Family Association, who worries about the destruction of Western civilization through acceptance of homosexuality, "plummeting ourselves, our children and grandchildren into an age of godlessness" (Edelman 2004, 16). Likewise, militants in the pro-life Army of God, were, in their words, willing "to disrupt and ultimately destroy Satan's power to kill our children, God's children" (22). It would seem they were after the antichrist. Edelman shows that the futurity of the Child is envisioned as part of a particularly apocalyptic futurity in which the Child becomes a signifier for all future, and for the fate of humanity.[18] His work thus opens a space, as I will show in chapter 6, for revaluation of the place

18. See also Edelman 2004, 75, 66, 91, 113–14.

of the antichrist as that queer element that will resist and disrupt the homo-phobic and sexist discourses that insist that sexual desires and gender roles be properly oriented toward the successful future of the (Christian) nation and humanity.

Homosexualized Enemy

Let me now turn to the way that political enemies are frequently homo-sexualized in the secular U.S. imagination. Independently of religious de-pictions of the antichrist as politically malicious or gay, other secular, often satiric, sites portray bin Laden and Hussein as homosexual. Portraying Sad-dam Hussein as homosexual—and thus bestial—goes back to the first Gulf War. For example, at that time, as the queer theorist Jonathan Goldberg has analyzed, *Rolling Stone* ran an ad for a T-shirt reading "America will not be Saddamized," with Saddam's head sketched over the ass of a camel (1992, 1–5). Since the beginning of the second Gulf War, such images have prolif-erated. For instance, a spoof *Queer Eye for the Straight Guy* poster advertised a show about the makeover of Hussein. Appealing to a different audience, *Weekly World News* launched stories of Hussein's and bin Laden's sexual preferences. Bold headlines tell of Saddam's sordid history as a porn star, his penchant for male lovers, his lurid diaries in which he confesses his love affair with bin Laden, their marriage, their broken penile implants, and their adopted ape baby. Other, less prominent media and political humor websites make use of similar themes. StrangeCosmos.com dis-played "Osama and his gay masochist pal," in which bin Laden's head has been photoshopped onto one party of a leather couple. The same site also hosted an animated image entitled "Saddam giving Osama bin Laden a 'Lewinsky!'" in which Hussein's head compulsively bobs up and down over bin Laden's lap, simulating a blow job. The political humor page at About.com contains dozens of photoshopped images of Hussein in drag (and several of G. W. Bush as well), including one of Hussein seductively posed as a pinup girl in a red devil suit. In an effort to interrogate the "hu-mor" that finds images of homosexualized Arabs funny, I would suggest that these political spoofs portraying Arab and Muslim political leaders as gay or gender queer are part of a larger tradition about humanity, nationalism, and sexuality in which the religious and the secular are intertwined.

Though in many ways different from the religious depictions of the political and gay antichrist that I have been discussing, these secular images of the queer Arab enemy can be understood as coming out of a combined religious and secular tradition that defines heterosexual marriage as a human trait.[19] Let me briefly point to two convergences between the secular and religious that form a tautological argument about the heterosexual human. First, in both secular and religious traditions, there is a slippage between the universal and the particular in conceptualizing humanity. As illustrated in the religious assessments of same-sex marriage discussed thus far, the use of apocalyptic language relates the category of human to the "universal truth" of Christianity. True humanity is saved. It is composed of those who have accepted Christ's salvation; true humanity will, in the next world, sit at the marriage supper of the Lamb. The human is particularized by the "truth" of Christianity. A similar slippage, this time between the universal human and the nation, appears in secular discussions of human rights. As Talal Asad points out in his book *Formations of the Secular*, the "human" in human rights is assumed to be universal, but is only protected by the laws of any given nation-state:[20] "The identification and application of human rights law has no meaning independent of the judicial institutions that belong to individual nation-states (or to several states bound together by treaty)" (Asad 2003, 129). He draws out the point that "the human" is simply an abstracted notion "imagined in a state of nature" (143) and therefore nowhere an actual reality in political terms. A tension arises, therefore, "between the moral invocation of 'universal humanity' and the power of the state to identify, apply, and maintain the law" (138). In both religious and secular discourse, then, the "universal" human is limited by the particular (religion or political governance).

Second, a commensurate overlap between religious and secular views of the body further defines the human in terms of sexual morality. Janet Jakob-

19. Per G. W. Bush's 2004 speech endorsing a constitutional amendment on marriage, discussed earlier.
20. Here Asad follows Hannah Arendt's similar observation in *The Origins of Totalitarianism* ([1950] 1973, 299–300).

sen and Ann Pellegrini explicate this dynamic in showing the central role that the body plays in joining religious and secular discourses. As they argue, the body is the site on which morality (secular in guise, though religious in form) is enacted. From early modernity into the contemporary period, they argue, religious views about the body were mandated by the secular state: "The newly secularized state enforced specifically religious ideas about, for example, 'natural' versus 'unnatural' sexual acts and appetites, precisely through enforcing body regulation" (2000, 2).[21] Christian values become secular human morality through the regulation of the nation-state.[22] Tautologically, heterosexuality becomes a human trait. Secular humor about the gay enemy is entangled with the temporal structure of apocalypse, as well as with discourses that affiliate the human with the nation. As we have seen, sexuality is regulated according to Christian values in order to save the nation and humanity. Universal humanity is particularized as Christian and safeguarded by the United States. Since the nation and humanity are ultimately preserved by heterosexuality, "true" humanity is "saved," affiliated with the United States, and heterosexual. The Christian discourses on the antichrist's sexuality and the threat of gay marriage to the nation that I have been discussing emphasize the roots of this "Christian secular" humor—to borrow a phrase from Jakobsen (2005).

Put another way, images of the queer Arab enemy come out of the same Christian secular apocalyptic regulation of desire as do depictions of the gay antichrist. Both define humanity in ways that mean it can be put into question via the representation of nonnormative desire. If sexual and civic desire must line up with the apocalyptic narrative of the nation and humanity, those considered to be outside of the narrative are represented through nonnormative sexual desire. Like human rights, "unnatural sexual acts and appetites" cannot be regulated outside of the nation. Without regulation they are assumed to be perverse. High-profile Muslims, seen as hostile to the nation and therefore to the Christian universal, are ascribed unnatural appetites and also assumed to be a threat to humanity.

21. For a longer discussion of the secular regulation of religious ideas about the body and sexuality, see Jakobsen 2005; Jakobsen and Pellegrini 2003.
22. For a discussion of the shift from religion to morality in modernity, see Baird 2000.

This tradition about the in/human queer Arab has, of course, long been part of orientalist discourse and art. Orientalist art is filled with virile, attractive, gender queer, and not-quite-human villains and antiheroes. Goldberg, for example, points out the way that English Renaissance texts repeatedly understand male homosexuality as a particularly Mediterranean and Islamic trait (1992, 3). Analyses of orientalist art have shown that nonnormative desire is not totally excluded from the realm of the human but rather is allowed to be present insofar as it can also signify cultural superiority for the viewer. In the words of the film theorist Adrienne McLean, orientalism acts "as a liminal dreamscape on which to project displaced Western erotic and political desires" (1997, 133).[23] McLean points to the work of other cultural critics, such as Susan White and Michael Moon, who notice that viewers' desires are inscribed in depictions of "corrupt sexuality, a degraded or treacherous femininity and male homoeroticism" (White 1988, 132) or in alternate masculinities, fantasized as intensely desirable, more human than human, and, at the same time, not quite human (Moon 1989, 28).

Such orientalist homophobic inscriptions on Muslim bodies seem more innocuous (although they are not) in the "humor" provoked by homosexualized images of political enemies, such as those of bin Laden and Hussein mentioned above. In these images, as in orientalist art, homoerotic desire is simultaneously permitted, explored, and demonized as politically antithetical and perhaps also spiritually hazardous. And because they depict enemies of the United States, these images insist that U.S. national identity is tied up with heteronormativity. Further, the masculinity of these figures appears as somehow out of the ordinary. As Goldberg notices of the "We will not be Saddamized" T-shirt, "Saddam—homosexual, bestial, foreign, inhuman, feminine—is the target of a proper masculinity," by which the United States will be on top (1992, 4–5). Yet this kind of heterogender is allowed to be homosexualized in the context of orientalism and war: The United States must penetrate the camel with a missile: "In a word, 'America' says, 'we will sodomize'" (4). One might say, as Gaylyn Studlar has said of orientalism in early film, these types of images allow "the viewer to

---

23. McLean analyzes Jack Cole's orientalist camp choreography in the 1940s and '50s.

project his 'unthinkable' sexual fantasies into an exotic imaginary space" (1997, 102). But erotic projection is done in a way that is safe because it justifies aggression toward the very object of desire. These images express "the Western male's externalization and vicarious destruction of his own fears and desires" (White 1988, 133). Nonnormative desire, fear, and aggression merge.

As Puar has analyzed, it is these kinds of images of sexual perversity and excess that the writers of *South Park* pick up on in satirizing (and representing) U.S. attitudes toward the Middle East and South Asia. She astutely draws out the orientalist subtexts in *South Park*'s Mr. Slave episode, in which Mr. Slave, the leather bottom, is called Pakistani (Puar 2007, 70–76). In similar fashion, in *Bigger, Longer and Uncut*, Saddam is portrayed as stereotypically male, wanting sex all the time—still, his humanity is in question because he has sex with Satan and enjoys torture. Conversely, Satan is more gender queer, a hard body with inner sensitivity, and ironically more human than Saddam. Satan's character, at least, has charm, and may provide a possibility for alternate points of queer identification. He is able to get out of his unhealthy heteromodeled relationship, in which he has to read *Saddam Is from Mars, Satan Is from Venus* in order to cope; he is able to move on to better things.[24] But Saddam is destroyed, skewered through the middle on a mountaintop in hell. To be sure, the orientalist and racist homophobia so typical of U.S. aggression toward the Middle East is parodied through the cartoon version of Saddam, evident in his death, and in Satan's angry parting insult to Saddam: "You sandy little butt hole." Still, Satan's character may depict the kind of U.S. exceptionalism that Puar criticizes. He is a more normative gay figure than Saddam; even Satan is better than Saddam.

Junaid Rana argues that the orientalizing, homosexualizing, and racializing of Muslim men are tied up with discourses on terror and on migrant workers. Rana's work shows how religious sexualization and racialization play into the larger discourse on biopolitics that I am exploring in this book, in which any bid for U.S. sovereignty is tied to the production of populations for markets. He writes, "Framing Muslim bodies through

---

24. I am grateful to my colleague Aaron Kunin for this insight that complicates a reading of the film as straightforwardly homophobic.

race, gender, and sexuality has naturalized the idea of the male body as a terrorist and, indeed, a migrant" (2011, 71). Rana's analysis of this trend shows how the war on terror works in tandem with markets to create a disposable work force of surplus labor, one that can be policed and regulated via the threat of deportation. The fear of the "Muslim terrorist"—intensified, through the fear of the sexualized antichrist—means that Muslim immigrant men are marked as noncitizens, living constantly live under the threat of detention and deportation (158). The ability of the United States to patrol and police migrant workers bolsters a sense of U.S. sovereignty and at the same time creates a resource of surplus labor (i.e., cheap labor) (156–60). The "homosexual Muslim antichrist" is part of a discourse that works to secure U.S. sovereignty at the same time that it requires market forces—in this case human labor—that go beyond state borders.

The Union of Antichrists: An Eschatology of the Exception

One of the homosexualized images of Hussein and bin Laden that circulated for a time on the Internet is the *Weekly World News* front page story of Osama and Saddam's gay wedding.[25] One can only wonder what this wedding portrait would signify to prophecy writers. Surely, even in jest, it would be an icon of everything gone wrong with the world: Two potential antichrists engaging in a truly godless ritual, defying both the family and the nation. From the perspective of an apocalyptic worldview, this image aligns enemies of the state with the enemies of the family: The threats to their futures merge. It depicts the antichrists' gay wedding par excellence.

This image and the apocalyptic scenarios with which it might intersect have both to do with anxieties about domestic policies and about foreign policies. Michael Cobb has called attention to precisely this "panic" over the "married gay terrorist" (borrowing a punch line from the Princeton

---

25. This image appeared on Political Humor, About.com; http://politicalhumor.about.com/library/images/blsaddamosamamarriage.htm. Accessed February 1, 2013. It may not be an original *World Weekly News* image; it did not appear in their archive and no one from the publication was willing to confirm it.

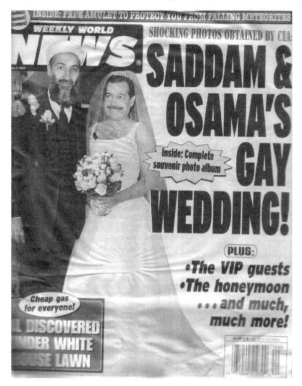

Figure 2. Tabloids tell of the marriage of two political enemies.

economist Paul Krugman's interview on the *Daily Show*) (Cobb 2006, 31–32). Cobb suggests that Krugman's joke urged contemplation of the "political effects of the unhappy marriage between religious rhetoric and national rhetoric" (32).

Lou Engle, a prayer warrior and evangelical leader, illustrated this very worry over the unhappy marriage of national threats when motivating a day of prayer and fasting in California on November 1, 2008. The day of prayer was to engage in spiritual warfare for Proposition 8, a state ballot measure asking voters to approve constitutional legislation against gay marriage. Engle is reported to have called pro-abortion, and pro–gay marriage legislation "antichristic legislation" (Posner 2008). The rally, available on Engle's God.TV, hosted speakers urging prayer against the spiritual enemy who lures the world into acceptance of new possibilities for marriage, gender roles, and women's reproductive health. The written call for the day of prayer adjures, *"This is not a time for hiding in caves. This is a time to resist mightily the spirit of peaceful coexistence and apathetic resignation in the face of this prevailing darkness."*[26] It is hard not to hear in this statement a reference to G. W. Bush's constant warning of "terrorists hiding in caves." Christians who do not defend heterosexual marriage are aligned with the nation's enemies, as well as with those seeking "peaceful coexistence," or, in Schmittian terms, liberal neutrality. Engle calls them to take a stand through spiritual and legal war (Posner 2008).

National rhetoric and religious rhetoric are more than married; the logic that grounds these rhetorics and the anxieties they produce is downright incestuous in that it comes from the same source: On both fronts the danger envisioned is to the future of the nation and to humanity, as well as to God's final kingdom. The antichrist and his followers (whether gay, or, as per Bush, Islamic radicals) are what block that future; they are portrayed as those who do not care about human life or the kingdom of God—indeed they are depicted as inhuman. Within this logic, they should be annihilated by constitutional amendment or by war; they should have no future. In an apocalyptically oriented religious worldview, the threat posed by the terrorist is ultimately the same as that posed by gay marriage: Both are a menace to the future of the nation and of humanity. It would appear that the fight against gay marriage and the fight against terror operate to protect the same set of apocalyptically oriented desires.

But what intrigues me, given the uniformity of apocalyptic desires, is the stark dissimilarity in the legal strategies used to pursue them on domestic and foreign fronts. On the domestic end, the tactic has been to fortify the law to ensure the nation's future. George W. Bush's proposed constitutional amendment prohibiting gay marriage precipitated a landslide of similar legal strategies on the state level.[27] By contrast, in war, and specifically with respect to torture in pursuing the war, the policy has been to undermine the law, by vetoing lawmaking at home and defying international law abroad. Why the explosion of legality in the proposed constitutional

26. Engle's account of the gathering is available from http://thecall.com/Groups/1000016919/TheCall/Gatherings/TheCall_California_Fall/TheCall_California_Fall.aspx.
27. For details, see Peterson 2004.

amendments about marriage when legality is eschewed in the more pressing issue of torture?

Perhaps not surprisingly, Bush's apocalyptically loaded speech of October 6, 2005, discussed above, in which he subtly compared Islamo-fascists to the antichrist (2005a), was given the day after the Senate voted in favor of an amendment to the Department of Defense Appropriations Act of 2006, which limited interrogation techniques (i.e., torture).[28] Bush's speech provided the religiophilosophical rhetoric for the administration's previously decided policy to counter any such amendments: A Statement of Administration Policy (2005), issued in response to the bill five days before the Senate's vote on torture, stated that the president should veto any attempt "to regulate the detention, treatment, or trial of terrorists captured in the war on terror." Practicality specified that such measures would "restrict the President's ability to conduct the war effectively under existing law" and would "restrict the President's authority to protect Americans effectively from terrorist attacks" (Statement of Administration Policy 2005). Given Bush's apocalyptic description of the war on terror, however, one wonders if such limitations on law have as much to do with the religiously framed descriptions of the in/humanity of the enemy as they have to do with practicality.

Of course, domestic law on torture is not the only social contract that the United States is prepared to disregard. Geneva Conventions' regulations on torture notwithstanding, the Bush administration was (in)famous for openly denying recognition of international legal bodies, including the International Criminal Court. *The National Security Strategy of the United States of America* states, "Americans are not impaired by the potential for investigations, inquiry, or prosecution by the International Criminal Court, whose jurisdiction does not extend to Americans and which we do not accept" (White House 2002, 31). The disregard of international law is perhaps more predictable, however, than the threat to veto any domestic U.S. law that would infringe on the progress of the war in Iraq. Why such trust in the power of law to regulate affairs within the United States and such dismissal of its ability to do so overseas? When U.S. officials insist on

---

28. See Babington and Murray 2005.

the importance of "the rule of law," why do they overlook exception to law? Certainly it is tempting to write off this dynamic as power-hungry cynicism, but I would like to suggest that there may be more at work—that it is precisely the apocalyptic determination of appropriate human desire that binds the proliferation of lawmaking at home to the refusal of law abroad.

Giorgio Agamben's ruminations on the limit between the human and the inhuman may be instructive in answering these questions. Agamben's work on power and politics—begun in *Homo Sacer: Sovereign Power and Bare Life* ([1995] 1998) and elaborated further in *State of Exception* ([2003] 2005)—seeks to interrogate the historical connections between what Foucault has distinguished as premodern and modern forms of power—that is, between authoritarian power and biopower. Agamben's discussion of the state of exception has been much referenced because, as he indicates, it provides a way of theorizing the operations of power in the present moment. Given Agamben's attention to exclusions within the operation of power, it is not surprising that queer theorists have been drawn to his work: for instance, Puar in her analysis of the events at Abu Ghraib and the war on terror (2007, 113, 116, 142–43) and Cobb in his analysis of the exclusion of queers from the symbolic order in the United States (2006, 33–35). When read alongside the apocalyptic logic I have been discussing, Agamben's genealogy of power explains the connection between the United States' differing approaches to law at home and abroad. Each enacts a form of exclusion that turns around the same apocalyptically determined distinction between human and inhuman orientation of desire.

Agamben explores a continuity between archaic and modern forms of power by looking at the way that the *excluded inclusion* of "bare life" is common to them both. He follows Aristotle to suggest that bare life is animal life that is not quite yet human. It is only through politics that bare life is sublated into the good life and the realm of the human. Only when biological life comes into the realm of language and law is it transformed into something that is no longer simply bare life; it becomes humanized as it enters into the realm of the political ([1995] 1998, 7–8). In becoming more than itself (i.e., in becoming humanized), bare life is effectively repudiated by, and excluded from, the political order. But, Agamben argues, bare life is also included in political life via exception to the law. In the ancient world, this happened through the sovereign's designation of the *homo sacer* (the sacred man), the person who could be killed with impunity, but not sacrificed. Through this exception to the usual laws of the land, bare life was exposed to death; it was left open and exposed to the will of the one making the exception (88–89). Analogously, Agamben argues, in the modern world the inclusion of bare life in the political realm comes about through the state of exception. For Agamben, the state of exception is a state of emergency that allows political leaders to suspend laws for their own purposes.[29]

Agamben's analysis shows that the state of exception makes use of the very thing that the political-juridical order eschews—that is, "bare life." In the state of exception, laws protecting some people's lives are suspended by the sovereign power ([1995] 1998, 83). Yet because it is life upon which power acts to assert itself as sovereign (101), bare life grounds the political (thereby also becoming human). Bare life is fodder for the political, the constituent outside to sovereignty. Indeed, Agamben suggests, politics is founded on this originary structure of inclusion and exclusion: "There is politics because humans are the living beings who, in language, separate and oppose themselves to their own bare life and, at the same time, maintain themselves in relation to that bare life in an inclusive exclusion" (8). What reappears in the state of exception is *bare life*, that is, biological life, that has been excluded from politics and the good life. Lee Spinks helpfully characterizes Agamben's notion of "bare life" as a limit marker for the human (2001, 26). In Agamben's terms, it is, "a threshold of indistinction and of passage between animal and man . . . precisely *neither man nor beast*" (105). Effectively, bare life is excluded as inhuman and included as human at the same time.

Read alongside the apocalyptic framework for desire made visible by the homosexual enemy as antichrist, Agamben's work explains perfectly the paradox I have been discussing, whereby law is increased at home and abandoned abroad. In order to establish U.S. sovereignty, bare life, or the in/human, is excluded from the social order at home while included abroad through exception to the law.

---

29. Agamben gives as an example Bush's November 13, 2001, order authorizing indefinite detention and military trial of noncitizens suspected of terrorism ([2003] 2005, 3–4).

Along these lines, let me posit, for a moment, raw sex as at least one aspect of bare life. By raw sex, I mean sexual expression of nonnormative desire. Raw sex is something like what Guy Hocquenghem calls (following the critique of Freud by Deleuze and Guattari), "polymorphously perverse non-human sex"—that is, sex that has not been brought into the realm of the human through the family relations of the Oedipus complex ([1972] 1993, 74–79). Raw sex is sexual expression understood simply through the desire and physicality of the moment rather than through some future goal, whether relating to the solidification of a monogamous relationship or the construction of a family. It is the opposite of heteronormative sex and of normative apocalyptically oriented desire. Let's call it Babylonian desire. In other words, it is the opposite of what the straight-queer theorist Calvin Thomas calls "justifiable," "teleologically narrativized sex: sex with a goal, a purpose, and a product [children]" (2000, 33). Raw sex is sexual expression that is not justifiable within this (apocalyptic) teleological narrative. In the United States, within the rhetoric of family values, raw sex is like bare life in that it is excluded from the social order. It is only included through the exception—as, for example, in orientalist art—or through discussions of the inhuman antichrist. Raw sex is considered inhuman, even demonic, the work of lawless, anarchic destroyers of institution. Within an apocalyptic framework, raw sex can move beyond the status of bare life only if it is brought into the "good life" of the polis—in other words, heterosexual family and nation. Sex becomes "human" only if it at least has the possibility of aiming at this particular eschatological goal. Indeed, in the homophobic imagination, any sex acts (including some imagined sexual practices) that do not fall into this trajectory are lumped together and become a site of fear and loathing. Yet—as Foucault has taught, as orientalist art illustrates, and as the industry build around "illegal" sexual activity demonstrates—the social order requires and even revels in the possibility of raw sex even as it tries to shut it down through fear or regulate it through law. Even as it is excluded, raw sex is included in the social order through exceptions to the law and the norms guiding law.

For conservative opponents of gay marriage, same-sex acts remain in the realm of raw sex, despite the arguments of those such as Andrew Sullivan who suggest that opening marriage up to include homosexuality is an incentive for gay monogamy and fidelity (1995, 107), thus bringing same-sex acts into the good life. For conservatives, same-sex unions remain raw sex precisely because the eschatology of the strong nation requires sex to produce children with mothers and fathers. Rights-based arguments about the economic disadvantages of being excluded from marriage (e.g., those of Human Rights Campaign)[30] are likewise dismissed because they disregard moral "truths" of heterosexuality and procreation. Oddly enough, conservative arguments against gay marriage do not worry about the threat to the heterosexual family that might come from the queer argument *against* marriage—predicting that gay marriage will stigmatize and regulate both the nonmonogamous sexual liberation achieved in the queer community and the alternate forms of family and relationship that have developed there.[31]

Offensive to the apocalyptic worldview, it seems, is the desire for the unattached pleasure made manifest in raw sex (or anything that is perceived to be raw sex): Such desire is not properly oriented to the future of the nation and of humanity. Perhaps any desire that is not circumscribed by these goals is a reminder of what Leo Bersani calls "a self-shattering and solipsistic *jouissance* that drives [people] apart" (1987, 222); such desire is in a way threateningly anticommunal. It also far more centered on pleasure than is comfortable for the national Protestant ethos. As Lee Edelman bitingly remarks, "The child of the two-parent family thus proves that its parents don't fuck and on its tiny shoulders it carries the burden of maintaining the fantasy of a time to come. . . . No fucking could ever effect such creation: all sensory experience, all pleasure of the flesh, must be borne away from this fantasy of futurity secured, eternity's plan fulfilled, as 'a new generation is carried forward'" (2004, 41). For those propounding heterosexual family values, fucking remains outside the future time of the good life. Not surprisingly, then, desire that does not conform to this eschatology is called unnatural and inhuman; it is the work of the antichrist. Law is seen as the avenue by which desire will be regulated and brought into conformity with the eschatology of the nation. National and state constitutional amendments flourish on this theology. In the United States, laws and proposed laws prohibiting gay marriage work hard to exclude at

30. See www.hrc.org/campaigns/marriage-center.
31. See Browning 1997; Butler 2004b; Ettelbrick 1997.

least one component of bare life—raw sex—and to bring that sex into the fold of the national future.

By way of stark contrast, the inclusion of bare life through the opposite approach to law overseas (i.e., contempt for it) is also necessary to ensure U.S. apocalyptic, nationalist, eschatology. In the state of exception, forever occasioned by the war on terror, domestic and international law is waived aside and torture is permitted. This fact—at issue in Guantánamo Bay and in the practice of rendering suspects to other countries where they are tortured—was made most visibly manifest in the sexualized abuse at Abu Ghraib prison. In the scenes of torture, in/human bare life and same-sex acts are somehow equated, a connection that is commensurate, as I have been arguing, with the future-oriented theology of the Bush II administration and its conservative bastion of support. Particularly shocking for a nation so aligned with heteronormativity was the fact that many of the photos used homophobia as a form of torture and dehumanization. Prisoners were piled naked, forced to simulate fellatio and to masturbate. Bare life looks, to the homophobic eye, much like the distorted and fearful-aggressive way it imagines raw sex (including its relation to the inhuman) to be.

Puar has shown that the media coverage of the Abu Ghraib scandal—both the photos and accompanying discourse—has followed the orientalist tradition of marking "the supposed Muslim terrorist . . . both as sexually conservative, modest and fearful of nudity . . . as well as queer, animalistic, barbarian, and unable to control his (or her) urges" (2007, 86). Puar points out the way in which the photos were glossed as doubly humiliating for the so-called sexually repressed cultures of Islam (further othering those tortured, and establishing a kind of U.S. sexual exceptionalism, wherein the United States is understood as a place that does not unhealthily repress sexuality). She makes the argument that those tortured become Agamben's *homo sacer*, both excluded from and fully integral to U.S. sovereignty (113) in ways that "redirect the devitalizing incident of torture toward a population targeted for death into revitalizing life-optimizing even for the American citizenry for whom it purports to securitize" (81).

Put another way, torture has become a policy that safeguards the eschatology of the United States, holding out the promise of safety (presumably to procreate) for its citizens. Maintenance of this eschatology requires the creation and pain of the in/human. Clearly, those tortured were considered what Agamben would call bare life: They could be killed with impunity (as some detainees were). They were seen as inhuman and treated accordingly. That the inclusion of bare life is a matter of policy became clear in reports following the release of the Abu Ghraib photos that showed that it was a higher command that ordered prisoners to be treated like animals (Blasberg and Blasberg 2005; Hersh 2004; Karpinski 2005, 210). Janis Karpinski, now demoted commanding Brigadier General of Abu Ghraib, recalls her superior, Major General Geoffrey Miller, telling soldiers "to treat these prisoners like dogs. . . . If they ever get the idea that they're anything more than dogs, you've lost control of your interrogation" (2005, 197–98). Yet such inhuman treatment is predicated precisely on detainees' humanity, their ability to talk, to inform, to be in human pain, to be humiliated. Though treated as inhuman, their humanity is necessary to the process. According to the Statement of Administration Policy (advocating that the president veto any regulations on "interrogation") allowing such treatment grounds the president's authority and, therefore, U.S. sovereignty.

Moreover, within the state of exception, U.S. soldiers' sadistic desire for these sexualized atrocities is permitted precisely because it still accedes to the (eschatological) goal of establishing U.S. superiority. As in the more "humorous" orientalist representations of the colonized person as gay or gender queer, here too desire is made safe because the seductive in/human object of desire can be aggressed at the same time as desire is enacted. One would think that conservative Christians would have condemned soldiers' deviance from the paradisic trajectory laid out for sexual relations in the national eschatology, that this would be considered a serious moral failure. But, as reported by *Christianity Today*, conservative Christian groups placed the blame for such acts on *other* purveyors of misguided desire: pornography, MTV, relativism, and, predictably, homosexuality (Olsen 2004). Indeed, Robert Knight, the director of the Culture and Family Institute (affiliated with the Family Research Council), proposed that U.S. Christians work to restore moral order by, among other things, trying to ban homosexuality in the military and by "strengthening state and federal marriage laws and ceasing the creation of civil unions and domestic partnerships" (R. Knight 2004). Thus the blame for the sadistic actions of the

U.S. soldiers at Abu Ghraib is laid, at least partially, at the feet of gay marriage. Further, Gary Bauer, president of Values, a nonprofit group for "life, marriage, family, faith, and freedom," suggests that enemy prisoners have no right to complain since they are "murderers and thugs," as are the enemies of the United States throughout the Muslim world (Bauer 2004). His language seems to mimic Bush's description of the enemy/antichrist as cold-blooded. According to this logic, if inhumanity at home meets inhumanity abroad, why should the latter complain?

Rana's discussion of the racialized, sexualized Muslim migrant worker suggests that bare life is also similarly created within the borders of the United States. If the discourse of the demonized gay enemy establishes law and sovereignty through procreating futures for good citizens and exception to law away from U.S. soil, the same dynamic also operates within the United States in the detention and policing of migrants. The fear of deceptive "sleeper cells" at work in creating fear of Muslim migrants (2011, 71–72, 81–85) may be compounded by an overlaid fear of spiritualized deception by the Muslim association with the antichrist. These fears lead to detention, mistreatment, and deportation. For Rana, "carceral violence is the state of exception that defines the U.S. nation-state" (164). He points to a 2003 U.S. Department of Justice report detailing the violence experienced by detainees in the wave of arrests after 9/11. The violence enacted on migrants is an attempt to regain sovereignty in the face of transnational migration. Sovereignty works through the uneven application of law: Laws are enforced for migrants (who may have been detained for breaking some law) at the same time as extralegal violence is permissible for guards to enact on detainees (Rana 2011, 163–66).

Law, Heteronormative Desire, Humanity

The writing and suspension of laws acts on bare life, that limit marker between the human and the inhuman. So much is clear from Agamben's work. But what the homosexualized antichrist as enemy makes visible is that a central determining factor in the limit between human and inhuman is the apocalyptic orientation of desire. Law or lack of law is about the regulation of desire, so that it conforms with the temporal ordering associated with U.S. determinations of the eschatological roles.[32] The move toward constitutional amendments for marriage assumes that law can reform, convert, or "heal" the bare life/raw sex of citizens (U.S. bare life); it can be brought into the potential of furthering humanity (and, of course, the nation). The suspension of law in the state of exception assumes that captured bare life (Middle Eastern bare life), bent on the sexually perverse end of destroying humanity, cannot be redeemed through law. The space outside the law is called Babylon. There, perverse desire is permitted and, indeed, enforced. In contrast, the U.S. state of exception must write and enforce heteronormative laws for its own population in order to define humanity.

The image of the homosexualized antichristic enemy is emblematic of the apocalyptic negotiations inherent in U.S. regulation of desire for the purposes of U.S. sovereignty. The logic that produces the homosexualized enemy as antichrist is the same logic that is central to the delimitation of the in/human, which enables the imperial project and the dehumanizing techniques that it requires. Within the graduated sovereignty of the nation (Ong 2006), laws protect the "human," composed of those who correctly desire integration into family, nation, and Christian secular humanity. Raw sex—or what is perceived as raw sex—is banished by law. Exceptions to law are made for those who are outside of this eschatological trajectory and who therefore must be associated with the hated (yet desired) raw sex.

The deceptive presence of the antichrist within—via raw sex—troubles the United States' suitability to protect heteronormative sex, and with it the family, the nation, humanity, and the very concept of the human. Of course, this is precisely why efforts are so strong to ban gay marriage: The protection of the future of humanity—U.S. hegemony—is at stake. This danger is what makes the figure of the antichrist so powerful. He cannot simply be recuperated as another point of identity; his deceptiveness threatens every identity. There is no telling who might be the antichrist, and whether or not there might be more than one. The antichrist could be anyone (even someone married). The double and separate identification of the antichrist—as political enemy and as gay—suggests that the political

---

32. See Castelli 2005 for an important analysis of the way in which U.S. foreign policy concerns itself with (other people's) practices of torture when it is understood as persecution for religious beliefs (where "religion" is closely associated with Christianity).

enemy might not be outside the nation at all, might not even wield weapons, but might simply desire wild, nonheteronormative, nonteleological sex. Indeed, the very capitalist mechanisms that the United States strives to protect alongside humanity depend on raw sex. Isn't everything sold through appeal to wildly promiscuous desire, even as the selling forecloses on desire and attaches it to telos?

In the next chapter I argue that uncertainty as to the locus of antichristic desires (domestic or foreign) works against the claims of empire. Although the racialized, homosexualized antichrist is essential to the production of the U.S. mission to save marriage and humanity, the inhuman antichrist within the nation troubles the straightforward assessment of the United States' relation to being, having, and saving universal humanity. Babylon crumbles from within.

Babelian Scripture: A Queerly Sublime Ethics of Reading

As witnessed in the preceding chapters, Babylon is particularly suited to the literalist-allegorical condensations of the problems of national sovereignty and transnational global capital because it can alternately condemn threats to sovereignty as threats *to* unity or as threats *of* a hostile unity. While cultivating the subject of interest, Babylonian fantasies seek to curb the political, economic, or ethnic "excess" produced in globalization by calling it moral failing (at home) and demanding pious, heteronormative, and patriarchal virtue as a corrective; or worse, calling it demonic (abroad) and violently punishing it. In these dynamics, a theodemocratic, anti-egalitarian complex consolidates around a political decisionism that is supported with reference and allusion to Babylon/Babel. Political and juridical authority is viewed in hierarchical terms that are supported by racialized norms of gender, sexuality, and reproduction, and authorized by transcendence. What motivates these dynamics and makes them effective is not so much the (composite) biblical figure itself but the cosmic "truths" by which it is allegorically understood. The notion of an animate evil, connected with a perverse sexuality, is particularly effective in generating defensive responses.

What I would like to offer in this final chapter is a different mode of reading the Babel/Babylon symbol and its queer cast of associated characters (the antichrist and the Whore), one that keeps at its center the ungovernable, queer, sublime impossibility of knowing truth, or evil. I do not want to repeat interpretations that mimic and secure the violent and hierarchizing dynamics of sovereignty and allegory or the horizontal, spreading dynamics of globalized markets and mobile diversity. Rather, I wish to halt these expansive and expanding interpretive moves by becoming attuned to *a queer opacity—that is, the sublime, liminal, undecidability of alterity—in the production of what is taken as transcendent.*

Such interpretive obstruction is signaled by the Babel story itself in Genesis 11. Of the people's univocality, God says, "If this is what they start to do, all that they plan to do will not be impossible for them" (Gn 11:6). To counteract infinite human potential, God creates multiple languages so that the one consolidated meaning to which the people aspire—"we will make for ourselves a name" (v. 4)—becomes impossible. Languages proliferate, perhaps ironically creating more avenues for possibility and creativity, but difference confounds complete signification and mutual understanding. The story can be read as placing value on impossibility, the preservation of a space of undecidability. (The reader cannot even know whether the deity is benevolent or malevolent in intention, a trickster or a pouter.) At the same time, the mythic worldview imagines humans as initially connected, if eventually sundered; there is some liminal connection retained by the very structure of the story, if impossible to fully bridge. It is these two aspects of impossible signification and liminal connection that I wish to pursue here.

The ambiguity in the narrative suggests an ethics of reading that is diametrically opposed to the norm of literalized allegory that governs the production of Babylon as theopolitical figure. Allegorical readings, with their presumption of fixed essences and rigid distinctions, are disrupted from the start. If all fixed and final meaning becomes impossible for humans, what can be said about the larger "immutable" truths of religion or about identifying the enemy on whom politics are decided? A Babelian approach to scripture takes as its starting point an always already uncertainty about knowing transcendent truths. I would like to demonstrate this approach by troubling certainty about evil and therefore about the decisions that can be made on the basis of discerning it. Reading for difference and liminality, I show the antichrist and the Whore of Babylon as perverse destabilizing figures that queerly share mythic lineages with what is taken as "truth." Their mythological derivations (Canaanite and Roman) connect them to the Christ figure. Like bare life, and like raw sex (chapter 5), Babylon, the antichrist, and the Whore are included and excluded in the political and religious symbolic order. They are liminal figures, although their inclusion is not recognized, only their exclusion as wholly other, so that those who are identified with them are physically threatened, tortured, and killed. In theoretical terms, the liminal alterity of these figures might be read as the sublime—that thing that is too big for reason to comprehend, producing pain and pleasure in the encounter. The sublime operates through a certain opacity; it makes one aware of the unknown without offering final meanings.

In this work, I hope to show the instability of the foundations on which decisions are made to fight evil and to imagine another way to confront the fear of difference. The argument progresses in stages. I first indicate how I understand the sublime, before moving into an extended discussion of the rereading of the sublime by the postcolonial feminist philosopher and literary critic Gayatri Chakravorty Spivak. I turn then to the writing of the African American artist Charles Gaines on metonymy and the sublime, which will help fill out what all of this means in terms of reading practice. Gaines says that the feeling of the sublime is actually one of social connection, one that can be provoked by metonymy. With metonymy in mind, then, I read the perversity of the antichrist and the Whore of Babylon in their queer relation to Christ, drawing on the work of other biblical scholars before me. The queerness of this reading is glossed through Lee Edelman's diagnosis of queerness as the death drive of the future-oriented social order and through Tim Dean's insistence on nonidentitarian connectivity (Caserio et al. 2006). A queerly sublime ethics of reading tries to disrupt the (sexually) orthodox futurity of a national superiority by observing the disavowed connection between opposing spiritual and political forces.

My method of reading is entirely influenced by what Spivak calls *detran-cendentalizing radical alterity*, and by what she calls the *impossible and singular ethical task of listening to the other*, both of which she relates, in places, to the sublime. The details of Spivak's reading of the sublime will take some time to develop, but it is important to note at the outset that Spivak advocates a turn to the literary and the aesthetic in a critique of transcendent grounds for certainty. In looking at religion, she does not want to think about tran-scendent truths (higher powers, moral wills) as much as about the possibili-ties that religious metaphors open up for the ethical interruption of (theo) political calculation. Spivak therefore argues for "a world where religion can shrink to [the] mundane normality" of "the weave of permissible narra-tives." In this world, religion would be understood as "idiom rather than ground of belief" (2004, 105, 111). Spivak's insistence on detranscendental-izing is helpful in thinking not only about how to disrupt political decision-ism, including its dependence on a particular conception of evil and the hierarchies it installs (see chapter 2), but also about how to build an alter-nate form of scriptural ethics. The move to the literary is instructive for disrupting the transcendental truths that are known through the literary text of the Bible; it shifts us away from biblical texts as signifiers of cosmic allegory to the sole auspices of biblical text as literature.[1] Reading this way, I seek to trace the systems of representation that produce the truth of evil, reading this production through the concept of the disruptive, queer sublime—the place of impossible, undecidable, liminal connection. But first, a much longer discussion of the sublime, and Spivak's theorization of it, is necessary.

Reading for the Sublime

Immanuel Kant famously described the sublime as the scary yet exhilarat-ing response to reason's inability to apprehend the vastness of nature or

---

1. This argument joins, from another direction, other feminist scholars of religion in trying to think beyond the power relations that are inscribed through transcendence, see Schüssler Fiorenza 2007; Pritchard 2006. For theological critiques of transcendence in the realm of the political, see Robbins 2011; Crockett 2011.

anything "absolutely great" ([1790] 2000, §27). As Kant describes it, the sublime feeling occurs when reason confronts a sublime object that suggests magnitude beyond comprehension. Such a moment causes pain in the inability to understand rationally and pleasure in the awareness of a supersensible order, that is, the idea that there is some higher purpose for reason to grasp (§27). The sublime pushes reason beyond itself. Because the sublime is said to be born in an encounter with the incomprehensible and the supersensible, it is a concept that has appealed to those (philosophers, theologians, and literary critics) wrestling with the relation of the divine, or simply of meaning, to the rational subject.[2]

Before becoming too enamored of the sublime, however, it is important to be aware, as the feminist theorist Barbara Claire Freeman has argued, that the traditional Kantian discourse of the sublime is a discourse of mastery, which justifies hierarchies of domination, including patriarchy and sexism.[3] As she puts it, "the central moment of the sublime marks the self's newly enhanced sense of identity; a will to power drives its style, a mode that establishes and maintains the self's domination over its objects of rapture" (Freeman 1995, 3). Reason confronts that which is too great to comprehend and masters it: the "[masculine, patriarchal] subject . . . maintains its borders by subordinating difference and by appropriating rather than identifying with that which presents itself as other" (4). Joanna Zylinska further elaborates the dominating function of Kant's sublime, pointing to

2. Although I do not undertake a full review of the extensive philosophical discussion of the sublime here, see work by the following. See Crockett 2001, 2007 for detailed discussion of Kant's sublime, its philosophical afterlives, and their relation to theology. See Battersby 2007 for a critical intellectual history, from the ancient Greek text on rhetoric by Longinus through discussions by Edmund Burke and Immanuel Kant on aesthetics; Friedrich Nietzsche and Jean-François Lyotard on being and subjectivity; and Hannah Arendt and Jacques Derrida on language and the political. Lyotard's reading of Kant ([1991] 1994) has been particularly groundbreaking in reinterpreting the sublime as the struggle with reason to represent the unrepresentable. For readings of the sublime that understand it as a mode of dealing with unrepresentable collective trauma, as for instance in slavery, or homophobic violence, see Gilroy 1993, Grindstaff 2008.

3. A number of feminist writers, writing at about the same time as Spivak, have looked at the way women are excluded from Burke's and Kant's accounts of the sublime, see Freeman 1995; Zylinska 2001; and Battersby 2007. Battersby extends the analysis of the exclusions made in the name of the sublime to racialization.

a passage in Kant's *Critique of Judgment* that is uncannily similar to the conservative discourses discussed in chapters 1 and 2. Kant writes,

> War . . . has something sublime about it, and gives nations . . . a stamp of mind only the more sublime the more numerous the dangers to which they are exposed. . . . On the other hand, a prolonged peace favours the predominance of a mere commercial spirit, and with it a debasing self-interest, cowardice and effeminacy. (1790, §28, quoted in Zylinska 2001, 22)

In this version of the Kantian story, the nation confronts the sublime object—the incomprehensible, dangerous enemy or battle—and produces a feeling of sublimity in mastering it. In the contemporary moment, we might call it sublime decisionism. The sublime feeling proves that decision makers are masculine and moral, over and against those characterized by effeminacy, commercialism, and self-interest.

The feminist and poststructural response to this narrative has been to delve into and appreciate the difference and excess of the sublime object. Along these lines, the literary critic George Hartley helpfully glosses the sublime as the abyss of representation. Reading Kant, he writes, "It is through the breakdown in representation, the point at which our representative faculties are confronted with their immanent limit, that the realm of the supersensible is opened up as the beyond of representation itself" (2003, 35). Hartley suggests that the supersensible "beyond of representation" is not transcendent, but "an inversion internal to appearance itself" (14).[4] In other words, the "beyond" is only "the limit internal to representation itself" (3), or, "the space of incommensurability . . . opened up between the figure and the concept . . . [without which] representation could not operate at all" (4). It is this liminal connection and incommensurability between knowing and not knowing, between otherness and transcendence that I wish to explore here.

Spivak implies that otherness, or radical alterity, provokes the feeling of overwhelming immensity and incomprehensibility that is known as the sublime. As I will show in more detail presently, in Spivak's critique of U.S. policy following 9/11, radical alterity stands in the same structural place as

---

4. Hartley draws on Marxist critics such as Fredric Jameson, Slavoj Žižek, and Spivak, who are all clearly influenced in some way by Lyotard.

the sublime object, pushing political calculation ("reason") into action. Because radical alterity is frequently understood as transcendence (good or evil), sometimes political calculation becomes theopolitical calculation. Spivak suggests that the challenge is to greet difference as a sublime, impossible, site for listening and negotiation rather than as a site of domination or regulation. Spivak shows, via destranscendentalizing, that the feeling of the sublime—evoked by alterity—is produced by systems of representation that are difficult to trace. Spivak's work thus provides an alternate way to approach the religious narratives that are used to master difference.

Detranscendentalizing the Sublime

Spivak brings together ideas of radical alterity, detranscendentalizing, the sublime, and listening to the other, in the published version of a talk called "Terror" given at Columbia University not long after 9/11. As is characteristic of Spivak's highly erudite writing, the theoretical connectors between these concepts are not made explicit; they require a certain degree of exegetical work, which will touch on other of her theoretical terms related to the working of the sublime: "effects of grace," "subreptive metalepsis," "ethical singularity," "permanent parabasis," and "invagination." Although it takes some unpacking, this theoretical constellation provides a rich resource for thinking beyond the theopolitical.

Let me begin with the sublime. As Spivak tells it in the essay "Terror," for Kant, the sublime "names a structure: the thing is too big for me to grasp; I am scared; Reason kicks in by the mind's immune system and shows me, by implication, that the big thing is mindless" (2004, 94). Elsewhere she shows, through a careful reading of Kant, how the sublime is a lack that reason supplements via assertions of God and morality. The concept of God "is what fills the abyss of fearful infinity with sublime denomination"; further, "God . . . must be presupposed to assert the law of our moral being" (1999, 23). A notion of God stands in the same place as the sublime as a grounding for morality. In "Terror" she suggests that political acts, such as the attack on the World Trade Center on 9/11 might *seem* sublime—too big to understand—and likewise provoke a political response, *as if* it were morality.

But she wants to read the sublime and religion very differently; she also wants to interrupt the kinds of political calculations that 9/11 produced, pitched as if they were moral obligations to the world. The problem of political calculation, she says, is in its dependence on epistemology, in "attempt[ing] to construct the other as object of knowledge . . . in order to punish or acquit rationally" (2004, 83). (In this description she names in another way the retributive structure discussed in chapter 4; revenge is a form of political calculation.) In her view, the ethical—that is the task of "listen[ing] to the other as if it were a self"—interrupts the certainties on which political calculation rests (as for instance we have seen in decision-ism). How, she asks—although not very directly—can secularism produce ethical action, or something close to morality, without being emptied of meaning by a system of political calculation?

In order to thus conceptualize a role for religion that does not justify political calculation, Spivak reframes the transcendent—and the sublime object—as radical alterity and then proceeds to detranscendentalize it. She writes, "Radical alterity, an otherness that reason needs but which reason cannot grasp, can be given many names. *God* in many languages is its most recognizable name" (2004, 102). Kant, she notes, gave it the name of *the transcendental*. In referring both to the transcendent and the transcendental, Spivak plays with a slippage in the way that radical alterity is sometimes understood as an omniscient power outside of knowledge—the transcendent—and sometimes as the condition of possibility for knowledge—the transcendental.[5] It also becomes evident that she is thinking about how human difference is sometimes pitched as radical alterity. In terms of this chapter, I will be arguing that evil is another name given to radical alterity. As shown in chapter 5, one does not have to look very deeply into U.S. political debates to find transcendent conceptions of evil thrown about, especially in the war on terror.[6]

5. Spivak moves away from understanding the transcendent(al)—i.e., radical alterity—as a kind of self-contained goodness that acts as an independent a priori; it is not a *causeless cause*, but something produced in social and cultural systems of signification (2004, 110n43).

6. To give another example, John McCain spoke in his 2008 presidential campaign of "the transcendental challenge of the century of radical Islamic terrorism . . . [in] the long twilight struggle against the greatest force of evil this country has ever seen." This speech, no longer available, was quoted in Gail Ober, "Supporters Greet McCain in Laconia," *Citizen of Laconia*,

For her project of detranscendentalizing, Spivak turns to a dense and compact deconstructive reading of Kant's *Religion within the Boundaries of Mere Reason* (Kant [1793] 1998). Spivak explains that, for Kant, religion is understood as that which supplements a moral lack in the realm of reason (Spivak 2004, 109). In Kant's terms, "Reason, conscious of its impotence to satisfy its moral needs, extends itself to extravagant ideas which might make up for this lack" ([1793] 1998, 72). Pure reason requires some help from elsewhere to produce moral capacity—hence, religion. One might expect, perhaps, that such help would come from transcendental intuitions, but instead it requires what Kant calls "effects of grace." As Spivak notes, the "effects of grace" are one of four secondary elements of religion within the bounds of pure reason—the others being miracles, mysteries, and means of grace (Spivak 2004, 102, 108–9; Kant [1793] 1998, 72).[7] In Kant's words, "These are, as it were, *parerga* [secondary elements] to religion within the boundaries of pure reason; they do not belong within it yet border on it" (72). He further explains that effects of grace, like the other parerga, are not available to cognition and so cannot be theoretically useful, but grace may be made available to the will from outside, although incomprehensible (73). Grace can help "make up for [reason's] moral impotence" (72).[8]

Like the sublime, grace appears to provoke the rational and moral will, as well as religious belief. Structurally, therefore, grace is homologous with the sublime. Both push reason beyond itself.

In the spirit of detranscendentalizing, however, Spivak suggests that what Kant calls the possibility of the invisible effect of the transcendent on the moral will ([1793] 1998, 184) can be understood in the realm of the aesthetic and the literary. To this end, Spivak seizes on the phrase "effects of grace"

January 2, 2008, http://www.citizen.com/apps/pbcs.dll/article?AID=/20080102/GJNEWS02/191050247/-1/CITNEWS0806 (accessed June 23, 2008). For a humorous take on McCain's use of the term "transcendental," with its slip between the epistemological and the theological, see *The Colbert Report*, June 18, 2008.

7. For Kant's other remarks on these parerga, see (1793) 1998, 98–102, 140–47, 182–91.

8. In his fourth general remark on the parerga to religion within the bounds of reason, Kant admits that accepting the idea of transcendent influence on morality is risky business, but he says it cannot be proven one way or the other and cannot be discounted. Some of these parerga, like belief in miracles, he finds unusable for "moral religion" (religion within the bounds of reason) ([1793] 1998, 101), whereas others, such as "effects of grace," he accepts as possibly necessary to supplement the moral will.

and reinterprets its function as parergon.[9] She hangs on to radical alterity of grace but also detranscendentalizes it. She suggests that the word *effect* implies causality and therefore points away from the theological and toward the secular and the aesthetic—understood, in this case, as the literary. If "effect" is moved into the aesthetic, or literary, then "grace," or radical alterity, must also be understood as related to that realm. Reason requires alterity for decision making and morality but cannot grasp it; reason requires effects of grace from alterity to induce moral action (rather than political calculation) but cannot apprehend grace through cognition or predict its effects. At the same time, if alterity is a space within signification, as alterity, it is a place of impossibility. It is something like the constitutive outside to rational possibility within discourse.

Grace, radical alterity, and the sublime, then, are no longer the transcendent(al) causeless causes of religion; they are more like an incalculable semantic possibility opened up by the aesthetic. Religion becomes the aesthetic. Grace becomes an "unverifiable effect of an effect." If *effect* is taken as something to do with aesthetics, it immediately disrupts calculation. Because Spivak calls the realm of the aesthetic (again following Kant) "purposiveness without purpose," it is not goal oriented; it is not calculative (2004, 109–9). Although the aesthetic will have an effect, it is not one that can be computed in advance.[10]

9. A footnote divulges that Spivak is engaging with Jacques Derrida's reading of Kant's *Religion within the Boundaries of Mere Reason*, which talks about, among other things, the dangers of misrecognizing Kant's parerga as religious knowledge or religious experience that can found a moral program. But she also clearly has in mind Derrida's earlier essay, "The Parergon," in which he analyzes Kant's discussion of parerga with respect to aesthetics. There he shows how difficult it is, in analyzing artworks, to separate out parerga—secondary or framing elements—from primary elements, as for instance, in his example of "the drapery on statues which simultaneously adorns and veils their nudity . . . clinging to the work's edges . . . but not a part of the representative whole." Along these lines, Spivak implies that detranscendentalization points to the bordering function for radical alterity as neither fully internal nor fully external to the system of reason, or the secular. See Derrida (1996) 2002, 48–53; (1978) 1979, 22; Spivak 2004, 108.

10. Spivak explicates her views on the aesthetic using Kant's description of beauty, "purposiveness without purpose." She indicates, without fully explicating, the connection Kant makes between beauty and morality. Her argument implies that aesthetic judgment can help with morality (or, for Spivak, the ethical) in a way that is not calculative. It seems as if she may concur with Henry E. Allison's *Kant's Theory of Taste: A Reading of the "Critique of Aesthetic Judgment"* (Allison 2001, 219–35), in which encounters with beauty and judgments of

Metalepsis and the Sublime

Grace and the sublime are akin to the figure of speech, metalepsis, Spivak suggests, moving the argument further into the realm of the aesthetic (2004, 108). In metalepsis, a chain of cause and effect works without being readily visible, as one metonym is substituted for another. In her earlier work, *A Critique of Postcolonial Reason*, she says that metalepsis works through *subreption*, defined by the *Oxford English Dictionary* as "a suppression of truth to obtain an indulgence" (1999, 11, 23).[11] Spivak may have the narratological sense of metalepsis in mind, so that an unmarked transition between narrative levels takes place so that a narrator's creation of a narrative effect goes unnoticed.[12] She also refers to Paul de Man, who in *Allegories of Reading*, suggests that allegory, like metaphor, uses literary mechanisms to assert what appear to be self-evident truths, "by means of a more or less hidden system of relays which allows the properties [referenced in the work] to enter into substitutions, exchanges, and crossings that appear to reconcile the incompatibilities of the inner with the outer world" (De Man 1979,

---

taste are *preparations* for morality as well as symbols of it. In this, Spivak is destabilizing the classical distinction between beauty and the sublime.

11. Spivak is also clearly drawing on Kant, who, in *Critique of Judgment*, says, "The feeling of sublime in nature is respect for our own vocation, which we show to an object in nature through a certain subreption (substitution of respect for the object instead of for the idea of humanity in our subject), which as it were makes intuitable the superiority of the rational vocation of our cognitive faculty over the greatest faculty of our sensibility" ([1790], 2000, §27). Lyotard glosses this as "subreption consists . . . in obtaining or in extracting a quasi presentation of the object, which is not presentable, in the presence of a magnitude of a natural force that is 'formless'" ([1991] 1994, 70).

12. See Gérard Genette: "Any intrusion by the extradiegetic narrator or narratee into the diegetic universe . . . or the inverse . . . produces an effect of strangeness that is either comical . . . or fantastic" ([1972] 1980, 234–35). He calls this transgressive "narrative metalepsis" and says it is related to the "narrative figure the classics called *author's metalepsis*, which consists of pretending that the poet 'himself brings about the effects he celebrates'" (235, 234, quoting Pierre Fontanier). As Genette puts it, these kinds of narrative conceits reveal "a shifting but sacred frontier between two worlds, the world in which one tells, the world of which one tells." Recognition of metalepsis is destabilizing because it presents "this unacceptable and insistent hypothesis, that the extradiegetic is perhaps always diegetic, and the narrator and his narratees—you and I—perhaps belong to some narrative" (136). Reading theological narratives as metalepsis destabilizes the boundary between material and spiritual.

60).[13] Metaphors and allegories work through such exchanges, even when they appear to make self-evident claims. In this same vein for Spivak, grace, or radical alterity, looks like the work of the transcendent but is the result of a hidden chain of cause and effect. When one encounters something called transcendent, the trick is to look for the connections that have been subreptively suppressed.

When Spivak speaks of subpretive metalepsis in *Critique of Postcolonial Reason*, however, she is not speaking of grace, as she does in the essay "Terror"—she is speaking of the sublime. Like grace, like religion, like the concept of God, the sublime is not transcendent(al); it is produced in an occluded series of relays. What is at the end of this chain of cause and effect? Hidden in Kant's description of the sublime, Spivak argues, is an imperial logic about the subhumanity of colonized peoples. In other words, the parergon to the sublime, itself a parergon to reason, is the colonized person (1999, 34). To gloss Spivak a little, it is not nature but rather an encounter with alterity that provokes the sense of lack that has to be filled with the feeling of the sublime and reason's "response" to it. She says that the sublime "is an imaginative exercise in experiencing the impossible—stepping into the *space of the other*—without which political solutions come drearily undone into the continuation of violence" (2004, 94, emphasis mine). Reading other passages from Spivak's *Critique*, Hartley argues that "the sublime object for Spivak is the possibility of a speaking subaltern" (2003, 235–43). The sublime is precisely the abyss of social, geopolitical alterity that reason sutures over. Spivak contrasts this approach to the sublime with an approach that would equate the violent events of 9/11 with the sublime and seek to master them via political calculation (2004, 94, 95–96). Instead, she wants to listen to the sublime voice of the other (radical alterity), as impossible as this may be.

Spivak brilliantly uncovers the series of significations at work in the very conceptualization of the sublime. She shows how Kant suggests that the moral will projects the feeling of the sublime onto the experience of incomprehensibility, but only for cultured persons; the "uncultured" "raw man" feels only terror. In Kant's words, "Without the development of moral ideas, that which we, prepared by culture, call the sublime presents itself to man in

---

13. De Man traces the way that metaphors in literary and philosophical texts (Proust, Rousseau, and Nietzsche) make epistemological and ontological claims.

the raw merely as terrible" (1790, §29, quoted in Spivak 1999, 12–13).[14] She notes that when colonized peoples are specifically named in Kant's text ("the New Hollanders or the inhabitants of Tierra del Fuego"), they are considered neither fully human nor fully natural and not even worthy of existence in Kant's mind (1790, §67, quoted in Spivak 1999, 26). They are therefore not even eligible for morality or the feeling of the sublime—or even the production of the sublime. In other words, in this view, the ability to feel sublimity requires "civilized" morality already to be in place. For Kant, as it turns out, the sublime does not actually produce that morality as if from the outside (i.e., kickstarting reason) but, rather, is produced by it. But this liminal exclusion of the "raw man" also shows that the concept of the sublime requires alterity. In order to be recognized as the prerogative of the civilized, the very notion of the sublime requires a set of "uncultured" persons who cannot access it. Thus colonized peoples, depicted as lacking full humanity, still stand as effects of grace, radically othered by the system, but pushing it to function.[15] The liminal alterity of the colonized subject is altogether excluded in the account of the sublime but is actually at work in its production.

Imagining sublime feeling not as something provoked by nature but by an occluded, and therefore impossible, alterity turns Kant's imperial logic on its head: Those who have benefited from colonization are the impoverished ones, since we have difficulty in feeling the sublime in response to radical alterity—we feel only terror when confronted with difference. We tend to call it evil.

Impossible Listening

Notably, when Spivak speaks of the sublime in her essay "Terror," she speaks of it terms of the project of attempting to hear the other. If the sublime is

14. Battersby notes the orientalism in this same section of Kant's *Critique* (2007, 32, 60). Kant compares the feeling of the sublime to the feeling felt by "Eastern voluptuaries . . . when they get their bodies as it were kneaded and all their muscles and joints softly pressed" ([1790] 2000, §29), but the difference from the actual sublime, for Kant, is that there is no connection to reason and so there is no edification.

15. For an extended discussion of Kant's orientalism in relation to the sublime, see Battersby 2007, 68–98.

an impossible to comprehend otherness within signification, encountering it involves listening. Spivak develops this idea in the essay only tangentially, however, through her discussion of religion as aesthetic. It may be helpful, therefore, to connect the project of detranscendentalized alterity in the "Terror" essay to the discussions of listening, ethics, religion, and radical alterity elsewhere in Spivak's writing.

Spivak advocates, in several places, for the impossible experience of ethical singularity, which is an impossible listening. Ethical singularity is the communication between two people, in which "slow attentive mind changing (on both sides)" can take place—it is produced in acts of true exchange (not charity), and with the recognition that even in this exchange something is always lost in the attempt at communication (1995, xxv, 201; 1999, 173, 383–84, 427). It is the recognition that, in any dialogue with the other, something does not get through; thus it can never ground an ongoing program of ethics—it is an impossible single encounter. It is the impossible sublime experience of imaginatively "stepping into the space of the other." Along these lines, Spivak "understand[s] the ethical . . . to be an interruption of the epistemological, which is the attempt to construct the other as object of knowledge" (2004, 83).

Ethical singularity is the famous way in which Spivak envisions love, which is precisely the detranscendentalized disruption of an epistemological "knowing" of the other. If the sublime object is radical alterity, the sublime feeling comes through attempted listening. Taking her example from one of Mahasweta Devi's stories, Spivak draws the conclusion that "we must learn 'love' (a simple name for ethical responsibility-in-singularity) . . . in view of the impossibility of communication. No individual transcendence theology . . . can bring us to this" (1995, 200). As Dawn Rae Davis glosses it in her essay on ethical singularity, "From this perspective, love is the impossible experience of knowing across radical difference, and simultaneously, that which requires ethical choice and action even in the face of the impossible" (2002, 146). Davis calls this sort of love a "not knowing" (152–57). Such impossible love interrupts colonial power relations predicated on knowing the other. Not knowing also disrupts the theological certainties through which calculations and decisions about the enemy are made. It is an impossible rapprochement.

How then does one listen to the other—who is sometimes figured as transcendent—through religion-as-aesthetic? How can this listening act as a sublime unbidden effect of grace? Again I turn to Spivak on the religious-as-literary. In her essay "Moving Devi" (on the Hindu goddess Mahadevi), Spivak theorizes the relation of radical alterity to the religious, using the literary term *permanent parabasis*, a phrase she borrows from Paul de Man, which refers to the persistent interruption in Greek comedy, whereby the chorus appears to comment on something apparently unrelated (Spivak 2001, 124–27). In deconstructive terms, she describes permanent parabasis as "invagination," a term she takes from Derrida. Invagination is "a participation without belonging—a taking part in without being part of. . . . The boundary of the set comes to form, by invagination, an internal pocket larger than the whole" (Derrida 1980, 206, quoted in Spivak 2001, 124). Alterity is, therefore, an *"impossible invagination in every instance of the other"* (2001, 124, emphasis mine). Invagination functions as a kind of undecidability; it is a permanent ironic interruption—a "nonpassage to the other side" (Spivak 2001, 127). It interrupts reason and political calculation.[16] Listening requires attending to the invagination of difference that will interrupt reason and political calculation.

Spivak's tactic of detranscendentalizing through the literary is a move toward the (im)possibility of *ethical* encounter. Once radical alterity has been detranscendentalized, a space is created to hear the actual other (as opposed to invoking the absolute other).[17] It allows for careful listening to alterity and ironic interruption of the truths produced through subreption—without foreknowledge of the outcomes. Much in the way that alterity operates as a sublime invagination or permanent parabasis to political reasoning, ethical singularity interrupts the kinds of political calculation that are often made

16. Spivak is interested in the principle of *dvaita*, or twoness, where divinity appears in a natural phenomenon. Although admitting she has "no disciplinary access to knowledge on this topic," Spivak reads the supernatural in Hinduism in the way that she advocates religion should be understood: as the weave of permissible narrative. *Dvaita*—that is, "the unanticipatable emergence of the supernatural in the natural"—becomes a way of understanding how radical alterity functions as an effect of grace.

17. Spivak stresses in *Critique* that ethical singularity is *not* an experience of radical alterity (1999, 384). She clarifies this point in her foreword to the Blackwell *Companion to Postcolonial Studies*, insisting that "the subaltern [with whom one might have an encounter of ethical singularity] is not the absolute other. (Nothing) (is) the absolute other" (Spivak 2000, xx).

in the name of ethics (invading other countries to "save" "their" women, for instance). Alterity is approached neither as the guarantor of hierarchical authority and moral judgment nor as evil to be avoided. Nor does it remain radically other, unavailable to cognition. Rather, on the horizontal level of the aesthetic, it is something to which to attend carefully—it is an invaginating constitutive outside, even if an inability to know means complete reception is impossible.

Scripture and the Sublime

I have tried to trace how Spivak imagines detranscendentalizing radical alterity (the sublime object): via interrogating the subreption that takes place in metalepsis in order to attempt the impossible, sublime work of ethical singularity, or, listening to the other (the sublime feeling). As indicated earlier, I suggest that *evil* is another name given to radical alterity. Detranscendentalizing evil requires attending to the grace of permanent parabasis and invagination of alterity within religious discourses. What does all of this mean for a Babelian reading of scripture and of the texts that come to represent transcendent notions of evil? What does it mean to read for the sublime? How does one listen for alterity in scripture? One way to do this work is to pay careful attention to the occluded literary relationships that might invaginate what has come to be "known" of the transcendent, as in the kind of literalist allegory discussed in chapter 4.

In this manner, I suggest reading biblical text with attention to metonymy rather than via allegory. As the de Manian thread within Spivak's work suggests, allegory, like signification in general, is only established through difference, association, and contingency, even if the final product obliterates those relationships. If allegory is subreptive in its production of transcendence, to deconstruct it one must look for literary and linguistic associations that have been suppressed. One must treat it as metonym.[18]

---

18. As an example of metonym, Merriam-Webster's dictionary gives the example of the term "Hollywood" standing in for the film industry with which it associated. Brent Plate points out that structuralist literary theory and linguistics suggest that allegory, like language more generally, works through both metaphor and metonymy, that is, through vertical and hori-

Interrogating the metonymic process whereby one thing may be named by another with which it is associated points to horizontal relationships and connections within the signifying chain, while allowing for the interruptive parabasis of difference.

Instructive in this regard is the African American artist and cultural critic Charles Gaines, who understands the sublime as an aesthetic ideal that can provoke social change, resistance, and transformation. For him, the feeling of the sublime can be evoked by art. He shows how listening and not knowing can happen at the same time. In his brilliant and provocative theoretical writing, Gaines explains his interest in transforming objects *metonymically* in order to show that "the thingness of an object is realized relationally, and not by its discrete separateness from other things" (2001, 6). Growing out of his own life experience of reified social boundaries produced by racialization, Gaines's work prioritizes the use of metonymy over metaphor. Metonymy, he argues, produces the sense of infinite relatedness and the sublime, rather than the distinct borders and cultural transcendence of traditional conceptions of beauty. The use of metonymy produces the affect (feeling) of incomprehensible vastness; metonymy continually points to other objects related by social agreements. Where metaphor gives the illusion of autonomy, totality, and universalism, thus fending off critique (2009, 54, 57), metonomy is *"based in contiguity, that is, social agreement . . .* formed in a part-to-whole or cause-and-effect relationship" (52, emphasis mine). Metonymy reveals hidden relationships, connections, agreements. Metaphor prioritizes a feeling that suppresses thinking (50); metonymy, in contrast, "provides a means for critique and discourse because it links words through substitution based on contiguity." Contiguity and substitution require social agreement and point to cultural knowledge (52). Gaines is certainly not alone in using metonymy as a critique of metaphor and as a political model, but his work stresses the sublime affect that accompanies the use of metonymy.[19] He suggests

---

zontal (subreptive and associative) linguistic systems (2005, 50–54). Thus, the task is to look for allegory's metonymic elements.

19. As Plate points out, feminist theorists, deconstructive literary critics, and religious scholars have critiqued the hierarchical nature of the linguistic structure of substitution that produces metaphors and allegories; they have turned to metonym instead (Plate 2005, 55–58); see the famous distinction between metaphor and metonym in Jakobsen (1956) 1987; see also Fuss 1989, for an explanation of the role of metonym for Luce Irigaray and Hélène Cixous. My

that the sublime feeling can be produced through metonymy in the realization of the infinity of difference and contiguity. His work seeks to provoke "the emotion that results when one cannot comprehend the totality of an object, idea, or experience" (2006, 53). Put another way, metonymy points to "an incomprehensible vastness, an allusion of limitlessness produced as an affect of meaning" (2001, 4).[20] Gaines develops his thinking on the sublime as part of his "anti-modern aesthetic realized in the space of alliances." In his critique of much modernist work, he seeks "an aesthetic that forms an alliance with sociocultural and political expression rather than transcending them or being strictly oppositional to them" (6). It is an "aesthetics that informs culture rather than functioning autonomously" as if above it, or outside it as a universal (2006, 45).

Spivak's move to the aesthetic corresponds very well with Gaines's argument for the aesthetic production of the feeling of the sublime. Where Gaines wants to harness the social agreement in metonymy, however, Spivak wants to show the occlusions made in signification that are one more step removed in metalepsis.[21] Both agree that the revealing work of understanding metonymy or metalepsis illuminates the chain of cause and effect. Attending to metonomy and metalepsis means looking for places where relationships have been suppressed so that they are difficult to see, thus producing the sense of fright that must be dominated. Still, even if relationships can be observed, difference remains a reality, blocking full understanding. In Spivak's terms, an ethical listening knows that there is always something that does not get through. Following Spivak and Gaines, I might say that reading for the sublime means reading for places of connection and impossibility. The vastness of connection and the simultaneous impossibility of comprehension combine to provoke the feeling of the sublime.

---

readings of biblical mythic and allegorical figures (and interpretations) through metonym follow in this earlier literary and feminist vein, connecting it to the kind of postcolonial and political concerns that Spivak and Gaines raise.

20. Gaines creates the feeling of limitlessness in his artwork by having one object point to other objects: "This gesture is the alterity of the object, realizing a mutable space in contrast to the object's presumed immutability, thus producing the infinite space that seems to surround it and blur its edges" (2001, 4).

21. For example, when Babylon stands in for "Hollywood," which stands in for the film industry.

To return to the readings that produce transcendent evil in relation to Babylon, the antichrist and the Whore, we might look there for the liminality that is figured as frightening lack. We might read it as the starting place of the sublime rather than of terror. The first step is to detranscendentalize, to see how the production of alterity invaginates these figures, to see subreption at work. If detranscendentalizing starts by interrogating the horizontal relays of signification, I would like to notice the textual relations between these figures of evil and the transcendent figure often used to authorize decisionism, Christ. The second step is to see what cannot get through, to see how the liminal alterity of these figures troubles the political symbolic order and political calculation. For instance, the antichrist is both human and inhuman, troubling the ability to recognize either category and therefore to base decisions on unwavering knowledge of good and evil. Similarly liminal, the Whore of Babylon abhors empire and attracts her readers to it; as it turns out, her evil is connected to early Christian anxiety over and ambivalence toward empire and their own positioning within it, thus blurring clear-cut determinations of who is evil. The final stage is to imagine how these figures produce the feeling of sublime, both through maintaining opacity and through opening up new sites of negotiation and agreement. Here queer theory is helpful in providing antiapocalyptic models for thinking about social connection.

Disrupting Decisionism, Invaginating Christ

I turn first to the figure of the antichrist to see what it might mean to detranscendentalize radical alterity and listen to the other, so as to receive effects of grace in the form of ironic interruption. In Daniel 7:1–14, one of the texts commonly used to fill out the form of the antichrist, an alterity usually associated with the antichrist comes to invaginate the Christ figure. Let me trace the chain of significations that produce and occlude these relations. Daniel 7:1–14 is thought by many apocalyptic interpreters to describe the antichrist. As readers of this text well know, the writer of Daniel uses the imagery of beasts to depict the political threat posed to the Judeans by their various colonizers, culminating in the Hellenizing project of

Antiochus Epiphanes IV. Yet, for apocalyptically oriented readers, the text tends not to be read as only, or primarily, about an ancient situation. The famous dream image of the boastful little horn rising to power through deceit is interpreted as the deceptive antichrist. In Daniel 7, the Ancient of Days defeats this figure and then appoints the Son of Man—who comes on the clouds—to reign forever.

Scholars of apocalyptic literature have tried to determine the historical background and mythic antecedents to Daniel 7, both for the succession of beasts and for the Son of Man. Scholars have argued over whether the text borrows from Babylonian or Canaanite myths of creation,[22] in both of which the favored god defeats the chaotic sea monster-god, to establish order, creation, or sovereignty. In the Canaanite myth, the rain god Baal, rider of the clouds, defeats the god of the sea (Yamm) and the god of death (Mot). Baal is therefore much like the Son of Man who comes upon the clouds to defeat the arrogant and deceitful little horn. John J. Collins argues that, in Daniel, Baal becomes the Son of Man. The later Christian tradition, specifically Mark 13:26, clearly reinterprets Daniel's Son of Man as the Christ who returns in the last days—"coming in the clouds with great power and glory" (1997, 143–46, 142). Not to put too fine a point on it, the Canaanite Baal becomes Christ.

Another series of signifiers connects Baal to the (racialized and sexualized) antichrist. Baal Haddad, who appears in the older Ugaritic Canaanite sources from which the writer of Daniel may have drawn, is often conflated by interpreters with the Baal frequently mentioned in the Hebrew Bible (likely a Phoenician Baal), to produce a generalized notion that Baal was a Canaanite fertility storm god depicted in bull form.[23] Thus, the name *Baal* has become a general signifier in much biblical interpretation for a supposed sexualized ancient Israelite idolatry against which the Hebrew scriptures rail.[24] Over time, the term *Baal* has come to represent all that is

22. J. J. Collins 1997; Lacocque 2001; Mosca 1986; Shea 1986; Walton 2001; and R. R. Wilson 2000.
23. See Oden 1977; M. S. Smith 2002, 65–75. For a discussion of the connection between bull iconography and Baal worship, see M. S. Smith 2002, 83–85; he points out that the bull iconography may also have been a symbol for Yahweh.
24. Biblical descriptions of Canaanite practice and the so-called Canaanite fertility cult are not attested in the ancient Near Eastern material and textual record, nor is a strong division

ungodly and must be stamped out. As an icon of idolatry, the (conflated) Baals' association with the bull form has also been affiliated with the antichrist beast in some versions of apocalyptic Christianity. Once Baal is connected with the idolatrous Canaan—the Bible's racialized and sexualized other—it is only a short interpretive hop for some interpreters to identify the inhuman antichrist with the racialized enemy, or with those practicing nonnormative forms of sexual expression.[25] Thus for some interpreters, the proud little horn in Daniel is mixed with an (embellished) immoral Baal in the extratextual figure of the antichrist.

Yet, as discussed, it is more than plausible that Baal (the Ugaritic version) *produces* Christ, by way of the Son of Man. Through a series of exchanges and substitutions, the Canaanite Baal gives rise both to the inhuman beast and to the victorious Son of Man figure, who becomes the divine-human son of God. The Christ figure is therefore replete with an alterity that is more or less impossible for many adherents of the Christian tradition. The antichrist is the boundary of the set that is the Christ; it forms an internal pocket larger than the whole. Christ is invaginated by cultural difference.

How, then, might this invagination function as a permanent parabasis to theopolitical reasoning? Briefly, let me offer several suggestions as to how it blurs the lines of certainty on which masculinist political decisions might be made in the name of the transcendent Christ. First, when the Ugaritic Baal cycle is read in its entirety, the figure of Baal can be read as ironically commenting, avant la lettre, on the narrative establishing Christ's divinity. Christ is understood to be the heroic final conqueror of death, but his Canaanite heritage reads differently. In the Baal cycle, the dying and rising god cannot conquer death without help from his sister Anat. It is actually Anat who slays the god of death and frees Baal. So, even if Baal is referred to as conqueror, he needs a little help. Here we have the invagination of cultural *and* gender difference. Can the saving work of the Baal-Christ still be claimed as masculine? Can it continue to justify the need for the patri-

---

in material culture between Israelite and Canaanite; M. S. Smith 2002, 5–9. See also Hillers 1985; Noll 2001, 259–61.

25. For example, the book *Islam—The Cloak of Antichrist* compares the Dome of the Rock to the high places of Baal (J. Smith 2011, 141). Baal is also connected with homosexuality in places; see Haraldsson 2011.

archal decision? This genealogy cannot help but undermine any claim to Christ as the exemplar of the masculine decision maker.

Second, when the antichrist poses as Christ, it troubles the waters of certainty, even if the similarity can now be understood as family resemblance rather than deception. It is truly difficult to tell the antichrist from the Christ. There is no telling who might be the antichrist. The antichrist could be anyone, even the most ostensibly upright person. The anti/Christ's apparent identifiers (gender, race, and geographical location) are no longer distinct. The grounds for political decisions about the enemy are destabilized.

Ultimately, the antichrist is a figure of undecidability—one that puts into question the prevalent calculations based on moral and ideological superiority. This indeterminacy acts as a permanent ironic interruption to the theological certainty of knowing the difference between the Christ and the antichrist, and those allied with either. It is a kind of not knowing. The antichrist troubles any certainty of arriving at an exacting moral judgment (per Schmitt [1922] 2005, 65; see chapter 2). Any decision might be false. In short, the indeterminate presence of the antichrist puts the heteronormative, masculinist, messianic decisions of the United States into question. Importantly, the undecidability of the antichrist illustrates that even if chains of occluded cause and effect are recognized, something still does not get through—perfect reception is not possible, preventing integration into a new political calculus.[26]

As a sublime figure of undecidability, the antichrist is (unthinkably, sublimely) a kind of grace—a permanent parabasis to the kinds of calculations and decisions that inspire war on the international front and limit the field of sexuality and kinship in the domestic arena. Invagination of radical al-

26. Proponents of a Schmittian decisionist politics might assert that Schmitt himself anticipated such an argument, even going so far as to describe political undecidability as part of the antichrist's evil. Recall that Schmitt referred to the antichrist in his fear of a mechanistic neutrality (see chapter 2). In his words, "The antichrist . . . knows to imitate Christ and so makes himself resemble Christ, and thus tricks everyone out of their souls. . . . His concealed power lies in his imitation of God. . . . The uncanny [*unheimlich*] enchanter re-creates the world in order to change the face of the earth and make nature submissive" ([1916] 1991, 61–62, translated and quoted in McCormick 1995, 60). Yet a Spivakian reading of Schmitt's antichrist would show that Schmitt's view of reality is fully dependent on the *metaphor* of transcendent activity (God's creation of the world). It would show the antichrist to be a metaleptic space that opens up within this metaphor, an effect of an effect that troubles the distinctions on which the metaphor is based.

terity problematizes the very notion of the enemy. It turns a discernible evil inside out. When the racialized, sexualized antichrist is read in the realm of the literary, the chains of signification to which this figure is attached become visible, showing it to be a narrative that is necessary to the political decisionism performed in the name of the transcendent. Like Kant's "raw man," the antichrist is not quite human; as we saw in chapter 5, he is depicted in sexual and racial terms that place him outside national belonging (but perhaps within national borders). Yet the antichrist's homosexualized in/humanity is the constituent outside to the "universal" (Christian, U.S., heterosexual) norms of the human. At the same time, the antichrist questions an ability to *know*: to know gender or sexuality, to know evil, or to know salvation when we see it. What has been so potentially threatening about the antichrist for apocalyptic exegetes through the ages is that he mixes the human and the inhuman to the degree that they cannot necessarily be told apart. To apply Davis's words, the antichrist is something like the site of an inability to know that "reconstitutes the will to know" so entwined with colonial processes and power relations (2002, 155). The process of detranscendentalizing the antichrist opens up a space in which the inability to know can be countenanced.

Subreption and the Masquerade of the Whore

Christ is big enough for several pockets. Equally queerly, the Whore of Babylon invaginates the Christ figure and, simultaneously, empire. To get to this, let me first interrogate the literary effects that produce the Whore's transcendent evil. I ask Gaines's question, what is the "thingness" of the Whore's evil? The subreptive production of evil that appears throughout the history of the Whore's interpretation, begins in the apocalyptic text of Revelation 17–18. A closer look will show that a sense of evil is produced by the juxtaposition of incompatible terms and contradictions: of affect, of the positioning of the reader, and, most significantly, of the many social roles the Whore encompasses. The Whore's evil resides in difference.[27]

---

27. As a number of scholars point out, the imagery of the Whore has its prototypes in earlier prophetic texts that describe Israel's sin of unfaithfulness to God via the imagery of harlotry

Fear *and* desire, hatred *and* attraction toward the Whore pulse through the text. The contradictory sets of affects produce conviction of her evil. The violence toward her is stronger because of censored desire for her. She is desired because she is powerful, wealthy, and sexually seductive. She is to be feared because she drinks the blood of saints (17:6); she is intoxicating with her "maddening wine" (18:3), thus wresting control from her partners; she is a dangerous associate, because she is so easily and quickly ruined (18:10). She is hated for all these things, but perhaps even more for combining desire and fear. This combination generates such strong discomfort that she must be called evil. Tina Pippin has beautifully elucidated these dynamics in her book *Death and Desire* (1992), in which she argues that staging Rome's power as female eroticism allows it to be contained.

Readers and interpreters are drawn into the production of the Whore's affect, and at the same time called to be separate from it. Rome's actual attractions and threats as an empire are intensified via the vague and hyperbolic language of mystification, demonization, and sexualization. Interpreters are left to fill in the details (ever proliferating) of her mystery (17:5), the identity of her evil spirits (18:2), and the contents of her cup of undefined abominations and filthy adulteries (17:4). The imprecise literary expression of Rome's power and seductiveness allows interpreters to insert their own desires and fears.

The power of the Whore's horror is largely produced by the juxtaposition of difference; she combines contradictory social roles within one figure. Although she is sumptuously dressed, and condemned for her luxury, she bears signs of being a slave. As Jennifer Glancy and Stephen Moore argue, the tattoo on the Whore's forehead, and the term *pornē* used to describe her sex work suggests that she is modeled on common prostitutes in Rome.[28] Different from courtesans, *pornai* were "slaves or other persons

---

(e.g., Hosea): Aune 1998, 930; Beale 1999, 855; Beasley-Murray 1974, 251; Ford, 1975, 283–86; Kim 1999, 69–70; Wengst 1994, 191–92. For feminist critiques of Revelation's imagery of the Whore, see Huber 2011; Ipsen 2009; Kim 1999; Nelavala 2009; Pippin 1992a, 1992b, 1999; Vander Stichele 2009.

28. In contrast to identifying prophetic castigation as the strongest influence on the writer, Glancy and Moore (2011) point to the immediate historical context of Roman sexual invective. They argue that the sexual invective directed toward the Whore would be familiar in

on the bottommost rungs of the social ladder" (Glancy and Moore 2011, 557). Tattoos, like that on the Whore's brow, were associated with slaves, administered as a form of punishment (Glancy and Moore 2011, 559; Koester 2008, 769n6). The Whore, therefore, "presents the paradox of an enthroned *pornē*" (Glancy and Moore 2011, 562)—queen and slave. Moreover, since slaves in the Roman empire were most often colonized peoples or the children of colonized peoples (C. Martin 2005, 101–2, Bauckham 1991, 74; Glancy 2006, 74–78), the Whore is both colonizer and colonized, queen and slave.

Further scrambling social expectations, the Whore's opulence resembles that of a slave trader. Craig Koester describes the grave stele of a slave trader in which the memorialized man reclines in luxury on a couch at a banquet, with a cup raised in his hand, overseeing the lower panels in which merchants trade wine and humans (2008, 773–74). There is strong resemblance between the imagery of this relief and the Whore. Yet slave traders would not be rulers; they would be merchants, like the ones doing business with "Babylon" (18:11–20), or possibly pirates (C. Martin 2005, 99). The incompatibility of the social roles (queen, slave, slave trader, merchant, pirate) adds to the sense of her wicked alterity.

And what would evil be without the difference of genderqueerness? In "Metonymies of Empire: Sexual Humiliation and Gender Masquerade in the Book of Revelation" (2009), Stephen Moore argues that the Whore is a parody of the Roman goddess Roma along with her own ambiguous gendering. Analyzing Roman iconography, he shows that the female Roma is remarkably masculine, depicted in military attire, with helmet, parazonium (short sword signifying high rank), and spear (2009, 77). Moore writes, "Roma is hegemonic Roman manhood encased in female flesh that is clad in hypermasculine garb . . . a man dressed as a woman dressed as a man" (87). The Whore of Babylon, as parody, is therefore in quadruple drag, "Roma stripped of her military attire and reclothed as a prostitute . . . a man dressed as a woman dressed as a man dressed as a woman" (87). As Whore, Rome's despised femininity is exposed as perverse and reviled excess.

---

the Roman world, as, for instance, in Juvenal's and Tacitus's descriptions of Valeria Messalina as empress-whore (2011, 564–69).

Moore posits that Roma's phallic femininity subtly represents the incorporation of the feminized, ethnic, colonized Asian and Greek other into the Roman empire. He points to places where Roman military leaders commented on the feminine softness of the Asian and Greek cities they were conquering, and the fear that their femininity would corrupt the soldiers. Roma thus illustrates an empire invaginated by some kind of lack, which as it turns out is the feminized, colonized other.

Where Roma is an image that can deal with this gender trouble by integrating foreign softness into her own masculinity, Babylon is one that emphasizes it and mocks it precisely through her vilified femininity (Moore 2009, 84–85). In Moore's words, "The Whore in combination with the Beast represents Rome as the collapse of masculinity back into the morass of femininity and animality" (2009, 92).[29] Moore's reading of the Whore's iconographic precursors raises the question of whether John is worried about the Babylonian and Persian influences that he has incorporated—and about his own masculinity. By protesting a little too much, might the seer be disavowing his own connection as a colonized person to the ethnic other, to the so-called softer masculinities of Asia, Babylon, Persia, and Greece, which he also sees in Roma? Like the common prostitute (*pornē*), the seer and his audience are colonized. The seer is quite likely a Hellenized Jew, exiled to Asia Minor.[30] Like him, his audience in Asia Minor would be marked by successive colonizations of their cities, by Persia, Greece, and Rome. They would be stereotyped as effeminate, in relation to the Romans. It would be their masculinity that the Whore exaggerates and mocks. The colonized churches are, therefore, included in the gender trouble of both Roma and her parody. There is an undecidability about the Whore's genderqueer, statusqueer, *evil attractiveness* that may have to do with the inclusion of the audience into her evil auspices.

Along similar lines, the ambivalence toward the Whore might be amplified by the fact that some within the churches of Asia Minor were involved in the very economic trade that the passage criticizes. As Richard Bauckham argues in his detailed analysis of Rome's economic exploitation, "It is not unlikely that John's readers would include merchants and others whose

29. For more on the feminization of non-Romans, see Frilingos 2004, 75; 2010, 348.
30. For an extended discussion of the seer's social location see A. Y. Collins 1984, 25–53.

business or livelihood was closely involved with the Roman political and economic system" (1991, 84). It is because they are so close to Rome's luxuries and her economic exploitation that they are called to come out of Babylon (85).[31]

Moreover, as Christopher Frilingos argues, the text enacts the desire for empire that it tries to control (2004). Frilingos innovatively notices that when the seer looks in amazement on the Whore of Babylon, the terms used, deriving from the verb *thaumazo*, are also ones he uses positively in places, thus signaling an ambivalent attraction to spectacle and to empire (2004, 50–52). In fact, the seer and his audience are imperial in their viewing, putting Rome on display in the same way that Rome displayed those subservient to it (2004, 42). As Moore writes, "John is secretly in love with Roma. . . . He loves her and hates her with equal passion. Which is why he deals so savagely with her" (2009, 88–89; see also 2006, 116–18).

If the colonized Asian churches invaginate the Whore, she in turn invaginates the Christ figure. As Moore says, "While one part of Revelation is busy shaming Roma by turning her into a prostitute, the other part of Revelation is busy modeling Jesus on Roma" (Moore 2009, 93). Moore indicates the various places in Revelation where Jesus has a sharp sword issuing from his mouth, recalling Roma's parazonium (a long triangular dagger; Rv 1:16; 2:12, 27; 19:5). In these descriptions, Christ is hypermasculine, but, around his breast is bound a golden girdle (1:13), not unlike the manner in which Roma is sometimes described (2009, 91).[32] Just as Christ is born from the same heritage as the antichrist, so also is John's messiah born of the same imperial logic as Roma.

The Whore of Babylon and God's kingdom are both Roma's offspring. One is called wicked and one righteous, but they can be read as the two

---

31. For more on the economic exploitation behind the image, see Perry 2007. Harry Maier suggests that the imagery of merchants mourning at Babylon's demise is a deliberate critique of the seer's opponents within the churches, such as the wealthy at Laodicea who might sympathize with the Empire (1997, 147, 150). Adela Yarbro Collins suggests that there was a strong conflict between rich merchants and the overtaxed working classes in Asia Minor (1983, 744). The difference in John's judgment of the churches seems to be related to this conflict.

32. This ambivalence toward empire is also made manifest by similarities between the Whore and God. Koester shows that the seer depicts God as a benevolent slave trader. God's people, including the seer, are called slaves (Rv 1:1, 10:7; 15:3). They are bought for God with the blood of Jesus (5:9; 14:3) and branded with God's seal (7:3; 14:1) (Koester 2008, 768–69).

sides of John's ambivalence about empire—one valuing it, and one horrified by it. As Moore points out, it is not too surprising that Jesus is eventually the founder of the new Rome (2009, 92–93). In Revelation, the empire of God is established using tactics not unlike the Roman empire, including "war and conquest, entailing, as always, mass-slaughter, but now on a surreal scale" (2009, 88; see also Moore 2006, 114–15; Pippin 1992a, 97–100). In her postcolonial analysis of the Whore, Surekha Nelavala considers this kind of reversal in Revelation to be a kind of colonial ambivalence, a love and hate of empire (2009).

Christ and his kingdom are invaginated by the Whore, who is invaginated by the goddess Roma, in turn invaginated by the genderqueer colonized other. Thus, the imagery of the Whore is more complex than simply separating the righteous self from the evil imperial other. Traits of the Whore become traits of God's kingdom, while traits of the seer and his audience become traits of the Whore. Indeed, the seer and his audience are implicated in the production of evil. But these continuities and relationships are made difficult to see in the metaleptic subreption that produces evil.

The undecidability of the gender performance of Roma and the Whore of Babylon might be well described by what Jennifer Friedlander, in her book *Feminine Look: Sexuation, Spectatorship, Subversion* (2008), has called imposture and masquerade. Drawing on other feminist Lacanians, Friedlander emphasizes the point that neither gender has the phallus, since it is a symbolic ideal. Attempts at masculinity constantly try to cover up this lack through imposture, and in so doing end up seeming feminine (in the case of Revelation, whorish). Imposture constantly and somewhat unsuccessfully tries to hide lack through attempts at mastery. Certainly John tries to prove that Rome does not have the power of phallus—Christ and his saints do. Nevertheless, as we have seen, as much as he might try to establish his virtuous self-control in her presence, thus modeling Roman ideals of masculinity (Moore 2009, 79–81), he not only desires her but also reviles his own stereotyped gendering through her.

The strategy of masquerade that Friedlander describes might allow us to see the connective possibilities of metonym. As she describes it, masquerade "accepts the knowledge that identity itself is an illusion" (2008, 64). It is ambiguous. Masquerade "articulate[s] rather than cover[s] over symbolic dissolution," or lack (71). It plays on surfaces rather than trying to cover a missing interior. In this sense, one could think about the Whore of Babylon's evil not as an insistence on the essence of Roma's lack—of virtue, of masculinity, of Romanness—but rather the articulation of John's ambivalence about empire. Identifying this conflictedness reveals that what initially appears as lack is actually a process of cause and effect. It shows the subreption at work in the production of the Whore's transcendent evil. "Lack" becomes a site of the infinite vastness of social agreement and negotiation.

In the end, Christ's invagination by the Whore shows up Roma, John, and the readers of Revelation for their masculine imposture, and it puts the attractions and invaginations of empire clearly on the table, not trying to cover them up or disavow them. The Whore, masquerading, reveals that her evil is metaleptically configured by difference, produced in subreption. If the original audience and their Christ figure is invaginated by the Whore, how might this also be true of those who use her to vilify others? Are the same ambivalences about the positioning of the "saints" in empire also operative?

Queerly Sublime

Invaginated by the enemy, a detranscendentalized Christ figure might be something like the figure of queer desire posited by Lee Edelman. Drawing on Leo Bersani's antipastoral, antisocial approach to sexuality, Edelman's project is to use the antisocial impulses of desire to deconstruct the oppressions made in the name of identity. Queer desire is oppositional: It embodies negativity; it disrupts rather than conjoins. The Whore and the antichrist offer sites of queer negativity that are somewhat outside of the usual candidates.[33] Edelman wishes to take queer difference seriously to reclaim the proliferation of queer desires as a negativity that can disrupt identity and the social. The point is to disrupt "normativity's singular truth" (Edelman 2004, 26). In his words, "Queerness attains its

33. For Judith Halberstam's critique of the "excessively small archive that represents queer negativity" in Edelman's work, as well as Edelman's response to this charge, see Caserio et al. 2006.

ethical value precisely insofar as it . . . accept[s] its figural status as resistance to the viability of the social while insisting on the inextricability of such resistance from every social structure" (3). For Edelman, queerness is that difference that has been repressed in the subject's entry into the heteronormative symbolic order for the sake of unity and coherence, yet without which difference the subject could not function. Queerness—like raw sex, bare life, the antichrist, and the Whore—is both included and excluded from the social order, and its exclusion must be tapped for its potential to disrupt the borders of inclusion. Queerness is like the death drive: It is that force emerging from "the gap or wound of the Real that inhabits the Symbolic's very core" (22).

In this sense, queerness operates in a way similar to that of the sublime in the radical theologian Clayton Crockett's reading. For Crockett, the sublime is akin to the Lacanian real. It is "the trace of the material in signification, the kernel of (meta) physical being that cannot be completely absorbed or represented in language, but that continues to exert distorting effects" (2007, 185). In his radical, materialist theology, Crockett puts the sublime in the place of God; it generates sublimation—the creative force producing meaning in and through the material realities of bodies. Crockett's theological sublime resonates with the way Judith Butler describes queer sexual practice and desire that is beyond the symbolic order: She calls it "the *sublime* within the field of sexual intelligibility" (2004b, 106, emphasis mine). She also sees queer practices inhabiting spaces of "uncertain ontology [and] difficult nomination" (108). But a queer sublime is not necessarily socially acceptable in the way we sometimes think of the work of sublimation. The invaginated Christ disrupts meaning through the proliferation of uncontainable desires (called perverse) and through deception. The antichrist and Whore demonstrate the abyss of representation. These are disruptive sites of not knowing and impossibility.

The queer sublime is produced in the process of detranscendentalizing, and produces a kind of antiapocalyptic mode of queer negativity. As Edelman argues, queerness moves backward, away from the future. Like the death drive, queerness "refuses identity or the absolute privilege of any goal." It denies teleology and "reject[s] . . . spiritualization through marriage to reproductive futurism" (2004, 27). Queer desire disrupts the future-oriented trajectory of identity and, with it, the social. Likewise, sublime alterity, sometimes named the antichrist, the Whore, or the colonized other/terrorist, invaginates what is held up as truth or righteousness, thus disrupting the eschatology of the nation and the compulsory heterosexuality that supports it.

The listening of ethical singularity—attending to the ambiguity of invagination that troubles the clear distinctions between good and evil—might be closer to the kind of queer connectivity proposed by Tim Dean in a panel conversation responding to the antisocial thesis in queer theory. As Dean argues, following an overlooked aspect of Bersani's work, even if the self/identity/future–shattering experience of queer desire is taken seriously, as in Edelman's antisocial queerness, some kind of collectivity might be forged across the fragments of time and self. It is a connectivity that acknowledges the impossibility of difference. In this vein, Dean suggests, it might be possible "to trace new forms of sociability, new ways of being together that are not grounded in imaginary identity [and the heteronormative apocalyptic future] or the struggle for intersubjective recognition." He further proposes that "we might speak of 'hooking up'—a visceral dramatization of the promiscuous sociability of unconscious desire when unconstrained by Oedipus" (Caserio et al. 2006, 827).[34]

Although Dean is thinking about actual sexual encounters, hooking up might also be a way of thinking about connection that is not goal oriented, that does not seek to create products (children, families, markets, wars) that secure superiority. Hooking up may be the place where impossible listening can take place, not based on intimacy, or conjoined identity, or futurity but rather liminality—the divisions between worlds that are mutually constitutive, even if negatively framed, and also incommensurable. Hooking up allows for momentary agreements across divides—the recognition of liminality and impossibility. The feeling of the sublime is that feeling of possibility and impossibility, connection and disconnection that can provoke creativity and desire outside of a search for superiority.

---

34. Dean is working with Guy Hocquenghem's critique ([1972] 1993) of the oedipal controls on libido in which the object of desire and the object of identification are separated within the constraints of the patriarchal family.

"Effects of Grace"

Via Spivak, I have read the sublime not in the traditional way as reason's confrontation with the inestimable, dangerous, sublime object but as that scary incomprehensibility of meaning in the face of social alterity. In this sense, a liminal, sublime, detranscendentalized alterity signifies a Babelian place of the impossibility of full communication, something like Hartley's abyss of representation but focused more closely on difference. Often, as we have seen, the incomprehensibility of difference is called evil and mastered by structures of domination. Transcendent notions of good and, especially, evil are frequently used to describe and control the a priori of difference and the frightening affect of the sublime. Superiority is secured in and for the United States through biblically authorized approaches to family, war, and economy; all that threatens these tactics or the goal of superiority is called evil. I have suggested that we look for places of connection and impossibility in the sexualized religious tropes that secure "superiority."[35] The recognition of creative connection with others and the simultaneous impossibility of full connection or full signification that haunts any achievementtogether reveal the fiction of superiority. I am arguing for an approach to scripture that values opacity, liminality, and undecidability; it looks for connections and disruptions, eschewing higher meanings.[36] In this way, Babel can be read as a metonym of the sublime (a metalepsis really). Applying this method of reading to the figures of the antichrist and the Whore destabilizes the grounds for decisionism: The contiguity of these figures with elements of Christian identity and belief troubles distinct theopolitical axes for making so-called moral decisions—about military action, the state of exception, torture, and so on

By moving the antichrist and the Whore out of the position of radical alterity and into the realm of the literary aesthetic, the recognition of cultural difference in the Christ/antichrist/Whore challenges the threat that the other poses. Those racialized and sexualized subjects normally associated

---

35. This project is something like Connolly's suggestion of looking for spaces of contestability within a tradition, as discussed in chapter 1.
36. In many ways, this approach borders on the listening Iñárritu proposes in his film *Babel* (see chapter 3), but unlike the film, it does not seek a common, marketable language.

with the antichrist/Baal or the Whore can no longer be associated with the satanic. The threat and taint of evil is removed (reduced to the mundane of literary genealogy). Once those called evil have been dissociated from transcendence, ethical encounter with the other (through listening) opens up as a possibility. Even if something is always missed in the attempt to listen, detranscendentalizing opens up a less spiritually invested space in which mind changing might become possible.

An alternative engagement requires a political ethics that does not depend on transcendent truth. It suggests a slow, attentive listening and mind changing that might go in an unexpected direction. It allows grace to play in detranscendentalized fields of religious metaphor as permanent interruptions to the guarantors of morality and the decision. Communal health, meaning, creativity, personal agency, and emotion—these can come through careful listening to the other: in religious text, in literature, in political discourse, in joint projects, or in conversation. Political theology may continually rebuild itself as sempiternal, but the delicate tasks of listening, rereading, and not knowing can slowly reduce its premises to mundane normalities and recast them into another kind of social network and politics.

Postlude: Roads to Babel

As we have seen throughout the book, Babylon is an uncertain symbol, alternately fetishized or demonized. Sometimes it is an object of desire. Frequently it signals dangerous incursions into national sovereignty and hierarchical authority. Babylon and its prince the antichrist are used to sanction the imperialist and heteroteleological project of the nation-state. The evil of Babylon and its prince the antichrist motivate preemptive wars, torture, and family values. The United States fights Babylonian tyranny and evil on behalf of the world, while it consolidates a sense of sovereignty for itself. Counterintuitively, images of Babylon and the antichrist also advance the subjectivities, interests, and bodies most conducive to a free market. The Babylon allegory centers and decenters, alternately valuing or derogating diversity or unity, as needed. If Babel's fall is read as a diversity that must be rebuilt by unity, Babel also becomes a symbol of inoculation against mindless unities. A dissolute Babylon (such as Hollywood Babylon) facilitates the dispersion of the market and cultivates the subject of interest, simultaneously curtailing and controlling political diffusion. Even Josephus's early retelling of the Babel story emphasizes the tension between a securitized political unity and the economic advantages of dispersion, suggesting that scattering into colonies is both mandated and governed by God.

Theodemocracy, as we have seen, is democracy for the subject of interest. Belief in the Jewish or Christian God is held up as central to U.S. national coherence. It guards the subject of interest from becoming the radically equal democratic subject; it ensures that hierarchies are enforced. Theodemocracy also allows for U.S. messianism, which protects good life in the world against bad life, or nonhuman life, and reinforces a sense of U.S. superiority. If there is a tension between national sovereignty and global market forces, between the juridical realm of social contracts and the subject of interest, Babylon shows us how theopolitics manages it. Capitalism is encouraged and held up as democratic; it is restrained and managed by families. The theological grounding for the family is the same as that which gives the United States the messianic mandate to assert its superiority, open up markets for itself, manage life across and within borders, and reinforce a sense of sovereignty for itself. As much as Babylon might conveniently kindle a (censored yet required) craving for capitalism, it can never shed its fatal flaw of excess. The United States is always better than Babylon. In contradistinction to the deceptive, excessive, spectacular, conquering Babylon, the United States sets itself up as a city on the hill, a place where militarism is for the biopolitical good of species life and where supposed immoderation is curbed by families. Yet the United States ends up looking awfully like Babylon in its pursuit of global superiority.

Such a theopolitics helps explain why family values are so obsessively pursued in the United States. The heterosexual family stands in the gap between unity and diversity, between Babylon and Babel. It becomes a central mediator against Babel's dissolution (neutrality, soft despotism, perverse Babylon), necessitating God as an arbiter of morality and truth (chapters 1 and 5). It hides U.S. Babylonian desires by creating the space where capitalist comforts can be conservatively enjoyed. It also provides a microcosm for the hierarchies of humanity, law, sovereignty, and economics. The family is the God-ordained place in which people are trained to take their place in the relations of capital and where these positions can be inherited; moreover, the family is the guarantor of transcendence through which these hierarchies are maintained.

In theodemocracy, democracy, equality, and political authority are viewed in hierarchical terms that are authorized by transcendent truths. On the basis of these truths—known through scripture, through law, through philosophy, or through the Spirit—strong decisions are taken to contravene tyrannical unities; laws are broken for righteousness. Transcendence frees people from the social contract, by guaranteeing control on another level. The authority of law is governed by a notion of some even higher authority, which allows a political actor to contravene particular laws and social unities, even as the very notion of law invests the decision maker with authority to do so. Conservative philosophers may understand the higher authority in abstract terms as truth, but this truth is disseminated to the population through religious language that apocalyptically frames human life as non-Babylonian, Christian, white, heteropatriarchal, U.S. American.

Transcendence reinforces the biopolitical. It provides cover for the groundlessness of market forces and the actual loss of sovereignty within global capital. A notion of transcendence theodemocratically preserves hierarchies within the decentering movements of globalization, market forces, and democratic processes. If the market is prioritized but does not need a sovereign to function, then something must fill in the gap, especially if the United States wants to continue to lay an ideological claim to world power, and if lines of wealth and privilege are to be protected against the tyranny of too much equality (i.e., revolt). Transcendence steps in. Good and evil are terms that subreptively invest populations within and between nations, cultivating, intensifying, or selling life for capital, and arranging it in graduated formations of possibility, privilege, and bodily health and comfort. Transcendence manages and obscures the decentering of globalization.

A process of scripturalizing is central to this theopolitics and the transcendence on which it relies. That Babylon gains its authority through scripture means that even when it is torn down, it is continually rebuilt as conquering truth. Literalist-allegorical interpretations of Babylon (chapter 4) metaleptically and subreptitiously produce transcendence (chapter 6). The link between reality and metaphoric language is almost absurdly associative. Interpreters bring together the literal (Iraq, Hussein, bin Laden, raw sex, excess democracy, ethnic difference, public services, the social safety net) and the metaphoric (Babylon/Babel/the antichrist) under the umbrella of "evil," itself a concept produced by a relay of significations, contradictions, and counteridentifications. Once Babylon/Babel is designated as evil or tyrannical, other associative substitutions can be made in which its demise becomes God's will and God's righteous judgment, or, philosophical truth. God, evil, or truth appear as transcendent entities operating in another realm, erasing the connections created in signification. The world of the interpreter and the spiritual world metaleptically merge. The political becomes the spiritual.

Allegory and subreption instill fear and create desire. The transcendence of evil is created through the swallowing up of incoherent elements, in which, as it turns out, the United States also resides. Babylon threatens to seduce its audience, and it does; those living in the United States are part of Babylon, and we participate in the production of its allure. We are lost in it, even as we try to separate ourselves from it. These losses of self and power, which also produce Babylon's fear, generate an incessant longing for power. The relationships and literary techniques that produce the feelings of desire and fear are forgotten.

Reading Otherwise

But this is a very particular view of scripture, one that demands the production of hierarchical authority through truth to secure political and spiritual dominion. There is continued work to be done in reconceptualizing scripture, rethinking the relation of scripture and law, and uncoupling the U.S. form of liberal democracy from the hierarchical authority and imperializing mission it seems, to many, to demand. New forms of reading must be imagined. Many have started on this project already, to which I hope I have contributed.[1]

I have offered one possible method of reading (chapter 6) that seeks to prioritize a queer sublime recognition of the vastness of (impossible, liminal, sublime) social connection. It is a detranscendentalizing mode of read-

---

1. See the Introduction for those working on understanding the power dynamics within scripturalizing, led by Vincent Wimbush and others.

ing, always looking for the hidden chain of cause and effect behind assertions of truth, good, and evil. It looks for places where difference queerly inhabits what is known as truth. What is called good and what is called evil become hard to separate, making it difficult for one or the other to ground political decisions. A queer sublime thus challenges the heteroteleology and messianism of a nation whose self-understanding and biopolitical mission relies on notions of transcendence. A queer sublime invaginates a nation that materially promotes and requires the conditions that produce the diversity it eschews, or at best, tolerates.

A reading practice thus grounded in undecidability holds out a vision for approaching the political that does not require a belief in an a priori to produce the authority on which to act. It is temporary and flexible, based on attentive engagement with the other, in the recognition that what does get through will be interruptive. It resists hierarchizations made in the name of good and evil, insisting instead on radical equality, shared lineages and shared responsibility for harm. Reading for the opacity and liminality of the queer sublime resists standard political critiques from the right and the left and presents a challenge to both. Neither is it mechanistically neutral or relativist, nor does it require notions of the transcendent(al) that shape recognition of the enemy. It opens up a space to envision an ethics and a politics based on ethical singularity rather than on the decision about the enemy, but it does not throw morality out the window. It offers a secularized view that can take on a materialist analysis without succumbing to a blind mechanism. Not only does it bypass the usual critiques, but it also might have appeal to many positions on the political spectrum, precisely because it is not a program that can be set in motion—radical unknowability disallows it, as does the singularity of each encounter. Listening across divides is essential. This work must go in all directions. It is worth recognizing—in the vein of listening to the other—that there are potentially common goals between the nonreligious left and the theopolitical right. These might include a struggle for meaning, community, the capacity to make change, the ability to recognize and address injustice, a place for emotional expression, and a sense of personal importance. The desire for individual agency and community building is made manifest as much in evangelical prayer vigils against the spiritual enemy as it is in progressive organizing. Surely, without hoping for complete agreement, such political goals can be cultivated across religious and political lines, even without transcendent certainties.

What are the chances of such listening? Certainly one cannot demand it from those who are hostile; but one might offer it; one might recognize that there are partially shared interests and affects, even if these are expressed in politically opposite ways. This is no easy task when the stakes around sovereignty, markets, comfort, gender, and sexuality are high. Struggle, resistance, firm stances, and decisions are much easier, safer, and perhaps more compelling on all sides. Being open to the sublime is much harder.

Perhaps, in drawing to a close, there is also a place for humor and self-critique in promoting radical democracy. I take my cue on this front from the appearance of Babel in the well-recognized social commentary provided by *The Simpsons*. In "Simpsons Bible Stories" (season 10, episode 18, 1999), Bart Simpson falls asleep in church and has a dream that he is King David. He takes it upon himself to revenge the deaths of his friends by killing the giant, Goliath II, who lives in the Tower of Babel. (It would seem that Josephus's Nimrod becomes Goliath.) Despite David-Bart's heroic confrontation with Goliath, it is the unheroic shepherd Ralph who finally kills Goliath. Nonetheless, King David-Bart takes credit for ridding the people of Goliath. They aren't grateful, however; they tell him, "But Goliath was the best king we ever had. He built roads, hospitals, libraries. To us, he was Goliath the consensus builder." So they have the police apprehend King David-Bart and take him away. Consciously or not, the writers create a Nimrod-like Goliath who is interested in collectivity, and they poke fun of Bart's misguided need to be the hero. Dissatisfied with the ungovernability of consensus making, David-Bart gets rid of it. Not to be quelled, however, the people voice and enact their own justice in response. Instead of being deemed a tyrant, Goliath is valued for his attempt at galvanizing collectivity and community. It is the reversal of expectation and the strange conjunction of imagery that make this retelling funny and pointed at the same time. The show thus pokes fun at the hierarchical, messianic theodemocracy of the United States. Humor is a necessary part of self-critique and imagination, one that needs further exploration.

This version of the Babel story brings me, finally, to organizing and protest. Given the theopolitical and theodemocratic response to globalization outlined throughout the book, it seems crucial to organize via radical equality and to protest the religiously grounded hierarchies that refuse this equality. Protest does not need to take the form of marches and rallies, but it has to be public. It can be funny, joyful, creative, and self-critical. It needs to integrate the ethical singularity of listening across political lines. Whatever the form, we need the public action of the ungovernable. Such action is not lawless, but it requires the difficult acknowledgment of "the absence of every title to govern" (Rancière 2006, 41; see chapter 1), that is, the ability of anyone at all to temporarily take on nonhierarchical leadership in collective political collaboration. Going beyond theodemocracy means working beyond hierarchies to find new modes of consensus making and new kinds of rhetoric that do not rely on transcendence. This is not to say that people will not continue to believe in transcendence, but only to say that such belief should not be the grounds for political certainty and authority. Rather, zones of unknowing, of difference, of queer, sublime impossible connectedness must be foregrounded, either in representations of transcendence or in other cultural and literary expressions of ethical and political ideals.

In short, this is a bid for a quashed Babelian collectivity. How can we govern ourselves, in the chaos of unknowing and indecision? Slowly, with much patience, with introspective humor, with an insistence on radical equality, impossible listening and connection, and without pretension to an anti-Babylonian messianism that causes unspeakable pain and death.

Adso de Montier-en-Der. (c. 950) 1979. "Letter on the Origin and Time of the Antichrist." In *Apocalyptic Spirituality: Treatises and Letters of Lactantius, Adso of Montier-en-Der, Joachim of Fiore, The Franciscan Spirituals, Savonarola,* edited and translated by Bernard McGinn, 89–96. New York: Paulist Press.

Agamben, Giorgio. (1995) 1998. *Homo Sacer: Sovereign Power and Bare Life.* Translated by Daniel Heller-Roazen. Stanford, Calif.: Stanford University Press.

———. (2000) 2005. *The Time That Remains: A Commentary on the Letter to the Romans.* Translated by Patricia Dailey. Stanford, Calif.: Stanford University Press.

———. (2003) 2005. *State of Exception.* Translated by Kevin Attell. Chicago: University of Chicago Press.

Ahn, John. 2008. "Psalm 137: Complex Communal Laments." *Journal of Biblical Literature* 127 (2): 267–89.

Aitken, Kenneth T. 1983. "The Oracles against Babylon in Jeremiah 50–51: Structures and Perspectives." Tyndale Old Testament Lecture. Published in *Tyndale Bulletin* 35 (1984): 25–63.

Allen, Leslie C. 1983. *Psalms 101–150.* Word Biblical Commentary 21. Waco, Texas: Word Books.

———. 1990. *Ezekiel 20–48.* Word Biblical Commentary 29. Dallas, Texas: Word Books.

Alliance for Revival and Reformation, prod. *God's Law and Society.* 1999. Narrated by Eric Holmberg. 240 min. DVD.

Allison, Henry E. 2001. *Kant's Theory of Taste: A Reading of the "Critique of Aesthetic Judgment."* Cambridge: Cambridge University Press.

Alster, Bendt. 1973. "An Aspect of 'Enmerkar and the Lord of Aratta.'" *Revue d'assyriologie et d'archéologie orientale* 67 (2): 101–10.

Anderson, A. A. 1981. *The Book of Psalms.* Vol. 2, *Psalms 73–150.* New Century Bible Commentary. Grand Rapids, Mich.: Eerdmans.

Anderson, Bernhard W. 1978. "Unity and Diversity in God's Creation: A Study of the Babel Story." *Currents in Theology and Mission* 5 (2): 69–81.

Andersson, Hilary. 2010. "Red Cross Confirms 'Second Jail' at Bagram, Afghanistan." *BBC News*, May 11. http://news.bbc.co.uk/2/hi/south_asia/8674179.stm.

Andrews, Dale. 2008. "A Tower of Pulpits." In *African American Religious Life and the Story of Nimrod*, edited by Anthony B. Pinn and Allen Dwight Callahan, 193–214. New York: Palgrave Macmillan.

Anger, Kenneth. 1975. *Hollywood Babylon*. New York: Dell.

Apocalypse of Elijah. 1983. Translated with an introduction by O. S. Wintermute. In *The Old Testament Pseudepigrapha: Apocalyptic Literature and Testament*, vol. 1, edited by James H. Charlesworth, 721–54. New York: Doubleday.

Arendt, Hannah. (1950) 1973. *The Origins of Totalitarianism*. New York: Harcourt Brace Jovanovich.

Aristotle. 1926. *Rhetoric*. Translated by J. H. Freese. Loeb Classical Library, vol. 22. London: William Heinemann; Cambridge, Mass.: Harvard University Press.

———. 1935. *Athenian Constitution*. Translated by H. Rackham. Loeb Classical Library, vol. 20. London: William Heinemann; Cambridge, Mass.: Harvard University Press.

———. (1946) 1962. *Politics*. Translated by Ernest Barker. Oxford: Oxford University Press.

———. 1998. *Nicomachean Ethics*. Translated by William David Ross. Oxford: Oxford University Press.

———. 2004. *Rhetoric*. Translated by W. Rhys Roberts. Oxford: Clarendon.

Asad, Talal. 2003. *Formations of the Secular: Christianity, Islam, Modernity*. Stanford, Calif.: Stanford University Press.

The Ascension of Isaiah. 1900. Translated and edited with an introduction and notes by R. H. Charles. London: Adam and Charles Black.

Associated Press. 2009. "Pentagon Briefings No Longer Quote Bible." MSNBC News. May 18. http://www.msnbc.msn.com/id/30814527/ns/us_news-military/t/pentagon-briefings-no-longer-quote-bible/#.TriSF3LG8vg.

Augustine. 1995. *Tractates on the First Epistle of John*. Translated by John W. Rettig. In *The Fathers of the Church*, vol. 92, 119–277. Washington, D.C.: Catholic University of America Press.

———. 2004. "Exposition on Psalm 137." Translated by Maria Boulding. In *Expositions of the Psalms 121–150, The Works of Saint Augustine*, pt. 3 vol. 20, 242–55. New York: New City Press.

Aune, David E. 1998. *Revelation 17–22*. Word Biblical Commentary 52C. Nashville, Tenn.: Thomas Nelson.

Avalos, Hector, Sarah Melcher, and Jeremy Schipper, eds. 2007. *The Abled Body: Rethinking Disabilities in Biblical Studies.* Semeia Studies 55. Atlanta: Society of Biblical Literature.

Axtmann, Roland. 2002. "What's Wrong with Cosmopolitan Democracy?" In *Global Citizenship: A Critical Introduction*, edited by Nigel Dower and John Williams, 101–13. New York: Routledge.

Babington, Charles, and Shailagh Murray. 2005. "Senate Supports Interrogation Limits: 90–9 Vote on the Treatment of Detainees Is a Bipartisan Rebuff of the White House." *Washington Post*, October 6. http://www.washingtonpost.com/wp-dyn/content/article/2005/10/05/AR2005100502062.html.

Bach, Alice. 2004. *Religion, Politics, Media in the Broadband Era.* Sheffield, Eng.: Sheffield Phoenix Press.

Bachmann, Holger. 2000. "The Production and Contemporary Reception of *Metropolis*." In *Fritz Lang's "Metropolis": Cinematic Visions of Technology and Fear*, edited by Michael Minden and Holger Bachmann, 1–45. Rochester, N.Y.: Camden.

Bachrach, Judy. 2006. "Washington Babylon." *Vanity Fair*, August. http://www.vanityfair.com/politics/features/2006/08/washington200608.

Bailey, Randall C., Cheryl A. Kirk-Duggan, Madipoane J. Masenya, and Rodney Steven Sadler. 2010. "African and African Diasporan Hermeneutics: Reading the Hebrew Bible and Journey, Exile, and Life through My/Our Place." In *The Africana Bible: Reading Israel's Scriptures from Africa and the African Diaspora*, edited by Hugh R. Page Jr. et al., 19–24. Minneapolis: Fortress.

Bailey, Randall C., Tat-Siong Benny Liew, and Fernando F. Segovia, eds. 2009. *They Were All Together in One Place? Toward Minority Biblical Criticism.* Semeia Studies 57. Atlanta: Society of Biblical Literature.

Baird, Robert J. 2000. "Late Secularism." *Social Text* 18 (3): 123–36.

Bal, Mieke. 2008. *Loving Yusuf: Conceptual Travels from Present to Past.* Afterlives of the Bible. Chicago: University of Chicago Press.

Barclay, John M. G. 2006. *Flavius Josephus: Translation and Commentary.* Edited by Steve Mason. Vol. 10, *Against Apion.* Leiden: Brill.

Bar-Efrat, Shimon. 1997. "Love of Zion: A Literary Interpretation of Psalm 137." In *Tehillah le-Moshe: Biblical and Judaic Studies in Honor of Moshe Greenberg*, edited by Mordechai Cogan, Barry L. Eichler, Jeffrey H. Tigay, 3–11. Winona Lake, Ind.: Eisenbrauns.

Barrera, Ashley. 2007. "Review of *Babel*." *Journal of Feminist Family Therapy* 19 (4): 78–82.

Barstad, Hans M. 1996. *The Myth of the Empty Land: A Study in the History and Archaeology of Judah During the "Exilic" Period.* Oslo: Scandinavian University Press.

Battersby, Christine. 2007. *The Sublime, Terror and Human Difference*. London: Routledge.

Bauckham, Richard. 1991. "The Economic Critique of Rome in Revelation 18." In *Images of Empire*, edited by Loveday Alexander, 47–90. Sheffield, Eng.: JSOT Press.

Bauer, Gary. 2004. "Frenzy over Abu Ghraib." Concerned Women for America, May 12. http://www.cwfa.org/articles/5661/CWA/misc/index.htm.

Baxley, Craig, dir. 2005. *Left Behind: World at War*. Produced by Peter and Paul Lalonde. Cloud Ten Films. DVD.

Beal, Timothy K. 2001. *Religion and Its Monsters*. New York: Routledge.

Beal, Timothy K., and Tod Linafelt, eds. 2005. *Mel Gibson's Bible: Religion, Popular Culture, and "The Passion of the Christ."* Afterlives of the Bible. Chicago: University of Chicago Press.

Beale, G. K. 1999. *The Book of Revelation: A Commentary on the Greek Text*. Grand Rapids, Mich.: Eerdmans.

Beasley-Murray, G. R. 1974. *The Book of Revelation*. New Century Bible Commentary. Grand Rapids, Mich.: Eerdmans.

Beck, Glenn. 2010. "Lessons from the Tower of Babel." *Fox News*. November 17. http://www.foxnews.com/story/0,2933,602223,00.html.

Bellah, Robert. 1975. *The Broken Covenant: American Civil Religion in Time of Trial*. Chicago: University of Chicago Press.

Bellis, Alice Ogden. 1995. *The Structure and Composition of Jeremiah 50:2–51:58*. Lewiston, N.Y.: Edwin Mellen.

Benjamin, Walter. (1921) 1986. "Critique of Violence." In *Reflections: Essays, Aphorisms and Autobiographical Writing*, edited by Peter Demetz and translated by Edmund Jephcott, 277–300. New York: Schocken Books.

———. (1928) 1998. *The Origin of German Tragic Drama*. Translated by John Osborne. London: Verso.

Benoit, David. 1997. "Man Targeted for Extinction." In *Foreshocks of the Antichrist*, edited by William T. James, 339–54. Eugene, Ore.: Harvest House.

Ben Zvi, Ehud, and Christoph Levin, eds. 2010. *The Concept of Exile in Ancient Israel and Its Historical Contexts*. Berlin: Walter de Gruyter.

Bercovitch, Sacvan. 1983. "The Biblical Basis of the American Myth." In *The Bible and American Arts and Letters*, edited by Giles Gunn, 221–32. Philadelphia: Fortress; Chico, Calif.: Scholars.

Berlant, Lauren. 1997. *The Queen of America Goes to Washington City: Essays on Sex and Citizenship*. Durham, N.C.: Duke University Press.

Berlin, Adele. 2005. "Psalms and the Literature of Exile: Psalms 137, 44, 69, and 78." In *The Book of Psalms: Composition and Reception*, edited by Peter W. Flint and Patrick D. Miller, 65–86. Leiden: Brill.

Berlinerblau, Jacques. 2005. *The Secular Bible: Why Nonbelievers Must Take Religion Seriously*. Cambridge: Cambridge University Press.

Bersani, Leo. 1987. "Is the Rectum a Grave?" *October* 43: 197–222.

Bhabha, Homi K. 1994. *The Location of Culture*. London: Routledge.

Bhattacharya, Sanjiv. 2004. "Look Back at Anger." *Guardian*, August 21. http://www.guardian.co.uk/books/2004/aug/22/fiction.features6.

Bickle, Mike. 2011. "Allegiance to Jesus: Exposing the Harlot Babylon Religion (Rev. 17)." International House of Prayer University. October 15. http://www.mikebickle.org.edgesuite.net/MikeBickleVOD/2011 /20111015_Allegiance_to_Jesus_Exposing_the_Harlot_Babylon_ Religion_P&P03.pdf.

Bielo, James S. 2009. *The Social Life of Scriptures: Cross-Cultural Perspectives on Biblicism*. New Brunswick, N.J.: Rutgers University Press.

Black, Fiona C., ed. 2006. *The Recycled Bible: Autobiography, Culture, and the Space Between*. Semeia Studies 51. Atlanta: Society of Biblical Literature.

———. 2012. "Reading the Bible in 'Our Home and Native Land': Exploring Some Margins and Migrations in Canadian Biblical Studies (through the Lens of Psalm 137)." In *The Future of the Biblical Past: Envisioning Biblical Studies on a Global Key*, edited by Roland Boer and Fernando Segovia, 237–62. Semeia Studies. Atlanta: Society of Biblical Literature.

Blasberg, Marian, and Anita Blasberg. 2005. "The Prisoner and the Guard: A Tale of Two Lives Destroyed by Abu Ghraib." *Spiegel Magazine Online*, September 26.

Blenkinsopp, Joseph. 1992. *The Pentateuch: An Introduction to the First Five Books of the Bible*. New York: Doubleday.

Boer, Roland. 2007. *Rescuing the Bible*. Blackwell Manifestos. Oxford: Blackwell.

———. 2008. *Last Stop before Antarctica: The Bible and Postcolonialism in Australia*. 2nd ed. Semeia Studies 64. Atlanta: Society of Biblical Literature.

———. 2009. *Political Myth: On the Use and Abuse of Biblical Themes*. Durham, N.C.: Duke University Press.

Boesak, Allan A. 1987. *Comfort and Protest: The Apocalypse from a South African Perspective*. Philadelphia: Westminster Press.

Bohrer, Frederick N. 2003. *Orientalism and Visual Culture: Imagining Mesopotamia in Nineteenth-Century Europe*. Cambridge: Cambridge University Press.

Bost, Hubert. 1985. *Babel: Du text au symbole*. Geneva: Labor et Fides.

Boston, Rob. 2006. "Is the Antichrist Gay? Stretching Scripture at the 'Values Voter Summit.'" Americans United for Separation of Church and State. Accessed December 22. http://www.au.org/site/News2?page=NewsArticle& id=8676&abbr=cs_.

Boyer, Paul. 1992. *When Time Shall Be No More: Prophecy Belief in Modern American Culture*. Cambridge, Mass.: Harvard University Press.

Brown, Wendy. 2005. *Edgework: Critical Essays on Knowledge and Politics*. Princeton, N.J.: Princeton University Press.

———. 2006. *Regulating Aversion: Tolerance in the Age of Identity and Empire.* Princeton, N.J.: Princeton University Press.

———. 2010. *Walled States: Waning Sovereignty.* New York: Zone Books.

Browning, Frank. 1997. "Why Marry?" In *Same-Sex Marriage: Pro and Con,* edited by Andrew Sullivan, 132–34. New York: Vintage Books.

Brueggemann, Walter. 1982. *Genesis.* Interpretation. Atlanta: John Knox.

———. 1984. *The Message of the Psalms.* Minneapolis: Augsburg.

Buchanan, Patrick. J. 1997. "Is America Still a Country?" Patrick J. Buchanan Official Website. August 8. http://buchanan.org/blog/pjb-is-america-still-a-country-370.

———. 2009. "It Can't Happen Here." Accessed August 1, 2011. http://buchanan.org/blog/pjb-it-cant-happen-here-1595.

———. 2012. *Suicide of a Superpower: Will America Survive to 2025?* New York: St. Martin's Press.

Burk, Denny. 2011. "First-Person: How Should Christians React to bin Laden's Death?" *Baptist Press,* May 2. http://www.bpnews.net/BPFirstPerson.asp?ID=35196.

Burlein, Ann. 2002. *Lift High the Cross: Where White Supremacy and the Christian Right Converge.* Durham, N.C.: Duke University Press.

Bush, George W. 2004. "President Calls for Constitutional Amendment Protecting Marriage." Washington, D.C., October 24. http://georgewbush-whitehouse.archives.gov/news/releases/2004/02/20040224-2.html.

———. 2005a. "President Discusses War on Terror at National Endowment for Democracy." Washington, D.C., October 6. http://georgewbush-whitehouse.archives.gov/news/releases/2005/10/20051006-3.html.

———. 2005b. "President's Statement on Signing of H.R. 2863, the 'Department of Defense, Emergency Supplemental Appropriations to Address Hurricanes in the Gulf of Mexico, and Pandemic Influenza Act, 2006.'" Washington, D.C., December 30. http://georgewbush-whitehouse.archives.gov/news/releases/2005/12/20051230-8.html.

———. 2006. "President Bush Nominates Rob Portman as Office of Management and Budget Director and Susan Schwab for U.S. Trade Representative." Washington, D.C., April 18. http://georgewbush-whitehouse.archives.gov/news/releases/2006/04/20060418-1.html.

Butler, Judith. 1990. *Gender Trouble.* New York: Routledge.

———. 1997. *The Psychic Life of Power: Theories in Subjection.* Stanford, Calif.: Stanford University Press.

———. 2004a. *Precarious Life: The Powers of Mourning and Violence.* London: Verso.

———. 2004b. *Undoing Gender.* New York: Routledge.

Cairns, Huntington. 1946. "Leibniz's Theory of Law." *Harvard Law Review* 60 (2): 200–32.

Callahan, Allen Dwight. 2006. *The Talking Book: African Americans and the Bible.* New Haven, Conn.: Yale University Press.

———. 2008. "The Strength of Collective Man: Nimrod and the Tower of Babel." In *African American Religious Life and the Story of Nimrod*, edited by Anthony B. Pinn and Allen Dwight Callahan, 147–62. New York: Palgrave Macmillan.

———. 2009. "Babylon Boycott: The Book of Revelation." *Interpretation* 63 (1): 48–54.

Carden, Michael. 1999. "Homophobia and Rape in Sodom and Gibeah: A Response to Ken Stone." *Journal for the Study of the New Testament* 24 (82): 3–96.

Carlsmith, Kevin M., and Avani Mehta Sood. 2009. "The Fine Line between Interrogation and Retribution." *Journal of Experimental Social Psychology* 45 (1): 191–96.

Carroll, Robert P. 1981. *From Chaos to Covenant: Prophecy in the Book of Jeremiah.* New York: Crossroad.

———. 1986. *Jeremiah: A Commentary.* Old Testament Library. Philadelphia: Westminster Press.

———. 2004. "The Polyphonic Jeremiah: A Reading of the Book of Jeremiah." In *Reading the Book of Jeremiah: A Search for Coherence*, edited by Martin Kessler, 77–85. Winona Lake, Ind.: Eisenbrauns.

Caserio, Robert L., Lee Edelman, Judith Halberstam, José Esteban Muñoz, and Tim Dean. 2006. "The Antisocial Thesis in Queer Theory." *PMLA* 121 (3): 819–28.

Cassuto, U. 1964. *A Commentary on the Book of Genesis.* Vol. 2, *From Noah to Abraham.* Jerusalem: Magnes Press, the Hebrew University.

Castelli, Elizabeth A. 2004. *Martyrdom and Memory: Early Christian Culture Making.* New York: Columbia University Press.

———. 2005. "Praying for the Persecuted Church: U.S. Christian Activism in the Global Arena." *Journal of Human Rights* 4 (3): 321–51.

———. 2006. "Notes from the War Room." *Revealer.* April 5. http://therevealer.org/archives/2378.

———, ed. 2007a. "God and Country." *differences: A Journal of Feminist Cultural Studies* 18 (3): 1–6.

———. 2007b. "Persecution Complexes: Identity Politics and the 'War on Christians.'" *Differences: A Journal of Feminist Cultural Studies* 18 (3): 152–80.

———. 2007c. "Theologizing Human Rights: Christian Activism and the Limits of Religious Freedom." In *Non-Governmental Politics*, edited by Michel Feher with Gaëlle Krikorian and Yates McKee, 673–87. New York: Zone Books.

Chambers, Joseph. 2005. "Same Sex Marriage: Defiling the 'Marriage of the Lamb.'" Paw Creek Ministries. Accessed October 12. http://www.pawcreek.org/end-times/same-sex-marriage.

Chambers, Samuel A., and Michael O'Rourke, eds. 2009. *Jacques Rancière on the Shores of Queer Theory. borderlands* 8 (2).

Chocano, Carina. 2006. "In a World of Hurt." *LA Times,* October 27. http://articles.latimes.com/2006/oct/27/entertainment/et-babel27.

Cobb, Michael. 2006. *God Hates Fags: The Rhetorics of Religious Violence.* New York: New York University Press.

Cockburn, Alexander, and Ken Silverstein. 1996. *Washington Babylon.* London: Verso.

Cohen, David. 1995. *Law, Violence, and Community in Classical Athens.* Cambridge: Cambridge University Press.

Cohen, Stanley. (1972) 2011. *Folk Devils and Moral Panics: The Creation of the Mods and Rockers.* Routledge Classics. New York: Routledge.

Collins, Adela Yarbro. 1983. "Persecution and Vengeance in the Book of Revelation." In *Apocalypticism in the Mediterranean World and the Near East: Proceedings of the International Colloquium on Apocalypticism, Uppsala 1979,* edited by David Hellholm, 729–50. Tübingen: Mohr Siebeck.

———. 1984. *Crisis and Catharsis: The Power of the Apocalypse.* Philadelphia: Westminster Press.

Collins, Christopher. 2007. *Homeland Mythology: Biblical Narratives in American Culture.* University Park: Pennsylvania State University Press.

Collins, John J. 1997. "Stirring up the Great Sea: The Religio-Historical Background of Daniel 7." In *Seers, Sybils and Sages in Hellenistic-Roman Judaism,* 139–55. Supplements, *Journal for the Study of Judaism.* Leiden: Brill.

Connolly, William E. 2000. *Why I Am Not a Secularist.* Minneapolis: University of Minnesota Press.

———. 2005. *Pluralism.* Durham, N.C.: Duke University Press.

Cooley, John K. 2005. *An Alliance against Babylon: The U.S., Israel, and Iraq.* London: Pluto.

Cooper, Phillip J. 2005. "George W. Bush, Edgar Allan Poe, and the Use and Abuse of Presidential Signing Statements." *Presidential Studies Quarterly* 35 (3): 515–32.

Coote, Robert B., and David Robert Ord. 1989. *The Bible's First History.* Philadelphia: Fortress.

Copeland, Rita, and Peter T. Struck. 2010. Introduction to *The Cambridge Companion to Allegory,* edited by Rita Copeland and Peter T. Struck, 1–11. Cambridge: Cambridge University Press.

Corbett, Christopher. 1997. "The U.S. and Other U.N. Serfdoms." In *Foreshocks of the Antichrist,* edited by William T. James, 203–30. Eugene, Ore.: Harvest House.

Crawford, Thomas Joseph. 2011. "Curating Gnosis: Discovery, Power and the Creation of (a) Discipline." PhD diss., Claremont Graduate University.

Cristi, Renato. 1998. *Carl Schmitt and Authoritarian Liberalism: Strong State, Free Economy*. Cardiff: University of Wales.

Critchley, Simon. 2006. "Crypto-Schmittianism." *State of Nature* 2. http://www.stateofnature.org/crypto-schmit.html.

Croatto, J. Severino. 1998. "A Reading of the Story of the Tower of Babel from the Perspective of Non-Identity." In *Teaching the Bible: The Discourses and Politics of Biblical Pedagogy*, edited by Fernando F. Segovia and Mary Ann Tolbert, 203–23. Maryknoll, N.Y.: Orbis Books.

Crocker, Thomas P. 2008. "Overcoming Necessity: Torture and the State of Constitutional Culture." *Southern Methodist University Law Review* 61 (2): 222–79.

Crockett, Clayton. 2001. *A Theology of the Sublime*. London: Routledge.

———. 2007. *Interstices of the Sublime: Theology and Psychoanalytic Theory*. New York: Fordham University Press.

———. 2011. *Radical Political Theology: Religion and Politics after Liberalism*. New York: Columbia University Press.

Crockett, Clayton, and Jeffery W. Robbins. 2012. *Religion, Politics, and the Earth: The New Materialism*. New York: Palgrave Macmillan.

Crossley, James. 2008. *Jesus in an Age of Terror: Scholarly Projects for a New American Century*. London: Equinox.

———. 2010. *Reading the New Testament: Contemporary Approaches*. New York: Routledge.

———. 2012. *Jesus in an Age of Neoliberalism: Scholarship, Intellectuals and Ideology*. London: Equinox.

Crozier, Michel J., Samuel P. Huntington, and Joji Watanuki. 1975. *The Crisis of Democracy: Report on the Governability of Democracies to the Trilateral Commission*. New York: New York University Press.

Culbertson, Philip, and Elaine M. Wainwright, eds. 2010. *The Bible in/and Popular Culture: A Creative Encounter*. Semeia Studies 65. Atlanta: Society of Biblical Literature.

Curti, Giorgio Hadi, John Davenport, and Edward L. Jackiewicz. 2007. "Concrete Babylon: Life between the Stars: To Dwell and Consume (with)in the Fold(s) of Hollywood, CA." *Yearbook of the Association of Pacific Coast Geographers* 69: 45–73.

Cusick, Suzanne G. 2006. "Music as Torture/Music as Weapon." *Revista Transcultural de Música/Transcultural Music Review* 10. http://www.sibetrans.com/trans/a152/music-as-torture-music-as-weapon.

Dahood, Mitchell. 1970. *Psalms III: 101–150*. Anchor Bible. Garden City, N.Y.: Doubleday.

Dalley, Stephanie, trans. 1989. *Myths from Mesopotamia: Creation, the Flood, Gilgamesh, and Others*. Oxford: Oxford University Press.

Daschke, Dereck. 2010. "'A Destroyer Will Come against Babylon': George W. Bush's Oracles against the Nations." In *A Cry Instead of Justice: The Bible and Cultures of Violence in Psychological Perspective*, edited by Andrew Kille, 156–81. New York: T & T Clark.

Davidson, Steed V. 2006. "Babylon in Rastafarian Discourse: Garvey, Rastafari, and Marley." *SBL Forum*. http://sbl-site.org/publications/article.aspx ?articleId=496.

Davis, Creston, John Milbank, and Slavoj Žižek, eds. 2005. *Theology and the Political: The New Debate*. Durham, N.C.: Duke University Press.

Davis, Dawn Rae. 2002. "(Love Is) The Ability of Not Knowing: Feminist Experience of the Impossible in Ethical Singularity." *Hypatia* 17 (2): 145–61.

DeGregory, Lane. 2004. "Iraq 'n' Roll." *St. Petersburg Times*, November 21. http://www.sptimes.com/2004/11/21/Floridian/Iraq_n_roll.shtml.

Deleuze, Gilles. 1992. "Postscript on the Societies of Control." *October* 59 (Winter): 3–7.

De Man, Paul. 1979. *Allegories of Reading: Figural Language in Rousseau, Nietzsche, Rilke, and Proust*. New Haven, Conn.: Yale University Press.

Derrida, Jacques. (1978) 1979. "The Parergon." Translated by Craig Owens. *October* 9 (Summer): 3–41.

———. 1980. "The Law of Genre." *Glyph: Textual Studies* 7 (Spring): 202–29.

———. (1980) 2002. "Des Tours de Babel." Translated by Joseph F. Graham. In *Acts of Religion*, edited by Gil Anidjar, 102–34. New York: Routledge.

———. (1989–90) 2002. "Force of Law: The 'Mystical Foundation of Authority.'" Translated by Mary Quaintance. In *Acts of Religion*, edited by Gil Anidjar, 230–98. New York: Routledge.

———. (1996) 2002. "Faith and Knowledge: The Two Sources of 'Religion' at the Limits of Reason Alone." In *Acts of Religion*, edited by Gil Anidjar, 40–101. New York: Routledge.

———. (2003) 2005. *Rogues: Two Essays on Reason*. Translated by Pascale-Anne Brault and Michael Naas. Stanford, Calif.: Stanford University Press.

Dershowitz, Samuel. 1994. "The Tower of Babel Revisited." *Jewish Bible Quarterly* 22 (3): 266–67.

Dever, William G. 2005. *Did God Have A Wife? Archaeology and Folk Religion in Ancient Israel*. Grand Rapids, Mich.: Eerdmans.

de Vries, Hent, and Lawrence E. Sullivan, eds. 2006. *Political Theologies: Public Religions in a Post-Secular World*. New York: Fordham University Press.

Diamond, Sara. 1995. *Roads to Dominion: Right-Wing Movements and Political Power in the United States*. New York: Guilford.

Dillon, Michael, and Julian Reid. 2009. *The Liberal Way of War: Killing to Make Life Live*. London: Routledge.

Dirks, Tim. 2008. "Intolerance." Filmsite. Accessed March 18. www.filmsite.org/into.html.

Dobson, James. 2004. *Marriage under Fire: Why We Must Win This War*. Sisters, Ore.: Multnomah Publishers.

Draper, Robert. 2009. "He Shall Be Judged." *GQ*. June. http://www.gq.com
/news-politics/newsmakers/200905/donald-rumsfeld-administration-peers
-detractors.

Drew, William. M. 1986. *D. W. Griffith's "Intolerance": Its Genesis and Its Vision.*
Jefferson, N.C.: McFarland.

Dreyfus, Georges. 2011. "Should We Be Scared? The Return of the Sacred and
the Rise of Religious Nationalism in South Asia." In *Crediting God: Sovereignty and Religion in the Age of Global Capitalism*, edited by Miguel Vatter,
117–41. New York: Fordham University Press.

Drury, Shadia B. 1997. *Leo Strauss and the American Right*. New York: St. Martin's Press.

Du Bois, W. E. B. 1920a. *Darkwater: Voices from within the Veil*. New York: Harcourt, Brace and Howe.

———. 1920b. "The Comet." In *Dark Matter: A Century of Speculative Fiction
from the African Diaspora*, edited by Sheree R. Thomas, 5–18. New York:
Warner Books, 2000.

Duggan, Lisa. 2003. *The Twilight of Equality: Neoliberalism, Cultural Politics and
the Attack on Democracy*. Boston: Beacon.

Economist. 1997. "The Whore of Babylon and the Horseman of Plague." April
10. http://www.economist.com/node/147341.

Eddlem, Thomas R. 2011. "Debate: Bachmann, Santorum Say Attack Iran;
Paul Warns That's Overreacting." *New American*, December 16. http://www
.thenewamerican.com/usnews/politics/item/9955-debate-bachmann-
santorum-say-attack-iran-paul-warns-thats-overreacting.

Edelman, Lee. 1995. "Queer Theory: Unstating Desire." *GLQ* 2 (4): 343–46.

———. 2004. *No Future: Queer Theory and the Death Drive*. Durham, N.C.:
Duke University Press.

Eisenstein, Sergei. (1944) 1977. "Dickens, Griffith, and the Film Today." In
Film Form: Essays in Film Theory, 195–255. San Diego: Harcourt.

Emmerson, Richard K. 1981. *Antichrist in the Middle Ages: A Study of Medieval Apocalypticism, Art, and Literature*. Seattle: University of Washington
Press.

Erlandsson, Seth. 1970. *The Burden of Babylon: A Study of Isaiah 13:2–14:23.*
Coniectanea Biblica Old Testament Series 4. Lund: Gleerup.

Erzen, Tanya. 2006. *Straight to Jesus: Sexual and Christian Conversions in the Ex-
Gay Movement*. Berkeley: University of California Press.

Ettelbrick, Paula. 1997. "Since When Is Marriage the Path to Liberation?" In
Same-Sex Marriage: Pro and Con, edited by Andrew Sullivan, 118–24. New
York: Vintage Books.

Evans, James H., Jr. 2008. "The Hunter and the Game: Reappropriating the
Legend of Nimrod from an African American Theological Perspective." In
African American Religious Life and the Story of Nimrod, edited by Anthony

B. Pinn and Allen Dwight Callahan, 15–26. New York: Palgrave Macmillan, 2008.

Exum, J. Cheryl, and Stephen D. Moore, eds. 1998. *Biblical Studies, Cultural Studies*. Sheffield, Eng.: Sheffield Academic Press.

Fardal, Randy. 2009. "Nimrod's Tower." *American Thinker*. September 27. http://www.americanthinker.com/2009/09/nimrods_tower.html.

Feinberg, Paul. 1997. "The Mideast March to Megiddo." In *Foreshocks of the Antichrist*, edited by William T. James, 255–73. Eugene, Ore.: Harvest House.

Feldman, Louis H. 1998a. *Studies in Josephus' Rewritten Bible*. Supplement, *Journal for the Study of Judaism* 58. Leiden: Brill.

———. 1998b. *Josephus's Interpretation of the Bible*. Berkeley: University of California Press.

———, trans. 2000. *Flavius Josephus: Translation and Commentary*, edited by Steve Mason. Vol. 3, *Judean Antiquities 1–4*. Leiden: Brill.

Felperin, Leslie. 2007. "Babel." *Sight and Sound* 17 (2): 41–42.

Fernandez, Eleazar S. 2002. "From Babel to Pentecost: Finding a Home in the Belly of the Empire." In "The Bible in Asian America," edited by Tat-siong Benny Liew, special issue, *Semeia* 90/91: 29–50.

———. 2009. "Diaspora, Babel, Pentecost, and the Strangers in Our Midst: Birthing a Church of Radical Hospitality." In *Postcolonial Interventions: Essays in Honor of R. S. Sugirtharajah*, edited by Tat-siong Benny Liew, 147–61. The Bible in the Modern World 23. Sheffield, Eng.: Sheffield Phoenix.

Fessenden, Tracy. 2007. *Culture and Redemption: Religion, the Secular, and American Literature*. Princeton, N.J.: Princeton University Press.

Fewell, Danna Nolan. 2001. "Building Babel." In *Postmodern Interpretations of the Bible: A Reader*, edited by A. K. M. Adam, 1–15. St. Louis, Mo.: Chalice.

Fewell, Danna Nolan, Gary Phillips, and Yvonne Sherwood, eds. 2008. *Representing the Irreparable: The Shoah, the Bible, and the Art of Samuel Bak*. Syracuse, N.Y.: Syracuse University Press.

Finkel, I. L., and M. J. Seymour. 2008. *Babylon*. Oxford: Oxford University Press.

Fletcher, Angus J. S. 2010. "Allegory without Ideas." In *Thinking Allegory Otherwise*, edited by B. Machosky, 9–33. Stanford, Calif.: Stanford University Press.

Fokkelman, J. P. 1975. *Narrative Art in Genesis: Specimens of Stylistic and Structural Analysis*. Amsterdam: Van Gorcum.

Ford, J. Massyngbaerde. 1975. *Revelation: Introduction, Translation and Commentary*. Anchor Bible. Garden City, N.Y.: Doubleday.

———. 1996. "The Physical Features of the Antichrist." *Journal for the Study of the Pseudepigrapha* 7 (14): 23–41.

Foucault, Michel. (1975) 1995. *Discipline and Punish: The Birth of the Prison.* Translated by Alan Sheridan. New York: Vintage.

———. (1976) 1990. *The History of Sexuality.* Vol. 1, *An Introduction.* Translated by Robert Hurley. New York: Vintage.

———. (1978) 1991. "Governmentality." In *The Foucault Effect: Studies in Governmentality,* edited by Graham Burchell, Colin Gordon, and Peter Miller, 87–104. Chicago: University of Chicago Press.

———. 2003. *Society Must Be Defended: Lectures at the Collège de France, 1975–1976.* Edited by Mauro Bertani and Alessandro Fontana. Translated by David Macey. New York: Picador.

———. 2008. *The Birth of Biopolitics: Lectures at the Collège de France, 1978–1979.* Edited by Michel Senellart. Translated by Graham Burchell. New York: Palgrave Macmillan.

Fox, Everett. 1983. *In the Beginning: A New English Rendition of the Book of Genesis.* New York: Schocken.

Franxman, Thomas W. 1979. *Genesis and the "Jewish Antiquities" of Flavius Josephus.* Biblica et Orientalia 35. Rome: Biblical Institute Press.

Freedman, David Noel. 1971. "The Structure of Psalm 137." In *Near Eastern Studies in Honor of William Foxwell Albright,* edited by Hans Goedicke, 187–205. Baltimore: Johns Hopkins Press.

Freeman, Barbara Claire. 1995. *The Feminine Sublime: Gender and Excess in Women's Fiction.* Berkeley: University of California Press.

Frei, Hans W. 1974. *The Eclipse of Biblical Narrative: A Study in Eighteenth- and Nineteenth-Century Hermeneutics.* New Haven, Conn.: Yale University Press.

Friedlander, Jennifer. 2008. *Feminine Look: Sexuation, Spectatorship, Subversion.* Albany: State University of New York Press.

Friedman, Richard Elliott. 2001. *Commentary on the Torah.* New York: Harper Collins.

Friedman, Sergeant Major Herbert A. 2013. "The Use of Music in Psychological Operations." Psyopswarrior.com. Accessed September 13. http://www.psywarrior.com/MusicUsePSYOP.html.

Frilingos, Christopher A. 2004. *Spectacles of Empire: Monsters, Martyrs, and the Book of Revelation.* Philadelphia: University of Pennsylvania Press.

———. 2010. "Wearing It Well: Gender at Work in the Shadow of Empire." In *Mapping Gender in Ancient Religious Discourses,* edited by Todd Penner and Caroline Vander Stichele, 333–49. Atlanta: Society of Biblical Literature.

Froese, Arno. 1997. "United Europe's Power Play." In *Foreshocks of the Antichrist,* edited by William T. James, 275–300. Eugene, Ore.: Harvest House.

Fukuyama, Francis. 1992. *The End of History and the Last Man.* New York: Free Press.

Fuller, Robert C. 1995. *Naming the Antichrist: The History of an American Obsession.* Oxford: Oxford University Press.

Fuss, Diana. 1989. *Essentially Speaking: Feminism, Nature, and Difference.* New York: Routledge.

Gaines, Charles. 2001. "Metonymy and the Defamiliarization of Objects." In *Lurid Stories: Charles Gaines: Projects from 1995 to 2001*, 2–7. Exhibition Catalogue. San Francisco Art Institute.

———. 2006. "Art and Culture: Metonymy and the Postmodern Sublime." In *Snake River*, by Charles Gaines and Edgar Arceneaux, 1:39–67. Los Angeles: Roy and Edna Disney / CalArts Theater.

———. 2009. "Reconsidering Metaphor/Metonymy: Art and the Suppression of Thought." *Art Lies* 64:48–57.

Gebauer, Matthias, John Goetz, and Britta Sandberg. 2009. "Detainee Abuse Continues at Bagram." *Salon*, September 21. http://www.salon.com/2009/09/21/bagram_5/.

Genette, Gérard. (1972) 1980. *Narrative Discourse: An Essay in Method.* Translated by Jane E. Lewin. Ithaca, N.Y.: Cornell University Press.

George, Andrew R. 2008. "A Tour of Nebuchadnezzar's Babylon" and "The Truth about Etemenanki, the Ziggurat of Babylon." In *Babylon*, edited by I. L. Finkel and M. J. Seymour, 54–59; 126–31. Oxford: Oxford University Press.

———. 2011. "A Stele of Nebuchadnezzar II." In *Cuneiform Royal Inscriptions and Related Texts in the Schøyen Collection*, Cornell University Studies in Assyriology and Sumerology 17, edited by A. R. George, 153–69. Bethesda, Md.: CDL Press.

Gershowitz, Hal, and Stephen Porter. 2010. "Liberty and Equality: Are They Compatible?" *Of Thee I Sing.* May 29. http://www.oftheeising1776.com/liberty-and-equality-are-they-compatible.

Gilroy, Paul. 1993. *The Black Atlantic: Modernity and Double Consciousness.* Cambridge, Mass.: Harvard University Press.

Gish, Lillian. 1969. *The Movies, Mr. Griffith, and Me.* Englewood Cliffs, N.J.: Prentice-Hall.

Glancy, Jennifer A. 2006. *Slavery in Early Christianity.* Minneapolis: Fortress.

Glancy, Jennifer A., and Stephen D. Moore. 2011. "How Typical a Roman Prostitute Is Revelation's 'Great Whore'?" *Journal of Biblical Literature* 130 (3): 551–69.

Gleason, Maud. 2001. "Mutilated Messengers: Body Language in Josephus." In *Being Greek under Rome: Cultural Identity, the Second Sophistic, and the Development of Empire*, edited by Simon Goldhill, 50–85. Cambridge: Cambridge University Press.

Goldberg, Jonathan. 1992. *Sodometries: Renaissance Texts, Modern Sexualities.* Stanford, Calif.: Stanford University Press.

Goldberg, Michelle. 2006. *Kingdom Coming: The Rise of Christian Nationalism.* New York: W. W. Norton.

Goldingay, John E. 1989. *Daniel.* Word Biblical Commentary 30. Dallas: Word Books.

Gordon, Colin. 1991. "Governmental Rationality: An Introduction." In *The Foucault Effect: Studies in Governmentality,* edited by Graham Burchell, Colin Gordon, and Peter Miller, 1–52. Chicago: University of Chicago Press.

Grady, Lee. 2008. "Can We Make a Deal for Peace?" *Forerunner.* http://forerunner.com/forerunner/X0308_Deal_for_Peace_.html.

Graves, Robert, and Raphael Patai. 1964. *Hebrew Myths: The Book of Genesis.* Garden City, N.Y.: Doubleday.

Greek Apocalypse of Ezra. 1983. Translated with an introduction by M. E. Stone. In *The Old Testament Pseudepigrapha: Apocalyptic Literature and Testament,* vol. 1, edited by James H. Charlesworth, 561–79. New York: Doubleday.

Gressman, Hugo. 1928. *The Tower of Babel.* New York: Jewish Institute of Religion.

Griffith, D. W. 1916. *The Rise and Fall of Free Speech in America.* Los Angeles: Larry Edmunds Bookshop.

Griffith, R. Marie. 2000. *God's Daughters: Evangelical Women and the Power of Submission.* Berkeley: University of California Press.

Grimstead, Jay, and E. Calvin Beisner, eds. 1986. "A Manifesto for the Christian Church." *Coalition on Revival.* http://65.175.91.69/Reformation_net/COR_Docs/Christian_Manifesto_Worldview.pdf.

———. 2000. "The Christian World View of Law." *Coalition on Revival.* http://65.175.91.69/Reformation_net/COR_Docs/Christian_Worldview_Law.pdf.

Grindstaff, Davin. 2008. "The Fist and the Corpse: Taming the Queer Sublime in *Brokeback Mountain.*" *Communication and Critical/Cultural Studies* 5 (3): 223–44.

Hagee, John. 2003. "The Final Dictator" (March 16 sermon). *Iraq: The Final War.* San Antonio, Texas: John Hagee Ministries. Audiocassette.

Halberstam, Judith. 2005. *In a Queer Time and Place: Transgender Bodies, Subcultural Lives.* New York: New York University Press.

Hall, Stuart. (1991) 1997. "The Local and the Global: Globalization and Ethnicity." In *Culture, Globalization and the World System,* edited by Anthony D. King, 19–40. Minneapolis: University of Minnesota Press.

Hamilton, Victor P. 1990. *The Book of Genesis Chapters 1–17.* Grand Rapids, Mich.: Eerdmans.

Hansen, Miriam. 1985. "Universal Language and Democratic Culture: Myths of Origin in Early American Cinema." In *Mythos und Aufklärung in der amerikanischen Literatur / Myth and Enlightenment in American Literature:*

Festschrift in Honor of Hans-Joachim Lang, edited by Dieter Meindl and Friedrich W. Horlacher, 321–51. Erlangen, Germany: University of Erlangen Nürnberg Press.

———. 1989. "Griffith's Real Intolerance." *Film Comment* 25 (5): 28–29.

———. 1991. *Babel and Babylon: Spectatorship in American Silent Film.* Cambridge, Mass.: Harvard University Press.

Hanson, Bernard. 1972. "D. W. Griffith: Some Sources." *Art Bulletin* 54 (4): 483–515.

Haraldsson, Hrafnkell. 2011."Rick Perry Ally Claims Homosexuality Is One of Baal's Strongholds." *Politicus USA.* July 14. http://archives.politicususa.com/2011/07/14/john-benefiel-claims-homosexuality-is-one-of-baals-strongholds.html.

Harding, James. 2012. *The Love of David and Jonathan: Ideology, Text, Reception.* BibleWorld. Sheffield, Eng.: Equinox Publishing.

Hardt, Michael, and Antonio Negri. 2000. *Empire.* Cambridge, Mass.: Harvard University Press.

———. 2004. *Multitude: War and Democracy in the Age of Empire.* London: Penguin.

Hartley, George. 2003. *The Abyss of Representation: Marxism and the Postmodern Sublime.* Post-Contemporary Interventions. Durham, N.C.: Duke University Press.

Hawkins, Peter S., and Lesleigh Cushing Stahlberg. 2009. *From the Margins.* Vol. 1, *Women of the Hebrew Bible and Their Afterlives.* Sheffield, Eng.: Sheffield Phoenix.

Hedges, Chris. 2004. "The Christian Right and the Rise of American Fascism." *Theocracy Watch.* November 15. http://www.theocracywatch.org/chris_hedges_nov24_04.htm.

Heidel, W. A. (1915) 1988. "Senate," in *The International Standard Bible Encyclopedia: Q–Z,* edited by Geoffrey W. Bromiley, 393. Grand Rapids, Mich.: Eerdmans.

Hendricks, Stephanie. 2005. *Divine Destruction: Wise Use, Dominion Theology, and the Making of American Environmental Policy.* Hoboken, N.J.: Melville House.

Herman, Didi. 1997. *The Anti-Gay Agenda: Orthodox Vision and the Christian Right.* Chicago: University of Chicago Press.

Hersh, Seymour M. 2004. "Torture at Abu Ghraib: American Soldiers Brutalized Iraqis. How Far Up Does the Responsibility Go?" *New Yorker,* May 10, p. 42.

———. 2007. "The General's Report." *New Yorker.* June 25. http://www.newyorker.com/reporting/2007/06/25/070625fa_fact_hersh.

Hidalgo, Jacqueline M. 2010. "California Dreaming: Scriptural Imaginaries and the Power of (No)Place from Aztlán to New Jerusalem." PhD diss., Claremont Graduate University.

Hiebert, Theodore. 2007. "The Tower of Babel and the Origin of the World's Cultures." *Journal of Biblical Literature* 126 (1): 29–58.

Hill, John. 1999. *Friend or Foe? The Figure of Babylon in the Book of Jeremiah MT.* Leiden: Brill.

———. 2009. "Writing the Prophetic Word: The Production of the Book of Jeremiah." *Australian Biblical Review* 57: 22–33.

Hillers, Delbert R. 1985. "Analyzing the Abominable: Our Understanding of Canaanite Religion." *Jewish Quarterly Review* 75 (3): 253–69.

Hilliker, Carl. 2007. "Coming Soon: One Pure Language." *Trumpet.* August/ September. http://www.thetrumpet.com/?q=4080.4868.97.0.

Hitchcock, Mark. 2003. *The Second Coming of Babylon.* Sisters, Ore.: Multnomah.

Hocquenghem, Guy. (1972) 1993. *Homosexual Desire.* Translated by Daniella Dangoor. Durham, N.C.: Duke University Press.

Holladay, William A. 1989. *Jeremiah*, vol. 2. Hermeneia Commentary. Minneapolis: Augsburg Fortress.

Holland, Shannon. 2009. "The 'Offending' Breast of Janet Jackson: Public Discourse Surrounding the Jackson/Timberlake Performance at Super Bowl XXXVIII." *Women's Studies in Communication* 32 (2): 129–50.

Hornsby, Teresa J., and Ken Stone, eds. 2011. *Bible Trouble: Queer Reading at the Boundaries of Biblical Scholarship.* Semeia Studies 67. Atlanta: Society of Biblical Literature.

Houck-Loomis, Tiffany. 2009. "Homogeneity: Safe or Profane? The Journey Toward the True Self: A Study of Genesis 11:1–9." *Reformed Review* 62 (2): 90–101.

Huber, Lynn R. 2011. "Gazing at the Whore: Reading Revelation Queerly." In *Bible Trouble: Queer Reading at the Boundaries of Biblical Scholarship*, edited by Teresa J. Hornsby and Ken Stone, 301–20. Semeia Studies 67. Atlanta: Society of Biblical Literature.

Humphreys, W. Lee. 2001. *The Character of God in the Book of Genesis: A Narrative Appraisal.* Louisville, Ky.: Westminster John Knox.

Hunter, Stephen. 2006. "'Babel's' World: Just a Big Ball of Yarns." *Washington Post*, November 3. http://www.washingtonpost.com/wp-dyn/content/article/2006/11/02/AR2006110201681.html.

Ibn Ezra. 1988. *Commentary on the Pentateuch: Genesis (Bereshit).* Translated by H. Norman Strickman and Arthur M. Silver. New York: Menorah.

Iñárritu, Alejandro González. 2006a. "Alejandro González Iñárritu." Interview with Stephan Littger. In *The Director's Cut: Picturing Hollywood in the 21st Century*, edited by Stephan Littger, 181–93. New York: Continuum.

———. 2006b. *Babel: A Film by Alejandro González Iñárritu.* Edited by María Eladia Hagerman. Los Angeles: Taschen.

————. 2007a. "Interview for On the Spot." Interview with Eleftheria Parpis. *Adweek* 48 (8): 21.

————. 2007b. "In a Global Age Films Must Portray Point of View of Others." Interview with Nathan Gardels. *New Perspectives Quarterly* 24 (Spring): 6–9.

Ingebretsen, Edward J. 1996. *Maps of Heaven, Maps of Hell: Religious Terror as Memory from the Puritans to Stephen King.* Armonk, N.Y.: M. E. Sharpe.

Ingersoll, Julie. 2009. "Mobilizing Evangelicals: Christian Reconstructionism and the Roots of the Religious Right." In *Evangelicals and Democracy in America.* Vol. 2, *Religion and Politics,* edited by Steven Brint and Jean Reith Schroedel, 179–208. New York: Russell Sage Foundation.

Inowlocki, Sabrina. 2005. "'Neither Adding Nor Omitting Anything': Josephus' Promise Not to Modify the Scriptures in Greek and Latin Context." *Journal of Jewish Studies* 56 (1): 48–65.

————. 2006. "Josephus' Rewriting of the Babel Narrative (Gen 11:1–9)." *Journal for the Study of Judaism in the Persian, Hellenistic and Roman Period* 37 (2): 169–91.

Ipsen, Avaren. 2009. *Sex Working and the Bible.* Sheffield, Eng.: Equinox.

Irenaeus. 1868–69. *Against Heresies.* Trans. Alexander Roberts and W. H. Rambout. Ante-Nicene Christian Library, vols. 5 and 9. Edinburgh: T & T Clark.

Jacobs, Andrew. 2004. *Remains of the Jews: The Holy Land and Christian Empire in Late Antiquity.* Stanford, Calif.: Stanford University Press.

Jacobs, Lewis. (1939) 1968. *The Rise of the American Film.* 4th ed. New York: Teachers College Press.

Jakobsen, Janet R. 2005. "Sex + Freedom = Regulation: Why?" *Social Text* 23 (3–4/84–85): 285–308.

Jakobsen, Janet R., and Ann Pellegrini. 2003. *Love the Sin: Sexual Regulation and the Limits of Religious Tolerance.* New York: New York University Press.

Jakobsen, Janet R., with Ann Pellegrini. 2000. "World Secularisms at the Millennium." *Social Text* 18 (3/ 64): 1–28.

Jakobson, Roman. (1956) 1987. "Two Aspects of Language and Two Types of Aphasic Disturbances." Chap. 7 in *Language and Literature,* 95–120. Cambridge, Mass.: Harvard University Press.

James, William T., ed. 1997. *Foreshocks of the Antichrist.* Eugene, Ore.: Harvest House.

Janoff-Bulman, Ronnie. 2007. "Erroneous Assumptions: Popular Belief in the Effectiveness of Torture Interrogation." *Peace and Conflict: Journal of Peace Psychology* 13 (4): 429–35.

Jastrow, Morris. 1915. *The Civilization of Babylonia and Assyria: Its Remains, Language, History, Religion, Commerce, Law, Art, and Literature.* Philadelphia: J. B. Lippincott.

Jaume, Lucien. 2011. "The Avatars of Religion in Tocqueville." Translated by Yves Winter. In *Crediting God: Sovereignty and Religion in the Age of Global Capitalism*, edited by Miguel Vatter, 273–84. New York: Fordham University Press.

Jenks, Gregory C. 1991. *The Origins and Early Development of the Antichrist Myth*. Berlin: Walter de Gruyter.

Joachim of Fiore. 1979. "Book of Figures, The Fourteenth Table, The Seven-Headed Dragon." In *Apocalyptic Spirituality: Treatises and Letters of Lactantius, Adso of Montier-en-Der, Joachim of Fiore, The Franciscan Spirituals, Savonarola*, edited and translated by Bernard McGinn, 136–41. New York: Paulist Press.

Johnson, Bradley A. 2006. "Currency of a Calling: The American Exception, the American Dream." *Postscripts* 2 (1): 87–95.

Johnson, Sylvester A. 2004. *The Myth of Ham in Nineteenth-Century American Christianity: Race, Heathens, and the People of God*. Black Religion, Womanist Thought, Social Justice. New York: Palgrave Macmillan.

Jones, C. P. 1987. "Stigma: Tattooing and Branding in Graeco-Roman Antiquity." *Journal of Roman Studies* 77: 139–55.

Josephus, Flavius. 1999. *The New Complete Works of Josephus*. Translated by William Whiston. Grand Rapids Mich.: Kregel.

Joyce, Paul. 2007. *Ezekiel: A Commentary*. New York: T & T Clark.

Kagan, Donald, Gary Schmitt, and Thomas Donnelly. 2000. *Rebuilding America's Defenses: Strategy, Forces and Resources for a New Century*. Project for the New American Century. http://www.newamericancentury.org/Rebuilding AmericasDefenses.pdf.

Kant, Immanuel. (1790) 2000. *Critique of the Power of Judgment*. Edited by Paul Guyer. Translated by Paul Guyer and Eric Matthews. Cambridge: Cambridge University Press.

———. (1793) 1998. *Religion within the Boundaries of Mere Reason and Other Writings*. Edited and translated by Allen Wood and George Di Giovanni. Cambridge: Cambridge University Press.

Kaplan, Amy. 2002. *The Anarchy of Empire in the Making of U.S. Culture*. Cambridge, Mass.: Harvard University Press.

Karpinski, Janis, with Steven Strasser. 2005. *One Woman's Army: The Commanding General of Abu Ghraib Tells Her Story*. New York: Hyperion.

Kass, Leon R. 2003. *The Beginning of Wisdom: Reading Genesis*. Chicago: University of Chicago Press.

Kaufman, Joanne. 2006. "'Babel' Mixes Plots, Pitt, Blanchett but Is a Mess in Any Language." *Wall Street Journal*, October 27. http://online.wsj.com/article/SB116190635292205389.html.

Keller, Catherine. 2005. *God and Power: Counter Apocalyptic Journeys*. Minneapolis: Augsburg Fortress.

Kelly, Henry Ansgar. 2006. *Satan: A Biography*. Cambridge: Cambridge University Press.

Kennedy, John F. 1961. "Address of President-Elect John F. Kennedy Delivered to a Joint Convention of the General Court of the Commonwealth of Massachusetts. Boston, January 9. http://www.jfklibrary.org/Asset-Viewer/OYhUZE2Qoo-ogdV7ok9ooA.aspx.

Kent, Jonathan. 2007. "Blair, Bush, in 'War Crimes Trial.'" *BBC News*, February 7. http://news.bbc.co.uk/2/hi/asia-pacific/6336333.stm.

Keown, Gerald L., Pamela J. Scalise, and Thomas G. Smothers. 1995. *Jeremiah 26–52*. Word Biblical Commentary 27. Dallas, Texas: Word.

Kessler, Martin. 2003. *Battle of the Gods: The God of Israel Versus Marduk of Babylon: A Literary/Theological Interpretation of Jeremiah 50–51*. Studia Semetica Neerlandica 42. Assen: Royal Van Gorcum.

———, ed. 2004. *Reading the Book of Jeremiah: A Search for Coherence*. Winona Lake, Ind.: Eisenbrauns.

Kidner, Derek. 1975. *Psalms 73–150*. Tyndale Old Testament Commentaries. Leicester: Inter-Varsity Press.

Kikawada, Isaac M. 1974. "The Shape of Genesis 11:1–9." In *Rhetorical Criticism: Essays in Honor of James Muilenburg*, edited by Jared J. Jackson and Martin Kessler, 18–32. Pittsburgh: Pickwick.

Kim, Jean K. 1999. "'Uncovering Her Wickedness': An Inter(con)textual Reading of Revelation 17 from a Postcolonial Feminist Perspective." *Journal for the Study of the New Testament* 21 (73): 61–81.

Kinkopf, Neil, and Peter Shane. 2007. "Index of Presidential Signing Statements: 2001–2007." *American Constitution Society for Law and Policy*. http://acslaw.org/node/5309.

Kintz, Linda. 1997. *Between Jesus and the Market: The Emotions That Matter in Right-Wing America*. Durham, N.C.: Duke University Press.

Kirschner, Robert. 1990. "Two Responses to Epochal Change: Augustine and the Rabbis on Psalm 137 (136). *Vigiliae Christianae* 44 (3): 242–62.

Kittredge, Cynthia Briggs, Ellen B. Aitken, and Jonathan A. Draper, eds. 2008. *The Bible in the Public Square: Reading the Signs of the Times*. Minneapolis: Fortress Press.

Kjos, Berit. 1997. "Classroom Earth: Educating for One World Order." In *Foreshocks of the Antichrist*, edited by William T. James, 45–80. Eugene, Ore.: Harvest House.

Kline, Scott. 2004. "The Culture War Gone Global: 'Family Values' and the Shape of U.S. Foreign Policy." *International Relations* 18 (4): 453–66.

Knight, Jason. 1995. *The Ascension of Isaiah*. Sheffield, Eng.: Sheffield Academic Press.

Knight, Robert. 2004. "Iraq Scandal Is 'Perfect Storm' of American Culture." May 12. http://www.wnd.com/2004/05/24595/.

Koester, Craig R. 2008. "Roman Slave Trade and the Critique of Babylon in Revelation 18." *Catholic Biblical Quarterly* 70 (4): 766–86.

Koldewey, Robert. 1914. *The Excavations at Babylon.* Translated by Agnes S. Johns. London: Macmillan.

Kraeling, E. G. H. 1920. "The Tower of Babel." *Journal of the American Oriental Society* 40: 276–81.

Kramer, Samuel Noah. 1968. "The 'Babel of Tongues': A Sumerian Version." *Journal of the American Oriental Society* 88 (1): 108–11.

Kraus, Hans-Joachim. 1988. *Psalms 60–150: A Commentary.* Translated by Hilton C. Oswald. Minneapolis: Augsburg.

Kraybill, J. Nelson. 1996. *Imperial Cult and Commerce in John's Apocalypse.* Supplement, *Journal for the Study of the New Testament* 132. Sheffield, Eng.: Sheffield Academic Press.

Kristol, Irving. 1960. "Democracy and Babel." *Columbia University Forum* 3 (3): 15–19.

———. 2003. "The Neoconservative Persuasion: What It Was and What It Is." *Weekly Standard* 8 (47). http://www.weeklystandard.com/Content/Public/Articles/000/000/003/000tzmlw.asp.

Kugel, James L. 1997. *The Bible as It Was.* Cambridge, Mass.: Belknap Press of Harvard University Press.

Kuklick, Bruce. 1996. *Puritans in Babylon: The Ancient Near East and American Intellectual Life, 1880–1930.* Princeton, N.J.: Princeton University Press.

Lackey, Michael. 2009. "Foucault, Secularization Theory, and the Theological Origins of Totalitarianism." In *Foucault's Legacy*, edited by C. G. Prado, 124–45. London: Continuum International.

Lacocque, André. 1976. *Le livre de Daniel.* Paris: Delachaux et Niestlé.

———. 2001. "Allusions to Creation in Daniel 7." In *The Book of Daniel: Composition and Reception*, vol. 1, edited by John J. Collins and Peter W. Flint, with Cameron VanEpps, 114–31. Leiden: Brill.

LaHaye, Timothy. 1999. *Revelation Unveiled.* Grand Rapids, Mich.: Zondervan.

Landsberger, Benno, and J. V. Kinnier Wilson. 1961. "The Fifth Tablet of Enuma Elish." *Journal of Near Eastern Studies* 20 (3): 154–79.

Lang, Berel. 1996. "Holocaust Memory and Revenge: The Presence of the Past." *Jewish Social* Studies 2 (2): 1–20.

Lee, Edmund. 2010. "Does Who Creates Content Matter to Marketers in a 'Pro-Am' Media World? *Examiner* Has 7.4 Million Readers, Local Ads and News—but Few Traditional Journalists." *AdvertisingAge*, June 7. http://adage.com/article/mediaworks/creates-content-matter-marketers/144286/.

Lefort, Claude. 2006. "The Permanence of the Theologico-Political?" In *Political Theologies: Public Religions in a Post-Secular World*, edited by Hent de Vries and Lawrence E. Sullivan, 148–87. New York: Fordham University Press.

Lennig, Arthur. 2005. "The Mother and the Law." *Film History* 17 (4): 403–30.

Lenowitz, Harris. 1987. "The Mock-Śimhâ of Psalm 137." In *Directions in Biblical Hebrew Poetry*, edited by Elaine R. Follis, 149–59. Sheffield, Eng.: Sheffield Academic Press.

Lerner, Robert E. 1985. "Antichrists and Antichrist in Joachim of Fiore." *Speculum* 60 (3): 553–70.

Levin, Yigal. 2002. "Nimrod the Mighty, King of Kish, King of Sumer and Akkad." *Vetus Testamentum* 52 (3): 350–66.

Levine, Daniel B. 1993. "Hubris in Josephus' Jewish Antiquities 1–4." *Hebrew Union College Annual* 64:51–87.

Liberman, Peter. 2006. "An Eye for an Eye: Public Support for War against Evildoers." *International Organization* 60 (3): 687–722.

Liew, Tat-siong Benny. 2008. *What Is Asian American Biblical Hermeneutics? Reading the New Testament*. Honolulu: University of Hawai'i Press.

Liew, Tat-siong Benny, and Gale A. Yee, eds. 2002. *The Bible in Asian America*. Semeia 90/91. Atlanta: Society of Biblical Literature.

Lifton, Robert Jay. 2003. *Superpower Syndrome: America's Apocalyptic Confrontation with the World*. New York: Nation Books.

Linafelt, Tod, ed. 2000. *Strange Fire: Reading the Bible after the Holocaust*. New York: New York University Press.

Lincoln, Bruce. 2004. "Words Matter: How Bush Speaks in Religious Code." *Boston Globe*, September 12. http://www.boston.com/news/globe/editorial_opinion/oped/articles/2004/09/12/words_matter.

———. 2006. *Holy Terrors: Thinking about Religion after September 11*. Chicago: University of Chicago Press.

Lindsay, Richard A. 2012. "The Camp and the Kerygma: Queer Readings of Hollywood Biblical Epics." PhD diss., Graduate Theological Union.

Lindsey, Hal. 2008. "How Obama Prepped the World for the Antichrist." *WorldNetDaily*. August 1. http://www.wnd.com/2008/08/71144/.

Long, Thomas L. 2005. *AIDS and American Apocalypticism: The Cultural Semiotics of an Epidemic*. Albany: State University of New York Press.

Louth, Andrew, ed. 2001. *Genesis 1–11: Ancient Christian Commentary on Scriptures*. Downers Grove, Ill.: InterVarsity.

Lowry, Robert. 2011. "'All Too Human' A Sermon on Psalm 137 Following the Death of Osama bin Laden." *Theology in Public*, May 15. http://presrevrob.blogspot.com/2011/05/all-too-human-sermon-on-psalm-137.html.

Luban, David. 2005. "Liberalism, Torture, and the Ticking Bomb." *Virginia Law Review* 91 (6): 1425–61.

Lundbom, Jack R. 1999. *Jeremiah 37–52*. Anchor Bible Commentaries. New Haven, Conn.: Yale University Press.

Lyon, David Gordon. 1918. "Recent Excavations at Babylon." *Harvard Theological Review* 11 (3): 307–21.

Lyons, William John. 2005. "A Man of Honour, a Man of Strength, a Man of Will?: A Canonical Approach to Psalm 137." *Didaskalia* 16 (2): 41–68.

Lyotard, Jean-François. (1991) 1994. *Lessons on the Analytic of the Sublime*. Meridian Crossing Aesthetics. Translated by Elizabeth Rottenberg. Stanford, Calif.: Stanford University Press.

Machosky, Brenda, ed. 2010. *Thinking Allegory Otherwise*. Stanford, Calif.: Stanford University Press.

Mader, Gottfried. 2000. *Josephus and the Politics of Historiography: Apologetic and Impression Management in the "Bellum Judaicum."* Leiden: Brill.

Mahlmann, Matthias. 2003. "Law and Force: 20th Century Radical Legal Philosophy, Post-modernism and the Foundations of Law." *Res Publica* 9 (1): 19–37.

Maier, Harry O. 1997. "Staging the Gaze: Early Christian Apocalypses and Narrative Self-Representation." *Harvard Theological Review* 90 (2): 131–54.

Maley, Willy. 1999. "Beyond the Law? The Justice of Deconstruction." *Law and Critique* 10 (1): 49–69.

Mansfield, Harvey C. 2006. *Manliness*. New Haven, Conn.: Yale University Press.

Martin, Clarice J. 2005. "Polishing the Unclouded Mirror: A Womanist Reading of Revelation 18:13." In *From Every People and Nation: The Book of Revelation in Intercultural Perspective*, edited by David M. Rhoads, 82–109. Minneapolis: Fortress Press.

Martin, Floyd W. 1983. "D. W. Griffith's 'Intolerance': A Note on Additional Visual Sources." *Art Journal* 43 (3): 231–33.

Marzahn, Joachim. 2008. "Koldewey's Babylon." In *Babylon*, edited by I. L. Finkel and M. J. Seymour, 46–53; 126–31. Oxford: Oxford University Press.

Mason, Steve. 2005. "Figured Speech and Irony in T. Flavius Josephus." In *Flavius Josephus and Flavian Rome*, edited by Jonathan Edmondson, Steve Mason, and James Rives, 243–88. Oxford: Oxford University Press.

Massegee, Charles. 2011. *The Rise and Fall of the Antichrist: Islam, Allah, and the Antichrist in Prophecy*. Parker, Colo.: Outskirts Press.

May, Lary. 1980. *Screening Out the Past: The Birth of Mass Culture and the Motion Picture Industry*. Oxford: Oxford University Press.

Mbembe, Achille. 2003. "Necropolitics." Translated by Libby Meintjes. *Public Culture* 15 (1): 11–40.

McCann, J. Clinton, Jr. 1996. "Psalms." In *The New Interpreter's Bible*, vol. 4, edited by Leander E. Keck et al., 639–1280. Nashville, Tenn.: Abingdon Press.

McCarthy, Rory, and Maev Kennedy. 2005. "Babylon Wrecked by War." *Guardian*, January 15. http://www.guardian.co.uk/world/2005/jan/15/iraq.arts1.

McCormick, John P. 1993. "Introduction to Schmitt's 'The Age of Neutraliza-tions and Depoliticizations.'" *Telos* 96 (Summer): 119–29.

———. 1995. "Dangers of Mythologizing Technology and Politics: Nietzsche, Schmitt, and the Antichrist." *Philosophy and Social Criticism* 21 (4): 55–92.

———. 1997. *Carl Schmitt's Critique of Liberalism: Against Politics as Technology.* Cambridge: Cambridge University Press.

McGinn, Bernard, ed. and trans. 1979. *Apocalyptic Spirituality: Treatises and Let-ters of Lactantius, Adso of Montier-en-Der, Joachim of Fiore, The Franciscan Spirituals, Savonarola.* New York: Paulist Press.

———. 1994. *Antichrist: Two Thousand Years of the Human Fascination with Evil.* San Francisco: Harper San Francisco.

McLaren, James S. 2005. "A Reluctant Provincial: Josephus and the Roman Empire in *Jewish War.*" In *The Gospel of Matthew in Its Roman Imperial Context*, edited by John Riches and David C. Sim, 34–48. London: T & T Clark.

McLean, Adrienne L. 1997. "The Thousand Ways There Are to Move: Camp and Orientalist Dance in the Hollywood Musicals of Jack Cole." In *Visions of the East: Orientalism in Film*, edited by Matthew Bernstein and Gaylyn Studlar, 130–57. New Brunswick, N.J.: Rutgers University Press.

McVicar, Michael J. 2007. "The Libertarian Theocrats: The Long, Strange His-tory of R. J. Rushdoony and Christian Reconstructionism." *Public Eye Maga-zine* 22 (3). http://www.publiceye.org/magazine/v22n3/libertarian.html.

Mein, Andrew. 2001. *Ezekiel and the Ethics of Exile.* Oxford: Oxford University Press.

Merritt, Russell. 1979. "On First Looking into Griffith's Babylon." *Wide Angle* 3 (1): 12–21.

Middleton, J. Richard. 2000. "Identity and Subversion in Babylon: 'Strategies for Resisting against the System' in the Music of Bob Marley and the Wail-ers." In *Religion, Culture, and Tradition in the Caribbean*, edited by Hemchand Gossai and Nathaniel Samuel Murrell, 181–204. New York: St. Martin's Press.

Milich, Klaus J. 2006. "Fundamentalism Hot and Cold: George W. Bush and the 'Return of the Sacred.'" *Cultural Critique* 62 (Winter): 92–125.

Miller, Keith D. 2007. "Second Isaiah Lands in Washington, D.C.: Martin Luther King, Jr.'s 'I Have a Dream' as Biblical Narrative and Biblical Her-meneutic." *Rhetoric Review* 26 (4): 405–24.

Miner, Alan C. 1996. *Step by Step through the Book of Mormon: A Cultural Com-mentary.* Accessed September 10, 2013. http://stepbystep.alancminer.com/home.

Mirzoeff, Nicholas. 2005. *Watching Babylon: The War in Iraq and Global Visual Culture.* New York: Routledge.

Moon, Michael. 1989. "Flaming Closets." *October* 51 (Winter): 19–54.

Moore, Stephen D. 1996. *God's Gym: Divine Male Bodies of the Bible.* New York: Routledge.

———. 2002. *God's Beauty Parlor: And Other Queer Spaces in and around the Bible.* Stanford, Calif.: Stanford University Press.

———. 2006. *Empire and Apocalypse: Postcolonialism and the New Testament.* Sheffield, Eng.: Sheffield Phoenix Press.

———. 2009. "Metonymies of Empire: Sexual Humiliation and Gender Masquerade in the Book of Revelation." In *Postcolonial Interventions: Essays in Honor of R. S. Sugirtharajah,* edited by Tat-siong Benny Liew, 71–97. Sheffield, Eng.: Sheffield Phoenix Press.

———. 2010. *The Bible in Theory: Critical and Postcritical Essays.* Atlanta: Society of Biblical Literature.

Morford, Mark. 2004. "Apocalypse Bush! Why Care for the Planet When the End Times Are Almost Here? Vote Bush and Hop On the Salvation Train!" *San Francisco Chronicle,* September 8. http://www.sfgate.com/entertainment/morford/article/Apocalypse-Bush-Why-care-for-the-planet-when-2727243.php.

Mosca, Paul. 1986. "Ugarit and Daniel 7: A Missing Link." *Biblica* 67 (1): 496–517.

Mowinckel, Sigmund. 1913. *Zur Komposition des Buches Jeremia.* Kristiania: Jacob Dybwad.

Müller, Jan-Werner. 2003. *A Dangerous Mind: Carl Schmitt in Post-War European Thought.* New Haven, Conn.: Yale University Press.

Murrell, Nathaniel Samuel 2000. "Dangerous Memories, Underdevelopment and the Bible in Colonial Caribbean Experience." In *Religion, Culture, and Tradition in the Caribbean,* edited by Hemchand Gossai and Nathaniel Samuel Murrell, 9–35. New York: St. Martin's Press.

National Security Council. 2006. "Overview of America's National Strategy for Combating Terrorism." http://georgewbush-whitehouse.archives.gov/nsc/nsct/2006/sectionI.html.

Nelavala, Surekha. 2009. "'Babylon the Great Mother of Whores' (Rev 17:5): A Postcolonial Feminist Perspective." *Expository Times* 121 (2): 60–65.

Nibley, Hugh W. 1988–90. *Teachings of the Book of Mormon: Semester 3.* American Fork, Utah: Covenant Communications.

Noll, K. L. 2001. *Canaan and Israel in Antiquity: An Introduction.* Biblical Seminar 83. Sheffield, Eng.: Sheffield Academic Press.

Norris, Andrew. 2000. "Carl Schmitt's Political Metaphysics: On the Secularization of 'the Outermost Sphere.'" *Theory and Event* 4 (1). http://muse.jhu.edu/journals/theory_&_event.

North, Gary. 1973. "Appendix 5: In Defense of Biblical Bribery." In *The Institutes of Biblical Law,* by R. Rushdoony, 837–46. Philadelphia: Presbyterian and Reformed Publishing.

Oates, Joan. 2008. *Babylon*. Rev. ed. London: Thames and Hudson.

Obama, Barack. 2010. "Remarks by the President at the National Prayer Breakfast." Washington, D.C. February 4. http://www.whitehouse.gov/the-press -office/remarks-president-national-prayer-breakfast.

———. 2012. "Remarks by the President in State of the Union Address." U.S. Capitol, Washington, D.C. January 24. http://www.whitehouse.gov/the-press -office/2012/01/24/remarks-president-state-union-address.

Odell, Margaret S. 2005. *Ezekiel*. Smyth and Helwys Bible Commentary. Macon, Ga.: Smyth and Helwys.

Oden, R. A., Jr. 1977. "Baal Samem and El." *Catholic Biblical Quarterly* 39 (4): 457–73.

O'Hehir, Andrew. 2006. "Babel." *Salon*, October 27. http://www.salon.com/2006 /10/27/babel/.

O'Keeffe, Alice. 2007. "Agent Provocateur." *New Statesman* 136 (January 15): 36–38.

O'Leary, Stephen D. 1994. *Arguing the Apocalypse: A Theory of Millennial Rhetoric*. New York: Oxford University Press.

Olsen, Ted. 2004. "Jim Dobson's New Political Organization: Plus: Christian Organizations Blame Porn for Abuse at Abu Ghraib." *Christianity Today Weblog*, May 1. http://www.christianitytoday.com/ct/2004/119/42.0.html.

Ong, Aihwa. 2006. *Neoliberalism as Exception: Mutations in Citizenship and Sovereignty*. Durham, N.C.: Duke University Press.

Origen. 1869–72. *Contra Celsum*. Translated by Frederick Crombie. *Ante-Nicene Christian Library*, vols. 10 and 23. Edinburgh: T & T Clark.

———. 1982. *Homilies on Genesis*. Translated by Ronald E. Heine, 1982. *The Fathers of the Church*, vol. 71, 47–224. Washington, D.C.: Catholic University of America Press.

Page, Hugh R., Jr. 1998. "'Ain't Gonna Lay My 'Ligion Down': African American Religion in the South." *Journal for the Scientific Study of Religion* 37 (2): 369–70.

———. 2009. "'Let My People Stay!' Researching the Old Testament in Africa: Report from a Research Project on Africanization of Old Testament studies." *Catholic Biblical Quarterly* 71 (4): 923–25.

Paine, Thomas. 1892. "The Tower of Babel." In *The Complete Religious and Theological Works of Thomas Paine*, 393–94. New York: Peter Eckler.

Pecora, Vincent P. 2006. *Secularization and Cultural Criticism: Religion, Nation, and Modernity*. Chicago: University of Chicago Press.

Peerbolte, L. J. Lietaert. 1996. *The Antecedents of Antichrist: A Traditio-Historical Study of the Earliest Christian Views on Eschatological Opponents*. Supplement, *Journal for the Study of Judaism* 49. Leiden: Brill.

Peisner, David. 2006. "Music as Torture: War Is Loud." *Spin*, November 30. http://www.spin.com/articles/music-torture-war-loud.

Perdue, Leo G., and Brian W. Kovacs. 1984. *A Prophet to the Nations: Essays in Jeremiah Studies*. Winona Lake, Ind.: Eisenbrauns.

Perry, Peter S. 2007. "Critiquing the Excess of Empire: A Synkrisis of John of Patmos and Dio of Prusa." *Journal for the Study of the New Testament* 29 (4): 473–96.

Peters, John P. 1919. "Notes on Isaiah." *Journal of Biblical Literature* 38 (2–3): 77–93.

Peterson, Kavan. 2004. "50-State Rundown on Gay Marriage Laws." *Stateline*, November 3. http://www.pewstates.org/projects/stateline/headlines/50-state -rundown-on-gay-marriage-laws-85899387500.

Phillips, Kevin. 2006. *American Theocracy: The Peril and Politics of Radical Religion, Oil, and Borrowed Money in the 21st Century*. New York: Viking.

Philo. 1993a. *On the Confusion of Tongues*. Translated by C. D. Yonge. In *The Works of Philo*, 234–52. Peabody, Mass.: Hendrickson Publishers.

———. 1993b. *Questions and Answers on Genesis*. Translated by C. D. Yonge. In *The Works of Philo*, 791–863. Peabody, Mass.: Hendrickson Publishers.

Pieslak, Jonathan. 2009. *Sound Targets: American Soldiers and Music in the Iraq War*. Bloomington: Indiana University Press.

Pinker, Aron. 1998. "Nimrod Found." *Jewish Bible Quarterly* 26 (4): 237–45.

———. 2000. "The Book of Zephaniah: Allusions to the Tower of Babel." *Jewish Bible Quarterly* 28 (1): 3–11.

Pinn, Anthony B., and Allen Dwight Callahan, eds. 2008. *African American Religious Life and the Story of Nimrod*. New York: Palgrave Macmillan.

Pippin, Tina. 1992a. *Death and Desire: The Rhetoric of Gender in the Apocalypse of John*. Louisville, Ky.: Westminster John Knox Press.

———. 1992b. "The Heroine and the Whore: Fantasy and the Female in the Apocalypse of John." *Semeia* 60:67–82.

———. 1999. *Apocalyptic Bodies: The Biblical End of the World in Text and Image*. London: Routledge.

Plank, Karl A. 2008. "By the Waters of a Death Camp: An Intertextual Reading of Psalm 137." *Literature and Theology* 22 (2): 180–94.

Plate, S. Brent. 2005. *Walter Benjamin, Religion, and Aesthetics: Rethinking Religion through the Arts*. New York: Routledge.

Plato. 1992. *Republic*. Translated by G. M. A. Grube and revised by C. D. C. Reeve. Indianapolis: Hackett.

Pope, Randy. 2011. "Should the Death of Osama Bin Laden Be the Cause for Rejoicing in Christendom?" *Examiner*, May 2. http://www.examiner.com/ religion-politics-in-akron/should-the-death-of-osama-bin-laden-be-the -cause-for-rejoicing-christendom

Porteous, Norman W. 1965. *Daniel: A Commentary*. Old Testament Library. Philadelphia: Westminster.

Portwood, Craig. 2010. "Part Two: The Beast Receives a Deadly Wound." *Examiner,* April 29. http://www.examiner.com/article/part-two-the-beast-receives-a-deadly-wound.

Posner, Sarah. 2008. "'The Call' Warns of Antichrist Legislation in California and Beyond." *Religion Dispatches.* October 29. http://www.religiondispatches .org/archive/politics/654/.

Povinelli, Elizabeth A. 2006. *The Empire of Love: Towards a Theory of Intimacy, Genealogy and Carnality.* Durham, N.C.: Duke University Press.

Preußischer Kulturbesitz. 2008. "Babylon: Myth and Truth." Staatliche Museen zu Berlin. Accessed February 23, 2012. http://www.smb.museum/smb/ kalender/details.php?objID=19235&lang=en&n=0&datum=05.10.2008.

———. 2012. "Museum of the Ancient Near East." Staatliche Museen zu Berlin. Accessed February 23. http://www.smb.museum/smb/sammlungen/ details.php?objID=23&n=15.

Priest, Josiah. 1843. *Slavery, as It Relates to the Negro, or African Race.* Albany, N.Y.: C. Van Benthuysen.

Prince, Stephen. 1992. *Visions of Empire: Political Imagery in Contemporary American Film.* New York: Praeger.

Pritchard, Elizabeth. 2006. "Agency without Transcendence." *Culture and Religion* 7 (3): 263–89.

Pseudo-Philo. 1996. *Biblical Antiquities.* Translated by Howard Jacobson. Arbeiten zur Geschichte des Antiken Judentums und des Urchristentums, vol. 31. Leiden: Brill.

Puar, Jasbir K. 2007. *Terrorist Assemblages: Homonationalism in Queer Times.* Next Wave: New Directions in Women's Studies. Durham, N.C.: Duke University Press.

Pyper, Hugh S. 2010a. "Cultivated Outrage: World Wrestling Entertainment and the Religious Excess of Violence." In *Holy Terror: Understanding Religion and Violence in Popular Culture,* edited by Eric Christianson and Christopher Partridge, 135–49. London: Equinox.

———. 2010b. "Rough Justice: Lars von Trier's Dogville and Manderlay and the Book of Amos." *Political Theology* 11 (3): 321–34.

———. 2012. *The Unchained Bible: Cultural Appropriations of Biblical Texts.* The Library of Hebrew Bible/Old Testament Studies. New York: T & T Clark.

Rahe, Paul A. 2009. *Soft Despotism, Democracy's Drift: Montesquieu, Rousseau, Tocqueville and the Modern Prospect.* New Haven, Conn.: Yale University Press.

———. 2011. "The 60 Second Update with Dr. Paul Rahe." VictoryNH: The Citizen Activist Network. http://60secondupdates.com/rahe/rahe-1.

Rajak, Tessa. 1985. "Jewish Rights in Greek Cities under Roman Rule: A New Approach." In *Approaches to Ancient Judaism.* Vol. 5, *Studies in Judaism in Its*

Greco-Roman Context, edited by W. S. Green, 19–35. Brown Judaic Studies 32. Atlanta: Scholars.

Rana, Junaid. 2011. *Terrifying Muslims: Race and Labor in the South Asian Diaspora.* Durham, N.C.: Duke University Press.

Rancière, Jacques. 2006. *Hatred of Democracy.* Translated by Steve Corcoran. London: Verso.

Reade, Julian. 2008. "Nineteenth-Century Exploration and Interpretation." In *Babylon*, edited by I. L. Finkel and M. J. Seymour, 34–39. Oxford: Oxford University Press.

Reagan, David R. 2005. "The Rise and Fall of the Antichrist." Lamb and Lion Ministries. http://www.lamblion.com/articles/articles_tribulation7 .php.

Reagan, Ronald. 1984. "Remarks Accepting the Presidential Nomination at the Republican National Convention." Dallas, August 23. http://www .reagan.utexas.edu/archives/speeches/1984/82384f.htm

Reimer, David J. 1993. *The Oracles against Babylon in Jeremiah 50–51: A Horror among the Nations.* San Francisco: Mellen Research University Press.

Rejali, Darius. 2007. *Torture and Democracy.* Princeton, N.J.: Princeton University Press.

Remnant of God. 1985–2005. "Characteristics of the Antichrist." Presents of God Ministry. http://www.remnantofgod.org/666-char.htm.

Renfroe, F. 1988. "Persiflage in Psalm 137." In *Ascribe to the Lord: Biblical and Other Studies in Memory of Peter C. Craigie*, edited by Lyle M. Eslinger and Glen Taylor, 509–27. Sheffield, Eng.: Journal for the Study of the Old Testament Press.

Renz, Art, and Sue Renz. 2005. "Osama bin Laden = 666?" His Sheep by the Shepherd's Voice. http://www.hissheep.org/special/prophecy/osama_bin_ laden_666.html.

Richardson, Joel. 2009. *The Islamic Antichrist: The Shocking Truth about the Real Nature of the Beast.* 2nd ed. New York: WND Books.

Ridley, Jim. 2006. "Communication Breakdown." *Village Voice*, October 17. http: //www.villagevoice.com/2006-10-17/film/communication-breakdown/.

Risse, Siegfried. 2006. "'Wohl dem, der deine kleinen Kinder packt und sie am Felsen zerschmettert': Zur Auslegungsgeschichte von Ps 137, 9." *Biblical Interpretation* 14 (4): 364–84.

Robbins, Jeffrey W. 2011. *Radical Democracy and Political Theology.* New York: Columbia University Press.

Rogers, Jay. 1994. "Van Tillian Presuppositional Theonomic Ethics." *Forerunner.* http://www.forerunner.com/forerunner/X0518_vantil.html.

Rogin, Michael. 1989. "The Great Mother Domesticated: Sexual Difference and Sexual Indifference in D. W. Griffith's Intolerance." *Critical Inquiry* 15 (3): 510–55.

———. 1990. "'Make My Day!' Spectacle as Amnesia in Imperial Politics." *Representations* 29 (Winter): 99–123.

Rose, Tom. 2006. "Contra Imperium: The Christian Case against American Imperialism and the Security/Police State." *Faith for All of Life* (November/December): 24–29.

Rosenstiehl, J.-M. 1967. "Le Portrait de L'Antichrist." In *Pseudépigraphes de l'ancien testament et manuscrits de la mer morte*, edited by Marc Philonenko, 45–60. Paris: Presses universitaires de France.

Rothfield, Lawrence. 2009. *The Rape of Mesopotamia: Behind the Looting of the Iraq Museum*. Chicago: University of Chicago Press.

Rove, Karl. 2010. "Karl Rove on Compassionate Conservatism." Interview with Jonathan Rauch. *Browser*, September 12. http://thebrowser.com/interviews/karl-rove-on-compassionate-conservatism.

Ruffin, Kimberly N. 2010. "The Hebrew Bible in Africana Art, Music, and Popular Culture." In *The Africana Bible: Reading Israel's Scriptures from Africa and the African Diaspora*, edited by Hugh R. Page Jr., et al., 52–57. Minneapolis: Fortress.

Runions, Erin. 2003. *How Hysterical: Identification and Resistance in the Bible and Film*. Religion/Culture/Critique. New York: Palgrave.

———. 2004. "Biblical Promise and Threat in U.S. Imperialist Rhetoric, Before and After 9/11." *Interventions: Activists and Academics Respond to Violence*, edited by Elizabeth A. Castelli and Janet R. Jakobsen, 71–88. New York: Palgrave.

———. 2005. "Desiring War: Apocalypse, Commodity Fetish, and the End of History." In *The Postcolonial Biblical Reader*, edited by R. Sugirtharajah, 112–28. Oxford: Blackwell.

———. 2007. "Theologico-Political Resonance: Carl Schmitt between the Neocons and Theonomists." *differences: A Journal of Feminist Cultural Studies* 18 (3): 43–80.

Rushdoony, Mark R. 2006. "From the President: Don't Pray for the Peace of Babylon." *Faith for All of Life* (November/December): 12–15.

Rushdoony, Rousas John. 1973. *The Institutes of Biblical Law*. Philadelphia: Presbyterian and Reformed Publishing.

Santner, Eric L. 2011. *The Royal Remains: The People's Two Bodies and the Endgames of Sovereignty*. Chicago: University of Chicago Press.

Sarna, Nahum M. 1989. *Genesis*. JPS Torah Commentary 1. Philadelphia: Jewish Publication Society.

Sarris, Andrew. (1968) 1996. *The American Cinema: Directors and Directions 1929–1968*. New York: Da Capo Press.

———. 2006. "Manipulative and Mean-Spirited, *Babel* Frustrates Despite Style." *New York Observer*, November 5. http://observer.com/2006/11/manipulative-and-meanspirited-ibabel-ifrustrates-despite-style/.

Sassen, Saskia. 1998. *Globalization and Its Discontents.* New York: New Press.

Sasson, Jack M. 1980. "The 'Tower of Babel' as a Clue to the Redactional Structuring of the Primeval History (Gen. 1:1–11.9)." In *The Bible World: Essays in Honor of Cyrus H. Gordon,* edited by Gary Rendsburg et al., 211–19. New York: KTAV.

Savage, Charlie. 2006a. "Bush Challenges Hundreds of Laws." *Boston Globe,* April 30. http://www.boston.com/news/nation/washington/articles/2006 /04/30/bush_challenges_hundreds_of_laws.

———. 2006b. "Bush Could Bypass New Torture Ban: Waiver Right Is Reserved." *Boston Globe,* January 4. http://www.boston.com/news/nation/ articles/2006/01/04/bush_could_bypass_new_torture_ban.

Savran, George. 2000. "'How Can We Sing a Song of the Lord?' The Strategy of Lament in Psalm 137." *Zeitschrift für die alttestamentliche Wissenschaft* 112 (1): 43–58.

Sawyer, John F. A., ed. 2006. *The Blackwell Companion to the Bible and Culture.* Oxford: Blackwell.

Sayce, A. H. 1897. *Lectures on the Origin and Growth of Religion as Illustrated by the Religions of the Ancient Babylonians.* Hibbert Lectures. London: Williams and Norgate.

Scheuerman, William E. 1999. *Carl Schmitt: The End of Law.* Lanham, Md.: Rowman and Littlefield.

Schlesinger, Arthur M., Jr. 1998. *The Disuniting of America: Reflections on a Multicultural Society.* 2nd ed. New York: W. W. Norton.

Schmitt, Carl. (1916) 1991. *Theodor Däublers 'Nordlicht': Drei Studien über die Elemente, den Geist und die Aktualität des Werkes.* Berlin: Duncker and Humblot.

———. (1922) 2005. *Political Theology: Four Chapters on the Concept of Sovereignty.* Translated by G. Schwab. Chicago: University of Chicago Press.

———. (1923) 1996. *Roman Catholicism and Political Form.* Translated by G. L. Ulmen. Westport, Conn.: Greenwood.

———. (1929) 1993. "The Age of Neutralizations and Depoliticizations." Translated by Matthias Konzett and John P. McCormick. *Telos* 96 (Summer): 130–42.

———. (1932) 1996. *The Concept of the Political.* Translated by G. Schwab. Chicago: University of Chicago Press.

Schüssler Fiorenza, Elisabeth. 1985. *The Book of Revelation: Justice and Judgment.* Philadelphia: Fortress.

———. 1991. *Revelation: Vision of a Just World.* Proclamation Commentaries. Minneapolis: Fortress.

———. 2007. *The Power of the Word: Scripture and the Rhetoric of Empire.* Philadelphia: Fortress.

Schwartz, Seth. 1990. *Josephus and Judaean Politics.* Columbia Studies in the Classical Tradition 18. Leiden: Brill.

Scott, A. O. 2006. "Emotion Needs No Translation." *New York Times*, October 27. http://movies.nytimes.com/2006/10/27/movies/27babe.html.

Scott, D., and C. Hirschkind, eds. 2006. *Powers of the Secular Modern: Talal Asad and His Interlocutors*. Stanford, Calif.: Stanford University Press.

Self, Robert O. 2003. *American Babylon: Race and the Struggle for Postwar Oakland*. Princeton, N.J.: Princeton University Press.

Seow, C. L. 2003. *Daniel*. Louisville, Ky.: Westminster John Knox Press.

Shalal, Ali. 2009. "Torture at Abu Ghraib: 'The Man Behind the Hood.'" A Full Transcript of Ali Shalal's Testimony. Global Research. April 27. http://www.globalresearch.ca/index.php?context=va&aid=13379.

Sharlet, Jeff. 2008. *The Family: Power, Politics, and Fundamentalism's Shadow Elite*. Queensland: University of Queensland Press.

———. 2010. *C Street: The Fundamentalist Threat to American Democracy*. New York: Little, Brown.

Sharp, Carolyn J. 2003. *Prophecy and Ideology in Jeremiah: Struggles for Authority in the Deutero-Jeremianic Prose*. Old Testament Studies. London: T & T Clark Ltd.

Sharrock, Justine. 2008a. "Am I a Torturer?" *Mother Jones*, March/April. http://motherjones.com/politics/2008/03/am-i-torturer.

———. 2008b. "The Torture Playlist." Interview with Justine Sharrock, by Gary Moskowitz. *Mother Jones*, February 22. http://motherjones.com/politics/2008/02/torture-playlist.

Shea, William H. 1986. "The Neo-Babylonian Historical Setting for Daniel 7." *Andrews University Seminar Studies* 24 (1): 31–36.

Shepherd, David, ed. 2008. *Images of the Word: Hollywood's Bible and Beyond*. Semeia Studies 54. Atlanta: Society of Biblical Literature.

Sherwood, Yvonne. 2000. *A Biblical Text and Its Afterlives: The Survival of Jonah in Western Culture*. Cambridge: Cambridge University Press.

———, ed. 2006. "Bush's Bible as a Liberal Bible (Strange though that Might Seem)." In *Postscripts: A Journal of Sacred Texts and Contemporary Worlds* 2 (1): 47–58.

———. 2008. "The God of Abraham and Exceptional States, or The Early Modern Rise of the Whig/Liberal Bible." *Journal of the American Academy of Religion* 76 (2): 312–43.

Singer, Peter. 2004. *The President of Good and Evil: The Ethics of George W. Bush*. New York: Dutton.

Skerrett, Kathleen. 2008. "Rawls: On Persons, Reciprocity and Force." Unpublished manuscript.

Slide, Anthony. 2010. *Inside the Hollywood Fan Magazine: A History of Star Makers, Fabricators, and Gossip Mongers*. Jackson: University Press of Mississippi.

Smelik, Klaas A. D. 2004. "The Function of Jeremiah 50 and 51 in the Book of Jeremiah." In *Reading the Book of Jeremiah: A Search for Coherence*, edited by Martin Kessler, 87–98. Winona Lake, Ind.: Eisenbrauns.

Smith, Abraham. 2008. "More than a Mighty Hunter: George Washington Williams, Nineteenth-Century Racialized Discourse and the Reclamation of Nimrod." In *African American Religious Life and the Story of Nimrod*, 69–84. New York: Palgrave Macmillan.

Smith, Clive Stafford. 2008. "Welcome to the 'Disco.'" *Guardian*, June 18. http://www.guardian.co.uk/world/2008/jun/19/usa.guantanamo.

Smith, Darryl A. 2007. "Droppin' Science ~~Fiction~~: Signification and Singularity in the Metapocalypse of Du Bois, Baraka, and Bell." *Science Fiction Studies* 34: 201–19.

Smith, Jack. 2011. *Islam—The Cloak of Antichrist*. Enumclaw, Wash.: WinePress Publishing.

Smith, Mark S. 2002. *The Early History of God: Yahweh and the Other Deities in Ancient Israel*. 2nd ed. Grand Rapids, Mich.: Eerdmans.

Smith, Wilfred Cantwell. 1993. *What Is Scripture? A Comparative Approach*. Minneapolis: Fortress.

Smith-Christopher, Daniel L. 2002. *A Biblical Theology of Exile*. Overtures to Biblical Theology. Fortress: Minneapolis.

Sources. 2004. "Photos of US Torture of Iraqi Prisoners at the Abu Ghraib Prison in Iraq." Indybay, April 30. http://www.indybay.org/newsitems/2004/04/30/16790301.php?show_comments=1.

Speiser, E. A. 1964. *Genesis*. Anchor Bible 1. New York: Doubleday.

Spilsbury, Paul. 1998. *The Image of the Jew in Flavius Josephus' Paraphrase of the Bible*. Texte und Studien zum Antiken Judentum 69. Tübingen: Mohr Siebeck.

Spinks, Lee. 2001. "Thinking the Post-Human: Literature, Affect, and the Politics of Style." *Textual Practice* 15 (1): 23–46.

Spivak, Gayatri Chakravorty. 1995. Translator's preface and afterword to *Imaginary Maps: Three Stories*, by Mahasweta Devi, xxiii–xxx and 197–205. Translated by Gayatri Chakravorty Spivak. New York: Routledge.

———. 1999. *A Critique of Postcolonial Reason: Toward a History of the Vanishing Present*. Cambridge, Mass.: Harvard University Press.

———. 2000. Foreword to *A Companion to Postcolonial Studies*, edited by Henry Schwarz and Sangeeta Ray, xv–xxii. Oxford: Blackwell.

———. 2001. "Moving Devi." *Cultural Critique* 47 (Winter): 120–63.

———. 2004. "Terror: A Speech after 9/11." *boundary 2* 31 (2): 81–111.

Stahlberg, Lesleigh Cushing. 2008a. "Modern-day Moabites: The Bible and the Debate about Same-sex Marriage." *Biblical Interpretation* 16 (5): 442–75.

———. 2008b. *Sustaining Fictions: Intertextuality, Midrash, Translation, and the Literary Afterlife of the Bible*. New York: T & T Clark.

Statement of Administration Policy, Department of Defense Appropriations Bill, FY 2006. 2005. H.R. 2863. September 30, http://www.presidency.ucsb.edu/ws/index.php?pid=24877.

Stephenson, Neal. 1992. *Snow Crash*. New York: Bantam.

Sterling, Joe, and Greg Botelho. 2013. "Algerian Hostage Crisis Enters 3rd Day with 'Ongoing Activity.'" *CNN*, January 18, 2013, www.cnn.com/2013/01/17/world/africa/algeria-hostage-crisis/.

Stevenson, Seth. 2010. "The Greatest Ad I've Ever Seen." *Slate*, June 7. http://www.slate.com/articles/business/ad_report_card/2010/06/the_greatest_ad_ive_ever_seen.2.html.

Stewart, Maria W. 1987. *America's First Black Woman Political Writer: Essays and Speeches*. Edited by Marilyn Richardson. Bloomington: Indiana University Press.

Strauss, Gideon. 2011. "Yes, Justice Has Been Done in the Killing of Osama bin Laden." *Christianity Today*, May 2. http://www.christianitytoday.com/ct/2011/mayweb-only/osama-celebration.html.

Stream, Carol. 2008. "Left Behind Authors Speak Out on the McCain Ad 'The One.'" *Christian Newswire*, August 8. http://www.christiannewswire.com/news/371367426.html.

Strong, John T. 2008. "Shattering the Image of God: A Response to Theodore Hiebert's Interpretation of the Story of the Tower of Babel." *Journal of the Society of Biblical Literature* 127 (4): 625–34.

Studlar, Gaylyn. 1997. "'Out-Salomeing Salome': Dance, the New Woman and the Fan Magazine Orientalism." In *Visions of the East: Orientalism in Film*, edited by Matthew Bernstein and Gaylyn Studlar, 99–129. New Brunswick, N.J.: Rutgers University Press.

Sugrue, Seana. 2006. "Soft Despotism and Same-Sex Marriage." In *The Meaning of Marriage: Family, State, Market, and Morals*, edited by Robert P. George and Jean Bethke Elshtain, 172–95. New York: Scepter.

Sullivan, Andrew. 1995. *Virtually Normal: An Argument about Homosexuality*. New York: Alfred A. Knopf.

Sweeney, Marvin A. 1996. *Isaiah 1–39: With an Introduction to Prophetic Literature*. Forms of the Old Testament Literature Commentary Series 16. Grand Rapids, Mich.: Eerdmans.

Teskey, Gordon. 1996. *Allegory and Violence*. Ithaca, N.Y.: Cornell University Press.

Thelle, Rannfrid I. 2009a. "MT Jeremiah: Reflections of a Discourse on Prophecy in the Persian Period." In *Production of Prophecy: Constructing Prophecy and Prophets in Yehud*, edited by Diana Vikander Edelman and Ehud Ben Zvi, 184–207. London: Equinox.

———. 2009b. "Babylon in the Book of Jeremiah (MT): Negotiating a Power Shift." In *Prophecy in the Book of Jeremiah*, edited by Hans M. Barstad and Reinhard G. Kratz, 187–232. Berlin: Walter de Gruyter.

Thomas, Calvin. 2000. "Straight with a Twist: Queer Theory and the Subject of Heterosexuality." In *Straight with a Twist: Queer Theory and the Subject of*

Heterosexuality, edited by Calvin Thomas, 11–44. Urbana: University of Illinois Press.

Thompson, Leonard L. 1990. *The Book of Revelation: Apocalypse and Empire.* Oxford: Oxford University Press.

Tierney, Dolores. 2009. "Alejandro González Iñárritu: Director without Borders." *New Cinemas: Journal of Contemporary Film* 7 (2): 101–17.

Tocqueville, Alexis de. (1835, 1840) 2000. *Democracy in America*, vols. 1–2. Translated and edited by Harvey C. Mansfield and Delba Winthrop. Chicago: University of Chicago Press.

Torchia, Christopher, and Ammar Al-Musawi. 2008. "Iraq: Can Ancient Babylon Be Rescued?" *MSNBC.* November 11. http://www.msnbc.msn.com/id/27669499/ns/technology_and_science-science/t/iraq-can-ancient-babylon-be-rescued/.

Towner, W. Sibley. 1985. *Daniel.* Interpretation. Atlanta: John Knox.

Twomey, Jay. 2007. "The Five That Remain: Versions of the Messianic in Battlestar Galactica." *Postscripts* 3 (2–3): 162–85.

———. 2009a. "Antonin Scalia v. Jonathan Edwards: Romans 13 and the American Theology of State." In *Sacred Tropes: Tanakh, New Testament, and Qur'an as Literature and Culture*, edited by Roberta Sterman Sabbath, 493–503. Leiden: Brill.

———. 2009b. *The Pastoral Epistles through the Centuries.* Oxford: Wiley-Blackwell.

Tyndale House Publishers. 2008. Left Behind. http://www.leftbehind.com/.

UNESCO. 2009. *Final Report on Damage Assessment in Babylon.* International Coordination Committee for the Safeguarding of the Cultural Heritage of Iraq. New York: UNESCO.

University of Virginia Library. 1999–2000. "Red, White, Blue and Brimstone: New World Literature and the American Millennium Exhibit." University of Virginia. http://www2.lib.virginia.edu/exhibits/brimstone/.

Urban, Hugh. 2004. "America 'Left Behind:' Bush, the Neocons and Evangelical Christian Fiction." *Counterpunch*, November 18. http://www.counterpunch.org/urban11182004.html.

Vanderhaeghe, Guy. 1996. *The Englishman's Boy.* Toronto: McClelland and Stewart.

Vanderhooft, David Stephen. 1999. *The Neo-Babylonian Empire and Babylon in the Latter Prophets.* Harvard Semitic Museum Monographs 50. Atlanta: Scholars.

Vander Stichele, Caroline. 2009. "Re-membering the Whore: The Fate of Babylon according to Revelation 17.16." In *A Feminist Companion to the Apocalypse of John*, edited by Amy-Jill Levine, with Maria Mayo Robbins, 106–20. New York: T & T Clark.

van der Toorn, Karel, and Pieter W. van der Horst. 1990. "Nimrod before and after the Bible." *Harvard Theological Review* 83 (1): 1–29.

Van Hecke, Pierre J. P. 2003. "Metaphorical Shifts in the Oracle against Baby-lon (Jeremiah 50–51)." *Scandinavian Journal of the Old Testament* 17 (1): 68–88.

Van Heest, Katrina. 2011. "Paul the Proprietor: Universal-Exclusivism and the Persistence of Metaphor." PhD diss., Claremont Graduate University.

Van Seters, John. 1992. *Prologue to History: The Yahwist as Historian in Genesis.* Louisville, Ky.: Westminster/John Knox.

———. 2003. *A Law Book for the Diaspora: Revision in the Study of the Covenant Code.* Oxford: Oxford University Press.

Van Wolde, Ellen. 1994. *Words Become Worlds: Semantic Studies of Genesis 1–11.* Leiden: Brill.

Vatter, Miguel, ed. 2011. *Crediting God: Sovereignty and Religion in the Age of Global Capitalism.* New York: Fordham University Press.

Von Rad, Gerhard. 1972. *Genesis: A Commentary.* Translated by John H. Marks. Philadelphia: Westminster.

Wall, Derek. 2005. *Babylon and Beyond: The Economics of Anti-Capitalist, Anti-Globalist and Radical Green Movements.* London: Pluto.

Walton, John H. 1995. "The Mesopotamian Background of the Tower of Babel Account and Its Implications." *Bulletin for Biblical Research* 5:155–75.

———. 2001. "The *Anzu* Myth as Relevant Background for Daniel 7?" In *The Book of Daniel: Composition and Reception,* vol. 1, edited by John J. Collins and Peter W. Flint, with Cameron VanEpps, 69–89. Leiden: Brill.

Warner, Michael, Jonathan VanAntwerpen, and Craig Calhoun, eds. 2010. *Varieties of Secularism in a Secular Age.* Cambridge, Mass.: Harvard University Press.

Webber, David. 1997. "Cyberspace: The Beast's Worldwide Spiderweb." In *Foreshocks of the Antichrist,* edited by William T. James, 125–62. Eugene, Ore.: Harvest House.

Weinrich, William C. 1985. "Antichrist in the Early Church." *Concordia Theological Quarterly* 49 (2–3): 135–47.

Weiser, Artur. (1959) 1962. *The Psalms: A Commentary.* Old Testament Library. Philadelphia: Westminster.

Wengst, Klaus. 1994. "Babylon the Great and the New Jerusalem: The Vision-ary View of Political Reality in the Revelation of John." In *Politics and Theo-politics in the Bible and Postbiblical Literature,* edited by Henning Graf Reventlow, Yair Hoffman, and Benjamin Uffenheimer, 189–202. Supplement, *Journal for the Study of the Old Testament.* Sheffield, Eng.: Sheffield Academic Press.

Wenham, Gordon J. 1987. *Genesis 1–15.* Word Biblical Commentary 1. Waco, Texas: Word Books.

White, Susan. 1988. "Male Bonding, Hollywood Orientalism, and the Repres-sion of the Feminine in Kubrick's *Full Metal Jacket*." *Arizona Quarterly* 44 (3): 120–44.

White House, Office of the Press Secretary. 2002. *The National Security Strategy of the United States of America*. Washington, D.C.: U.S. Government Printing House.

———. 2005. "The National Strategy for Maritime Security." Department of Homeland Security. September 20. http://georgewbush-whitehouse .archives.gov/homeland/maritime-security.html.

———. 2007. "2007 U.S.-EU Summit Promoting Peace, Human Rights and Democracy Worldwide." April 30. http://georgewbush-whitehouse.archives .gov/news/releases/2007/04/20070430-13.html.

———. 2010. *The National Security Strategy of the United States of America*. Washington, D.C.: U.S. Government Printing House.

Wilson, Bruce. 2008. "Source/Information Page for New John Hagee Video." Talk to Action: Reclaiming Citizenship, History, and Faith. June 1. http:// www.talk2action.org/story/2008/6/1/163843/2726.

Wilson, Robert R. 2000. "Creation and New Creation: The Role of Creation Imagery in the Book of Daniel." In *The God Who Creates: Essays in Honor of W. Sibley Towner*, edited by William P. Brown and S. Dean McBride Jr., 190–203. Grand Rapids, Mich.: Eerdmans.

Wimbush, Vincent. 2008a. "Introduction: TEXTureS, Gestures, Power: Orientation to Radical Excavation." In *Theorizing Scriptures: New Critical Orientations to a Cultural Phenomenon*, edited by Vincent Wimbush, 1–21. Signifying (on) Scriptures. New Brunswick, N.J.: Rutgers University Press.

———, ed. 2008b. *Theorizing Scriptures: New Critical Orientations to a Cultural Phenomenon*. Signifying (on) Scriptures. New Brunswick, N.J.: Rutgers University Press.

———. 2012. *White Men's Magic: Scripturalization as Slavery*. Oxford: Oxford University Press.

Wolfe, Alan. 2004. "A Fascist Philosopher Helps Us Understand Contemporary Politics." *Chronicle of Higher Education*, April 2. http://chronicle.com/ free/v50/i30/30b01601.htm.

Wolin, Sheldon. 2003. *Tocqueville between Two Worlds: The Making of a Political and Theoretical Life*. Princeton, N.J.: Princeton University Press.

Worthen, Molly. 2008. "The Chalcedon Problem: Rousas John Rushdoony and the Origins of Christian Reconstructionism." *Church History* 77 (2): 399–437.

Wright, David P. 2009. *Inventing God's Law: How the Covenant Code of the Bible Used and Revised the Laws of Hammurabi*. Oxford: Oxford University Press.

Yurica, Katherine. 2004. "The Despoiling of America: How George W. Bush Became the Head of the New American Dominionist Church/State." *Yurica Report*. February 11. http://www.yuricareport.com/Dominionism/ TheDespoilingOfAmerica.htm. Accessed August 7, 2008.

Zenor, Jon. 2011. "Should Christians Celebrate the Death of Osama bin Laden?" Eternal Truth Ministry. May 3. http://www.eternaltruthministry .com/2011/05/should-christians-celebrate-the-death-of-osama-bin-laden/.

Zylinska, Joanna. 2001. *On Spiders, Cyborgs and Being Scared: The Feminine and the Sublime*. Manchester: Manchester University Press.